David Mitchell
~~37 Forest Avenue~~

~~Aberdeen~~

~~AB1 6TU~~ .

4 BERNHAM CRES .

STONEHAVEN
KINCARDINESHIRE
AB3 2WQ .
(0569) 765528

D0530762

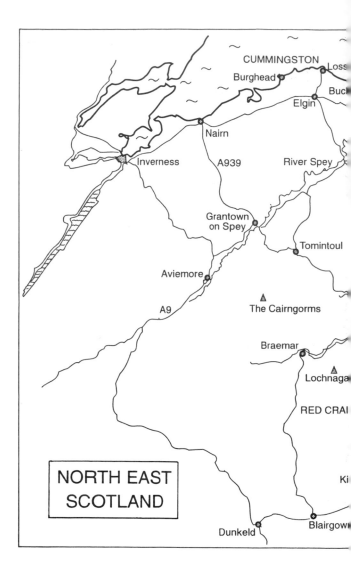

NORTH EAST
SCOTLAND

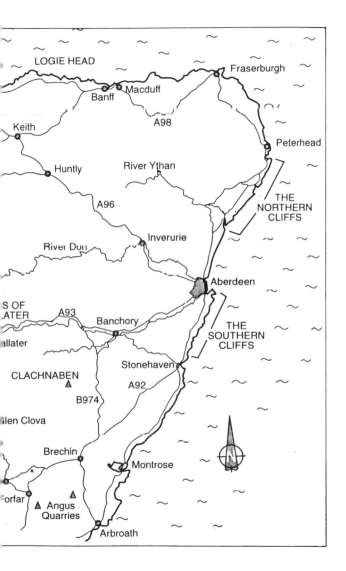

This guidebook is compiled from the most recent information and experience provided by members of the Scottish Mountaineering Club and other contributors. The book is published by the Scottish Mountaineering Trust, which is a charitable trust.

Revenue from the sale of books published by the Trust is used for the continuation of its publishing programme and for charitable purposes associated with Scottish mountains and mountaineering.

Northeast Outcrops

Including

the Aberdeen, Moray and Banff sea-cliffs, Deeside, Glen Clova and the Angus quarries

Compiled by Neil Morrison

With contributions from Grant Farquhar, Martin Forsyth, Wilson Moir, Neil Morrison, Kevin Murphy, Andy Nisbet, Niall Ritchie, Alastair Ross and Neil Shepherd

Edited by Neil Morrison
Series Editor: Roger Everett

SCOTTISH MOUNTAINEERING CLUB
CLIMBERS' GUIDE

Published in Great Britain by the Scottish Mountaineering Trust,
1994
Copyright © the Scottish Mountaineering Club

British Library Cataloguing in Publication Data

Northeast Outcrops. — 2 Rev.ed
I.   Morrison, Neil
796.52209411

ISBN 0-907521-41-X

Maps drawn by Ronnie Robb and Harry Salisbury
Diagrams drawn by Ronnie Robb, Ian Davidson, Charlie Cook,
      Andrew Nisbet and Neil Morrison
Production by Scottish Mountaineering Trust (Publications) Ltd
Typeset by Elliot Robertson, Westec, North Connel
Colour separations by Par Graphics, Kirkcaldy
Graphic work by Elliot Robertson, Westec, North Connel
Printed by St Edmundsbury Press, Bury St Edmunds
Bound by Hunter and Foulis, Edinburgh

Distributed by Cordee, 3a DeMontfort Street, Leicester, LE1 7HD

Contents

The Coast South from Aberdeen

List of Illustrations

List of Diagrams and Maps

The Climber and the Mountain Environment

With increasing numbers of walkers and climbers going to the Scottish hills, it is important that all of us who do so should recognise our responsibilities to those who live and work among the hills and glens, to our fellow climbers and to the mountain environment in which we find our pleasure and recreation.

The Scottish Mountaineering Club and Trust, who jointly produce this and other guidebooks, wish to impress on all who avail themselves of the information in these books that it is essential at times to consider the sporting and proprietory rights of landowners and farmers. The description of a climbing, walking or skiing route in any of these books does not imply that a right of way exists, and it is the responsibility of all climbers to ascertain the position before setting out. In cases of doubt it is best to enquire locally.

During stalking and shooting seasons in particular, much harm can be done in deer forests and on grouse moors by people walking through them. Normally the deer stalking season is from 1st July to 20th October, when stag shooting ends. Hinds may continue to be culled until 15th February. The grouse shooting season is from 12th August until 10th December. These are not merely sporting activities, but are essential for the economy of many Highland estates. During these seasons, therefore, especial care should be taken to consult the local landowner, factor or keeper before taking to the hills.

Climbers and hillwalkers are recommended to consult the book HEADING FOR THE SCOTTISH HILLS, published by the Scottish Mountaineering Trust on behalf of the Mountaineering Council of Scotland and the Scottish Landowners Federation, which gives the names and addresses of factors and keepers who may be contacted for information regarding access to the hills.

It is important to avoid disturbance to sheep, particularly during the lambing season between March and May. Dogs should not be taken onto the hills at this time, and should always be kept under control.

Always try to follow a path or track through cultivated land and forests,and avoid causing damage to fences, dykes and gates by climbing over them carelessly. Do not leave litter anywhere, but take it down from the hill in your rucksack.

The number of walkers and climbers on the hills is leading to increased, and in some cases very unsightly erosion of footpaths and hillsides. Some of the revenue from the sale of this and other SMC guidebooks is used by the Trust to assist financially the work being carried out to repair and maintain hill paths in Scotland. However, it is important for all of us to recognise our responsibility to minimise the erosive effect of our passage over the hills so that the enjoyment of future climbers is not spoiled by landscape damage.

As a general rule, where a path exists walkers should follow it and even where it is wet and muddy should avoid walking along its edges, the effect of which is to extend erosion sideways. Do not take short-cuts at the corners of zigzag paths. Remember that the worst effects of erosion are likely to be caused during or soon after prolonged wet weather when the ground is soft and waterlogged. A route on a stony or rocky hillside is likely to cause less erosion than on a grassy one at such times.

Although the use of bicycles can often be very helpful for reaching remote crags and hills, the erosion damage that can be caused by them when used 'off road' on soft footpaths and open hillsides is such that their use on such terrain must cause concern. It is the editorial policy of the Scottish Mountaineering Club that the use of bicycles in hill country may be recommended on hard roads such as forest roads or private roads following rights of way, but it is not recommended on footpaths or open hillsides where the environmental damage that they cause may be considerable. Readers are asked to bear these points in mind, particularly when the ground is wet and soft after rain.

The proliferation of cairns on hills detracts from the feeling of wildness, and may be confusing rather than helpful as regards route-finding. The indiscriminate building of cairns on the hills is therefore discouraged.

Climbers are reminded that they should not drive along private estate roads without permission, and when parking their cars should avoid blocking access to private roads and land, and should avoid causing any hazard to other road users.

Finally, the Scottish Mountaineering Club and the Scottish Mountaineering Trust can accept no liability for damage to property nor for personal injury resulting from the use of any route described in their publications.

The Mountaineering Council of Scotland is the representative body for climbers and walkers in Scotland. One of its primary concerns is the continued free access to the hills and crags that we now enjoy. Information about bird restrictions, stalking and general access issues can be obtained from the National Officer of the MCofS. Should any climber or walker encounter problems regarding access they should contact the National Officer of the MCofS, whose current address is published in CLIMBER AND HILLWALKER magazine.

The Bird Nesting Season

Many of the crags described in this guidebook, both sea-cliffs and those inland, are nesting sites for a wide variety of birds. It is important that climbers respect the needs of birds during the nesting season. Where there are particular potential problems these are highlighted in the Introduction and the text. While the sheer numbers of birds on some sea-cliffs, and the resultant mess, smell and noise, act as a very effective deterrent, climbers should comply politely with any request by wildlife wardens to avoid climbing at particular locations at specified times of the year.

Acknowledgments

Thanks are due to all the people who have contributed to this guidebook, in particular those who were involved with the previous editions, which have provided the basis for the present work. Greg Strange, Dougie Dinwoodie, Brian Lawrie and Bob Duncan have been of particular help with advice on the text and the task in general.

Lucy Burnett put all the text onto disc whilst Sue Hartley transported that text to her. Ian Davidson produced some excellent new diagrams, whilst Charlie Cook and Harry Salisbury revised Ronnie Robb's original maps and diagrams. Many others have contributed with comments on grades, proof reading, opinions, slides etc. Their help was invaluable and greatly appreciated.

Introduction

This guide covers all the outcrops in the north east of Scotland, including the sea cliffs and inland outcrops of the north-east shoulder of Scotland extending from Forfar in the south to Cummingston on the Moray Coast in the north. It is a comprehensive guidebook covering all the outcrop activity in this area. It is the fifth edition of a body of work started by the Etchachan Club's *Rock Climber's Guide to the North-East Coastline of Scotland* first published in 1960. With the growing importance of outcrops it has grown to encompass the whole north-east and stewardship has been passed to the Scottish Mountaineering Trust. The various sections were farmed out to eager local experts who have updated, added to and revised the work done for the fourth edition.

Scotland as a whole lacks good low lying outcrop areas and whilst the north-east is no real exception it has an amazing diversity of climbing with respect to both rock types and settings. Its geographical isolation has kept it at a safe distance from the rest of Scottish climbing with few outwith the area aware of what it has to offer. This isolation and uncrowded nature is indeed one of its attractions, let us hope it is not lost.

The Inland Crags

There are only four inland centres worthy of inclusion in this guide: Glen Clova, Pass of Ballater (Deeside), Clachnaben and the Angus Quarries. Clova and Ballater can be loosely classed together. Both hold several scattered crags or buttresses and both lie just above the roadside on the fringe of the mountain massif. They are often dry when the higher crags are cold and wet. The other two could hardly be more dissimilar in character. Clachnaben sits austere and exposed, a hilltop tor providing views of Lower Deeside, The Cairngorms and the Mearns, its rounded rocks rough and weather worn. The Angus quarries stand in total contrast and are a new area to this guide in more ways than one. Firstly, they lack the scenery and beauty found elsewhere and are drab holes in the ground. Secondly, they have bolt protected climbing, anathema to other areas in this guidebook. What they may lack in aestheticism they make up for in terms of providing excellent climbing in an area previously lacking.

The Coast

If the area does not abound in inland crags, this is more than compensated for by the coast. The coastal crags are well spread out, and, in the main, still very much on an outcrop scale. In this context, however, they stand out for the sheer volume of routes and variety of climbing found. Varying from small granite crags within the Aberdeen city boundary, the Gothic structures of Findon, the pink Buchan granite to the sandstone of Cummingston and Covesea. Whilst far from the mainstream of Scottish climbing, the proximity of these areas to Aberdeen, or in Moray, to Elgin, make them close enough for summer evenings.

A few general pointers are worth noting when considering climbing on the coast. Firstly, the bird situation is very bad on some cliffs and voluntary bans have not been necessary with the birds providing sufficient deterrent themselves. Outwith the nesting season there is no problem, although after the birds have left it may be necessary to clean your intended route or wait until high seas do this service. Alternatively, there are a large number of cliffs which are not really affected by bird colonies and can be visited all year round. The second point concerns the weather. Cool sunny spring or autumn days are the best, although many areas offer year round climbing if you pick your day. On humid days, the coast can be greasy and unpleasant, particularly south of Aberdeen. In spring, the haar or sea mist can wreak havoc on your evening's cragging. Seas running from the south or south-east often leave the coast damp and inhospitable. An attempt has been made to highlight the good and bad points of the different crags. Given consideration of the above points, and a bit of perseverance, the coast provides an excellent and varied climbing ground.

The coastal fringe is the driest part of the north-east and sunny weather can often be found here when even the inland outcrops catch the Cairngorm rains. Added incentives are the short walks, so important these days, and the quiet of the coastal areas. The coast can be classed roughly in three different sections: the coast south of Aberdeen; the coast north of Aberdeen, mainly centred around Longhaven; and the extensive Banff-Moray coast, running west towards Inverness. Quite possibly there is no climbing ground in Britain with such a great variety of rock types. This applies in particular to the southern section around Aberdeen with its granites, slates, dolerites and motley metamorphics.

The southern area consists of a near continuous line of cliffs running south to Stonehaven. Much of it vegetated or rotten with climbing spread out on the more attractive and cleaner crags. The surroundings are a dour landscape of windswept farmland with the occasional fishing village now surrounded by new housing. Towards Aberdeen the scene is even less appealing with commuter housing and industry. Development is fortunately forbidden east of the railway line which lies to the coast side of the main dual carriageway and clips the head of the deepest inlets. The traveller from the south might see little worth preserving and even less to climb on. This is misleading, however, because on descending to the cliffs a secluded underworld appears with some fine crags and the developments above hidden from sight. No less pleasant is the strip of rough ground hemmed in between clifftop and farmer's field, often alive with butterflies, bees and flowers. This is particularly true of the broader patches of unfarmed ground in the Clashrodney and Findon area where a few roe deer still manage to survive.

Immediately south of Aberdeen lies an area of crags extending south towards Cove village. They lie within the city boundary and being so accessible, it seems worth recording many trivial little climbs which might be ignored elsewhere. Although uninspiring initially, many of the smaller crags excel in the quality of their rock, for example Souter Head. Additionally, they offer introductory crags for beginners with Black Rock Gulch, Souter and Deceptive Wall the best. Unfortunately the area is blighted by industrial developments and the council's tip but these are forgotten when down at the cliffs and their accessibility makes them popular on summer evenings, although beware of the haar. At South Cove, the cliffs are bigger and more complex with awkward approaches often involving abseiling. However, some of the routes on offer are amongst the best in the area. Birds can be a bit of a problem and some of the cliffs suffer from a lack of sunshine. Further south at Findon the rock type changes to metamorphic and the scale increases again. The rock is sometimes less than perfect but the atmosphere and settings are impressive. Standing as the finest example of this is the primeval Earnsheugh, off-putting at first acquaintance but offering superb climbing in the middle to upper grades. Northerly winds hold the key to the best days on the Findon cliffs.

Moving south from Findon, cliffs are dotted along the coastline. There is nothing of the same scale as at Findon but excellent quality crags abound. Berrymuir Head at Downies offers a variety of fine hard routes but is badly birded in the nesting season and has an awkward descent. Floor's Craig offers a number of fine extremes plus some good steep VSs and HVSs, the crag is open and has no bird problems. Craig Stirling comes into its own at E3 and above, its only drawbacks are its tidal nature and retiring aspect which can combine to make it greasy. Around Newtonhill the cliffs are steep and short. The Harbour Wall is very open and receives sun well into the afternoon. Much of the rock around Muchalls is disappointing but Brown Crag offers a number of routes from HVS to E3 in a sunny sheltered location with no birds, the only proviso is to go after a dry spell as the crag can seep badly.

Moving north of Aberdeen the first area encountered is at Collieston. This area has been neglected but is excellent for the middle grade climber with a large number of routes on generally sound and bird-free rock. The Graip, in particular, is an open sunny crag receiving sunshine on summers evenings, and what little loose rock that exists will clean up with traffic.

The red granite cliffs away north of Aberdeen have an instant appeal, largely because the rock is of such obvious excellence and wonderfully clean. The cliffs tend to be more open than in the south, although most of them do lose the sun in early to mid-afternoon. The first and most popular area encountered is around Meikle Partans and offers a large number of routes in the middle grades on cliffs unaffected by birds. This area provides possibly the best introduction to the northern cliffs and is ideal for the introduction of beginners. Slightly further north lies Grey Mare Slabs which provides good low grade routes although access involves abseil or down climbing. The wildly overhanging prow of Arthur Fowlie is host to a number of quality extremes but is severely affected by birds and their debris. Additionally, the prow itself can remain a bit damp and greasy.

The next area is centred around the Longhaven quarries and has several fine cliffs, particularly for the extreme leader. The down side is that access is often difficult and the cliffs are host to large seabird colonies, so they can only be visited early or late in the year. Cliffs affected in this way include the Red Wall, Rob's Butt, the south end of Scimitar Ridge and the Bloody Wall. A partial exception to this is Alligator which provides pleasant middle grade routes and is not too birdy. Munich Buttress in the heart of the quarries is also unaffected by birds, and it hosts a few good extremes and faces south. It is also set well away from the sea and as such can save the day when rough seas rule out other cliffs.

Murdo or Murdoch Head offers some outstanding routes in the upper grades, however, problems do exist. The Escarpment wall requires an abseil and is affected by rough seas. On a hot day it can be very humid and greasy. The Round Tower is set well above the sea and so can be a fine location. However, the routes from Stoneface southwards are very heavily birded. The best time for the Round Tower is often September.

North again Meackie Point offers a number of extremes on excellent rock with a south-facing aspect. Its only problem is that large swells will swamp the cliff base even at low tide. Many of the other areas north of here are small and limited but there is a concentration of good extremes around Herring Cove and Robie Gow's Prison, all of which are unaffected by birds.

If the north-east coast should fail you, then the alternatives of Cummingston, Logie Head and Mull Cleave exist on the north coast. Their advantages are covered in detail elsewhere but for the hardened devotee of the coast their real plus is that the haar rarely affects them.

History

The Aberdeenshire Coast *by Neil Morrison*

The earliest reference to Aberdeenshire climbing is to be found in Sir Walter Scott's "The Antiquary" where there is mention of one "Francis O'Fowlsheugh, the finest cragsman that ever speeled a heugh, who brak his neck on the Dunbuy O'Slains". No doubt the unfortunate Francis and his contemporaries were in it for the money, seeking eggs and the birds themselves. Other visitors to the coast were fishermen using the sheltered inlets. It is not unlikely that the same inlets also saw more illicit activities in the shape of smuggling.

Next came the quarrymen, carving open the pink granite of Longhaven. This was used as dress stone for the bridges and buildings of the Victorians. Another use was in the construction of the breakwater for Peterhead's Harbour of Refuge, the work being carried out by prisoners from Peterhead. The quarries must have been an awesome sight in their heyday, with hundreds of workers and massive blasting. The quarrymen's scars do not heal easily but have created many of Longhaven's most striking features with ridges, towers and aretes all lending to the atmosphere of the area. South of Aberdeen the quarrying was not as extensive but can be seen at South Cove.

The first records of actual rock climbing on the North-East coast date from before the Great War, when H.G. Drummond and others of the then youthful Cairngorm Club scaled the Long Slough Pinnacle. They were also active at Clashrodney, Souter Head and elsewhere. James McCoss established a variety of routes including Slab Top Chimney at Souter and at least six routes at Blowup Nose. Actual routes are difficult to identify from the records, but obviously the area south of Aberdeen was being well explored.

The Great War appears, as elsewhere, to have left a gap and it was in the late 1920s and early 1930s that development restarted. The only link with the pre-war years seems to have been James McCoss, with records showing that he was still climbing in the 1930s. G.T.R. Watt, R.P. Yunnie and Miss D.M. Carle were pioneering routes such as the Milestone and Overhang Crack at Souter. In the 1930s, the Cairngorm Club was holding Club Outings to Souter, Clashrodney and Longhaven. Aitken's Pinnacle near Souter was climbed by W.N. Aitken in 1934; tactics involved a top rope passed over the pinnacle and a flag on a pole was hoisted on top.

The coast south of the city was frequently visited, with the Cairngorm Club particularly active. Whilst much of this may have been seen as training for the mountains, it is clear that the coast had its devotees. Despite this activity, little seems to have been achieved north of Aberdeen, probably due to the difficulties of getting there, but possibly because few records were kept. Certainly, the Tewnions had visited some of the now classic routes, including Scimitar Ridge, in the course of bird studies and whilst on holiday at their uncle's farm.

During the Second World War activity was limited. However, W.T. Hendry, a founder member of the University Lairig Club, was active most notably with Sickle at Souter in 1944. This route was a leap in difficulty and significantly harder than anything from the 1930s or indeed 1940s. In 1945, Hendry produced the first real documentation of climbing in the North-East with his *Short Guide to Souter Head* in the Cairngorm Club Journal.

The next phase of development began in the period 1949-52 when Morrison, Patey and Taylor began a systematic exploration of the coastline between Collieston and Peterhead. They were shortly to be joined by Brooker who was operating independently at the start of this period, mainly south of Aberdeen.

At this time, and in fact through to the present day, the coast and outcrop climbing in general has been viewed by many in the North-East as a poor relation to the mountains, not as something complimentary. Even more so than the rest of Scotland, the North-East retains a strong mountain tradition, with many preferring a day on the hill to a visit to the coast. The 1950s through to the 1970s were the epitome of this with the Cairngorm bothies used every weekend regardless of weather for climbing or socialising. The coast was rarely visited, and even today some climbers scarcely visit the coast. The effect this had on development was to limit it to a training ground for the majority and to hold back the pushing of standards.

The systematic exploration by Patey and friends took them first to Collieston. Here, Patey put up his first new route with the ascent of Crab's Wall, a 10m Difficult. The rest is history. These pioneers then moved their attentions to the quarries of Longhaven, presumably attracted by the mountaineering atmosphere of the place with its ridges and summits. Scimitar, Walrus and Alligator Ridges plus the Red and Round Towers were named and ascended in this period. Few of the routes done were technically hard, however Patey and Charlie Morrison's Hallelujah Staircase and The Great Diedre were solid VS and big cliffs such as the Red Wall were opened up. Areas south of Longhaven seem to have been dismissed as too small, although it is interesting to note that the party credited with discovering Grey Mare Slabs in the 1960s did find old pitons from earlier unknown visitors.

South of Aberdeen, the scale of routes may have been smaller but technically the developments equalled or surpassed those to the north. Jerry Smith led the short but stiff White Seam in nails, whilst The Pobble and the bold South-East Diedre (all at Souter) date from this period. Numerous other routes were done at this time, mainly at Clashrodney and South Cove. Perhaps the most audacious attempt of the early 1950s was when Patey, Brooker and Taylor ventured onto the awesome knife blade edge of the Spigolo at Cove. They found the rock "indescribably bad, part of an overhang crumbled away under the leader leaving him hanging by his hands". The climb was completed on a top rope. The route had to wait until 1969 for its first true lead, when, with questionable sanity, Richie Maguire and Dave Innes climbed the route.

The 1950s continued with routes both north and south of the city with new areas opened up. Morrison's Slabs at Longhaven (by Charlie Morrison), the Cock's Caim near Boddam with routes by Patey and Freddy Malcolm, with his Cyprus Wall. The Graip at Collieston, an excellent cliff, was climbed upon only to disappear when guidebooks came out. The metamorphic rocks south of Clashrodney were still avoided, perhaps regarded as too loose and unappealing. The decade finished on a high note with the development of Bruin Cove by John Hay. His ascent of Pandrop at a stiff and steep HVS 5b lasted as the hardest route on the coast well into the 1960s. In 1960, the first guidebook to the sea-cliffs came out edited by Patey and Hay.

With the 1960s the group led by Patey, Taylor and Brooker were less prominent on the local scene, and the coast experienced a slack period of development. A similar lull hung over the Cairngorms but a new young wave was on its way, which started to make its mark on the coast in the latter half of the decade.

North of Aberdeen several important areas previously dismissed were developed, with Dave Duncan leading the way. Others who followed his example included Greg Strange, Brian Findlay and Mike Rennie. The stretch of coastline south of Longhaven close to Dunbuy was checked out. Perhaps the most important discoveries from this period were Meikle Partans, Fulmar Wall, Harper's Wall and Grey Mare Slabs. Routes on perfect granite such as Epistrophe (Strange and Duncan), the bold Band of Hope (Rennie and Strange), Albatross (Findlay) and Groovin' High (Duncan) epitomise what this stretch of coast has to offer. Elsewhere, 1966 had seen Allen Fyffe and Paul Hindmarsh making the first real dent in the Round Tower with The Present (although 2 pegs were required to overcome copious guano in the top corner). Findlay and Strange put up the fine and atmospheric Zwango near Perdonlie Inlet.

South of the city, Jerry Light had traversed both walls of North Doonies Yawn, the south wall giving a particularly fine route. Harry Smith and Dave Stuart produced the classic Insect Groove and the granite of Clashrodney saw further development from both Duncan and Fyffe. In 1969, a new guidebook edited by Duncan was published. The 1960s had seen a development of the coast's potential, but relatively little in the way of technical advance. Rennie's ascent of Mythical Wall at Souter, after top roping, showed that the harder lines could be climbed but this was not much harder than Hay's Pandrop from 10 years before. Hard lines seem to have been given a wide berth, presumably due to the number of lines available at easier standards.

The 1970s kicked off well and now incomers to the area were starting to make their mark. In 1971, a young student, Dougie Dinwoodie, appeared on the scene with the impressive and bold Crocodile at Seal's Cave, the start of a lengthy series of outstanding new routes. Over the following years, Dinwoodie established himself as the coast's most important and enduring pioneer. Andrew Maxfield (later killed exploring beyond Alligator Ridge) arrived in the North-East and led the first successful climbing trip to Dunbuy, ascending the oft admired Dunbuy Diedre. Aid climbing was in vogue and both Dinwoodie and Maxfield made their mark on the impressive prow of Arthur Fowlie. University students Richie Maguire and Dave Innes accounted for further development at South Cove and put up the excellent Birthday Treat at Clashrodney. The rest of the early 1970s saw a slower pace. The odd gem appeared such as John Mothersele's Wandering of the One Toed Wizard, Dinwoodie's Billy the Kid, Mungo Ross's

Talisker and The Hedonist by Dave Wright and Steve Bateson. Whilst all excellent, none of these routes pushed up standards. Development was at a leisurely pace.

The 1970s might have continued like this but for the arrival, in 1975, of Spaff Ackerley, an outgoing American from the Shawangunks. Using his experience, Spaff forced some five first class lines, a couple of which were technical breakthroughs locally. Subline on the Red Wall takes a thin crack up a leaning wall and fell at a stiff E2 5c (now thought to be E3). However, the American Route on Munich Buttress, another E2, grabs the attention standing boldly over Longhaven quarries. Locals had known of the potential that these routes pointed to and had been making gradual in-roads. However, things were now set for a boost. Bob Smith appeared on the scene and quickly showed a keenness to take on the big or hard lines. He accounted for Knacker's Crack (although with a sling for aid), then the Sorcerer at Arthur Fowlie whilst also discovering a new cliff on the metamorphic rocks south of Aberdeen, the Red Band Cliff. Tony Barley, a Yorkshireman, was also active, starting with Newtonhill. Smith had begun developing the cliff but it was Barley who led the very steep and, at the time, bold Acapulco. April 1978 saw the publication of the Etchachan Club guide to Sea Cliff Climbs in the Aberdeen Area. An altogether bigger affair than its predecessors, it took the then bold step of including three routes graded Extremely Severe.

Possibly as a consequence of the new guide, the final years of the 1970s saw an unprecedented period of enthusiasm for the sea-cliffs. 1978 was a boom year; outstanding lines were found up and down the entire coast. Although routes such as Brian Lawrie's Purple Emperor at the Red Cliff and the excellent Strawclutchers Wall at Meikle Partans took obvious gaps on well known cliffs, it was the development of three neglected cliffs that pushed standards and added a greater depth of routes.

The unmistakable overhanging prow of Arthur Fowlie had seen developments previously, and actually held one of the coast's first extremes. But The Gallows and The Bouncer by Dinwoodie and Lawrie plus Incubus by Smith took things a step further. A year later Murray Hamilton added the free ascent of the wildly leaning North Crack.

Murdoch Head near the true Longhaven yielded up a host of excellent (if often birded) routes at its two distinct sections. The Red Tower saw Dinwoodie add the exciting Neanderthal Man to a big open face whilst Lawrie climbed his Jungle Book. However, it was at the Round Tower that most development took place. The strikingly obvious Tyrant Crack was done by Dinwoodie but not before Smith had spent himself fixing gear and trying the crux.

South of Aberdeen on Craig Stirling a string of fine routes were added by incomers, such as Electric Blue and Omnivore by Dick Renshaw and John Mothersele respectively. However, it was Pat Littlejohn who stole the limelight, soloing Depth Charge then grabbing the "sensational overhanging flake crack" of Lean Meat.

The impetus of the previous year carried into 1979 with more important ascents. Perhaps most notable was the long-awaited Red Death at Long Slough.

This line had been tried frequently and it was Bob Smith who gained the flake and groove by the traverse in from the Doo's Nest. Red Death has become a benchmark for aspiring locals, who fling themselves at its vicious bouldery start until, with usually flagging arms, they gain the dubious sanctuary of the groove. At Bruin Cove Smith and Lawrie added Mind Games and the horribly birdy Thieves' Route. Up north, the same team added Atlantis and Silver Surfer to the Round Tower. Elsewhere, Harper's Wall was being developed, the highlight proving to be Strange and Archbold's aptly named 1,2,3, Go. South of Aberdeen, Floor's Craig was discovered and then developed over the next few years. However, the find of the year was made when Smith, Lawrie and Dinwoodie ascended Earnsheugh Ridge. The ridge opened up the crag but it was Deathcap that showed what the cliff had to offer. Earnsheugh had been dismissed previously as just too hideous, loose and steep. Closer inspection showed that under its skin Earnsheugh had a lot to offer for the future in terms of both climbing quality and experience.

Away from the actual climbing the late 1970s and early 1980s saw a major threat to climbing around Longhaven. Attempts were made by a large quarry firm to open a super quarry at Longhaven. The proposal involved taking away some of the natural cliffs with the granite ground down to roadstone and exported to Europe by boat. A protracted campaign was mounted as the forces of venture capitalism sought to confuse dupe and harass both local councils and government departments into allowing the project to go ahead. Eventually the bid was defeated, and although quarrying does take place, it is of a limited nature and the coastal strip around Longhaven quarries is now owned by the Scottish Wildlife Trust.

Back on the climbing front, 1980 and 1981 were years of consolidation with obvious gaps being filled. Earnsheugh's potential began to be tapped notably with the fine Pterodactyl. Bob Smith found Sea Cat at Craig Stirling. Dinwoodie freed the once aided and bolted Cirrhosis and was the prime mover in the development of the Shag's Cave Face and Robie's Haven routes in the north. Unfortunately the northerly aspect and birdy nature of the latter two cliffs has left them languishing in obscurity after initial enthusiasm. Brian Lawrie's contribution was the superb lower section of Stoneface at the Round Tower, probably the area's first E4. The fine upper crack was added in 1982 by Smith, 1981 also saw Brian Sprunt add new routes with his Animal and the vicious Red Wall at Cove. Perhaps his finest addition that year was when he fought his way up Black Velvet at Long Slough.

1982 was a landmark year, with outstanding contributions including the first E5s on the North-East Coast. Bob Smith climbed Prehistoric Monster at Earnsheugh, the first route up the imposing Thug Wall. Three pitches in impressive surroundings created a real classic. Dougie Dinwoodie trod the eye and nose of the "stone face" at Round Tower to produce Sungod. Its technical traverse and bold upper wall took later repeats to upwardly adjust its original E4 grade. Brian Sprunt's route was Yahoochie at Craig Stirling, achieved after a rather inadequate cleaning and top rope practice. The top roping only slightly detracts from what was a harrowing ascent for both leader and spectators. Subsequent cleaning and more thought for runners has made the route a bit less frightening. However, it still stands out as a stiff lead.

In addition to these developments, a host of other significant ascents took place in 1982. Brian Lawrie added the viciously technical Upside Downies, Willie Todd did Roof Roof, whilst Dinwoodie produced the Paranormal, all at Downies. Craig Stirling saw additions in the form of Colin MacLean's Greedy Pig and Dinwoodie's bold Wet Pussy. Up north, Smith and Lawrie found the beautiful Hidden Treasure, on the same day they added two routes to Robie Gow's Prison and a further two to Harper's Wall. At Munich Buttress, Dinwoodie solved Monkey Puzzle, whilst MacLean added a stopper with Jammy Dodger. Lovers of the esoteric would have noticed the arrival of the charmingly-named Boglesheugh this year; its dank and depressing ruin makes Earnsheugh a relative delight. However, with a drying northerly wind it is an experience not to be missed for those who like adventure.

After 1982, development slowed down but a new guidebook began to take shape. Previous editions had been purely local affairs, for this one the scale was too big and the S.M.T. agreed to publish it. The first developments of 1983 saw further routes added to the Red Wall by Hamilton and Dinwoodie, who took advantage of good weather prior to the birds' return. Bob Smith succeeded on his Overhang at Long Slough. All of this was over-shadowed by the death, in July, of Bob Smith whilst attempting to rope solo a new line at Sickle Row. His contribution to the local scene had been enormous and the loss was heavily felt. Within a year Brian Sprunt was to die on the Matterhorn, leaving another gap.

The remainder of 1983 saw little of real significance as the guidebook headed for publication. Brian Davison, an Englishman resident in the area, produced a string of routes, usually notable for their chossy rock. However, he did manage a slightly flawed Usurper at Newtonhill. Graeme Livingston, still a schoolboy, put his endless hours on the Rosemount Viaduct walls to good effect with Levitator and Nazi Swing, at Longhaven; hardly major but a start. With the guidebook deadline near, Dinwoodie and MacLean ventured into the Red Hole at Cove to produce the outstanding Space Rats, surely one of Scotland's best outcrop routes. Unfortunately darkness forced them to aid out the top pitch. MacLean returned early in 1984 to sort this out, but the route had to wait until 1986 for a complete ascent in its free form by Brian Lawrie.

1984 saw the steady development of several crags. Dinwoodie and friends produced a string of routes at Berrymuir Head, Downies. Alistair Ross added routes to Fulmar Wall and Harper's Wall. In October, the neglected south end of Scimitar Ridge produced several fine routes to Lawrie, Dinwoodie and friends. Meackie Point, clearly visible from the Round Tower but ignored since the late 1970s, produced the first of a fine string of routes. However the highlights of 1984 took place at Earnsheugh. Dinwoodie added the unrelenting Thugosaurus to the wall left of Prehistoric Monster, then went on to produce Necromancer, less strenuous but of equal quality.

The main activists in 1985 were Dinwoodie and Livingston. Livingston added the exciting Double Dyno at Long Slough but produced possibly his finest new route on the coast with The Truth Hurts up a lovely golden wall at Grey Mare.

Dinwoodie produced the sensational and technical Running Wild at Craig Stirling, the slippery Octopussy at Scimitar Ridge and the beautiful Hole in the Wall at Murdoch Head. Others filled the gaps with the discovery of Hidden Inlet by Alistair Ross. Neil Morrison and Brian Lawrie found some good lines at Meackie Point and I lerring Cove. Bloodhunt, the pick of the bunch, was siogod into submission by Morrison. In October, Dinwoodie and Lawrie finished developments for the year by adding Red Planet at Cove's Red Hole.

Dinwoodie returned to the Red Hole in 1986 with Ewen Todd to add the stunning Cracks in Reality up the huge Pink Wall. Those with a traditional bent will be glad to know that a fine bomb-bay chimney tops this sustained wall route. The same team freed the obvious challenge of Hamish Towler's aid route Procrastination. This provides two stiff E5 pitches in fantastic surroundings, only marred by the difficulty of finding the bottom pitch dry. Dinwoodie also set to at Earnsheugh sorting out the Thug Wall. A fine series of routes culminated in the desperate eliminate Grim Spectre. Activity north of Aberdeen saw Dinwoodie and Lawrie climb the remaining lines at Meackie Point in one day. Meackie Point now boasts a clutch of excellent routes on a bird-free south-facing cliff. Alistair Ross was also active in the Longhaven area, climbing the serious Squid Vicious at Scimitar Ridge.

New route activity was slow to take off in 1987. However, when it did, several major hard lines were climbed at Longhaven. Dinwoodie laid siege to the stunning wall right of Hole in the Wall at Murdoch Head and, after much effort, came away with Bagheera. The 1984 guide had touted Main Crack at Arthur Fowlie as a challenge for "a steel armed android". Dinwoodie fitted the bill perfectly and he muscled his way up both Main Crack and the thin flake crack of Ultima Thule. Dinwoodie's next big addition was at the Round Tower where he climbed through Sungod to give Raingod, a firstly technical then bold route. South of Aberdeen he climbed The Black Sleep in the Red Hole. This latter route completed a superb series of routes ranking with anything in the country. Elsewhere, Brian Lawrie had been beavering away at Floor's Craig with a variety of partners. A fine string of routes culminated in the ascent of Pugilist by Bob Duncan. Lawrie, pipped at the post, returned the following night for his lead of the route. A year later, Wilson Moir was to add the equally fine Manassa Mauler to the wall left of Pugilist.

Of note in 1987 and 1988 was series of ascents by Owen Hayward. He repeated several hard coast routes including Cracks in Reality, Black Sleep and Yahoochie. These were done in fine style and without the knowledge gained from being part of the local scene. In addition to these ascents, Wilson Moir started to work his way through the card with ascents of a number of the hardest routes. Encouraged by this, other locals and visitors also began to repeat these climbs.

On the new route scene, 1988 was a fairly quite year. At Murdoch Head, the obvious challenge of the thin cracks left of Hole in the Wall was tackled by Alistair Ross. The route was climbed over three days and is very sustained and technical. Unfortunately, four peg runners mar one of the coast's most striking pieces of rock. Of greater interest to the majority of climbers was the development of Brown Crag at Muchalls by Ross and friends. This provides several pleasant sunny routes at amenable grades.

Wilson Moir took over the pioneering role in 1989 and added four hard new routes at Sickle Row, rarely visited since Bob Smith's fatal accident there. The hardest of the routes was his free version of the old aid route Band Aid-Glasnost. At South Cove he added the elegant rib of Gallipolli and the neighbouring Woomera to Australia Wall. Various other routes were done up and down the coast but little of real significance. On the repeats scene, the Earnsheugh and Red Hole routes' reputations had spread and they were starting to see more traffic.

Thin pickings with regard to new routes continued into 1990. Moir's Teetering on the Brink of Madness at South Cove gave a very technical problem, whilst Alistair Ross returned to Scimitar Ridge's marbly rock to add two hard and serious routes beside Octopussy. Two new crags were also discovered that year. Brian Lawrie and friends developed Coble Boards, the highlight here being Niall Ritchie's Jihad, a wildly overhanging flake crack. Wilson Moir, Paul Allen and friends found and worked out Dyke's Cliff at Newtonhill. This crag is visible from the Harbour Wall at Newtonhill, but had been dismissed. Its development has provided an excellent, if short, venue with a clutch of easy extremes.

1991 saw Wilson Moir and Julian Lines add four routes to the Whisky Cliff, long neglected despite being so close to the city. At Earnsheugh, the same pair added two routes left of Death Rattle Roofs and repeated Grant Farquhar's route of the previous year, Grimly Fiendish. On the Humpback at Altens they added two vicious little technical problems. Their best route was at Craig Stirling, where they found Between the Devil and the Deep Blue Sea. Moir was also responsible for several second ascents with, amongst others, Procrastination, Raingod, Usurper and Running Wild. As before, others followed, Running Wild quickly receiving a further four ascents in two weeks: it had waited six years for the second ascent. Later in the year Moir added Animal Magnetism to the Smuggler's Cliff at Collieston. Fine weather late in the year allowed Lines to climb Plutonic Verses at Murdo Head, and on a bitterly cold day, Moir plugged the last real gap on Munich Buttress with Azerbaijani. 1992 came in with a bang when Moir worked then led the technical and serious Lunatic Fringe at South Cove to give the coast possibly its hardest route to date. The year continued with a steady trickle of new routes from both Moir and Julian Lines, the highlights being Redshift at South Cove by Moir and Making Windows at Harper's Wall by Lines. South Cove was very much the crag of the year with a number of new routes by Lines and partners, and repeats of the existing routes. Up north at Murdoch Head, both Shere Khan and Bagheera received their probable second ascents.

In 1993 attention shifted once again, with Craig Stirling becoming the "in" crag. Moir, usually partnered by Paul Allen, added a number of routes, notably Bone Machine and When the North Wind Blows. As well as all this new route and early repeat activity, the coast now sees steady traffic. On a fine summer evening, Souter Head, Black Rock Gulch and even Long Slough can seem almost busy!

The Moray Coast by Neil Morrison and Andy Nisbet
Much of the history of this area is relatively recent. However, the Journals of the Moray Mountaineering Club show that Covesea was a popular venue for club

meets in the 1930s with several routes and traverses worked out. Unfortunately, their exact whereabouts are unclear. Rusting remnants of old pitons give clues of activity. Cummingston itself does not appear to have become popular until much later; this seems unlikely and perhaps details were never recorded. Certainly the 1970s saw activity at Cummingston with routes recorded and both Moray Sea School and RAF personnel active. Most of the routes on the Doubt Wall and Cornflake Walls were climbed during this period. Again, actual details are difficult to relate to today's routes. However, Graffiti Wall, Diedre of Doubt and Classic Wall plus others, all seem to date from this period. Undated routes can be assumed to have been climbed prior to 1975.

The late 1970s saw John MacKenzie showing an interest in the area and with friends such as M.Birch, D.Butterfield and F.Adams, a large number of routes were established. They developed the areas east of the central bay, such as Gutbuster Bay and Prophet Walls, as well as filling many obvious gaps in the western half. MacKenzie led the classics Kneewrecker Chimney, Legbuster and The Prophet. Richard McHardy teamed up with MacKenzie for the fine Gutbuster and soloed Route Two. In the early 1980s, Aberdeen-based climbers began to take an increasing interest in Cummingston, and a number of lines fell. Colin MacLean freed the formerly aided Hernia Corner and added Skelp and King Swing. Dougie Dinwoodie produced The Nest, Sandy Volestrangler and Fingers Wall. While preparing Cummingston for the 1984 Guide, Alf Robertson climbed most of the remaining easier gaps, particularly several on The Stack. The Guide was the first detailed publication and established Cummingston as a major crag. This opened the way for a flurry of activity by Dinwoodie who grabbed many lines including Aesthetic Ape, the tiring Bat's Wall and several routes on the Orange Wall. Alistair Ross was involved with many of these ascents and added his own routes with Sea Witch and the very sandy Melting Clock. Murray Hamilton visited to add two routes in the collapsed cave.

Covesea had apparently remained untouched since the 1930s but 1985 brought a change when Dinwoodie started to work his way through the lines at Boulder's Bay, with Banana Republic and The Domino Effect. This year and the next saw steady development of the area around Boulder's Bay, the routes generally being longer and having more substance than their Cummingston counterparts. The hardest route produced was Dinwoodie's Fascist Octopus. Other routes came from others including Doug Hawthorn and Colin Murray. Alistair Ross was responsible for a variety of routes, including the development of the esoteric Honeycomb Wall. Development of Covesea has continued to date with a variety of routes, notably Graeme Livingston's ascent of the vicious roof crack in Boulder's Bay, and the area is now a very worthy companion to Cummingston.

The late eighties and early nineties have seen Cummingston reach maturity with the majority of lines ascended. Dinwoodie climbed the Prow on the sea-stack and various routes were added by RAF climbers, the highlight being Nick Clements bold and powerful stretches over the bulge then roof right of Hernia Corner. The area has grown in popularity and perhaps unfortunately it is rare to have the cliffs to yourself.

Logie Head *by Neil Morrison and Andy Nisbet*

Logie Head's history appears to be very recent despite its prominent position on the coast east of Cullen. In 1983, Alfie Robertson came upon the place and added the first routes. He leaked the potential to friends in Aberdeen who duly arrived for a day of new routing when some 10 to 15 routes were added. Richard McHardy climbed Dark Star, Andy Nisbet Sea Anemone, and Dave Lawrence added his Dilemma. Activity was then steady for several years with a variety of people active. Dougie Dinwoodie added Holy Ground. Andy Cunningham and Andy Nisbet climbed Central Belt, and others from Glenmore Lodge added a variety of routes. In 1990, John Hall and friends added several routes to the stack, although these may have been climbed previously by RAF climbers. Logie Head has been developed in a relatively short time into an excellent crag which has gained in popularity. It appears to be worked out, but its setting and the quality of climbing should ensure its continuing popularity.

Clach na Beinn *by Alistair Ross*

The Cairn o' Mounth has been used since prehistoric times as one of the main "ways" to Aberdeen from the south of the country. Over the centuries Edward I and Bonnie Dundee used the Mounth on their campaigns; MacBeth may well have passed by on his way to Lumphanan and in February 1746 the infamous Butcher Cumberland used the Mounth route on his way to Culloden Moor.

However the climbing history of the tor is of a much more recent vintage. It was not until the latter years of the 19th century, that the Cairngorm Club made their early visits to Clach na Beinn. An important result of this patronage was the earliest recorded route on any of the north-east outcrops when W.Garden climbed No.1 Gully in 1901 (now called Cairngorm Club Crack) with the aid of a top rope. Dr J R Levack visited the cliff in 1919 and declared the "bare rock face itself" to be "manifestly impossible". However, the gullies were obviously a different proposition and in the company of, Messrs Garden, J.A.Parker and D.P.Levack he climbed No.2 Gully, being hauled up the last section. In March 1925, Dr Levack returned and climbed Microline without a top rope "giving no great trouble to the leader" and Central Gully was top roped with some "assistance" for the older members of the party.

The next recorded burst of activity came in 1947 when W.D.Brooker ascended The Platform Climb and over the next year (with three school friends) he climbed six new routes including the fine lines of Window Chimney and Square Chimney.

In 1978 the start of a long overdue phase of activity was marked when the three challenging cracks right of Cairngorm Club Crack were assaulted. Although the advent of Friends has made them easier to protect nowadays, these cracks still present a painful struggle for the uninitiated or unwary. Thereafter, it was realised that even the scrappier looking pieces of rock would yield worthwhile routes. For the next four years spasmodic development continued and a number of fine lines were produced, particularly B.Sprunt's Bogendreip Buttress, M.Mac-Donald's route Twilight Zone and G.Strange's Crack o' the Mearns. This period of activity was brought to a fitting close in 1982 with Dinwoodie's lead of Erk. At E3 this is still the crags hardest route with a ground fall a distinct possibility. A quiet spell ensued until 1989 when a further six routes were added by A.Ross, I.Davidson and M.Sutherland whilst checking out grades for the current guide.

Upper Deeside *by Alistair Ross*

Scotland's kings have for centuries hunted the Dee valley from the Braemar area downwards, showing that the prefix "Royal" is not just a modern phenomenon. In 1760, the beneficial properties of the Pannanich Wells were discovered and the fame of the waters soon spread; indeed the building of the village of Ballater was a direct result of this popularity. The next 100 years were to see Victoria lay the foundation stone for the new Balmoral Castle (1853) and in 1866, the Deeside Railway was opened to Ballater. Around this time, quarrying started with granite, silver and lead extracted from the Pass and the granite workings at Cambus o'May were opened.

In comparison to all this, the climbing history of the area is relatively recent, the earliest known ascent being Bill Ewen's Pannanich Cave pitch in 1928. Strangely, there are no records of climbing at the Pass until 1965 when Jim McArtney, Derek Pyper and Alan Corbett climbed Bluter Groove after a morning's drinking in Ballater. This ascent, using wooden wedges amongst other things, was an isolated case as climbing in the hills was of prime importance. Indeed, anyone claiming routes here at this time would have been laughed at.

Although the years 1965-1970 produced a handful of routes, it was during 1971 that the true potential of the Pass was first indicated. Lucky Strike, Medium Cool and Original Route were climbed and Anger and Lust aided. In addition, one of the then hardest routes in the north-east, Black Custard, was led by John Mothersele, a prize line much eyed and top roped by other parties. 1977 was a fruitful year for two southern raiders, Tony Barley and Jerry Peel. Firstly, they freed the upper corner of what is now Pretzel Logic, then overshadowed anything else in the north-east with Peel's Wall. This route was a full two grades harder than anything previously climbed and did much to encourage local climbers to higher levels of fitness and effort. 1980 saw the number of routes at the Pass almost triple. An unprecedented increase which was sustained for a number of years. At this time, Bob Smith nipped in to grab the first free ascent of Anger and Lust. Cadha Dubh was opened up during this period with the ascents of Backwoodsman and Run Rabbit Run. 1982 saw Murray Hamilton, Pete Whillance and Rab Anderson climb Bluter Groove using the arete right of the original route (now Bluter Crack). This was one of the first 6b's in the north-east and is still a demanding test piece.

During 1983, Dougie Dinwoodie climbed Lech Gates and freed Cold Rage to produce a pair of classics. However, the main event was to be the ascent of Smith's Arete. The first E5 in the Pass solved a long standing problem only slightly flawed by a pre-placed runner. Sadly, this was to be Bob Smith's last significant new route. The following year, Graeme Livingston made the first free ascent of the original aided Bluter Groove naming it Bluter Crack to save any confusion with Hamilton's route. In the same year he repeated Smith's Arete in good style and the year culminated with the publishing of the 1984 *North-East Outcrops* Guide.

Hot on the heels of the new guide, Livingston opened up the Upper Gully Wall with the fine Captain Copout. Dinwoodie stepped in to solve the two major problems of Drambo and Demon Drink. Later in the year, he freed the fantastic right-hand finish to Anger and Lust. General Anaesthetic, Distemper and Hot Temper were added in 1986 when Willy Todd joined forces with Graeme Livingston. January 1987 saw Livingston, Strange and Callum Henderson claim the first winter ascent of the Cave Pitch at Pannanich. The summer of 1987 saw various fillers in and Alastair Ross red-pointed his Private Parts on the Upper Gully wall.

Pannanich had been inspected on several occasions prior to August 1987, but it was dismissed as too vegetated for development. That summer Chris Forrest visited the cliff. Frantic and enthusiastic cleaning operations were initiated in secrecy. That September, as well as Freebird and Cool as a Cat, in one days climbing, he accounted for German Holidays, Flush with Pride, Wondrous Stories and Pannanich Wall.

Immediately after the events at Pannanich, Ian Davidson and Alastair Ross returned to the Cadha Dubh and in a two month period literally unearthed nine new routes between VS and E3. Tales of spades, brushes and tied off tree runners have done little to further the acceptance or popularity of these routes. The spring of 1988 saw the same team, plus Colin Stewart and others develop Cambus o'May Quarries, a clutch of routes were produced, including Idiot Savant and No Rest for the Wicked by Ross. The remaining lines at Pannanich were mopped up and the crag's near neighbour, Crag X, was developed. Back at the Pass, Wilson Moir led Bottle of Smoke at the second attempt having been rained off the finishing moves on the first try. Ross also contributed with the impending groove left of Lucky Strike to give Ton Ton Macoute.

Although 1989 and 1990 saw some new routes, the years were ones of consolidation with the majority of the earlier hard routes seeing repeats. At this stage, the Pass seems worked out, perhaps the outlying crags will provide something for the keen new router. However, on a more sobering note, the Pass has become exceptionally popular, erosion of the paths, falling stones from damaged paths and litter are now serious problems. Large school and youth parties who come to abseil and climb leave litter and cause erosion. Climbers who should know better are not blameless with fag packets, tin cans and chalk wrappers littering the crag. Please treat the area with care and concern before the damage is irreparable.

Glen Clova by Grant Farquhar

The first recorded rock climb in the area is H.G.Drummond and H.Alexander's ascent of Craig Maud's Pinnacle Ridge in 1911. In 1934, R.Scott and J.Beedie climbed the steep Diagonal Crack on Juanjorge, an impressive ascent for the time and probably unrepeated! Climbing on the Red Craigs began in 1938 when the 3Js of Scroggie, Scott and Ferguson chimneyed their way up the route of that name on the South-East Crag. In 1939, J.Nisbet and Ferguson discovered the splendid 20 Minute Route up the left edge of the Lower North-West Crag. Later in the year, W.H.Ward and Ferguson climbed the classic Flake Route on the South-East Crag and the awkward Hanging Chimney on the Upper North-West Crag. The following year, Ferguson and G.S.Ritchie wandered up the face right of Flake Route to give the excellent Parapet Route. In the early 1950s, the Upper North-West Crag received some attention. First of all, I.Sutherland and D.Watt grovelled their way up the cleft of the High Level Traverse and then climbed the open chimney on the right of the crag to give W + S Chimney. HLT gained a direct finish from D.Thomas, J.Fleming and G.B.Leslie. Around the same time, D.Brown found a way up the steep exposed face right of the HLT to give Alder.

In 1954, local Forfar climber, Andy Mitchell climbed the open corner on the right of the Lower Crag, Monster's Crack, and Tom Patey shinned up The Beanstalk. The following year, W.K.Divers and K.A.Sturrock added a direct finish to Patey's route with Dander. Two years later the same pair revisited the crags and employed some aid to add Zigzag to the Upper North-West Crag and the fine Wander to the Lower Crag. both of these outings being described as "VS in rubbers".

Up till then, the intimidating main face of the Lower Doonie had remained unclimbed. However, the Dundee-based Carn Dearg MC regularly climbed in the Glen and in 1958, a Carn Dearg party comprising Fred Old, George Malloch, Frank Anderson and Alex Ferguson forced a line up the left hand side to create the superb and sustained Guinness. Two bolts some 6 to 8 inches long were required to overcome a black leaning corner on the second pitch. Also in the 1950s, Jack Ellis fought vegetation to climb his Jungle Route. During the next few years, George Malloch added another couple of excellent routes with his ascents of the exposed face right of Guiness and the bold arete left of Monster's Crack to give Special Brew and Proud Corner respectively. Around this time, B.Forbes used pegs and wooden wedges to aid the central crack on The Red Wall and Martin Hendry gave Guinness its Variation 1.

In the 1960s another Dundee climber, Doug Lang, started climbing in the Glen and among other things, put up Zigzag Direct on the Upper North-West Crag. In 1964, D.Crabbe, J.Howe and Lang pegged their way across the large roof on the left of the crag; Roman Candle was A3.

In the early 1970s, aid continued to be used on most ascents in the Glen. In 1972, J.Cadger and J.Thomson engineered their way up the Upper Doonie to create Vindaloo (VS and A2), a disgraceful ascent involving 6 pegs, 3 bolts, 1 rurp and 1 nut for aid. Also that year, Mick Tighe and the Nevis Guides visited the Glen and climbed what is now pitch 1 of Zigzag Double Direct. In 1976, another aid line appeared on the Upper Doonie when D.Myatt and C.Robinson climbed Cream Cracker (HVS and A2), although this was partly in common with a route known as Trapeze, climbed in the early 1960s.

However, the mid-seventies saw several significant free ascents. In 1974/75, Ged and Ian Reilly freed Guiness and dispensed with the sling on Special Brew. Steve Scott with Ian Reilly freed Zigzag Direct. In 1976, Murray Hamilton with Dave Brown freed The Red Wall and Witches Tooth. Also that year, Pat Standing and Roy Tait added Variation 2 to Guiness and furthered the alcoholic tradition of the crag with Heinekin.

In 1982, Alec 'Tam' Thomson and Ian Shepherd, part of a large contingent of Forfar-based climbers who regularly climbed in the Glen, forced the line of Puddin' Fingers with 3 aid points. The following year, Hamilton. with Duncan MacCallum and Rab Anderson, made an on-sight free ascent of Roman Candle and with John 'Spider' Mackenzie, breached the fearsome Central Crag with Mearns' Wall. That year, the long-neglected Juanjorge received its first modern routes with Roslin Riviera from Hamilton and Greg Strange and Ladies of the Canyon from Kenny Spence and Hamilton, both these excellent routes being on immaculate granite. Around this time, Neil Shepherd from Arbroath added the superb Wandered and the strenuous Taken by Force to the Lower North-West Crag. Hamilton teamed up with Shepherd to climb the crack left of Roman Candle which became Just Another Sparkler. The Altduthrie Slabs also received its first route, Solution Socket, by Ged Reilly and Alistair 'Plod' Ross.

During 1985 several new lines were found on the crags. Nick Sharpe freed the overhang of Cream Cracker and boldly stole the much-eyed line of Special Brew Direct. On the same day in May, Chris Flewitt and Shepherd surmounted the large overhang to the left of The Doonie; Solar Wind, and climbed up the flake ladder of Summer's Over. Shepherd also soloed the first ascent of Halloween and with Graeme Woodfine, scaled the sharp arete of Mandy. A number of Aberdeen-based climbers also made fruitful trips to the Glen. On the Upper North-West Crag, Colin Maclean conjured up The Sorcerer and his Apprentice. Hamilton made the second ascent of The Sorcerer, running both pitches together in the process. Also on this crag, Alistair Ross and Ged Reilly climbed Kremlin Control, although the top pitch had been recorded by Lang as a variation to Alder in 1968.

Over on the Upper Doonie, Ross and Reilly with Forrest Templeton, added Jungle Warfare to the extreme right-hand edge of the crag. On the Central Crag, Dougie Dinwoodie climbed the improbable fangs of Black Adder. Also that year, a group of young Dundee-based climbers including Simon Stewart, Graeme Ettle and Grant Farquhar, who had served their 'apprenticeship' in the Glen, discovered some new lines including Guinless, Zigzag Double Direct, Rocketman and the first free ascent of the strenuous Puddin' Fingers.

Over the excellent summer of 1986, Stewart partnered variously by Catherine Smith, Chris Cracknell, Bruce Strachan, Lee Delaney, Ettle and Farquhar added a batch of new routes including The Thin Wall, Four Corner's Route, Sun Goes Down, Carn Dearg Corner, Kremlin Control Direct, 999, Jailbreak, Monster Munch, Belhaven and almost single-handedly, developed the Upper Doonie with Dancin' in the Ruins, Vindaloo Direct (after chopping the bolts), The Slicer, The Grater and Fastbreeder. Chris Cracknell added Headspread and The Catwalk to this crag and Agrajaz to the quarry. Over on the Central Crag, Ettle climbed West Side Story and Dinwoodie completed the trilogy of E4s with his excellent Empire of the Sun. Down on the South-East Crag, Brian Lawrie found his Clairvoyant Reality which was quickly superseded by Neil Shepherd's Wildebeest and Stewart's Spider. On Juanjorge, Dinwoodie and Strange climbed Rhiannon while across the Glen, Alec Thomson and Ian Shepherd added two routes to the slabs of Altduthrie. Late in the season, Farquhar and Stewart girdled the Lower Doonie with The Pub Crawl and Ettle and Strachan added Elliptical Dreams to the Upper Doonie.

In 1987 Stewart filled some more gaps with The Cosmic Pump, Ion Drive, Sidestep, Jug Wall, Shadow on the Wall and Chitteroo. Dinwoodie revisited Juanjorge to add Granite Fields and John Morgan and Steve Hill had some Trouble With Lichen on Craig Maud. In May, Ettle top roped the overhanging arete in the centre of the Upper Doonie, eventually leading it with pre-placed runners to create the Glen's hardest and most serious route. Graded E6 6a for an on-sight ascent, DRI remains unrepeated at the time of writing. The crags were deserted until September when Stewart, who had been put out of action by a bad fall at Creag Dubh, returned to add Green Shield, Green Bunny and Henry's Cat to the Upper Doonie. Later that month, over the same weekend, Farquhar and Ettle crossed the Upper and Lower North-West Crags and the South-East Crag to give their respective girdle traverses. Farquhar and Stewart returned a few days after and climbed The Cold War, Faulty Towers, The Supernatural Anaesthetist and Catbird. The last route of the year went to Ettle, when after extensive practice he led the bold Cinderella with a rest point on the top peg.

Early in 1988 Farquhar found The Furstenberg Finish and The Whoremistress on The Doonie, while Stewart developed the High Crag with a batch of small routes. Going on-sight, Gary Latter and Kev Howett freed Cinderella of her rest point. Later in the year, Farquhar and Mark McGowan wobbled their way up the unfriendly Taste Me! on sight.

The crags were very quiet in 1989 with only two routes recorded; Stuart Cameron's pre-practised ascent of The Flying Cabbage Heads in the quarry and Overhanging Coroner with Grant Campbell.

In 1990, Farquhar and Arthur Collins established A Vanishing Breed which was quickly repeated by Malcolm Smith and Stuart Cameron in red-point style. Also that year, Farquhar and Clare Carolan added Scoopy Doo and Ride My Face to Chicago. This brings the history of climbing in this Angus Glen up to date. Unfortunately, details of the pre-1980s routes are a bit vague. Sadly some routes have been lost in the mists of time; for instance on The Doonie, where are Elephant's Slab, Cornfoot's Corner and Mewat's Renege?

The Angus Quarries by Neil Shepherd
First visited during the mid-1970s, Legaston and Balmashanner Quarries were used by the Royal Marines from Condor for abseiling and aid practice with some development of easier free climbs. At Legaston a large deep pool prevented access to many of the faces whilst Balmashanner's radical right wall proved insurmountable. However in 1977, the Legaston pool was filled in, improving access, and an ambitious low level traverse was chipped at Balmashanner, which remained unclimbed in one push until 1989.

In 1981 and 1982, the first properly documented free climbs were established at Legaston by David McKelvie and Neil Shepherd, who later added routes to Ring Buttress with Kenny Edwards. Meanwhile a group of Marines were adding easier routes to Main wall and painting on the route names. During the good summers of 1983 and 1984, Shepherd with Malcolm Cameron and Graham

Woodfine climbed and repeated a large number of routes and other climbers started to visit the quarry and add routes of their own. Inclement weather during 1985 curtailed activity, however Legaston's first 6b was added by Malcolm Cameron with Brian the Snail Direct Start and Spider MacKenzie made a bold bolt free lead of No Remorse.

Attention switched the following year to Balmashanner's right wall where Shepherd cleaned and bolted what was later to become Savage Amusement and Richard Worth and Graeme Ettle independently cleaned and top roped the line of Hell Bent. At Legaston Shepherd produced the notable Spandex Ballet. Little of note was done in 1987 except for the theft of all the in situ gear at Legaston and Ken Clarke's "discovery" of the Red Head's potential near Inverkeilor with mammoth cleaning sessions producing The Engine Driver.

During 1988, most local attention was focused on Balmashanner and in June, 17-year old Dave Douglas led the first route to breach the right wall with Hell Bent for Lycra. Other routes then fell quickly to both Shepherd and Douglas, ranging from E3 to E5, many being repeated by others including Grant Farquhar and Mark McGowan. New routing began early in 1989 with Shepherd climbing Start the Fire in January at Balmashanner, whilst at Legaston the bold Hunt the Ratbag was added by Myles Bright. Farquhar and Douglas repeated Spandex Ballet. In June, Shepherd led Manifestations at Balmashanner, quickly repeated by Douglas who went on to climb the very powerful Delivery Man as well as completing the whole low level traverse in one push. Finally, 15-year old Stuart Cameron excelled to make the second ascent of Savage Amusement.

1990 saw little new route activity, but the popularity of both quarries increased. The in situ equipment was improved, particularly at Balmashanner. However, before the rains arrived Grant Farquhar and Stuart Cameron redpointed the bolted project at Balmashanner to give Gravity's Rainbow. A year later Cameron added The Niche, and then upped the ante yet again in 1992 with his Merchant of Menace. The quality and quantity of the in situ gear at both Legaston and Balmashanner was improved on a regular basis throughout 1992 and 1993, turning both into excellent sports climbing venues with welcome lower-off points. Also in 1992 and 1993, Ley Quarry near Forfar was developed as a sports crag by Neil Shepherd and George Ridge and friends. Well bolted, south-facing and quick drying, it provides an excellent early and late season venue.

Notes on the Use of the Guide

Grading of Rock Climbs

The normal British grading system of Easy, Moderate, Difficult, Very Difficult, Severe, Very Severe (VS), Hard Very Severe (HVS) and Extremely Severe is used. The Extreme grade is sub-divided into E1, E2, E3, E4, E5, E6 and E7.

Technical grades have been given where known. The normal range of technical grades expected on routes of the given overall grade are as follows: VS - 4b, 4c, 5a; HVS - 4c, 5a, 5b; E1 - 5a, 5b, 5c; E2 - 5b, 5c, 6a; E3 - 5c, 6a; E4 - 5c, 6a, 6b; E5 - 6a, 6b. Routes with a technical grade at the lower end of the range will be sustained or poorly protected, while those with grades at the upper end of the expected range will have a short and generally well protected crux section.

Although the British system is thought second to none by those who use it, it is known to confuse visitors from abroad. For their benefit, it can be assumed that 5a, 5b, 5c and 6a correspond approximately to the American grades of 5.9, 5.10a/b, 5.10c/d and 5.11a/b respectively. A number bolt protected climbs have been produced in the last few years. These have been given French grades, which are more suitable for this style of hard climb. As a rough guide, F6b is approximately British 5c and F6c is British 6a; F6c climbs would be in the E3 and E4 range. At higher French grades the situation becomes more complicated, but if you can climb at that standard you'll know all about it anyway.

An attempt has been made to equate the grades with those of the bigger mountain crags, rather than with those of typically harsh and undergraded outcrop areas. This is not to say that the climber should not be wary of the odd undergrading as a number of climbs in this guide are unchecked and unrepeated. Additionally there may be some variations between areas in the guide. All gradings are for on-sight leading of routes without prior top-roping, sieging, inspection or advice. It is regrettable to note that not all of the routes in this guide have been led on sight. One can only hope that future generations will put this right with pure on sight leads of previously sieged routes.

Bolts

After extensive consultation with all interested parties, the Mountaineering Council of Scotland has issued a policy statement on the use of bolts in Scotland. This policy is endorsed by the Publications Sub-Committee of the Scottish Mountaineering Club.

"The MCofS acknowledge that there is a place for bolts in the future development of Scottish climbing. However, to ensure that the highly regarded ethos of, and future development of, traditional climbing (involving the use of leader-placed and second-removed protection) is not threatened, it is felt that the use of bolts should be limited to the production of sport climbs. There should be no retrospective bolting of established climbs for protection or belays, and there should be no minimalist bolting.

The production of sport climbs with bolts is acceptable on natural rock only when all the following conditions have been satisfied:

(1) On low-lying cliffs, provided that such development is not against the wishes of the landowner. Bolts are inappropriate on mountain cliffs and sea-cliffs.

(2) On routes where natural protection is absent or is inadequate for the repeated falls that such routes necessitate.

(3) Where the rock is steep and provides climbs of a high order of difficulty, at the forefront of developments of the day.

(4) Where there is no historical or local anti-bolt ethic.

Concerning quarried rock, it is felt that any future development should be constrained only by points (2) and (4) above.

Finally, it is felt that bolts should be located to ensure minimum visual impact and should be placed according to current best practices.

It is intended that these principles are not seen as simply restrictive rules, but as a guide to promote the positive development of Scottish climbing, where sports climbing, rather than becoming a substitute for traditional climbing, grows alongside it."

Terminology

Left and right refer to a climber facing the cliff or facing downhill in descent. In cases of potential ambiguity a compass direction is also given. Pegs and other fixed gear are for protection only, except where specifically stated that they are for direct aid. Do not assume that they will either be in place or in a safe state of repair.

Diagrams

Some of the crags have accompanying diagrams to aid the identification of the climbs. In these instances the descriptions in the text have numbers which correspond to the numbers of the lines on the diagrams. If a numbered route is not shown on the diagram then it will be found in numerical order with respect to those that are.

Recommended Routes

No list of recommended climbs is given, instead a star grading system for quality has been used. Three stars indicates a route of the highest quality. If a route has no star this does not necessarily mean that it is poor, it may also indicate that insufficient is known about that route properly to assess its quality. Star ratings may be found to be inconsistent. It is hoped that climbers using this guide will inform the authors of such inconsistencies so that future editions of the guide can be improved.

Crag quality is perhaps even more subjective but crucial to avoid disappointment. Each section's introduction attempts to give an indication of crag quality and offers tips about conditions, birds, etc. This is particularly important on the sea cliffs where crag quality will be affected by weather conditions and the bird situation.

New Routes
New routes can be recorded in the Aberdeen New Route book which at the time of going to print is kept in Rocky Crags, George Street, Aberdeen. New routes can also be sent to the New Routes Editor of the Scottish Mountaineering Club.

First Ascentionists
The year of first ascent, where known, is given in the text. However, due to the constraints of space the full list of first ascentionists has not been reproduced. This has been archived by members of the Etchachan Club. More details of the more notable and influential first ascents may be gleaned from the detailed historical sections.

Maps and Other Sources of Information
Place names and map references have in general been taken from the OS 1:50000 Landranger Series maps. The maps that are required are: sheet 38 (Aberdeen); sheet 45 (Stonehaven); sheet 30 (Fraserburgh); sheet 29 (Banff); sheet 28 (Elgin); sheet 44 (Ballater); and sheet 54 (Dundee).
    The meanings and pronunciations of local place names can be found in *Scottish Hill and Mountain Names* by Peter Drummond, published by the Scottish Mountaineering Trust (1991). Much useful information, particularly about the areas surrounding the inland crags, can be found in the Scottish Mountaineering Club District Guide *The Cairngorms* (1992), published by the Scottish Mountaineering Trust.

Mountain Rescue
In case of an accident requiring rescue or medical attention, contact the Police. Try to leave someone with the victim, who should in any case be made as comfortable as possible. Some knowledge of rudimentary first aid is a desirable thing for a climber to have, so it is wise to consult one of the large number of suitable books on mountaineering first aid and rescue techniques.

Nigg Bay to Cove Bay

Despite the proximity of the outskirts of Aberdeen, the backdrop of industrial estate and rubbish tip detracts little from the pleasant atmosphere of the coastal fringe. Perhaps the most striking feature of this stretch of coast is the tremendous variety of rock. Although rather small, the cliffs still provide many worthwhile climbs and some long sea-level traverses on generally steep sound rock.

This well developed and popular area has many routes in the lower grades, which makes this the best area on the coast for the beginner. Deceptive Wall and Black Rock Gulch in particular offer some excellent easier routes. Souter Head guarantees good climbing with quality routes at all grades up to E3. For those in search of sterner stuff, Long Slough is the place to go, with its impressive collection of overhanging classics. It is also one of the few cliffs on the coast sufficiently warm and dry to allow regular climbing in winter. In fact, winter and early spring are the best times of the year to visit the largest cliff in the area, The Red Cliff, which unfortunately turns white in summer when it is festooned with birds. Elsewhere in this section, birds do not pose problems except at Long Slough Red Rocks, where a few routes have recently been colonised.

Finally, it should be noted that although most of the smaller cliffs dry quickly after rain, virtually all climbing here is impracticable in high seas.

Access
The coastal road and footpath traversing from Nigg Bay to Cove Bay (see map) provide easy access to all the cliffs. Buses from the city centre to Balnagask (Torry) and Cove Village currently come within 10 minutes walk of the first cliffs. The railway line must be crossed, best done at one of four points, each giving the best access to the following cliffs:

Black Dyke to Dead McIvor Gulch — About 150 metres south of the Coastguard Station, the coastal road turns sharp right to cross the railway line. Instead of crossing this bridge, continue down the dirt track on the left, where cars can be parked.

Deceptive Wall and Long Slough to Alan's Cliff — A bridge crosses the railway at Doonies Model Farm. About 250 metres south of this a farm track goes under the railway. Parking is on both sides of road.

The Humpback and Humpback Gulch, and Seal's Hole — A farm track goes under the railway at the junction of Altens Farm Road and the coastal road. Limited parking.

Black Rock Gulch to The Red Cliff — About 200 metres south of Altens Farm Road, a bridge crosses the railway beside the recently renovated Burnbanks village. Plentiful parking.

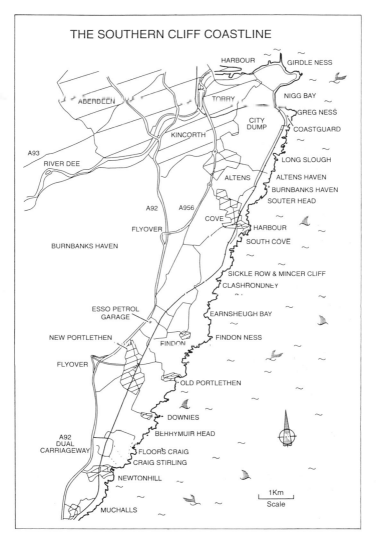

THE SOUTHERN CLIFF COASTLINE

HARBOUR
GIRDLE NESS
ABERDEEN
TORRY
NIGG BAY
GREG NESS
COASTGUARD
CITY DUMP
KINCORTH
A93
LONG SLOUGH
RIVER DEE
ALTENS
ALTENS HAVEN
BURNBANKS HAVEN
SOUTER HEAD
A92   A956
COVE
FLYOVER
HARBOUR
BURNBANKS HAVEN
SOUTH COVE
SICKLE ROW & MINCER CLIFF
CLASHRONDNEY
ESSO PETROL
GARAGE
EARNSHEUGH BAY
NEW PORTLETHEN
FINDON NESS
FINDON
FLYOVER
OLD PORTLETHEN
DOWNIES
BEHHYMUIR HEAD
A92
DUAL
CARRIAGEWAY
FLOORS CRAIG
CRAIG STIRLING
NEWTONHILL
MUCHALLS

1Km
Scale

THE BLACK DYKE   *(Map Ref 969 038)*

From where the coastal road crosses the railway line, follow the coastal path straight down towards the sea, and then northwards for about 100 metres to where a narrow grass topped ridge runs out north-east. The ridge is a dyke of unusual dark rock (dolerite) which provides almost gritstone-like climbing. Descent of the ridge (Moderate by the north-west corner) leads down past a steep snout to a large platform from where access may be gained to the Black Dyke and the Whisky Cliff.

There are a number of excellent steep problems in the vicinity of the snout and also along the south-east facing wall. The steep black north-west wall is often greasy, but when dry the seaward section gives good steep climbing on sound rock. A traverse at sea-level from the platform across this wall is Mild Severe. A 15m route starts from a point where the traverse reaches the boulders at the back of the inlet. Climb up to a small roof and break out right to a grassy finish (Severe).

THE WHISKY CLIFF

This is the extensive south-east facing wall of the Black Dyke. It runs back from the snout for some 120 metres to terminate at a rather off-putting rubbish tip, the descent of which is definitely not recommended. The wall is separated from an island by a narrow tidal channel. At very low tide it is possible to scramble over to this island, which can be easily traversed then descended to reach the climbs. Otherwise, access is by abseil (the third large fence post along the path is directly above the routes) or by the following route:

Whisky Traverse   90m   Mild Severe *   (1960s)
Start from the platform below the snout. Follow ledges near high water mark, move up to higher ledges then continue, descending slightly to a point where the wall overhangs. Traverse below overhangs to shelves and the foot of the rubbish dump. The final section is occasionally wet and slimy and in such conditions problematical.

Gable End   12m   VS 4b
At a point on the traverse where the upper wall becomes overhanging there is a left-trending groove. Climb this groove with a very awkward start (it is easier to traverse in a few feet higher than girdle ledge). Ignore ledges on the left and climb a steep crack above to easy ground.

Diagonal   25m   Severe *
Beyond the main overhang and the wettest section of the cliff there is an isolated overhang with a large ledge above. Diagonal takes the obvious right-slanting line passing the isolated overhang on the right. Continue right to a break in the upper cliff.

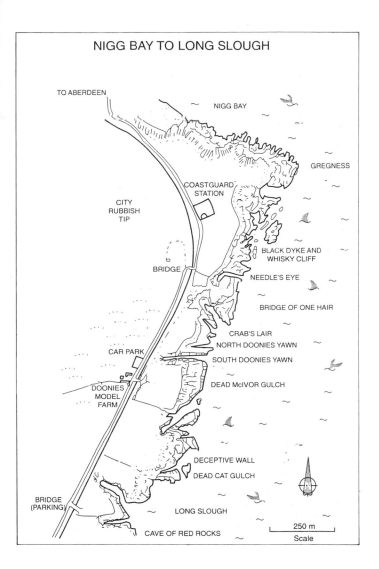

NIGG BAY TO LONG SLOUGH

TO ABERDEEN

NIGG BAY

GREGNESS

COASTGUARD
STATION

CITY
RUBBISH
TIP

BLACK DYKE AND
WHISKY CLIFF

BRIDGE

NEEDLE'S EYE

BRIDGE OF ONE HAIR

CRAB'S LAIR
NORTH DOONIES YAWN

CAR PARK

SOUTH DOONIES YAWN

DOONIES
MODEL
FARM

DEAD McIVOR GULCH

DECEPTIVE WALL

DEAD CAT GULCH

BRIDGE
(PARKING)

LONG SLOUGH

250 m

CAVE OF RED ROCKS

Scale

Fiskavaig   20m   VS 4c *   (1981)
Start directly below the isolated overhang. Go up slightly left, move right and climb a short wall above the overhang to the big ledge. Climb the wall above to exit past a prominent detached flake. There is a belay stake up the grass bank on the left.

Islander   20m   E3 5c **   (1991)
Start 5 metres left of Fiskavaig, climb straight up blocks and a short groove to make an awkward move right onto the large ledge of Fiskavaig. From the left end of the ledge, climb the bulging wall via cracks direct to the top. The top section usually seeps, but is still climbable.

The Belles, The Belles   20m   E4 6b **   (1991)
Start directly below the centre of the bulging wall, move up to an obvious square-cut black ledge, then continue up and left via cracks in the bulging wall to a small ledge, and climb direct to the top.

Talisker   20m   E1 5a ***   (1972)
Left of Fiskavaig the cliff is very steep and compact, the only obvious feature being a triangular niche 12m up. This fine intimidating route gains the niche then climbs out right to the top. Start directly below the niche where the boulders are only covered at high tide. Climb up left until a traverse right leads into the niche. Move out right and up vertical wall above. Very exposed.

The MacAllan Finish   5m   E2 5c *   (1991)
This pulls directly through the Talisker roof where that route traverses right.

Neat and Cool   20m   E2 5c ***   (1991)
Start 3 metres left of Talisker, climb a faint groove line to a ledge below a steep wall. Climb the steep wall and pull through the overhang on huge holds. Wild.

The Malt Ramp   25m   Mild Severe **
Start beside Talisker and climb up left for about 10m. Move up right and climb the prominent hanging ramp left of the steep Talisker prow.

There have been other routes made on the Whisky Cliff, particularly on the easier-angled section at the seaward end. However, apart from the routes described these tend to lack definition or interest.

BRIDGE OF ONE HAIR

This is the large promontory immediately east of where the coast road crosses the railway. It has a triangulation point on its flat top and is surrounded by a large chain link fence; the best access is to squeeze round the fence at either end. Recently, several pits have been sunk into the promontory. These are currently being used as a dumping ground for chemical sludge. This revolting stuff has a hideous glistening appearance and a disturbing aroma. On warm days following dumping, the stench can become overpowering.

The vista from the tip of the headland can be overwhelmingly bleak; it is often possible to discern the City's sewage outflow snaking gently out to sea. If you are not too depressed by this stage, access to the climbs (on unpolluted and odourless rock) is by an easy scramble down the north-east tip to reach a broad platform on the seaward face. Alternatively, climbs on the very steep North Wall can be reached by crossing the old rubbish tip at the foot of the Whisky Cliff. Low tide required.

NORTH WALL

This is separated from the neighbouring island by a narrow gap known as the Needle's Eye. The traverse of this wall gives an interesting climb. It is best started from the landward end, but can be climbed in either direction at the same grade.

North-Facing Wall   60m   Mild VS 4b   (1965)
From foot of rubbish dump climb diagonally left round an arete into a prominent corner. Descent to near high water level and continue traversing to a good halfway ledge. Climb steeply up left to gain ramp. Go up this, then swing down and continue at about one-third height to reach the broad platform on the seaward face. A combination of this traverse, the Whisky Traverse and the traverse of the north-west facing wall of the Black Dyke gives fair value.

North-West Corner   25m   Severe
The prominent corner at the landward end.

The following two climbs begin at different points on the North Wall traverse. Neither is likely to become popular.

Rubbish   20m   HVS 5a   (1983)
Start at a ledge directly below the right-hand end of a large grass ledge at two-thirds height. Climb wall to the right end of the ledge. Finish up the wall just right of the obvious groove.

Dreadlock Holiday   20m   E1 5a   (1983)
This climbs the overhanging section of the north-facing wall towards the seaward end. Start at the next ledge left from the 'Rubbish' ledge (the 'first ledge' if traversing from the seaward end). Climb up to a flake, move right, then go 2 metres left across the wall. Finish up right at a block at top.

On the seaward face a series of short walls above a broad platform provide many good fingery problems. The obvious short corner at the southern end is Hard Severe, while the sizeable smooth wall 6 metres to its right is HVS 5a.

Last Thread Traverse   30m   Difficult **
This is the traverse south from the platform. Here a steep 12m wall drops into the sea. The wall is covered in good holds and may be climbed at any point, nowhere exceeding Severe. The traverse threads the cliff at about mid-height and provides exciting climbing for the grade.

CRABS' LAIR

About 100 metres south of Bridge of One Hair, and 40 metres after the coastal path takes a sharp turn southwards, the steep pink-splashed north-facing wall of Crabs' Lair can be seen. A useful descent ramp (Moderate) leads down the back wall to the foot of a wet black corner. Directly below the ramp is a short right-angled corner, **Johnny's Corner**, an awkward one move problem (4c).

Right-Hand Corner   8m   VS 5a   (1960s)
The steep groove left of the wet back corner has some brittle rock.

Central Arete   8m   Hard Severe *   (1960s)
The obvious arete left of Right-Hand Corner gives a super little pitch.

Central Groove   8m   Hard Severe   (1960s)
Climb the shallow groove left of the arete, moving onto the arete at the top.

Turnpike   10m   Severe   (1960s)
Climb the overhang left of Central Groove to a ledge. Continue up the corner.

Pike Wall   10m   VS 4c   (1960s)
Start directly below a red quartz wall. Climb straight up to the ledge of Turnpike, then continue up red wall with poor rock at top.

Shield   10m   Severe
Immediately south is another north-facing wall above the sea. Climb the left side of the prominent shield of rock (loose).

NORTH DOONIES YAWN

South of Crabs' Lair and about 100 metres north of Doonies Model Farm (where a farm track crosses the railway) are two major inlets. North Doonies Yawn, the smaller of the two inlets, has two excellent traverses. South Doonies Yawn has no worthwhile climbs.

Fall Out Chimney   10m   Moderate   (1950s)
The obvious chimney near the seaward end of the north wall provides a useful means of descent.

North Wall Traverse   45m   VS 4b *   (1960s)
Low tide required. Start at the seaward end. The bulges at halfway are best taken direct, but other ways are possible. Thereafter, much variation is possible, but it is best to keep low.

Jerry Light's Traverse   45m   HVS 5a **   (1965)
This is the traverse of the south wall. Low tide essential. Traverse from the seaward end (passing at one point below an impressive overhanging and unclimbed crack) and finish diagonally up the obvious ledge exiting left.

DEAD McIVOR GULCH

This is the small dry ravine directly opposite the Doonies Farm Bridge, approximately 100 metres south of South Doonies Yawn. Descend grassy slopes to reach the ravine, which has an undercut south wall and a slabby north wall (easily descended).

Spider's Walk   10m   VS 4c   (1976)
Climb the obvious arete, surmounting an unlikely roof at the start.

Thirty metres south of Dead McIvor Gulch some short steep walls above a ramp provide interesting problems on slightly brittle rock. The next few cliffs are best approached via the farm track under the railway about 250 metres south of Doonies Farm Bridge. Once under the bridge, a short cut across the field on the left gives quick access to The Long Slough. However, this is usually very muddy and it is probably always best to take the long way round by the coastal path.

DECEPTIVE WALL   *(Map Ref 967 030)*

About 100 metres north of Long Slough a very narrow inlet (Dead Cat Gulch) cuts inland for 25 metres. Follow flat clifftop rocks north from this inlet until an easy chockstone gully gives access to a broad tidal platform below this straight section of cliff. The cliff is pleasantly situated and provides good, well protected climbing in the lower grades on generally excellent rock.

Yawn Pillar   10m   Mild VS 4a
Just north of the descent gully is a steep edge, near the head of a narrow tidal channel. Climb straight up north-east face of the pillar.
   The steep wall to the left has been climbed (Very Difficult).

Cormorant   6m   Very Difficult
Climb the groove just round the corner from the descent gully.

All Quiet   6m   VS 4c   (1981)
Climb to the overhang, then the short corner above just left of Cormorant. Rather artificial.

Waves   6m   Hard Severe
Climb to overhang of All Quiet. Move left and continue up a crack.

The Somme   10m   Mild VS 4b *
Climb the steep wall left of Waves, with some long reaches between superb holds.

Big Daddy   10m   Severe *
The obvious crack leads to a niche, then climb the wall above.

Fretted Socket   10m   Severe *
Climb thin cracks bending left from the start of Big Daddy.

Cod Eyes   10m   Mild VS 4b
The right-hand of twin cracks. Swing left through the bulge at top.
Fishbone Variation: Severe
Traverse right to finish in the obvious short corner at the top of Fretted Socket.

Untroubled Blue   10m   Mild Severe *
Climb the left-hand crack.

Diversion   10m   Mild Severe
Climb wall left of Untroubled Blue to the overhang. Move right, then go up to the top.

Cruise   8m   VS 4b *
Climb the bulge near the south end of the wall direct.

Damp Start   8m   Difficult *
The obvious corner at the end of the wall.

Deceptive Traverse   45m   Very Difficult   (1950s)
The sea-level traverse of this wall from north to south gives some enjoyable climbing, best at high tide. The traverse ends in Dead Cat Gulch. The walls of this can be bridged to finish. Alternatively, cross the gulch and follow ledges and short walls to eventually reach Long Slough.

THE LONG SLOUGH   *(Map Ref 966 029)*

This is the largest inlet on this section of the coast. It runs back as far as the railway line and is characterised by a prominent stack on the south side, the Long Slough Pinnacle.

NORTH WALL

At the seaward end of the North Wall there are a number of large overhangs above a broad rock shelf. These give some of the best climbing on the cliffs south of Aberdeen, and also the only decent bouldering within easy access of the city.
   To gain the broad shelf, walk down grass slopes at the seaward end of the inlet and descend easy rocks behind a squat tower at a point where a short steep south-facing wall runs out towards the sea. All the obvious features on this wall have been climbed, but the rock is suspect. Just round the corner from the descent the first steep wall has an overhang at half-height and a ledge on the left. This is the seaward face of the squat tower.

Heir Apparent   8m   HVS 5a   (1981)
Climb the brittle lower wall and go straight over the overhang via an obvious large pocket to the top, without stepping onto the platform. Strenuous.

The next section of cliff is higher, but at an easier angle. It leads round a corner past a little bulging crack (Very Difficult) and a black corner (Severe) to the first overhang. The next two routes ascend the short overhang above the obvious right-trending slab ramp (Very Difficult).

Internal Haemorrhage   8m   HVS 5a   (1981)
Climb the slab to an overhang. Continue up the groove above using a conspicuous undercut knob to start.

Brain Death   8m   E2 5b *   (1981)
Climb the slab to the overhang as for Internal Haemorrhage. Swing out left on flat holds. Once established above the roof a testing move out left leads to easier ground.

The next overhanging bay has a prominent black corner (Very Difficult, often wet).

Quartz Deviant   10m   Severe
Start up the black corner then move onto the left wall above the overhang. Climb the quartz fault, moving right at the top. A direct start provides an acrobatic problem. Climb the overhang using a flat hold. Nothing less than a pull onto the top quartz flake satisfies the requirement of this problem (6a). There are other hard problems on the overhang on the left.

The overhangs above the next bay provide the best of the climbing here. The overhangs are underlain by a broad platform, which according to a previous guide "forms a sheltered sun trap from which to watch the antics of young tigers"!

Zombie Right-Hand   10m   VS 5b *   (1978)
This is the first line of weakness round the edge to the left of Quartz Deviant. Climb the initial overhang (crux) and swing up right into a short groove below the next overhang. Surmount this and continue straight up to join Zombie at the bulge.

Twisted Crack   10m   HVS 5a *   (1972)
Climb the bulge left of Zombie Right-Hand to gain the slab of Zombie. Continue straight over the overhang above.

Zombie   12m   Severe *
Climb the short corner left of Twisted Crack to gain a slab below the overhang. Traverse up right (crossing Twisted Crack) across a slab, then go over a slight bulge to a ledge. Climb the short wall to the top.

Bob's Overhang   10m   E4 6a ***   (1983)
In the middle of the main overhang left of Zombie is a prominent triangular flake. Gain and climb the flake to its apex, then make testing moves out right and pull over the top.

Double Dyno or Die   10m   E5 6b **   (1985)
As the route implies, this is a bold and committing route involving some dynamic climbing. It is a direct variant of Bob's Overhang, climbing the full height of the roof. Follow Bob's to the end of the big flake, move up and left, then make a move to a hold at the bottom of a small flake. It is possible to reach left at this point to place a Friend 1 or 2. Continue up the flake to make hard moves round the lip.

Black Velvet   10m   E4 6b ***   (1981)
The spectacular overhanging groove on the left of the main overhang left of Zombie. Climb up to a niche (where pigeons sometimes nest) and move up into the groove. The perplexing exit at the top is the crux. From a cramped resting position below the final roof pull out left onto the top of the left wall.

Red Death   10m   E3 6b ***   (1979)
The hanging red groove on the left wall of this bay has become the classic test piece on this section of the coast. Climb up impending rock moving slightly right to gain a tantalising flake at base of groove. Continue more easily up a groove to the top. The initial section has lost holds and is now harder. The original start is harder and traverses in from the "doos' nest niche" of Black Velvet (6b). A metre or so right of the usual start, another variation start gains the flake at 6b.

The Immaculate Collection   15m   E4 6b   (1991)
Climb Red Death to a traverse line into Black Velvet. Step up to its cramped rest then move right to finish up Double Dyno. Not much new climbing but fun.

Mad Dogs and Englishmen   10m   E4 6a *   (1983)
The arete and flake left of Red Death. Start up Zeta until it is possible to gain the first large hold on the arete. Follow the arete to the flake then climb round it to a large hold on Red Death. Either finish up this, or better, climb the overhang on the right direct (5b).

The Jobbie Stabber's Finish   10m   E4 6a *   (1987)
A direct up the arete of Mad Dogs and Englishmen. Follow this route to the flake. Reach up for incuts and traverse left along these to the arete. Finish straight up the arete on its right side.

Zeta   10m   Mild VS 4a   (1950s)
Start in the corner left of Red Death and climb steeply up and left to the crest of the rib. Climb to the final steepening where a pull up right on suspect rock leads to the top.

Android   10m   VS 4c   (1970s)
Climb the break in the overhang just left of Zeta and continue up the steep groove to finish left of Zeta.

Sneak   10m   VS 4b *   (1972)
Start left of Android and about 3 metres left of Zeta. Pull up leftwards through the overhang and follow shallow grooves to the top.

LONG SLOUGH TO SOUTH COVE

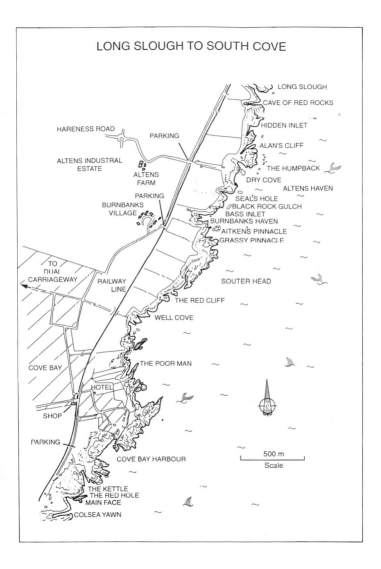

LONG SLOUGH
CAVE OF RED ROCKS
HIDDEN INLET
ALAN'S CLIFF
THE HUMPBACK
DRY COVE
ALTENS HAVEN
SEAL'S HOLE
BLACK ROCK GULCH
BASS INLET
BURNBANKS HAVEN
AITKEN'S PINNACLE
GRASSY PINNACLE

HARENESS ROAD
PARKING
ALTENS INDUSTRIAL ESTATE
ALTENS FARM
PARKING
BURNBANKS VILLAGE

TO DUAL CARRIAGEWAY
RAILWAY LINE
SOUTER HEAD
THE RED CLIFF
WELL COVE

COVE BAY
HOTEL
SHOP
PARKING

THE POOR MAN

COVE BAY HARBOUR

500 m
Scale

THE KETTLE
THE RED HOLE
MAIN FACE
COLSEA YAWN

Leaning Meanie   12m   E1 5a *   (1978)
The overhanging groove in the recess left of Sneak is sustained and strenuous
with some dubious rock near the top. Well protected and worthwhile, but
sometimes wet.

It is possible to make a low level traverse across the whole of this section of
cliff from Sneak to Heir Apparent. The climbing need never be more than a few
metres above the deck (6a).

The Great Cave Route   110m   Severe   (1948)
This is the traverse of the whole north wall starting from the rock shelf at the
seaward end. It is technically Severe, but involves two intimidating jumps and
some unreliable rock. A low tide and calm sea is recommended. Start below the
Zombie-Zeta overhangs and descend almost to sea-level. Traverse below the
overhang and continue at more or less the same level, jumping the two prominent caves. (The first cave is known as the Great Cave). An interesting and
memorable expedition.

THE LONG SLOUGH PINNACLE

From the back of the Slough flat tidal rocks lead out beneath unpleasant
vegetated cliffs to a prominent stack about halfway along the south wall. This
interesting large fin of rock may be ascended by climbing from the neck joining
it to the main cliff. The rock is poor and the climbing Very Difficult. A more
enjoyable way to climb the pinnacle is to traverse just above sea-level from the
western end and climb straight up the middle of the slabby north face (Mild
Severe).

THE LONG SLOUGH RED ROCKS

Beyond the pinnacle the south wall is quite different in character. A broad
horizontal band of red felsite is sandwiched between a top and bottom layer of
darker rock. The red rock is very sound and compact but tends to feel damp in
humid weather. In places, the dark rock should be treated with caution. A number
of good climbs have been made here. Unfortunately, recent summers have
witnessed the invasion by a considerable number of nesting birds. These tend
to congregate towards the right of the cliff. However, only the routes from
Pedestal Corner rightwards are affected.

Access is possible by traversing from the neck behind the pinnacle (usually
Difficult), although the normal approach is from the seaward end. Descend easy
rocks on the Long Slough side of the headland to an iron spike above a
steepening. Move awkwardly down to the left across a lichen-covered slab to
shelves leading inland (Difficult). Descent is also possible going right from the
spike, then down a steep edge on big jugs (Very Difficult).

About 20 metres back from the descent is a recessed bay with rock pools.

The Exit Crack   13m   Mild Severe   (1967)
This is the right-bending flake crack in the red rock left of the obvious black wet fault.

Black Chimney   13m   Very Difficult   (1967)
The black fault at back of recess is often wet. A Severe variation goes up the right wall.

A few metres right of Black Chimney are two prominent grooves in the red rock.

Black Groove   12m   E1 5b   (1981)
Climb the left-hand groove and finish straight up on big holds.

Jester   12m   E1 5b *   (1981)
The right-hand groove, really a shallow corner with a black finger crack.

Blue Dot   12m   E2 5c **   (1981)
Just right of Jester is a smooth arete. Round the corner from this, on the main face, there is a steep smooth diedre capped by an overhang. Climb the diedre, move left, surmount the overhang and climb a crack to finish slightly left.

The Red Knife   15m   E4 5c   (1987)
This route climbs the right side of the impressive hanging arete right of Blue Dot, gained by a left-rising traverse from a few metres up Pedestal Corner. Sparsely protected by RPs, the best of which is in a crack round on the left side of the arete.

Pedestal Corner   13m   VS 4c *   (1981)
This corner has twin cracks and a rock pedestal at the base of the red rock. Climb the corner with awkward exit onto big ledge at junction with red and dark rock. From right end of ledge, climb to the top on dubious rock.

Firebird   12m   E1 5b *   (1981)
The shallow hanging groove right of Pedestal Corner. Step in from the left and finish as for Pedestal Corner.

Red Face   12m   VS 4c   (1981)
Starting right of Firebird, climb a short overhanging right-leaning corner-crack to the top of the red rock. Hand traverse left to the ledge of Pedestal Corner and finish as for that route.

Trog   20m   HVS 5a *   (1980)
The prominent overhanging groove right of Red Face and approximately 20 metres east of the Long Slough Pinnacle. The crack in the back is often wet, but can be avoided by bridging.

Lucky Jim   20m   HVS 5a   (1981)
Start just left of the second last rib in the red rock, about halfway between Trog and the Pinnacle. Climb converging cracks and a short overhanging corner to a ledge on the right, on top of the red rock. Climb away up left on poor and badly protected rock. The climbing on the red rock is good, and a safer finish looks possible out right.

THE INLETS OF THE RED ROCKS

Immediately south of Long Slough there are two inlets where the band of red rock is continuous along both walls. The seaward end of the south wall of the southerly inlet has a tower formation which provides a few problems. The larger northerly inlet is known as the Cave of the Red Rocks, after the large dripping cave at its head. The north wall may be traversed by an obvious platform, but the steep rocks above are often wet and repulsive. Access to this wall is via the descent to Long Slough South Wall. The main seaward arete beside this descent is Mild Severe.

The following climb is on the south wall. Descend the promontory between the northerly and southerly inlets.

Vibrator   20m   E1 5b   (1978)
This is a prominent clean-cut jamming crack near the seaward end of the red rocks. Find a way traversing in from the seaward end. Climb up grey rocks to the crack left of a smooth corner. The crack is strenuous and impending and the nasty finish requires further cleaning.

HIDDEN INLET
This narrow hidden inlet lies 20 metres east of the tower in the southerly inlet. It runs in a north-east to south-west direction and leads to a rock pool at the landward end. The landward wall offers a variety of problems, the best starting from the obvious recess.

THE DIVING BOARD
Thirty metres south of the rock pool mentioned above, there is an obvious rock platform protruding horizontally out over the sea. The rock hereabouts is excellent and there are a number of interesting little problems.

ALAN'S CLIFF
The section of cliff containing The Diving Board continues for some 75 metres to a cave, beyond which a low grass-topped headland reaches further seawards to a steep little wall above a diagonal inlet. Climbing is possible almost anywhere and there are many interesting problems. Only the better features are described. The usual descent is via a short water chute at the north end of the steepest section of the cliff.

Cobra   8m   Mild VS 4b   (1974)
This is the right-leaning groove on the overhanging pillar immediately left of the water chute.

Central Corner   10m   Mild Severe   (1974)
The prominent black corner about 6 metres south of Cobra. It starts with an awkward and slightly overhanging chimney.

Hanging Slab   8m   VS 4c   (1974)
There is a big overhang left of Central Corner with a delicate slab poised above. Climb the slab from left to right.

Left of the slab there are two lines of weakness which break through the overhang above a diagonal shelf, **First** and **Second Overhangs**, both HVS and very strenuous.

THE HUMPBACK   *(Map Ref 964 024)*

Altens Haven, with its open bay, sea-stack, whitewashed bothy and thatched cottage was once a very attractive place. Now the buildings are burnt out and graffiti daubed, there is evidence of rogue dumping and the bay is polluted by a drainage outfall. Nevertheless there is good climbing on and beside the big stack. The best approach is along the farm track below the railway from the junction of the coast road and Altens farm road.

The Humpback is the big sea-stack at the end of the easily descended promontory which divides the bay. It is only cut off in rough seas or at very high tide. The stack is a long wedge of rock with a very steep landward face, best seen in profile from the cliff top path just south of Alan's Cliff. In places, the rock requires careful handling. The easiest way up and down is at the north end (Difficult).

Humpback Girdle   45m   Very Difficult
Start at the access point at the north end of the landward face. Fine steep climbing along the landward face leads to an overhanging prow at the south end. An awkward move round this at sea-level leads to ledges on the seaward face. The finish is straightforward.

LANDWARD FACE

Quartzite Crack   8m   VS 4c   (1978)
The obvious very steep right-leaning crack near the north end of the face. Finish out left.

Left Face   10m   Hard Severe   (1960s)
In the middle of the wall there is a vague scooped line of weakness. Climb the left side of this, trending left.

Right Face   10m   Hard Severe   (1978)
Climb the right side of the scoop, starting up a flake crack. Again finish out left.

Humpback Crack   10m   VS 4b *   (1960s)
This is the fine steep crack splitting the face towards the south end.

The Black Ramp   10m   HVS 5a *   (1960s)
The obvious left-trending black ramp near the south end. Climb a steep slab to
a small bulge. Bridge up over this, then finish more easily. A good ledge at the
foot of this climb is only uncovered at lowish tide.

(Only Love can be) Stranger than Fiction   10m   E5 6a *   (1991)
The obvious line up the black impending wall right of The Black Ramp. Reach
the flaky line from the left and follow it, with the hardest moves at the top. There
is a crucial RP5 (sideways) at two-thirds height.

Hanging Block Climb   6m   Hard Severe   (1950s)
Climb the short steep cleft between the Black Ramp and the prow.

SEAWARD FACE
Moving round to the seaward face from the north end, the first feature is a steep
wall above an overhang.

The Brush-off   8m   E2 5b *   (1978)
Climb the centre of this gold-coloured wall: surmount an overhang, go up right
then finish straight up.

Legover   8m   E2 6a *   (1983)
The severely overhanging crack and lichenous hanging corner right of the gold
wall gives an amusing technical problem.

Gold Cracks   8m   Hard Severe
Climb the cracks in the left side of the gold wall.

Seaward Chimney   10m   Very Difficult
The obvious shallow fault in the middle of this face.

At the south end are three obvious quartz bands. One is very steep, going up
the prow. The other two give good easier routes.

Prowess   8m   E5 6b *   (1991)
The steep quartz band leading up the prow. Clip a peg runner in the quartz band,
then go out left using the obvious sidepull. Now climb the prow (Rock 3 high up;
hard to place and clip).

Ricketyploon   10m   Severe
Follow the right-hand band to a small roof. Surmount this then follow an obvious right-slanting slab-ramp to the top.

Quarts Dernor   10m   Mild Severe '
The left-hand band is steep, with some very satisfying holds.

HUMPBACK GULCH

This is the little boulder-strewn inlet on the inner side of the descent ridge to the Humpback. It has a very steep south-west facing wall. At high tide (when some of the routes are inaccessible) the best descent is by the grassy ridge immediately south.

Boundary Corners   10m   Severe   (1968)
Climb the obvious corners on the left-side of the steep wall.

Nooky Wall   10m   HVS 5a   (1979)
This is on the wall right of Boundary Corners. Start up a thin crack line, traverse right to move up into the obvious niche and pull over this to the top.

Central Crack   10m   VS 4c   (1969)
The obvious break in the centre, right of Nooky Wall. The holds improve after a hard start.

Golden Shot   8m   E3 6a **   (1983)
Right of Central Cracks is a large overhang. Climb the black wall to the highest point in the overhang. Pull over and finish up the wall split by the obvious crack. The crucial Friend runner is very hard to place, except for the very tall.

Tales of the Unexpected   6m   E2 5b *   (1982)
Climb the overhang right of Golden Shot.

The next two routes are only accessible at low tide.

Bernie   8m   Severe
Climb the corner right of Tales of the Unexpected.

The Bolt   8m   Severe
The corner right of Bernie has a steep start.

THE DRY COVIE

About 100 metres south of the Humpback there is a small rock promontory separated from the land by a narrow gap. The north wall of this may be climbed by the obvious black streak (Mild Severe). Running inland from the promontory is a small dry very sheltered cove, known as the Dry Covie or V.S. Cove. There are a some good problems, especially on the steep rocks at the back of the cove.

SEAL'S HOLE

This, the only major inlet between Altens and Burnbanks Havens, contains a large flake island which is separated from the main wall by as little as 2 metres. The traverse of the Cove's main (north) wall gives a good route (low tide and calm sea advisable).

Vengeance   45m   VS 4c *   (1950s)
Start traversing from the seaward end. After 10 metres it is possible to step across onto the island. Resist this temptation and continue round a bulge and up over a small black cave. Further steep climbing leads to another cave in the middle of the face. The easiest way to finish is to climb up out of the cave, then traverse up left on a steep slab to the top. Alternatively, continue downwards to sea-level to reach a broad ledge at the western end. A deep chimney-like cave (the western end of the fault containing the Dry Covie) must be crossed (very thin) to reach the back of the inlet.

The obvious hanging diedre left of the central cave is another alternative finish (Hard Severe). It is exposed and has loose rock.

The remaining cliffs on this section of the coast are probably best reached from the bridge over the railway 200 metres south of Altens Farm Road junction. Opposite this bridge is the small village of Burnbanks, recently renovated after years of dereliction.

BLACK ROCK GULCH   *(Map Ref 963 022)*

This pleasant gulch is sunny and open and offers some good routes in the easier grades, making it an excellent place for beginners. To reach it, follow the coastal path north from the bridge, past the deep inlet of Burnbanks Haven and the narrow gash of Bass Inlet. Eighty metres north of this, and 30 metres south of Seal's Hole, grassy slopes lead down to the top of the crag. Descent is by a simple scramble at the southern end, leading to a little pool. The main cliff faces south-east and is distinctly divided into two sections: a steep slab and a near vertical wall.

The Shute   4m   Mild Severe   (1950s)
Climb the awkward V-groove above the little pool.

RED SLAB

This is the smooth steep slab, about 10 metres wide, just right of the rock pool. The slab can be ascended by some half dozen climbs, none exceeding Severe, though the climbing is quite thin and technical in places.

RED WALL

This is the steep 10m wall right of Red Slab. The steepest section of this wall, immediately right of the slab, has poorer rock than the rest of the cliff.

The Stick-Up   10m   HVS 5a   (1978)
On the steepest section there are bulges with a prominent scoop. Climb the left
side of the scoop and the wall above.

Mellow Yellow   10m   Severe   (1972)
In the middle of the wall is an obvious chimney. Start left of the foot of the
chimney and go up left to below a short right-angled corner. Traverse left above
the bulges, then continue to the top.

Windy Ledge   10m   Very Difficult   (1950s)
Climb Mellow Yellow to the right-angled corner, then follow it to the top.

Astra   10m   Very Difficult   (1950s)
Climb the fine groove just left of the chimney, finishing straight over the bulge at
the top.

Black Rock Chimney   10m   Moderate   (1950s)
The obvious chimney provides a useful descent.

Yellow Edge   10m   Mild Severe **   (1960s)
The pillar right of the chimney gives steep airy climbing: a little classic.

Yellow Diedre   10m   Mild Severe *   (1960s)
Climb the steep right-angled corner right of Yellow Edge.

At the back of the inlet, on the south wall, are some black damp walls. There
are three climbs: The first goes directly up the big overhang on the left; well worth
doing (HVS). The second takes twin cracks left of centre (Severe). The third goes
up the V-corner on the right-hand end (Very Difficult).

The Purple Way   45m   Difficult   (1950s)
This is the traverse between Black Rock Gulch and Bass Inlet. Most of the
climbing is on ledges, the only difficulty being moving round an awkward bulging
wall directly above the sea. A more entertaining line starts at the top of The
Plumbline, slants down to reach a corner at 20m, then traverses the awkward
bulging wall (Very Difficult).

The Bean   8m   Severe *   (1960s)
Climb strenuously up the awkward bulging wall which is traversed by The Purple
Way.

The wall just to the right gives a good climb (Severe).

Has Been   8m   VS 5a   (1985)
Midway between Black Rock Gulch and The Bean is a short overhanging wall.
Climb this using good finger jugs.

BASS INLET

This is the small sea-filled inlet south of Black Rock Gulch. The north wall comprises a steep pillar with a broken slab on its left (Moderate) and easy rocks on the right. It is reached by either descending these, or traversing in via The Purple Way.

The Plumbline   10m   Difficult *   (1950s)
The right side of the pillar. Start from a large ledge and climb by flakes and cracks, moving right near the top.

Dancin' Fool   10m   HVS 5a **   (1981)
The wall of Plumbline is bounded on the left by a blunt undercut arete with a hanging slab topped by a groove. Climb the wall right of the arete for a few moves then cross left onto the edge at an obvious horizontal break. Go up and move left to the base of the groove. The original route finished up this. However, it is much better to continue straight up the wall on the right to finish over a little bulge. Excellent climbing on small incuts.

Plum Jam   8m   VS 4c
The jamming crack in the wall left of Dancin' Fool.

The dank south wall is very steep and has no climbs at present. However, at the seaward end a steep undercut buttress faces out to sea, giving the following routes.

Bass Buttress   10m   Severe   (1950s)
The large undercut buttress is bounded on the left by an easy chimney. Start at the foot of the chimney and traverse out right. Where the ledges end, pull up strenuously to a large ledge on the right edge. Finish straight up easier rock.

Willie's Way   10m   Hard Severe   (1950s)
Start as for Bass Buttress, then climb straight up the overhanging wall on big jugs.

Jaunt   8m   Very Difficult
On the left of the easy chimney is a small corner with an awkward start. Move up into the corner, ignore the easy left exit and sidle up right to finish.

BURNBANKS HAVEN

This is the large cove with a small slipway and a fisherman's bothy at its head. It is bisected by an evil disintegrating knife edge ridge (Very Difficult). The south wall traverse round to Aitken's Pinnacle is Difficult. The north wall may be traversed with little difficulty from the beach end (easier at low tide) but an awkward move (Severe) has to be negotiated at sea-level before reaching Bass Inlet.

NORTH WALL

At the seaward end of the north wall there are two areas of steep clean rock, most conveniently approached by scrambling down the broken rocks just south of Bass Inlet. The following route starts at the back of the large alcove with overhangs above, just round to the south of the descent.

Labyrinth Nose   10m   Mild VS 4b *   (1950s)
Climb up left on huge jugs, making for an obvious break in the overhangs. Once above the level of the roof, traverse right and finish straight up.

Beyond this alcove is the 'Severe' move of the north wall traverse. It involves climbing round a proud corner just above sea-level. A ramp then leads up left below a steep wall of good rock.

Sunfun   8m   VS 4b   (1979)
The most obvious feature on this wall is a shallow rock arch. Climb this, then a thin crack above to a rock bench near the top of the cliff.

Expecting to Fly   8m   E2 5c *   (1985)
A direct ascent of the wall between Sunfun and Sunfair, starting just right of the rock arch.

Sunfair   8m   HVS 5a   (1984)
Start in the short overhanging corner right of Expecting to Fly. Climb straight up in the line of an incipient crack to finish over a small bulge.

SOUTER HEAD   *(Map Ref 963 018)*

This, the headland south of Burnbanks Haven, is one of the best-known climbing areas on the Aberdeen coast, having been developed as early as the 1950s. With its high concentration of short technical climbs on generally excellent rock, the place is justifiably popular. From the bridge at Burnbanks, cross a fence, then go straight down the edge of a field to the cliff-top footpath. Nearby, a slippery path descends to the grassy hollow behind the rocks. Alternatively, if there are crops in the field, walk round by Burnbanks Haven.

AITKEN'S PINNACLE

The 6m pinnacle lying just to the north of Souter Head is an obvious landmark. It is accessible at low tide by a narrow neck of rock.

Direct Route   6m   Severe   (1944)
Climb straight up the centre of the landward face. The initial moves are the hardest.

Southern Diagonal Traverse   8m   Very Difficult   (1934)
Start from the neck and traverse right and up to a ledge on the edge. Continue
easily to top. This is the easiest descent route, but there is also a metal ring on
the summit from which to abseil.

THE GRASSY PINNACLE
This fine square tower forms the northern limit of Souter Head proper, and is
surrounded on three sides by the sea. It provides some excellent steep climbing.
The rock is generally sound and completely free from vegetation, apart from the
grass cap on the summit, from which it derives its name.

SOUTH WALL
The largest and most impressive of the three main faces. It has a distinctly red
appearance and faces the normal approach from the descent path. A sloping
shelf runs down below the routes into the sea.

The Pobble   10m   VS 4b **   (1950s)
Start at the overhung recess at the south-west corner. Climb up right on
magnificent jugs to a sloping mid-way ledge. Step up left onto a narrow ramp,
then go slightly right and up to the top. Strenuous.

Mythical Wall   10m   E1 5b ***   (1969)
Probably the most celebrated route on this section of the coast. As a result, a
few well loved holds have gone missing in recent years. The route begins at the
obvious crack where the wall starts to impend. Climb the strenuous crack to a
prominent overhang. Move left onto the sloping mid-way ledge, then climb the
obvious thin vertical crack to the top. Sustained and well protected. A left-hand
start (5b) slants up to the overhang, starting somewhat left of the normal start.
Chockstone Start: 4m   5c *
Climb the bulge immediately left of the left-hand start, using a conspicuous
chockstone.

Over the Top   10m   E2 5b **   (1980)
Climb Mythical Wall left-hand start to the overhang. Pull over, then climb the wall
right of Mythical's final crack, finishing up left by flakes. Very sustained.

American Graffiti   10m   E3 6a **   (1983)
Start just right of Mythical. Palm along a narrow shelf, then go up right across the
overhanging wall on small holds to climb a crack through the bulge into South-
East Diedre. Climb the right edge for a good finish.

Davy Jones' Locker   10m   E3 6a   (1983)
Climb cracks just right of American Graffiti, then continue up the arete by
palming. An escape right is possible on the hard lower section. Low tide required.

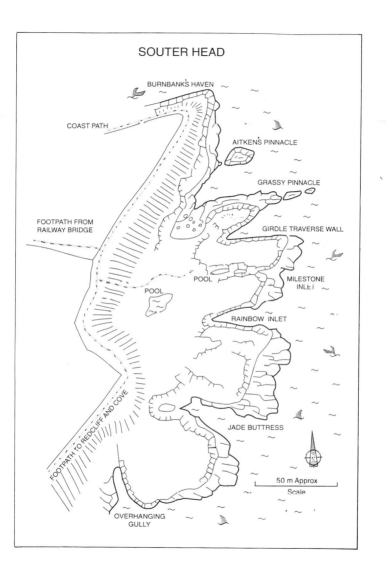

SOUTER HEAD

BURNBANK'S HAVEN

COAST PATH

AITKEN'S PINNACLE

GRASSY PINNACLE

FOOTPATH FROM
RAILWAY BRIDGE

GIRDLE TRAVERSE WALL

POOL

POOL

MILESTONE
INLET

RAINBOW INLET

FOOTPATH TO REDCLIFF AND COVE

JADE BUTTRESS

50 m Approx
Scale

OVERHANGING
GULLY

NORTH WALL

On the north side of The Grassy Pinnacle an easy slab abuts a short vertical wall. All the routes on this face start from the slab.

Gangplank   8m   Mild VS 4b   (1950s)
Start at the junction of the slab and wall. Work out horizontally right until round the corner, then go straight up. Some loose rock.

The Rack   6m   VS 4c   (1950s)
Start as for Gangplank but climb straight up via a delightfully delicate mantel-shelf.

Eunach Yummick   4m   E1 5c   (1984)
The very thin crack line between The Rack and Tiger's Terror is protected by small wires and RPs.

Tiger's Terror   4m   VS 4c   (1950s)
Short and awkward. Climb the crack starting in a small recess at the left-hand end of the main slab. Move out left at the bulge.

North-East Edge   8m   E1 5b   (1950s)
Climb first by short steps in a shallow corner, then go straight up to finish at the top of East Wall. No protection, with the crux at the top.

EAST WALL

This pockmarked wall has two identifying features, namely a shallow rectangular recess low down on the right and a small niche at two-thirds height.

Seawall   8m   E1 5b **   (1976)
Start in the recess and climb up slightly left to the niche. Finish straight up. There is good protection at the niche.

Pickpocket   10m   E2 5c *   (1980)
Climb the left side of the wall by small pockets (micronuts useful) to gain the niche. Exit up left.

South-East Diedre   10m   HVS 4c ***   (1950s)
The diedre itself is on the south wall. Start as for Pickpocket. Move left to the edge then go up and step round onto the south wall. Move left and climb the diedre to the top. A very sustained climb with a sparsely protected lower section.

The Vicious Circle   20m   E1 5b   (1977)
A girdle of the east and south walls, starting up North-East Edge, crossing via the niche into South-East Diedre, then continuing under the overhang of Mythical Wall to finish up Pobble. The traverse of the north wall is possible, but trivial.

GIRDLE TRAVERSE WALL
This is the long wall opposite The Grassy Pinnacle.

Girdle Traverse   60m   Severe **   (1948)
The wall may be traversed at various levels and in both directions. The most popular route starts from the landward end. Start at mid-height and scramble down a shelf to a small recess below a triangular overhang. Pull up out of this and go horizontally across ledges below the easy upper corner of Bootlace Crack. The ledges continue diagonally down as a black fault. Descend vertically a little and traverse across the fault to a prominent black corner (often wet). Step up into the corner and go up left. Continue horizontally to another corner and go up this to a good stance on a diagonal ramp (belay). Go down the ramp, swing round a vertical nose and move up onto another ledge. Continue descending slightly via three undercut ledges (crux). From the farthest ledge pull onto a steep lichenous slab, climb up left, then continue traversing out left to finish.

Bootlace Crack   10m   HVS 5a   (1978)
Near the landward end of the wall an obvious crack splits a black overlap. Climb this teasing bulge and cross the Girdle to finish up the easier corner. The upper corner was originally called Parallel Cracks.

Winkle-Picker   8m   HVS 5a   (1985)
The left arete of the easy upper corner of Bootlace Crack provides a good finish to that route.

Black Corner   10m   Severe   (1950s)
The prominent black corner one-third way along the girdle may be climbed either from the Girdle or from sea-level via the diagonal black fault.

Beyond the Black Corner, the lower half of the wall overhangs. The next three climbs start below the overhang from a series of ledges almost at sea-level. At low tide it is possible to scramble along barnacled rocks from the seaward end. However, a better way is to follow the Girdle and continue down the diagonal black fault to reach the ledges (Severe).

Man-o'-War   20m   HVS 5a   (1982)
Climb the most prominent corner (second from the right) to an overhang. Move left and continue up to the level of the diagonal ramp. Climb up right onto a ramp beside the vertical nose of the Girdle Traverse. Move up right, then climb a right-facing corner to the top (ignoring the easy grassy exit out left)

Conger   20m   VS 4c *   (1982)
This takes the next line left of Man-o'-War. Climb straight up (crossing the diagonal ramp) through a slight bulge to the middle of the three undercut ledges on the Girdle. Move left, pull onto a slab, then climb up right to finish at the highest point of the wall.

Scyphozoa   20m   VS 4c *   (1982)
The most easterly line (the start of the diagonal ramp). Climb overhanging rock
to easier ground. Ignore the obvious exit left to the ledge on the seaward start
(see below) and continue up the groove to reach the upper slab just left of the
third undercut ledge of the Girdle. Finish straight up.

Seaward Start   10m   Severe   (1948)
This is the seaward start to the Girdle Traverse. It may be climbed for its own
sake. Start from some red rocks just above high water. Climb up the edge
between Girdle Traverse Wall and the Seaward Wall to reach an overhang.
Move right over this onto a slab. Traverse right to a ledge, then climb the crack
to the top. If it is intended to continue the Girdle, quit the crack at half-height, go
right, then descend to the leftmost of the three undercut ledges of the Girdle.

Round the corner from the seaward start, on the north-east point of the
headland, is a small wall with a central vertical crack. This is **Nog Crack**
(Moderate). The steep wall to its left is Mild Severe and the wall to the right is
Nigg Wall (Difficult).

THE POOLS
These pools are at the end of the path down from the cliff-top path, and are
usually the colour of cold tea. The murky shallows of the landward pool await
anyone who should part company with the renowned **P & J Overhang** on its
north side. Opinions on the grade of this climb vary anywhere from Very Difficult
to VS, so beware! The holds have been painted, presumably as an aid to
short-sighted climbers. The seaward pool has two short traverses on its south
side. One at mid-height, and one at water level (Very Difficult).

THE MILESTONE INLET
The small inlet on the seaward side of the pools is characterised by a prominent
'milestone' sticking out from the rock on the north wall. It is best reached by
descending easy slabby rock just to the north. At the back of the inlet is a through
route (Moderate), which gives an enjoyable squirm.

Milestone Direct   10m   Very Difficult *   (pre 1933)
The slabby north wall can be climbed at any point. The best route starts directly
below the milestone. Climb up to and over the milestone, then continue straight
up to a slight overhang. Step left and finish on good holds. The overhang may
be climbed direct (Severe).

RAINBOW INLET
The next inlet south is steep-sided and has some of the best climbing at Souter
Head. The easiest descent to the base of the climbs is by a shallow depression
at the south-west corner of the inlet. The first five climbs are on the north wall.

Rainbow Wall   6m   Difficult   (pre 1945)
At the back of the inlet is a smooth slab. Climb its centre, much more easily than
it looks.

Rainbow Crack   6m   Very Difficult   (1950)
The corner right of Rainbow Wall.

Puffin Wall   10m   Very Difficult
Climb the steep wall right of Rainbow Corner, crossing a ledge below the
steepest part of the wall.

Puffin's Perch   10m   Moderate   (pre 1945)
Starting right of Puffin Wall, climb a steep left-slanting shelf, then traverse the
ledge across Puffin Wall to finish just right of Rainbow Crack.

Puffin Overhang   10m   Severe   (1948)
Start up the ramp of the Perch then climb the two-tiered overhang above direct.
Continue directly via another small overlap.

   Right of Puffin Overhang there are two short undercut cracks: **Westerly** (Mild
VS) and **Easterly** (Severe): The Twin Overhangs.
   The following climbs are on the south wall.

Swing Seam   10m   Severe *   (1948)
The prominent crack just right of the steepest part of the wall. Move awkwardly
up to a sloping shelf and continue straight up the crack above.

Tyke   10m   E3 5b *   (1976)
This is on the very steep buttress between Slab Top Chimney and Swing Seam.
Start just left of Swing Seam. Climb straight up for a few metres, then move out
onto the left edge. Continue up until a delicate move gains the obvious break in
the final overhang. Finish straight up. Poorly protected.

Mo's Traverse   10m   HVS 5a   (1961)
Start up Swing Seam, then traverse left (descending slightly) across the face to
join Tyke. Exit left to top of Slab Top Chimney.

Slab Top Chimney   10m   Difficult **   (pre 1933)
Climb the obvious chimney with a constricted top.

Brooker's Arete   10m   Severe ***   (1948)
The arete left of Slab Top Chimney. Start at the foot of the Chimney and move
left onto the crest. Continue directly up the crest on good holds to the top.

Long Step Crack   10m   Mild Severe   (pre 1945)
Climb the crack left of Brooker's Arete.

JADE BUTTRESS AREA

South of Rainbow Inlet lies an amphitheatre containing a small circular pool. All the climbs in this area are on the large mass of rock south of this pool. At its north-west corner there is a slightly undercut grey wall.

The Sickle   10m   HVS 5b   (pre 1945)
Start a few metres up the gully above the pool. Work up right across the face to a small recessed overhang. Continue round and finish up a right-slanting crack. Very Strenuous. The rock is less sound than elsewhere at Souter Head.

The Last Post   4m   Very Difficult
Step over to the grey wall from a point 4m above the pool, then climb the slanting crack of Sickle.

Bird's Nest Crack   6m   Easy   (pre 1945)
The easy-angled narrow crack above the pool provides a useful descent, and E-points for beginners.

Overhang Crack   10m   Mild Severe *   (pre 1933)
The obvious corner on the north wall starts with an overhang and finishes on a shelf slanting off to the right. Swing up over the overhang into the corner with the help of an excellent time-honoured flake (crux) and continue up the corner.

Jade Traverse and Jade Buttress   12m   VS 4c *   (1950s)
These two climbs combine to make a worthwhile and fairly sustained route. Start 3 metres right of Overhang Crack. Traverse horizontally left across a slab beneath an overhang to the corner of Overhang Crack. Continue with difficulty round the crest. Follow the crest to the final steep wall, which is climbed on small holds to the top (crux).
   The crux of Jade Buttress is often climbed by traversing in from the shelf below the White Seam (VS 4c).

St Andrew's Crack   4m   Moderate   (1944)
The crack line left of Overhang Crack leads to the big shelf below the White Seam. The climb is named after a characteristic white quartzite cross on the finishing ledge.

Tension Crack   4m   Severe   (1950s)
The crack left of St Andrew's Crack is really a right-angled corner with a prominent square-cut overhang at its base.

The White Seam   4m   HVS 5a   (1949)
On the steep wall above St Andrew's ledge and about 4 metres left of upper Jade Buttress is a white quartzite seam. This route follows a line as close to the quartz as holds will allow. A popular test-piece of yesteryear, which was originally led in nails.

The Go Between   4m   VS 4c   (1960s)
Climb the wall between Jade Buttress and White Seam.

The Rat Trap   4m   Very Difficult
Climb the wall 3 metres left of The White Seam, finishing at the top of a small
sloping shelf.

The Catwalk   4m   Difficult
Climb the sloping shelf up right. A paltry offering.

OVERHANGING GULLY
The large mass of rock which contains Jade Buttress is bounded on the
south-west side by a steep wall which is undercut by a ledge sloping down to the
sea. Above the higher end of this sloping ledge is a slightly recessed open
corner.

Scylla   8m   Very Difficult   (pre 1945)
Go straight up on good holds over the bulge at the back of the recess.

Charybdis   8m   Very Difficult   (pre 1945)
Traverse right from the foot of Scylla to the bottom of a large flake, then climb up
left using the flake.

Cerberus   4m   VS 5a   (1950s)
Further down the sloping ledge is an obvious round pothole. Climb the shallow
indefinite corner above this.

The Styx   4m   Very Difficult
Start at the pothole and climb the rib on the left.

Hades   4m   HVS 5b   (1950s)
Work diagonally out right from the pothole, over a bulging overhang.

Cadaver   6m   VS 5a   (1950s)
The big overhang down on the right. A short traverse from the left is needed to
start it, and low tide is necessary.

THE RED CLIFF   *(Map Ref 958 016)*

The Red Cliff lies about 250 metres south of Souter Head and comprises a steep
granite wall opposite the large flat-topped Bunstane. There is some good
climbing here, but unfortunately the cliff suffers an annual invasion by nesting
gulls, which occupy most of the holds from April to August. Their mess is usually
slow to clear, and nesting residue may prohibit climbing here well into the winter.

Red Grooves and Purple Emperor usually lose their nests quite quickly, but an autumn ascent of the routes to the left will usually entail digging for holds through mouldering beastie-infested nests.

The cliff has a sunny aspect, and is best visited during the winter and early spring when (following a reasonable dry spell) it becomes a good place to climb.

Access
From Souter Head, follow the cliff-top path south for 200 metres, passing a sewer outlet with a metal surround down on the left. (This was once a narrow ravine containing a good, strenuous climb — Chamonix Crack). Forty metres beyond this, there is an obvious right-angled zigzag in the landward fence. Go down grassy slopes at this point to reach a rocky headland. Descend a moderate slabby shallow chimney on the seaward face of this headland, then traverse south below a steep prow. (The vertical corner between the descent chimney and the prow is Severe and the prow itself is HVS 5a.) A tedious traverse of about 100 metres along ledges and over walls now leads to the foot of the cliff.

Before embarking on this descent and traverse, it is a good idea to walk along the clifftop path for a further 150 metres to a point overlooking the Bunstane, from where the condition of the Red Cliff can be determined.

Broken Buttress   25m   Difficult   (1950s)
The indefinite buttress lying between the steep main cliff and an unpleasant vegetated depression on the right. Start about 5 metres right of Red Grooves and follow the line of least resistance on good rock. The easiest finish is out left at the top of Red Grooves.

Red Grooves   25m   Hard Severe **   (1957)
The obvious line of steep corners and grooves on the wall forming the northern flank of the main face.

The Purple Emperor   25m   E1 5c *   (1978)
This climbs the prominent seam of white quartz on the crest of the rib between Red Grooves and Butterfly Wall. Start from the left end of a big flat ledge at the foot of Red Grooves. After the initial moves on the bulging wall (crux) an awkward overhanging wall at half-height leads to an obvious finishing groove.

An awkward move at sea-level must be negotiated to reach the rest of the climbs here.

Butterfly Wall   25m   HVS 5a **   (1950s)
This climbs the broad band of quartz left of Purple Emperor. The band actually forms a corner for the first 6m. Continue straight up by the obvious line until near the top, where a strenuous pull out right gains easy ground.

Grey Groove   25m   Mild VS 4b   (1950s)
This follows the line of an indefinite groove left of Butterfly Wall. Start on slightly
overhanging rock a few metres left of Butterfly Wall. Go up on good holds then
move left into the groove. Continue more easily up this and finish out right where
it becomes steep again at the top. Heavily birded.
Variation Finish: 12m   E1 5c *   (1981)
A technical finish on excellent rock. Follow Grey Groove until below the moves
out right. Move up to the obvious leaning corner on the left, then follow this to a
ledge and so to the top.

Rest in Pieces   25m   E2 5b *   (1981)
Left of Grey Groove and past a jutting nose is another groove, with a left-trending
grey groove at its top. Gain the groove via a slab and follow it, initially on its right
wall, to a square-cut overhang. Pull over this and go out left to the end of the
smooth ramp. Pull back right to the top. Strenuous with good protection.

Fritillary   25m   VS 4c   (1981)
The rock rib left of an obvious crumbling groove left of the main wall. Start left of
the rib and climb a short steep wall to enter a groove. Follow this until it is possible
to exit right onto the rib. Step down and hand traverse right to a ledge in the
unpleasant groove. Return immediately left to the rib and follow an awkward
crack to reach vegetated ground. The rock remains good to the top.

Leaping Lawyer   25m   E1 5a   (1983)
Climb Fritillary for 10m, traverse left across a slab, go up a short groove, then
climb cracks to the overhanging headwall. Now traverse right to re-join Fritillary.

BUNSTANE WALL
Immediately south is the impressive Bunstane Cave. Just south of this is a steep
wall of clean and very sound black rock. To reach it, walk 100 metres south from
Bunstane cave to the next inlet with a cave: Well Cove. Easy shelving rock
descends to the sea on the north side of the inlet. Traverse back north to reach
the routes. The wall is north-facing and often greasy, but does not take long to
dry out. There are no birds.

The Fartin' Freckle   20m   Mild VS 4b   (1974)
Start at a crack just left of the sloping ledge underlying the main wall. Climb it to
where it thins, then traverse out right to a ledge on the edge of the main wall.
Climb the wall above directly, with one awkward move stretching for a jug.

Bunstane Wall   20m   E2 5c *   (1991)
Just right of The Fartin' Freckle is an overhung ramp. Step onto the slab above
and move into a corner (good runners). Pull up on pinches over a bulge to good
holds on a ledge. Finish straight up the leaning wall.

BLACK COVE

South of Well Cove is the large bay of Black Cove. It is best reached by following a track from where the coast road turns west into Cove Village. This track leads down under the railway to the cliff top path at the head of Black Cove.

The north wall of Black Cove is one of the most impressive features of the whole coast. It is about 50m high and exceptionally steep. Unfortunately the cliff is thronged with birds in the summer, and the rock is of inferior quality. However, the cliff may merit closer inspection. No routes have been recorded here except for the traverse of the north wall following the conspicuous red band of rock (VS 4b). The traverse may be finished by climbing a steep wall on the little headland between Well Cove and Black Cove. There are two routes recorded here; both Very Difficult and indefinite.

THE POOR MAN

This sea-stack lies about 100 metres south of the descent into Black Cove. It does not provide a good climb (at least Very Difficult on poor rock) but its situation is interesting. There is a free-standing waterfall on the mainland cliff.

The cliff south of the Poor Man has been traversed round to another inlet (**Winter Boot Wall**; Very Difficult). A calm sea is required.

Cove Bay to Clashrodney

There are five principal groups of crags spread out along this 3km section of coastline. From north to south these are: South Cove, Bruin Cove, Sickle Row, the Mincer Cliff and Clashrodney. Situated only a short distance from the city, and having a reasonable bus service, these crags are quite accessible. This applies in particular to the South and Bruin Cove complex, which provides a fine range of routes of varying grades. This is one of the most popular climbing areas on the coast. Of the other climbing grounds, Clashrodney is the most secluded, providing climbing of a friendly and sunny nature. Sickle Row and the Mincer Cliff, situated a stone's throw from each other, provide more serious climbing and little in the way of easier routes. Nesting birds only affect a fraction of the routes in this section, mainly in parts of South Cove and Bruin Cove. The nearest village is Cove Bay, where food and drink can be bought. The Cove Bay Hotel is a useful hostelry.

Access

South and Bruin Coves are reached from Cove Village, while Sickle Row, the Mincer Cliff and Clashrodney are reached from the coastal road branching off south from the southerly road running into Cove. Cove Village lies about 3km (2 miles) south of Aberdeen and is approached via the A956 (Harbour Road). When coming from the south, turn off the A92 at the signs marked Aberdeen Harbour. Turn off the A956 at the signpost to Cove and follow the road towards the coast. Turn off right along Loirston Road into the village. Follow the road where a long straight leads south to a shop at a sharp right-hand bend. Turn left at this bend, go over a railway bridge and turn immediately right. Go straight on and along a track beside the railway to parking spaces 100 metres short of a cottage. South Cove cliffs are now nearby, lying around the fringe of an old grassy quarry, 150 metres east of the parking. Bruin Cove lies further south along the railway line, past the cottage.

SOUTH COVE   *(Map Ref 953 003)*

This is quite a complex area, but most of the climbs lie in the vicinity of the grassy quarry. This is best reached by a path leading down from the parking area to its north side. The flat seaward side of the quarry overlooks the spectacular walls of the Red Hole. Climbers usually gear up here or else on the rocky crest of the Main Face immediately south. The quarry itself provides a little bouldering, most notably on the graffiti-adorned little buttress at the south side of the quarry mouth. Here, from left to right, is a friction slab, a corner and an overhang most challengingly climbed by a daring mantelshelf. The climbing sections are described from north to south.

THE PRIEST

This is the promontory just south of Cove Harbour. It can be reached by traversing from the harbour but is usually gained from the grassy quarry area by walking round the big inlet of the Kettle. Going down the rim of the east side of the Kettle, an interesting cave with a blow-hole is reached. This cave may be traversed at very low tide with a calm sea. Start from the south-east extremity of The Priest, which lies east of the cave. Traverse to the cave, which is entered with difficulty, jumped at a convenient narrow point, then continue the traverse along the north-east wall of the Kettle on deteriorating rock. The traverse can be continued along the south wall of the inlet to exit at the Hospital Wall — an interesting excursion. There are three routes on the small headland of The Priest.

The Mitre   15m   VS 4c *   (1974)
The rocks of The Priest form a distinct prow jutting out into a small inlet. The Mitre takes the obvious corner on the south wall, gained by a short traverse from the south.

The Spinechiller   10m   HVS 5a *   (1975)
Climb the prow, gained from the north side. A good little pitch.

El Dorado   10m   VS 4c   (1975)
The obvious crack on the north-facing wall.

Old Tawny Traverse   30m   Severe
To the north of the above routes is a small inlet with a steep south-facing wall. Traverse this from left to right at low tide.

THE KETTLE WALLS

These are the big walls on the south-west side of the Kettle inlet, forming one boundary of the quarry area. They have a relatively sombre atmosphere and some of the routes are affected by birds in summer. The most prominent feature is the great knife edge of The Spigolo. South of this is Australia Wall, separated from The Spigolo by a repulsive fault. South again, more broken rocks run along to the promontory underneath the Hospital Wall of the Red Hole.

Access
1. As for Hospital Wall (see Red Hole North Section). From the sloping rocks below this wall, descend a chimney on the nose of the promontory and traverse round past a clean cut groove (Leg Up) to reach easier rocks leading into the inlet.
2. By abseil from stakes above Australia Wall. These stakes are 50 metres north of the Red Hole, at a flat grassy patch on the broad hummocky ridge bordering the quarry (overlooking The Spigolo). The stakes are sited 10 metres back from the cliff top.

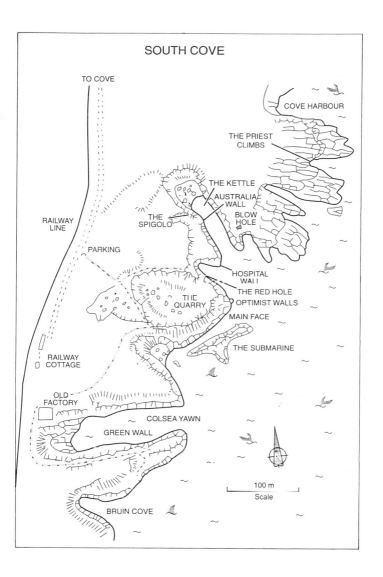

SOUTH COVE

Leg-Up   10m   HVS 5b   (1979)
This route takes the clean-cut groove mentioned in the descent. An amusing
boulder problem, but trivial as a route. There is a good little platform under the
groove. Climb the groove and the avoidable nose above. Using holds on the right
edge the standard is 5b, but it is far better to climb the V-groove direct (6a).

Directly below the descent chimney for the Kettle Walls is a miniature box inlet.
The following routes are gained by abseil to a ledge at the bottom, just above the
sea.

The Wideboys   10m   E1 5c   (1989)
The right-hand line. Bridge up rightwards and climb the clean-cut corner direct
to the top.

The Waterboys   10m   E3 6a *   (1989)
The obvious crack line gives fine climbing.

The Wildboys   13m   E4 5c *
This sustained and technical climb takes the groove line just left of The Waterboys. Layback up the edge to gain a standing position on a big hold (RP2 and
two RP1s). "Escape" left and return right to finish up the groove.

The following routes are on Australia Wall, and are described from left to right.

Ale and Farewell   25m   VS 4c   (1975)
The obvious left arete of the wall, just left of the prominent groove of Drongo. The
arete is bounded on the left by a vegetated gully. A choice of cracks leads into
the gully. Go up this for a few feet, then gain the arete to follow this steeply to
the top.

Drongo   25m   E1 5b *   (1982)
The recessed crack line tucked into the left side of the main wall. Start up the
obvious thin crack. Climb to a roof and pull round right (crux) to the base of the
groove. Climb the groove to a ledge near the top, finishing on the left as for Ale
and Farewell. A good lower section but chossy and dirty above.

Gallipoli   25m   E5 6a **   (1989)
This climbs the pillar right of Drongo by the thin blind crack line. Start at the top
of a slab ramp running right from the base of Drongo. A hard start leads to a peg
runner at 5m (Friend 0 above). Step left, then go up to a break with crucial runner
placements (RP3 and HB4 in the short vertical crack, RP2 in the horizontal
crack). Reach left and climb up to a vibrating flange to pull out right and enter a
corner. Climb the corner, step right, and follow twin cracks to the top.

Woomera   25m   E3 5c   (1989)
This climbs the thin left-bending crack line to join Gallipoli's corner. Start up on
good holds just right of the crack, then follow the crack. Continue, using the right
arete before quitting the crack by moving to a perch on the left. Reach back up
right into the crack line and follow it leftwards to gain the corner on Gallipoli.
Follow this route to the top.

Dingaroo   25m   HVS 5a   (1982)
The long groove right of Woomera. The first section is rather loose and dirty but
the rock improves with height. The crux is at mid-height where a long reach gains
good holds. The final chimney is rotten, but the left rib gives a good finish.

Sonata Rib   25m   VS 4b   (1975)
This is the broad rib right of the main wall proper and separated from it by a
grassy chute. Start up indefinite messy rocks on the left side and move up close
to the crest to a ledge where the rib steepens. Move up onto the wall beside the
gully to traverse right onto the face of the rib. From here, climb directly to the top.

The Spigolo   45m   E1 5a *   (1969)
One of the most impressive rock formations in the area gives a climb of
considerable character and still a serious expedition, despite having been
cleaned up by abseil. Start up grooves slanting up right of the crest for 13m, then
traverse left over a vertical cracked wall onto the crest. Go up this to a large
pointed block. It is probably best to belay here using the thin crack directly above
the block. Swing up the overhanging wall immediately right of the block, and so
onto the edge and another crack above. Continue up, keeping on the right side,
to finish some 8m right of the edge, or finish up the edge (distinctly loose). A good
route if you're insane.

THE RED HOLE

Immediately below the mouth of the grassy quarry, the cliffs overhang a small
inlet, the Red Hole. At the back is a curious slanting cave. This runs back a good
distance into the cliff and its exploration provides a very interesting excursion for
the enthusiastic troglodyte. A fixed line normally being necessary for entry and
exit, and a head torch is recommended as is a low tide (unless squeezing
through underwater apertures is your particular delight).

The stunning walls and overhangs around the cave are the showpiece of
Cove. This superb arena has some great routes and is one of the top centres for
hard climbing in the north-east. Most the routes are unaffected by kittiwake nests.
Fine climbing is also available on the more amenable walls both to the north and
south of the cave (which effectively divides the climbs into two sections with
different access).

RED HOLE NORTH (HOSPITAL WALL)

The wall to the right of the main roofs is quite striking, comprising a number of clean-cut tilted grooves which dwindle away on the right.

Access

At the north-side of the quarry mouth is another flat-faced boulder with the usual inscriptions. A split block provides a good abseil point, the usual descent line being Vasectomy, the tallest and most obvious of the grooves. An alternative is to down-climb or abseil the right bounding nose of the wall (an awkward and exposed Severe). Climbs are described from right to left.

The first of the well-defined grooves is La Rainure, with a prominent crack running up its back. Lobotomy is a hanging, scooped groove line to its right and Lob-Off subsidiary grooves just right again, close to the descent nose.

Lob-Off   10m   E1 5b *   (1979)
Start up the obvious line of Lobotomy and step right to surmount the obvious roof, swinging out right. Finish up the well-defined upper groove.

Lobotomy   15m   HVS 5a   (1971)
Climb the groove line, which is rather loose high up.

La Rainure   15m   VS 4c *   (1971)
The first main groove is sustained, with the crux at the top bulge, moving left and up. Some dodgy rock.

Cirrhosis   20m   E3 6a ***   (1981)
This classic route takes the fine smooth yellow groove left of La Rainure. It is an old aid route and there is a rusty old bolt at the bottom. Start by swinging up a subsidiary groove (arrow) and go up left to climb the groove (poor protection) to a bridging rest at mid-height. Now move up the groove to gain the right arete, finishing at the same point as La Rainure. It is also possible (slightly harder) to finish directly up the groove.

A poor filler-in starts up Cirrhosis then breaks right to follow a diagonal crack into La Rainure (E1 5b).

Exploding Laxative   20m   E5 6a *   (1982/83)
This is the groove between Cirrhosis and Vasectomy. The first part is very thin and joins Vasectomy at mid-height. The first ascent followed Vasectomy to the top (E4 6a); instead, mantelshelf out onto the arete on the right and follow it to the top (bold).

Vasectomy   20m   HVS 5b **
The big groove with a hanging block near the bottom. Gaining a standing position on the block is difficult. Usually a layback in from the right is employed. Follow the corner direct to the top.

Superbrat   20m   E2 6a *   (1981)
The furthest left of the groove lines. The initial crux bulge is slow to dry. Surmount
the bulge and move up into the groove. Move up left across the slab and over
into the undercut base of the left-hand groove. Finish up this.

CAVE WALLS

These magnificent walls face north-east and are sheltered from prevailing winds.
Consequently dampness can be a problem, particularly in humid summer
weather. For optimum conditions a favourable breeze is recommended.

Red Planet   40m   E4 6a ***   (1985)
A fine route, low in the grade although not recommended in the nesting season
(Kittiwakes on the hanging red slabs).
1. 10m 6a   Space Rats, pitch 1 (the crux).
2. 10m 5c   Layback up into the left corner of the slot. Step up and cross right
out of the slot onto small ledges on the slabs.
3. 20m 5b   Move diagonally right up the slabs and take the obvious fault with
some dubious rock through the overhangs to finish.
The Patrick Moore Finish: 20m   5b **   (1988)
An alternative last pitch to Red Planet. From the belay, step down and traverse
along the red slabs on the lip of the overhangs. Move up to climb twin cracks
through the bulge to enter the corner, then follow this to the top. Better than the
normal finish, but less direct.
The Redshift Finish: 20m   E5 6a ***   (1992)
From the belay on the red slabs at the end of pitch 2, move up to the big roof
(Friend 3) and gain an obvious flange (Rock 3 above). Climb the wild roof, bridge
up the groove and follow cracks to the top. Low in the grade.

Space Rats   40m   E5 6a ***   (1983/86)
Above the rounded slabs (often wet) at the cave mouth, a prominent feature of
the crag is a smooth square-cut slot some 12m up, and at the left side of the
main roofs. This impressive route gains the red slabs under the slot, then
traverses left to take the obvious left-slanting line. It is free of nests all year round.
1 10m 6a   Start at the most accessible part of the undercut wall at the cave
mouth; peg belay. Step onto the wall (peg runner) and move up a vague open
corner to pull up to roofs. Move right and up a groove to pull out left onto the
hanging red slab. Move right to belay under the main roofs.
2. 15m 6a   Traverse the slab leftwards for 8m to a small exposed perch (there
is a crucial wet underclHng halfway). Climb the crux overhang above and go up
the slabby corner to take a hanging belay under more roofs.
3. 15m 5c   Move up onto the edge and climb the roof. Go up left to finish up
the big slanting crack of Procrastination.

Procrastination   45m   E5 6b ***   (1986)
A magnificent route with good protection. Immediately left of the cave is a very
impressive red wall. This old peg route gains the red wall by a slanting crack
(unfortunately slow to dry) below the start of Space Rats.
1. 15m 6b   Step onto the wall as for Space Rats (peg runner) and follow a crack
down left to the base of a slanting crack. Climb this (peg runner) to a jug under
a small roof. Swing left to climb up onto a slab under the big corner crack. Peg
and nut belay.
2. 30m 6a   Climb the corner until it is possible to pull out right under a big roof
to rest on the slab alongside. Climb the roof on its right side then sneak right
under another roof to finish up the big crack in the slab.

Cracks in Reality   35m   E5 6a ***   (1986)
An outstanding route, well protected with large nuts, giving superb sustained
climbing in an impressive position. It takes cracks up the centre of the big red
wall. The traverse in is the best approach when dry, but it is sea-washed and
usually greasy. Alternatively, abseil down the line of the final groove to the
hanging belay on the edge of the wall. It is necessary to maintain a swing to gain
the stance. Jumars are handy for escape.
1. 30m 5a   Start at the bottom of Hedonist (peg belay). Move down and find a
way across rounded slabs under bulges to climb diagonally up to the hanging
peg and nut belay. A belay right on the edge is necessary to prevent rope drag
and to view the leader.
2. 35m 6a   Traverse right using undercuts in black rock to reach the crack.
Climb this to a big jug, then continue to a big loose undercut and pull up left to a
poor rest. Move right and up another crack line to a resting place under the
overhangs. Move right onto a slab then back left into the chimney. Pull up the
final awkward overhang to finish up the final easy groove.

The Black Sleep   40m   E5 6b **   (1987)
This route climbs the red wall left of Cracks in Reality to an obvious black spring,
then moves out left above the roofs into the boundary corner. Another fine climb.
1. 30m 6b   From the hanging belay, climb straight up the edge to the right end
of the roof (Friend runners). Go slightly right then left up the wall to traverse left
to a resting place above the roof. Move out left and up the wall until possible to
move into the corner. Climb the corner exiting out left over a bulge to a ledge.
2. 10m 5c   Finish up the deceptive groove on the left.

RED HOLE SOUTH (OPTIMIST'S WALLS)

This is the tall slabby face left of the red wall, cut by several slanting grooves in
its upper reaches. Losing the sun early on, the crag has a gloomy atmosphere.
The southern boundary is the Leaning Tower where the cliff curves round to form
the Main Face.
    It is usual to descend or abseil Optimists Gully (Severe). The gully reaches
the cliff top beside the crest of the main face at the top of the North Descent. It
is grassy at the top.

Hairy Rib   30m   VS 4c   (1976)
The left-hand rib of Optimist's Gully gives good climbing but reaching its base is
tedious. It has been reached by climbing down from where Optimist's Gully
peters out and also by traversing from below Akimbo Crack at low tide (better).
It is usually easier to abseil. Climb cracks in the rib to the large flake where
Optimist's route crosses. Continue up the slabby arete and finish up a crack on
the right of the final bulge.

Butterlegs   12m   E4 6b *   (1992)
This takes the clean overhanging groove left of Hairy Rib, but access is even
more awkward. Either abseil to belay low on the left edge of Hairy Rib, or better,
approach from the base of Akimbo Crack at lowish tide and belay directly
beneath the route. Cross a black hanging slab to gain a small red triangular slab
at the base of the groove (peg runner). Continue up the groove (peg runner) to
jugs and a belay ledge. Scrambling remains.

Bongo Fury   15m   HVS 5a *   (1981)
This route is right of Optimist's Gully, starting halfway down the gully and directly
below an overhung recess at about 10m. Climb up into the recess, then go
directly through the overhang above and follow easier grooves to the top.

Day Tripper   15m   VS 4c *   (1969)
Start as for Bongo Fury. Climb the slab to a right-slanting diedre with an obvious
layback crack. Move up this and finish up a short slabby V-groove (grassy and
sometimes damp).

The Hedonist   30m   HVS 5a ***   (1974)
A fairly serious route in an intimidating position, overlooking the red wall and the
cave. Start where Optimist's Gully drops steeply down to the sea, about 6m
below. Traverse out right horizontally across a slab to its right edge. Climb the
edge over a small overhang until a small green slab on the right can be crossed
to reach a steep shattered wall. Climb this, trending right to a large flake and
resting perch. From here move into the groove above and left (crux). Climb the
groove, hand traverse the right wall and move up and back left to a grassy groove
which leads to the top.

Orbital Ejection   50m   E3 ***   (1992)
An exciting traverse across the Red Hole, superb but a little hybrid. Start as for
Hedonist at the foot of Optimist's Gully.
1. 4c   Follow The Hedonist to the perch and belay on its right side at the
junction with red rock.
2. 5c   Climb the corner forming the left edge of the red rock to the overhangs,
then undercut right to a belay surrounded by overhangs on the Cracks in Reality
slab.
3. 5c   Move down and right under an overhang to pull into a groove (as for
Procrastination). Now finish up the wide open groove to the right.

THE MAIN FACE

While the Red Hole has plenty of routes in the upper grades, the Main Face is justly one of the most popular cliffs on the coast for routes in the lower grades. It has a pleasant, sunny aspect and most routes are on fine rock with good protection. The wall lies opposite a rocky islet nicknamed The Submarine. Some of the routes are birded in summer, mainly those left of The Bifurcator. Some minor routes have been done on the Submarine itself.

Access

North Descent is often used, but many prefer to abseil down Insect Groove. There are embedded pieces of rusty metal in a small rocky hollow at the top of this route.

North Descent   25m   Moderate *   (pre 1960)
A good climb for its grade, but quite tricky and exposed at first acquaintance in descent. Start almost opposite the east tip of the Submarine, close to the eastern corner of the face. Descend directly for 5m down slabs with a blunt arete to a platform (the top of the Leaning Tower). Climb down the steep groove on the left (facing in) which bulges awkwardly at the bottom. This is most easily negotiated swinging right and down, then stepping back left to easier ledges leading west to the centre of the face.

From these ledges the most prominent feature of the cliff is the large corner of Insect Groove. The wall left of this is steep and marked by a number of cracks and grooves. The right wall is less steep and has three routes; protection is not particularly good. The climbs are described from right to left.

Painted Wall   15m   Very Difficult   (pre 1960)
Starting immediately left of North Descent, this ill-defined and uninspiring line takes shallow cracks which lead slightly left in the upper part.

Painted Groove   10m   VS 4c   (1988)
Start at the foot of North Descent. Climb an awkward ramp up left and the continuation V-groove to finish at the top of Insect Wall.

Insect Wall   15m   Very Difficult *   (pre 1960)
Start 5 metres left of Painted Groove at a tapering slab leading left towards Insect Groove. Start up the slab for a few metres, then traverse right to a short groove. At the top of this groove, step left and climb up briefly before moving out right to an exposed position. Finish straight up the upper walls on good holds.

Insect Flake   20m   E1 5b *   (1975)
An eliminate line with good climbing. Start beside Insect Wall. Instead of taking the initial slab, pull over the bulge below the traverse directly and take the rib left of the first groove, then ascend moving slightly left to gain a ledge below a vertical corner. Climb the flake crack in the corner, and a final technical but avoidable crack to the top.

Red Wall   10m   E4 6a *   (1981)
This climbs the compact overhanging headwall right of Insect Groove by thin
quartz cracks, starting by Insect Groove or Flake.

Insect Groove   30m   VS 5a ***   (1969)
A classic well protected line. Start directly up rounded slabby rocks into a vague
crack, then take the groove direct to the top.

The Bifurcator   30m   VS 4c **   (1971)
Another fine route up the wall left of Insect Groove. Start 5 metres left of Insect
Groove below a steep wide crack (taken by Nicol's Eliminate). Climb the slab
corner right of this crack to join Insect Groove for a few feet before moving left
to climb the overhanging V-groove. Finish straight up the wall above.

The Eliminator   30m   HVS 5a   (1979)
An eliminate line moving left from the base of the hanging groove of Bifurcator
to finish by the variation of Nicol's Eliminate.

Nicol's Eliminate   30m   Mild VS 4b *   (1950s)
This good line is an eliminate in name only. Starting as for Bifurcator, climb the
wide crack to a ledge below an overhang which is climbed directly to gain a
groove on the left, at the top of which is a large ledge. Two finishes are possible.
Original Finish: Very Difficult
Climb cracks on the left to large ledge then up the short wall above.
Variation Finish: Severe
Pull over the bulge on the right to gain a slab. Step back left and into a groove
which is climbed on good holds (better).

The Slide   30m   VS 4c **   (1971)
From the ledges at the foot of Nicol's Eliminate, cross the slab on the left and
step up onto a square-cut ledge. Climb the short groove above and pull out onto
another ledge below a fine steep groove. Climb the groove for 10m to its
termination below a bulge. Here it is possible to finish out right, but the moves
which give the climb its name lie out over the slabby edge on the left to reach
easy ground.

Brooker's Original Route   35m   Hard Severe   (1950)
Start up The Slide to the base of the steep groove. From here traverse ledges
leftwards, then take a short groove, pulling up left onto a large ledge a little
higher. From here, move left and up a short crack above which a final groove
and some scrambling leads to the top.

Right of the North Descent is The Leaning Tower, an impressive square-cut
buttress. Halfway up its south-east face is a platform above which the rock
overhangs. Four routes on excellent rock climb the short slightly overhanging

wall below this platform. They can be reached by descending wave-worn rounded rocks from the central ledges, followed by a short traverse right just above the sea. Access is problematical at high tide. On the left side of the wall are three thin crack lines.

Aqualung   10m   E2 6a *   (1989)
The left-hand of the three thin crack lines, the exit being the crux.

Aquarius   10m   E1 5c *   (1988)
The right-hand crack line.

The Waterline   7m   VS 4c
This takes the obvious break right of Aquarius, a wide crack with an awkward bottleneck.

The Waterfront   7m   VS 4c
This is the flared groove just to the right, starting from a lower barnacled ledge up a steep wall.

The following route climbs the frontal face of the Leaning Tower above the previous routes. At the time of writing it is the hardest non-bolted route in the North-East.

Lunatic Fringe   15m   E7 6c ***   (1992)
Start from the ledge. Climb cracks diagonally rightwards to a jug on the arete (Rock 6). Move left of an undercling and go up to sloping holds. Continue up (dangerous) to a horizontal break (Peg and Friend 1 runners on the right). Gain the next break, using the right arete (crux),(RP5). Finish on the slab above.

At very low tide it is possible to continue traversing the barnacled ledges round to a platform under the north-east wall of The Leaning Tower. However, Optimist's Route is the usual approach.

Optimist's Route   35m   Severe   (1950s)
Seldom climbed for its own sake, but a useful access route. Once down the awkward bulge of the North Descent go down a short chimney to gain the halfway platform of The Leaning Tower. Traverse right around the arete onto the steep north-east face of the Tower. Continue traversing right and descend the twin cracks of Akimbo Crack to a platform. Now climb obliquely up right (under a nose of quartz) and round a leaning arete into a chimney-fault (Tower Chimney). Cross this directly and climb up to a prominent pointed flake or block on the crest of the rib beyond (Hairy Rib). Traverse into the hanging gully beyond (Optimist's Gully) and finish up this (grassy at the top).

Teetering on the Brink of Madness   15m   E5 6c **   (1990)
This route takes the arete left of Akimbo Crack. Belay on the quartz platform
below Akimbo. Climb Akimbo Crack to the niche, then take the right side of the
arete to a horizontal break (peg runner). Gain a standing position on the break
with great difficulty to reach a good incut under an overlap (Friend 0 on right).
Final technical moves lead up the arete to finish.

Threshold of Insanity   20m   E5 6c *   (1992)
Climb the previous route to the peg runner. Move below the vertical crack and
gain a standing position on the break. Shuffle left until a move up gains sloping
holds (Friend 0 on the left). A hard move gains the horizontal break, then further
difficulties lead right then up to the top.

Akimbo Crack   15m   VS 4c *   (1972)
The obvious crooked crack on the north-east wall of the Tower. The bottom can
be reached via Optimist's Route, along the barnacled ledges under the lower
wall of the Tower (low tide), by descending Tower Chimney (dirty) or by abseil.
Climb the twin cracks and crack above to a niche then follow the crack out right
into the upper part of Tower Chimney.

A scrappy eliminate climbs Akimbo Crack to the niche, then mantles out of the
jam crack to a good side pull. Delicate moves lead to the top (E2 5c).

Tower Chimney   15m   Very Difficult
The bordering fault on the right side of the Tower.

The South Descent is little more than a scramble down the south-west side
of the cliff. It is identifiable by scree slopes at the top, just east of the rocky step
on the grassy access ridge of the quarry.

Rock Bottom Traverse   30m   Difficult *   (1950s)
This goes north-east along the base of the cliff to link with the central ledges.
When combined with an exit via North Descent it provides a good easy expedition. From the foot of the South Descent, traverse right across a slab below an
overhanging wall (calm sea and low tide advisable). Move down then pull
rightwards into a crack and so gain the central ledges.

Ecky's Crack   20m   Hard Severe *
This is the left-slanting crack on the left side of the wall. It rises in two steps,
escapable at the easement. Climb a wide crack then the corner crack above,
negotiating a block.

Quartz Bicycle   20m   VS 4c *   (1972)
Climb the crack just right of Ecky's, then move right and up a short groove to
small ledges. From here the wall above may be climbed directly (HVS) or by
moving left to follow a right-trending crack to easier ground.

The Wandering of the One-Toed Wizard   30m   HVS 5a **   (1972)
This belies its name by climbing the right side of the wall fairly directly. Start on top of a pedestal beside the overhanging wall overlooking Rock Bottom Traverse. Climb directly up the steep wall to ledges. Climb the shallow groove above and so to the top.

The Main Girdle (Puck's Route)   55m   VS 4c *   (1950s)
A girdle of the main face. Halfway down the South Descent a slanting crack cuts out onto the cliff. Follow this for 8m until it steepens, where an exposed move down right leads into the short groove of Quartz Bicycle. Traverse right to large ledges and continue right to the foot of the groove of the slide. A difficult move round the arete allows entry into a groove alongside Nicol's Eliminate which leads to its large ledge and belay. Pull over the overhang on the right and cross the slab until an awkward step can be made into Insect Groove. Descend this for 4m, then traverse right and finish up any of the routes on the right.

THE SOUTH SLABS

Further south from the South Descent the cliffs form a small inlet containing a deep cave. The high north wall of this inlet is very dirty and vegetated in its lower half but the upper part holds a belt of smooth exposed slabs. The rock is dubious and protection is indifferent. Nevertheless, the climbing is unusual and interesting. There are two routes both starting from an earth ledge halfway up the cliff. This can be reached by a very insecure traverse from the north, or by abseil.

Aardvark   30m   HVS 4c *   (1971)
The best line. From the earth ledge move briefly up a slab before traversing left across a grassy groove into a parallel groove. About 5m up this, move up left following a thin crack to gain the slabs under a larger overlap (after surmounting a small bulge). Use a small break on the left of the overlap to gain a groove. Follow this to the top on deteriorating rock.

The Blue Baboon   30m   E1 5a   (1975)
Climb Aardvark for 8m, then break out right and climb steep slabs to a corner 5m right of the final groove of Aardvark (runner in the blocks to the right). Climb the loose corner to the top.

   Instead of traversing right to climb the corner, it is possible to climb directly up onto the upper face, following the right-hand edge to the top. This has better rock but is harder and still poorly protected.

COLSEA YAWN   *(Map Ref 952 001)*

This is the large inlet south from the South Cove cliffs, overlooked by a long-disused fish manure factory. From the cottage, follow the railway line south for about 30 metres where an easy slope descends to the stony beach. Climbing interest on the north side of the Yawn is limited to a few short problems on overhanging rock near the seaward end. They can be reached by a pleasant moderate traverse taking broad ledges 7m or 8m above the sea. The steep wall halfway along this traverse has been climbed direct (Difficult). The south side of the Yawn has a small slab at the seaward end which gives a short Difficult route up the centre.

The big green wall further right provides some climbing. The wall is well seen from the vicinity of the disused factory. It has an obvious stepped overlap at mid-height. Access is by traversing from the pebble beach (low tide) or by going down the grassy shoulder of the inlet (as for Bruin Cove) then climbing down the immediate east side of the wall (Moderate). The top part is an obvious cutting. The wall is north-facing, sheltered and can be rather green. A favourable breeze is desirable for optimum conditions.

Beryl the Peryl   20m   VS 4c *   (1982)
This takes a direct line up the centre of the wall. Swing left over the overlap from the bottom of a short corner formed by a step in the overlap, and finish by the obvious hanging chimney.

A Taste for Treason   20m   HVS 5a **   (1985)
The obvious crack line right of Beryl the Peryl, finishing out right under the bulge at the top.

A Basket of Rogues   15m   E1 5b *   (1989)
About 3 metres right of A Taste for Treason is a thin crack line which peters out after 3m. Climb this, then ascend directly to join and climb another crack line to the top. Exit by a grassy alcove on the right.

Pansy Potter   15m   VS 4c   (1989)
The obvious corner to the right. A crumbly start leads to better climbing in the upper corner. Finish up a small slab on the left.

BRUIN COVE   *(Map Ref 952 000)*

This is the next inlet just south of Colsea Yawn. It contains a superb sea cave, above and left of which is an impressive unclimbed wall, alas topped by loose rock and very steep grass. The steep north wall holds the existing routes. The rock is fairly solid granite, which catches the sun in the morning and early afternoon and provides good climbing in a relaxed atmosphere. There are a lot of birds in the nesting season, mainly affecting the routes left of Pandrop. The other routes are usually quite clean.

Access
Descend the southern shoulder of Colsea Yawn to reach rocky ledges near sea-level, then cut back into the cove. At high tide there is an awkward wall to negotiate. The routes are described from right to left.

1 Back Drop 20m Hard Severe * (1958)
The first main feature on the approach is a short open book corner. Climb this corner to a ledge then go up a slab and the groove above. Swing out right over a small arete to follow another groove to the top.

2 Green Rosetta 20m VS * (1979)
Climb the bulges below the ledge of Back Drop on jugs, then go up the slab and rib left of Back Drop to the top.

3 Acid Drop 20m Hard Severe *** (1958)
An obvious feature of the cliff is a large impending corner at the top, left of Back Drop. This route climbs an initial steep fault, then follows the corner on excellent holds to the top.

4 The Pretender 20m E1 5b * (1981)
Left of Acid Drop are twin niches in the lower wall. Pandrop takes the left-hand niche and Pretender the right-hand. Climb the niche going directly through the slot, then follow large holds directly up the wall above to an easy ramp. Finish directly by a layback round a block.

5 Pandrop 20m HVS 5a ** (1958)
Move up into the left-hand niche, then surmount the bulge on the left leading to the base of a left-slanting ramp. From the top of the ramp swing up right across a steep wall to a shallow groove and crack which leads to the top.

6 Eve's Drop 25m Very Difficult (1958)
Climb the deep left-slanting chimney crack and the continuation crack to the top.

7 Mind Games 20m E2 5b ** (1979)
The obvious groove line left of Eve's Drop is Drop Not. This sustained route takes the thin crack line in the wall to its right. Gain the crack by a layback in from the left, round a small roof. Follow the crack to easier ground and the top.

8 Drop Not 20m VS 4b * (1958)
Where the broad ledges peter out into the steep wall of the cave, there is a steep crack and groove. Follow this, with some dodgy rock near the top.

9 Thieves' Route 25m E2 5b (1979)
From the bottom of Drop Not, climb down left to a lower belay ledge. Start up a flake forming the base of a peculiar arched corner, then traverse out left to obvious little perches. Climb back up right above the arch and so up close to the arete, to finish by the left-finishing groove of the Girdle Traverse. Severely stricken by nests.

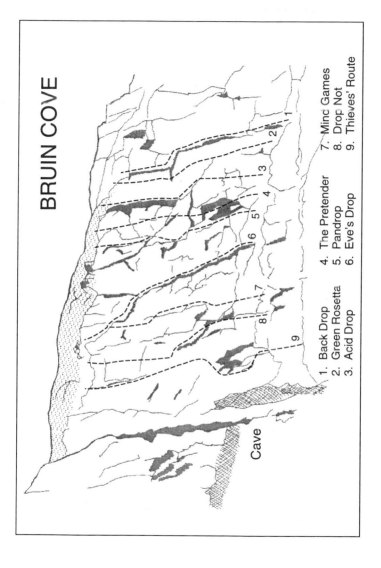

BRUIN COVE

Cave

1. Back Drop
2. Green Rosetta
3. Acid Drop
4. The Pretender
5. Pandrop
6. Eve's Drop
7. Mind Games
8. Drop Not
9. Thieves' Route

Girdle Traverse   35m   VS 4c *   (1972)
Start at the seaward end and cross Back Drop above the initial corner. Continue
over ledges and a slab and round an edge to belay on the platform of Acid Drop.
Descend awkwardly onto the foot of the ramp of Pandrop. Climb the ramp and
swing round on the wall on the left (intimidating); cross this on jugs to a belay on
Eve's Drop. Continue at the same level to finish up Drop Not, or else by a groove
a few metres further left.

In the bay south of Bruin, a couple of icefalls can form after a mini ice-age;
they provide some good sport.

HARENESS   *(Map Ref 953 998)*

This is the next headland south of the inlet south of Bruin Cove. There are
miniature disused quarries with spoil tips of rubble at the cliff top (midway
between Bruin and Sickle Row). The biggest quarry is under the main rubble tip.
The 15m slab at the back is Jigsaw Slab. In the lower part of the quarry is a
relatively tall flaring groove on the north side, which gives the route Rusty Halo.
The slab wall to its right gives a few interesting problems.

Jigsaw Slab   15m   VS 4b *   (1989)
Start up the obvious line in the centre of the slab and move right to follow grooves
to the top. Poor Protection.

Rusty Halo   15m   E2 5b *   (1989)
Climb the flaring groove finishing on the left. Sparse protection.

About 50 metres south of the quarry is an attractive 10m slabby wall facing
out to sea. It gives the following routes.

Pink Crack   10m   HVS 5a
The obvious left-slanting crack.

Finger Jive   7m   E3 6a   (1992)
Start as for Pink Crack and move right onto a finger ramp. Follow this with a
rockover left to finish.

Bottom Boys   10m   E4 6a *   (1987)
This takes a line of quartz flakes up the wall left of Pink Crack, starting at a
pointed block. Climb up and slightly left, then go slightly right and up to finish at
the top of Pink Crack. Fine climbing but poorly protected.

THE MINCER CLIFF   *(Map Ref 948 994)*

This cliff lies close to Sickle Row. Both cliffs provide a number of interesting
climbs, only one of which is below VS. The rock of Sickle Row is quite good and
similar to that at Bruin Cove. The Mincer Cliff is very steep and the rock distinctly

unsound. Both cliffs catch a great deal of sunshine. Birds are not a significant problem on these crags.

Access

Take the minor road south from the southern road leading into Cove Bay. This is marked Blackhills Quarry and is only a couple of hundred metres from the junction. After about 400 metres the track for Blackhills Quarry branches off left. Take the road immediately beyond this one, marked Haven Cottage. Follow this past a farm to park on verges just before a lorry yard. Follow a track downhill and through the railway arch to end on a tip overlooking an inlet (The Horse Shoe).

The Mincer Cliff is the north wall of the Horse Shoe inlet. It could not be called an attractive place. From the tip a muddy slope sweeps down to the sea alongside the cliff where there are strewn bizarre lumps of metal from the foundry. The cliff itself is very steep and of unhealthy looking shades of red and orange. The rock is very worrying and calls for a lot of care. In the event of disaster, it may be of some comfort to consider that descent will generally be through mid-air into deep water. Despite its drawbacks, the cliff does have a certain Gogarth-like character and the challenge of the main central part remains unclimbed.

Descent for the left hand routes is via the central ridge of the Horse Shoe, overlooking the tip. It is exposed and requires care. Access for the two right-hand routes is by traversing steeply in from the seaward end. The routes are described from left to right.

The Mincer 35m   VS 4b *   (1958)
The most prominent feature of the cliff, and the original line which gave the cliff its name, is a chimney crack near the left end. The first 15m are loose but easy. The ensuing vertical section is worryingly lacking in protection until a welcome chockstone is gained. Thereafter, enjoyable climbing on better rock leads to the top. Tom Patey and Mac Smith originally climbed the route largely by squirming inside the chimney, hence the name. It has since been found easier to bridge all the way.

The Green Manalishi 35m   VS 4b   (1972)
This takes a right-trending line from the base of the Mincer crack. Rotten and poorly protected, give it a miss.

Girdle Traverse 65m   HVS 5a **   (1969)
A good left to right traverse at a low level and a fine way to savour the atmosphere of the cliff in relative safety. Traverse right along ledges a few metres above the sea to an overhanging corner. Climb this (crux), then move right to ledges below the overhanging central prow of the cliff. Descend rightwards and follow the easiest line about 3m above the sea on steep rock to easy ledges at the seaward end.

Rotwand   40m   E1 5a *   (1972)
A steep and serious route in an impressive position, taking a hanging corner right
of centre. Traverse into the wall from the seaward end and go up left, heading
for the obvious overhanging corner on the right of the prominent rib. Climb the
steep wall to a block overhang in the corner. Climb this (crux) and go up the
corner above (loose) until an escape to the right can be made. Climb up and left
to an optional belay (pegs useful) on a poor stance on an edge overlooking the
corner. Continue up the disintegrating wall to a fence post belay.

Nightrake   35m   HVS 4c   (1976)
This takes the right wall of Rotwand. Traverse in from the seaward end to a point
where the cliff begins to overhang. A band of brittle rock ascends slightly right
from the same point. Climb up and left, following the easiest line, to a good ledge
and belays. Climb a short corner right of the stance, then continue up left on
easier ground to the top. Another serious route.

SICKLE ROW   *(Map Ref 950 995)*

This cliff lies about 100 metres north of the Horse Shoe inlet. It faces east but
the high north end curves out into the sea to form an impressive south-facing
wall. This wall takes quite a lot of drainage from marshy ground above and the
central part can often be wet. The cliff is usually free of birds in summer.

Access is by a simple scramble at the south end to reach the flat rocks and
pools below the crag. Routes are described from left to right. The first two routes
lie just to the right of the short undercut wall at the left end of the crag. They start
either side of, and meet above, an overhung niche. Both routes are awkward and
poorly protected.

Antic   10m   HVS 5a   (1975)
The left-hand line, climbed diagonally right below a slanting overlap.

Frolic   10m   HVS 5a   (1975)
The right-hand line, climbed up and left above the niche.

Pioneer Grit   10m   HVS 5a *   (1979)
An eliminate taking the wall right of Frolic. Start up a puckered wall and follow
the obvious left-slanting line to a down-pointing roof. Climb through the roof and
move right to finish by a deep crack.

Mong   15m   E1 5a *   (1971)
A good line, steep and strenuous and sparsely protected. Climb the cracked wall
just right of the puckered wall of Pioneer Grit to an easement halfway up the crag.
Finish out left by a line of holds on the overhanging upper wall.

THE FINDON CLIFFS

TO COVE
BACKHILL
BLACK QUARRY
SOUTH BLACKHILL FARM
HARENESS
PIONEER GRIT FOUNDRY
QUARRIES
SICKLE ROW
MINCER CLIFF
CLASHRODNEY
BACKHILLS OF CAIRNROBIN
BARESIDE POINT
WATERFALL
BAREARSE POINT
PIPERS HOLE
RAILWAY
BLOW-UP NOSE
NORTH MAINS OF HUTTON
MIDDLETON FARM
GRAVEL QUARRY
FOWLS HEUGH
RED MANTLE
SEALS' CAVES
EARNSHEUGH BAY
MAIN CLIFF
PINK BAND CLIFF
FROM DUAL CARRIAGEWAY
EARNSHEUGH TONGUE
PARKING
BOGLESHEUGH
DUMP
FINDON MOOR
FINDON VILLAGE
KAYHOLE
FINDON NESS
GREY WALL
UNILEVER RESEARCH LAB.
DOO COVE
POW KEBBUCK
ARNNOT BOO
FINDON SHORE

500 m
Scale

move right to finish by a deep crack.

Mong   15m   E1 5a *   (1971)
A good line, steep and strenuous and sparsely protected. Climb the cracked wall
just right of the puckered wall of Pioneer Grit to an easement halfway up the crag.
Finish out left by a line of holds on the overhanging upper wall.

Trunk   15m   E1 5a *   (1971)
Another strenuous and not very well protected route. Start at the base of an
obvious crack line of Mao and take a left-slanting slab to a grey-stained wall. Go
up this (crux) to an oval depression in the face. Climb cracks above the right side
of the depression to the top.

Mao   15m   E1 5b *   (1979)
Climb directly up the obvious crack line just left of an arching recess (The Open
Sesame Cave).

The Shape of Things to Come   20m   E2 5b   (1983)
Climb the right corner of the Open Sesame Cave to the overhang. Move right
onto the arete then into a groove to climb up to a ledge. Go right under an
overhang round a rib and continue to the top. Exceedingly loose and uninspiring.

Vicious Love   20m   HVS 5a   (1975)
Start 10 metres right of the cave and climb a cracked wall by the right-hand of
the two obvious lines to a ledge at 6m. Continue by the obvious left-trending line.

The cliff changes angle at a messy wet corner. The impressive face to the
right has four fine routes. A dry spell of weather is necessary, especially for
Glasnost and Perestroika.

Glasnost   20m   E5 6b *   (1989)
The old aid route Band Aid takes the slanting crack line (quartz-filled in places),
surmounting the overhang to the right of the main roofs, just left of the obvious
short corner of Perestroika. Climb the line to the roof and gain a hold above it,
right of the quartz crack, to place a nut strenuously. Continue up using holds
either side of the quartz crack until it is possible to pull across right to a resting
ledge. Step back left into the line and follow it to the top. As long as the seepage
below the roof and in the quartz crack above is not too bad, the holds remain dry.

Perestroika   25m   E4 6a **   (1989)
The obvious line parallel to and just right of Glasnost. It breaks through the roof
by the obvious short corner, which gives the crux. From the resting ledge reach
left to join and finish up Glasnost.

Red Army Blues   25m   E4 6a **   (1989)
The fine obvious line to the hanging corner at two-thirds height. Climb the line
to a short quartz corner. Pull over this (peg runner over the bulge on the right)
and continue up to pull out left to a semi-rest below and left of the hanging corner.
Step right and enter the corner (crux). Climb this to a resting ledge on the right,
then continue directly to the top. The runners in the top corner (RP5 at the base,
Rocks 3 and 4 a little higher) are placed blind.

Babooshka   20m   E4 5c   (1993)
The corners and grooves between Red Army Blues and Spinnaker Direct give
good climbing, but the rock is not as good as on the routes further left and the
first 10m are unprotected. The crux is the entry into the hanging V-corner at
two-thirds height.

Spinnaker   20m   Hard Severe **   (1970)
An excellent route at a reasonable standard, taking the wall on the right where
the angle relents. Start up a shallow corner where slabs dip smoothly into the
sea. From a sloping ledge at 8m move right and up to a narrow ramp. Move right
then up to the top by easier climbing.

Spinnaker Direct   20m   HVS 4c
Start as for Spinnaker but continue straight up the groove until a move right leads
to a sloping ramp. Climb the steep flaky crack on poor rock to the top.

The Joker   10m   E1 5b *   (1983)
Right of Spinnaker there is a short steep area of fine rock with a crack in it (HVS).
The Joker climbs a very steep wall up and left to join the crack line. Continue up
left on steep rock to easy ground near the top of Spinnaker.

CLASHRODNEY NORTH

This recently developed crag lies between The Mincer Cliff and Clashrodney.
Follow signs for Haven Cottage and park by Tom Shanks' depot, or continue
down the track to park through the railway arch. Enter the field to the south and
follow the fence on its seaward side for 100 metres. Just after a pile of boulders,
cross the fence and follow a grassy ridge down to the top of the crag and descend
on its north side. The crag has numerous quartz veins, faces south-east and is
non-tidal. The routes are described from left to right.

The Friability Drive   20m   HVS 4c   (1993)
Climb the big quartz slab, finishing by a groove 2 metres right of a grassy corner.

Wild Hearted Son   20m   E3 5c *   (1993)
Climb easy rocks to a Friend 1 placement, then move right and climb a tiny
left-facing corner. Hand traverse left, then go up right through a roof to the slab
above.

Skills for Adolescents   15m   HVS 5a   (1993)
Start up the crack of All Stripped Down, then move left across the wall to a niche.
Finish up the slab above.

All Stripped Down   15m   HVS 5a   (1993)
Start up easy rocks and continue up the obvious crack line.

CLASHRODNEY (BARESIDE POINT)   *(Map Ref 947 991)*

This is the most southerly outcrop of granite on the north-east coast and
comprises a number of pleasant sunny walls. Bareside Point is the headland
south of the Clashrodney inlet and it is in this vicinity that all the climbing lies.
The routes are generally free of nesting birds and there are a good number of
suitable routes for the beginner and lower grade climber. There is a fair amount
of yellow lichen around, but when dry it is not troublesome.

Access
See South Cove and Sickle Row and Mincer Cliff sections for general access to
the coast road which runs south towards Findon Village. Go south past the
Pioneer Grit turn off for 500 metres and turn off left down a short dirt track
immediately before a sharp bend, where the road dips down alongside the
railway. Parking space is very limited and care needs to be taken to avoid
blocking the track.
   Cross the railway then follow a fence coastwards in a vague grassy hollow
with a gorse-strewn left bank. Cross a fence and follow a vague path slightly
leftwards across the heather to cross a stream (which ends in a waterfall beside
some of the routes). Keep going north-east to look down on a small inlet, the
Lagoon. There is an iron spike on bare rocks in a vague hollow. By descending
from the iron spike all but The Causeway climbs can be reached. Descend the
short wall by another convenient spike. The Central Buttress is the wall just to
the north, overlooking the head of the Lagoon, whilst the Pink Slab is the cracked
slab dipping into the Lagoon itself.
   The Causeway climbs are on the continuation of the crag to the north. They
can be reached by heading north along the cliff top and descending the north
side of the tip of the headland, then traversing back in underneath a 10m cracked
wall (only recommended at low tide). Otherwise descend The Slant (Moderate)
or abseil. From above, The Slant may be identified by a peculiar horizontal rock
cutting going back from the clifftop.
   The Waterfall climbs lie to the south of the iron spike descent and Cairnrobin
Point, some 50 metres south beyond the waterfall.

THE CAUSEWAY CLIMBS

Corbett's Crack   15m   Severe *   (1967)
This lies on the cracked wall mentioned above. At the top of the fine crack easier
rock leads to the top.

Mac's Route   20m   Hard Severe *   (1967)
Round left from Corbett's Crack is an obvious V-shaped chimney. Climb this until a mantelshelf can be made to a ledge (optional belay). A steep ledge system on the right leads to the top.

Birthday Treat   20m   HVS 5a ***   (1971)
Climb the obvious steep crack just left of Mac's Route to a ledge. Step left onto an undercut wall, then climb this to the top. An excellent pitch.

Blind Faith   20m   E3 5c **   (1979)
The fierce overhanging groove left of Birthday Treat. The crux is surmounting the overhang to enter the hanging groove. Break out right towards the top. A fine line.

The Slant   20m   Moderate   (Pre 1912)
The easiest way up the rib and fault left of Blind Faith, and a useful descent.

Grimace   10m   E2 5b
The short corner above easy slabs between Grimble and The Slant. The crux is exiting left at the top of the corner.

Grimble   10m   E2 5b
This is the steep shallow corner on the left wall of the rib of The Slant. Climb the corner, finishing on the right wall.

Creased Slab   10m   Moderate   (Pre 1912)
Take the easiest line up slabs and grooves left of Grimble.

Pipeyard Blues   15m   Mild Severe   (1981)
The left boundary of the creased slab is a slabby inset diedre. Move up this for a short way, then move across left to climb another corner alongside a prominent edge. Artificial.

Rose Rib   15m   Difficult   (1950s)
This is the rib left of Pipeyard Blues, gained by starting up the inset diedre. It is actually the right edge of the Pink Slab.

THE PINK SLAB

This provides some nice climbing, gained by walking in from the descent below the iron spikes. The fastest descent from the routes is to go down a broken gully (Moderate) at the west end of the slab or by walking across under Central Buttress. There are four obvious crack lines. The climbs finish on a ledge, although it is possible to extend them by finishing up the steeper headwall.

The Hairline   10m   Severe *   (1949)
The left-hand crack gives a classic little route.

Stiletto   15m   Hard Severe **   (1958)
The next crack line has a tricky start. Thereafter it gives fine climbing on small
delicate holds.

Gorgon   15m   VS 5a **
The crack line 2 metres right of Stiletto. Start on the small ledge at its right side.
Pull up right over the bulge on quartz jugs and follow the crack to the top.

Medusa   20m   Severe *   (1966)
The next crack, around the corner. Start up a recessed corner (low tide required)
to gain the crack line.

Serpent   20m   VS 5a   (1992)
Approach from the north at low tide. Climb the corner right of Medusa to the roof,
then turn this using the left edge to gain the slab. Finish easily up the crack on
the right.

Suicide Blonde   15m   E5 6b *   (1991)
The little corner and big roof right of Medusa. Climb the arete and make a
technical move to gain holds over the lip. Cut loose, heelhook right and power
over onto the easy slab.

Pink Slab Traverse   25m   Severe *   (1966)
A diagonal traverse of the slab from left to right. Start at the foot of the Hairline
and slant right across the other routes to finish up Rose Rib, the right bounding
edge.

CENTRAL BUTTRESS
This is the small steep buttress facing out to sea up above the back of the
Lagoon. The routes are described from left to right.

Robb's Revenge   10m   Very Difficult   (1981)
The left rib of the obvious chimney, keeping to the crest.

Chisel Chimney   10m   Very Difficult *   (1949)
The chimney has an overhanging block near the bottom and is climbed direct.

Stone Roses   10m   E2 5b *   (1986)
Climb the smooth corner to the right, exiting right to gain a standing position on
the obvious spike (crux). Move up to an overhang, traverse left into a recess and
finish easily.

Capitol Wall   10m   Mild VS *   (1958)
Climb the face right of Stone Roses by the left-slanting line, finishing up a bulging
niche.

Quick Corner   10m   Severe
The right-hand corner.

THE WATERFALL CLIMBS

These lie on the short walls running south from the Iron Spikes, bounded on the south by a waterfall, the final gesture of the little burn. The climbs are described from right to left.

Yellow Peril   10m   E1 5b *   (1980)
The best line on this section of cliff, taking the obvious hanging corner on the first steep wall below the rocky promontory. Pull up onto the right edge of the lower scoop and go up the rib to a bulge. Swing up left over the bulge to gain the groove leading to the top.

The Prisoner   12m   E3 6a *   (1992)
A good but escapable climb. Start at the base of the wall down and left of Yellow Peril. Climb boldly to a peg runner, then pull up and right. Climb the upper wall centrally, with the crux at the top.

Oat   10m   VS 4c   (1981)
There are overhangs left of Yellow Peril and a slab left of a niche. Pull directly up onto the slab via a thin crack. Go up the slab and a short corner to the top.

   The slabby rocks left of the slab are Difficult and useful in descent.

Gristwood's Gutties   6m   Mild Severe   (1981)
The obvious roofed corner round left from Oaf.

The Nose   5m   VS 4c
The obvious nose between the previous route and the waterfall.

CAIRNROBIN POINT   *(Map Ref 946 989)*

These routes lie 50 metres south of the waterfall, at a small headland. Although short, there are some good routes, often on excellent rock. The climbs are described from north to south.

Schoolboy Alcoholic   10m   VS 4c *   (1981)
This lies up the first steep slab, split midway by a thin horizontal crack. Follow the right edge of the slab on small holds to a jug and pull onto a block. Move right to finish up a tricky thin crack.

Streetwise   10m   HVS 5a   (1986)
Climb the smooth arete left of Schoolboy Alcoholic and continue over a bulge to finish just right of Glaswegian Snotter.

Glaswegian Snotter   10m   Hard Severe *   (1981)
This takes the left edge of the slabby face. Start up the obvious left-trending shelf
and climb directly up to reach an excellent finger crack in the top wall. There is
an interesting direct start at 5a.

Shrinking Baa's   6m   E2 6a   (1987)
Climb the wall right of Johnnie's Dangler via an undercut to reach a small ledge.
Finish straight up.

Johnnie's Dangler   6m   E1 5b *   (1981)
The obvious notch in the leaning wall gives a good little problem.

Johnny B Good   6m   E3 6b
A problem up the thin crack left of Johnnie's Dangler.

Digital Torquer   6m   E3 6a   (1986)
Climb the overhang left of Johnny B Good via an obvious foot ledge and obscure
pocket.

Mask   15m   Difficult   (Pre-1912)
The obvious corner-gully several metres to the south provides a useful descent.

Cloak   10m   Very Difficult *   (1981)
Starting just right of Mask, climb up right over a bulge on jugs and finish straight
up.

Visor   10m   Hard Severe *   (1981)
Take a direct line through the roof immediately right of Mask, then continue
direct.

Scratch   10m   Mild Severe *   (1981)
The arete forming the left edge of Mask's left wall. Start directly up the arete, then
move onto the right side to finish up a slabby corner, or straight over a bulge on
the right.

Onassis   10m   E3 5c   (1989)
The central line on the leaning wall left of Scratch, swinging right at the top. Short,
yet rich and powerful.

   One route has been climbed in the inlet south of Scratch.

Look Sharp   25m   E1 5b   (1991)
Climb a crack 3 metres right of the nose, then go left to exit onto a ledge.
Continue up the capped corner, avoiding the roof on the left. Finish up the slabby
ramp on the left.

BLOWUP NOSE   *(Map Ref 946 987)*

This is the next headland south, beyond the bay with a free-standing waterfall where the Diney Burn tumbles over the cliff. Immediately south of the descent over the blow-hole there is an inlet with a north-facing wall. At the back of the inlet are two parallel trap dykes which were climbed pre-1912 by members of the Cairngorm Club. The right-hand dyke was named Waterpipe Chimney due to its resemblance to the well known gully on Sgurr na Fheadain in the Coulin. Just left of the left-hand dyke a fault curves up left on the north-facing wall to reach a mid-height terrace. This fault (**The Stomach Crawl**) was also climbed by the early pioneers who finished by traversing the terrace out to the end of the promontory below a short steep red band. The prominent corner in the red band immediately round on the seaward side is Mild VS.

The Crack   25m   Hard Severe   (1991)
About 8 metres left of the Stomach Crawl there is a large boulder at the high water level. Climb the prominent crack directly above the boulder to a recess on the terrace below a roof. Traverse round right of the roof and climb the wall of grey rock to the top (crux).

Beconase   10m   E1 5b   (1991)
The wall left of the crack. Start at the foot of the crack and traverse left to a thin vertical crack. Climb this, then a short right-facing shallow corner to the terrace.

The early pioneers also climbed on the north-facing wall of the next inlet south. Access is from the back of the inlet via Slabby Shelves (old metal spikes).

Findon Cliffs

Climbing started in the Findon area in the late 1970s with the discovery of the solid and attractive Red Band Cliff. The obvious bigger cliffs were largely written off as being too horrible, being largely north-facing with drab and apparently loose rock. However, it became apparent that the rock at Earnsheugh was more solid than it looked, and it also ran to good flat holds. The great exposure promised to make up for any shortcomings, and the resultant explorations made it clear that a climbing ground of great character had been found. Earnsheugh is the biggest crag near Aberdeen; while not everyone's cup of tea, the atmosphere and exposure of its best routes make most other crags seem tame in comparison. It is also one of the few cliffs where climbers can enjoy multi-pitch routes.

The crags at Findon Ness also offer some worthwhile climbing. Systematic cleaning at Boglesheugh, another hideous-looking cliff, produced some remarkable climbing in the distinct Earnsheugh style.

The bigger Findon cliffs are unsuitable for beginners, and climbers wanting something more sunny and light-hearted would do better at the Red Band Cliff, Clashrodney or elsewhere. Even the Red Band Cliff has few easier routes and the approach to it involves a committing abseil.

Access
Findon, a small village 8km (5 miles) south of Aberdeen, is the birthplace of the widely appreciated "Finnan Haddies". There are no pubs or shops. From Aberdeen there are two approaches:

1. Via the coast road splitting south from the south road into Cove (Findon is 3km from this junction). This is as for Sickle Row and Mincer Cliff.
2. More directly and quickly from the main dual carriageway, south of the flyover. There are two turn-offs marked Findon, the most convenient is 50 metres north of a petrol station (on the coast side of the carriageway). Follow the twisty road which veers south, then take the second of twin left-hand turn-offs to follow the road bending right and through the village, see map.

Earnsheugh, the Red Band Cliff and Boglesheugh are best reached from the last house at the north-west end of the village where a dirt track leads down to a small tip. It is best to park at the start of the track or in the village. The gate is usually locked. Keep bearing left to the end of the dump. For Earnsheugh, from the left extremity of the dump take a path leading down left and left again over the heathery moor to the clifftop. For Boglesheugh, take the path leading down left, then take the right branch down the moor until it runs along a dry-stane dyke. Follow the dyke for about 50 metres, then cut directly over the fields, following

Neil Morrison on Long Slough

another dyke to reach the head of an inlet with a big vegetated south wall. Boglesheugh is the next big cliff just south of this. The Red Band Cliff can be reached by either way, or more directly across the fields.

The headland of Findon Ness can also be reached from the dump, but is much quicker to follow a track down through the houses. From the last house described, turn down Old Inn Road, which becomes a dirt track, and turn left before the last house to park where the track deteriorates at the edge of the moor. Do not obstruct the track. Follow the track to where a choice of diverging paths lead to the Kay Hole and the Ness.

EARNSHEUGH   *(Map Ref 944 981)*

This is the big fortress-like crag dominating Earnsheugh Bay. From pleasant pastoral surroundings, the cliff drops in a sudden vertical plunge to the boulders and sea below. The name may mean Eagles Cliff; sea-eagles may have nested here long ago. It would be a fitting haunt because the place is one of the most impressive on the whole coast.

The cliff is gloomy and ruinous with an air of age and decay. The rock is of a crude slatey sort and varies from downright bad to perfectly solid. The climbs are relatively big and serious, the exposure often dramatic. The horizontal strata makes for good flat holds and ledges. Protection is usually quite adequate and the belays are good. All the routes were cleaned to a greater or lesser extent by abseil.

The crag is divided into left and right walls by the great central ridge. The left wall, messy in the centre, is about 55m high and drops sheer into the sea at high tide. There are two caves at the bottom, accessible at low tide by a scramble round the base of the ridge. The right wall, arrayed with corners and roofs, holds most of the climbing. It is about 45m high but tapers up to the right above a steep grass bank. There are good ledges on top of the bank, linked to the clifftop by the Descent Route which runs up the small but exposed right end of the crag.

The crag faces north-east and gets little sun, although it usually dries quickly after rain, even sometimes remaining dry if the wind is from the west. In stormy seas and spray conditions, the right wall may be one of the few dry crags on the coast. The crag is very sheltered from prevailing winds so in milder spells it is often possible to climb in November, sometimes December, and early in the year. However, the sheltered nature of the place can lead to dampness, particularly in humid weather. For optimum conditions a northerly breeze is normally required.

The nearby gun club have clay pigeon shooting on most weekends and occasionally on weekdays. This is not usually a problem, although spent shot can sometimes rain down near or even on the crag. Some climbers may find the noise of gunfire off-putting.

The left wall holds a spectacular colony of kittiwakes, guillemots and razorbills in the nesting season. The right wall is relatively bird-free but scattered fulmars occupy strategic ledges. There may also be the odd pair on the Descent Route.

Running Wild, Craig Stirling (Climber Kenny McIvor)

Descent

There are three usual ways of reaching the base of the cliff.

1. By a scramble down stony slopes 200 metres north of the crag. A jutting rocky nose marks the start. Do not try to make a closer descent. Nettle Gully flanking the cliff is obnoxious and the grassy rakes are either discontinuous or else lead into the gully. This is the best descent on a first visit, leading round the boulder beach to the base of Earnsheugh Ridge.

2. By the Descent Route, a rather unpleasant Very Difficult. This leads down onto the grass bank under the right wall. Start down a short deep chimney-crack to reach a splintered platform. From the left end of the platform (facing in) descend a wall and go down to the grass below (tricky and exposed on first acquaintance). It is then possible to walk beneath the crag.

3. By abseil down the full height of the cliff, usually down the line of Necromancer (at the top of which are stakes and other anchors). Extra ropes are needed since pulling the ropes down is impractical.

The climbs are described from left to right.

1   Batty Bat   80m   HVS 5a   (1980)

The bent crack system left of Hissing Sid, venturing out onto the upper part of the left wall, gives a remarkable and wildly exposed line. Unfortunately it was only lightly cleaned and is still pretty loose. Gain the final platform by the Ridge, Hissing Sid or The Lost World. From the platform climb left up the crack line until it is possible to move left round the arete. Follow the crack system which soon cuts back up right to the top.

2   Hissing Sid   75m   HVS 5a *   (1980)

The chimney crack splitting the roof just left of the final rib of the Ridge route gives another striking line. Again, it was only lightly cleaned, so it is loose and often slimy in the arching corner.

1. 30m A start can be made by the first pitch of The Lost World, which is possible even at high tide. Otherwise, the best start is by the Ridge to gain the neck behind the tower.

2. 25m 4c Turn the gendarme on the left, then make an exposed diagonal traverse left across the face for some 15m. Now climb a bulging wall to clamber up right (beware of poised blocks) to gain the big platform under the headwall.

3. 20m 5a Climb the arching corner up left into a niche under the Chimney. Climb this through the roof and move up right into the notch at the top of the Ridge route.

3   Earnsheugh Ridge   75m   HVS 5a *   (1979)

The original climb, taking the overgrown central ridge, provides a unique route in a commanding position. The ridge crest is fairly easy whilst the fine headwall pitch is poorly protected. There are fulmars in the nesting season, the worst of which can be avoided by taking pitch 3 of Hissing Sid. There is a big tower at the bottom, its right flank hanging with grass. This feature juts out into the sea (low tide required). Gain a curious flat platform up on the seaward end of the tower.

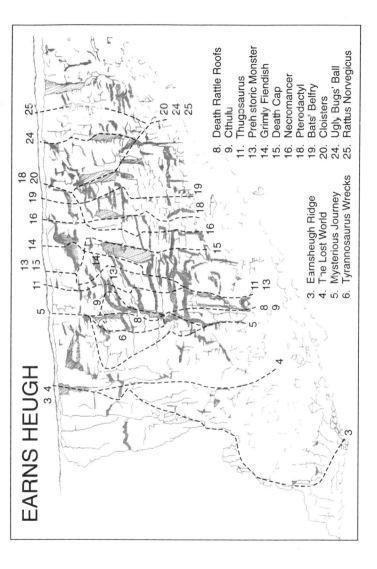

EARNS HEUGH

3. Earnsheugh Ridge
4. The Lost World
5. Mysterious Journey
6. Tyrannosaurus Wrecks

8. Death Rattle Roofs
9. Cthulu
11. Thugosaurus
13. Prehistoric Monster
14. Grimly Fiendish
15. Death Cap
16. Necromancer
18. Pterodactyl
19. Bats' Belfry
20. Cloisters
24. Ugly Bugs' Ball
25. Rattus Norvegicus

1. 20m 4c Move back right into a groove and go up to a ledge to climb a thin crack to a platform under the crest of the tower.
2. 30m Work right across the cracked face of the tower to the neck at the far end. It is also possible to climb to the top of the tower, although descent at the far end is awkward. From the neck, go up the crest turning a gendarme on the left, then go on and up a short wall to easier ground leading up left to a spacious platform under the steep headwall.
3. 25m 5a The obvious rib. Swing out onto the face of the rib and climb up slightly right to the right end of a small roof. Traverse left under the roof and go up the left side to bigger holds leading to the final notch.

4   The Lost World   40m   HVS 5a *   (1980)
The twin cracks on the right side of the upper rib of the Ridge route provide the easiest way up the main crag, unaffected by tide, but there is a grass section. The very overgrown face below the twin cracks has a prominent cavity formed by great blocks. The route starts up gardened grooves running up the right side of this, left of a narrow slab-ramp.
1. 20m 4b Traverse left along a ledge and climb the right side of a tall dubious block, then pull over a bulge into a short V-groove (just right of the cave). Climb this and continue up grass. Go right up grass to belay under the twin cracks.
2. 20m 5a Climb the cracks to a ledge, then slink left round the bulge directly above, and so up the wall to the notch at the top of the Ridge route.

5   Mysterious Journey   65m   E1 5b *   (1980)
This winds a way up the big shattered wall right of the Ridge, the highest part of the Right Wall. Although it looks disgusting, this is an interesting route with fine situations. Start at the base of the great wall, down left from the big Death Cap corner on top of some piled blocks just left of the start of Cthulu.
1. 20m 4b Climb the groove system directly above the blocks to move out left onto a belay ledge.
2. 25m 4c A poorly protected pitch with some bad rock. Traverse left and climb a short groove to step right onto another ledge. Trend diagonally left up the face to a perfect belay stance on top of a steep rib.
3. 20m 5b Traverse away right by small ledges under the overhangs (fulmars in summer), and step down onto a platform. Swing up right into a steep corner with a "crack for thin fingers". Finish up this (crux); good rock and well protected.

A white quartz band cuts through the roofs above the start of Mysterious Journey. This is the line of Death Rattle Roofs. The following two routes take lines left of this and start from the belay ledges above pitch 1 of that route.

6   Tyrannosaurus Wrecks   30m   E3 6a *   (1991)
The corner line left of Death Rattle Roofs' main pitch. Traverse across the ledges and climb a break in the wall to a peg belay below the corner.
1. 20m 6a Climb the corner with crux moves out right, then go up over bulges before pulling out right to belay below the final corner of Mysterious Journey.
2. 10m 5b Finish up the final pitch of Mysterious Journey.

7 Ichthyosaurus 30m E4 6a * (1991)
1. 20m 6a Start up the corner of Death Rattle Roofs, but instead of going right, go straight up to a break (peg runner). Use the obvious handrail to swing left and pull over the roof with difficulty. Climb the wall above to belay below the final pitch of Mysterious Journey.
2. 10m 5b Finish up Mysterious Journey.

8 Death Rattle Roofs 55m E4 6a ** (1985)
This takes the quartz band going up double overhangs left of the Prehistoric Monster Wall. Both this route and Cthulu tend to be damp and really need a favourable breeze to dry them out.
1. 25m 4c Start up Mysterious Journey, then go straight up to belay under bulges (at a level 6m above the Thugosaurus-Prehistoric belay).
2. 20m 6a Climb the great bulge up the line of the quartz (left of a peg runner in a pocket), crux. Continue over the second overhang (easier than it looks) to an easy ramp leading up to the last corner of Mysterious Journey.
3. 10m 5b Finish up Mysterious Journey.

9 Cthulu 65m E5 6a * (1985)
1. 30m 5c Climb the obvious groove with a bulge just left of Prehistoric Monster to join Death Rattle Roofs, follow this to its belay.
2. 25m 6a Climb powerfully up the bulge past the peg runner, then traverse right onto the big wall and go up to a poor resting place (hidden peg runner above the first bulge). Climb straight up the bulges on big improving jugs to the block just left of Thugosaurus, then pull out left using a big flat jug to escape onto the previous route just above its second roof. Climb this to the belay.
3. 10m 5b Finish up Mysterious Journey.

10 Grim Spectre 50m E6 6b * (1986)
An eliminate up the wall left of Thugosaurus. This is the hardest Earnsheugh route, the section up to and over the bulge giving very technical moves.
1. 20m 5b Prehistoric Monster, pitch 1.
2. 20m 6b Traverse left along the ledge and go up to a vague recess under the main wall. Climb out right onto a good foothold on an obvious projection. Climb up left using a good pocket and traverse left to a rest on the belay platform of Death Rattle Roofs. Traverse back right and up to a peg runner (serious) under a vague break in the overlap. Use a good pocket right of the peg and surmount the overlap to gain a raised jug directly above the centre of the break (crux). From here, it looks easier to swing out left, but this is not the case. Climb up and left to the poor rest on Cthulu (hidden peg runner over the bulge). Now either climb the bulges as for Cthulu to reach an awkward rest on the right side of the block, or traverse right and climb Thugosaurus to the same point. Climb the final overhang as for Thugosaurus to peg belays.
3. 10m 5b Climb the overhang as for Thug, then traverse left to finish up an obvious crack just right of the final corner of Mysterious Journey.

11   Thugosaurus   50m   E5 6a ***   (1985)
The magnificent crack line up the centre of the Prehistoric Monster wall.
1. 20m 5b Prehistoric Monster, pitch 1.
2. 20m 6a Climb straight up the crack line over a bulge to a small foot ledge
(semi-rest) under the overlap. Move up right to a crack in the overlap and pull
out left to traverse along the lip using pockets. Move up left and go up to big holds
under the overhangs. Move right to a good flange (poor rest but good runners).
Swing up left and surmount the overhang direct to a stance with peg belays. A
superbly pumpy pitch.
3. 10m 6a Climb the overhang above the belay to a small ledge. Climb the
headwall direct past a pocket and by a vague thin crack line, veering slightly right.

12   Thugosaurus Direct   50m   E5 6a **   (1986)
This is more technical than the ordinary way. At the staggered overlap, continue
straight up the crack line to a break with good runners (Friend 1½, Rock 7,
Friend 1). Climb directly (slightly left) to gain the flange-rest on Thugosaurus
(crux). Move right and climb the double overlap direct with a long reach. Good
flat jugs above lead to the Prehistoric Monster belay. Excellent climbing.

13   Prehistoric Monster   60m   E5 6b ***   (1982)
An impressive and now classic route at the lower limit of its grade.
1. 20m 5b Start at the base of the wall and climb the obvious line up into a small
hanging corner and so on up to belay ledges on the left.
2. 25m 6b Traverse right and gain a standing position on the big block at the
base of the wall. Climb straight up to a hand rail which permits moves out right.
Climb the bulging section up into the crack line where the climbing is less
strenuous (good runners). Move up the crack and gain the smooth triangular
niche from the left (very awkward no hands rest). Climb over the bulge and up a
small corner (crux) to a broken ledge on the right (Friend 3). Step back above
the corner and climb up left to peg belays in a shallow recess.
3. 15m 5b Step left from the recess and climb the wall immediately above, using
a superb pocket to reach the left end of the hand traverse break of Stratosfear.
Reverse this rightwards for 6m to join Death Cap on the undercut arete just below
the top bulge. Climb the bulge and wall to the top.

14   Grimly Fiendish   35m   E4 *   (1990)
This takes the hanging arete between Prehistoric Monster and Death Cap. Start
on the ledge below Death Cap.
1. 25m 5c Move up and left to the belay ledge below the main pitch of Prehistoric
Monster. Follow Prehistoric Monster to the base of the crack line below its niche.
Traverse right along footholds on the lip of the big roof to the arete. Go up the
arete on good jugs to a small sloping ledge. Continue boldly up the shallow
corner above to a rest on the right side of the broken ledge of Prehistoric
Monster. Step right and climb the juggy wall directly to the eyrie belay of Death
Cap.
2. 10m 6a Climb directly through the roof above (peg runner), then go up the
short wall to the top.

From the belay ledges above Pitch 1 of Prehistoric Monster it is possible to traverse right past the standing block and round to the base of Death Cap (Very Difficult).

15   Death Cap   35m   E1 5a ***   (1979)
Right of the great wall the grass bank runs up to good ledges. Death Cap is the big corner hanging above the left extremity of the ledges. Although the rock is slightly poorer than on the routes to its right, it is a classic route of great character, taking the most obvious line on the Right Wall.
1. 25m 5a Climb directly up bulging rock into the corner. Follow it up and right by a sentry box and turn the final overhang on the right. Return left to belay in an exposed eyrie under a big roof.
2. 10m 5a Turn the roof on the left by a difficult bulge and go up the short wall to the top. Very exposed.

16   Necromancer   40m   E5 6a ***   (1985)
This strenuous route, with first class wall and crack climbing, takes the wall right of Death Cap by the central crack line. Start 5 metres right of Death Cap.
1. 10m 5c Climb a crack to a projecting block, then pull over the roof direct using an obvious jam. Peg belay on the ledge on left (Friend 1½ above).
2. 20m 6a Pull up right over the bulge onto the wall, then go straight up over another small bulge to move left and up to a break (crux). Pull up to gain a superb hold and nut placement on the right. Trend right up the wall and go straight up to the belay ledges of Pterodactyl.
3. 10m 5b Climb the obvious crack line just up and left from the belay.

17   Weird Sister   45m   E3 5c *   (1986)
A good eliminate between Necromancer and Pterodactyl.
1. 10m 5a Start just right of Necromancer and climb a bulge direct onto a shelf. Turn the roof on the right and return left to the Necromancer belay.
2. 20m 5c Climb up right over the bulge as for Necromancer, then continue traversing right and up to join Pterodactyl under the overhang. Step left to a peg runner and pull up the overlap to traverse right to a foothold on the arete (crux). Climb the arete to the Pterodactyl belay.
3. 15m Finish as for Pterodactyl or Bats' Belfry.

18   Pterodactyl   45m   E1 5b ***   (1980)
A terrific route taking the hanging corner right of Necromancer. Start at the centre of the grey lower wall at a shallow right-facing corner, under the fall line of the hanging corner. The first two pitches may be combined.
1. 15m 5a Climb the corner moving left at the bulge, then go straight up a notch in the bulging nose above to traverse right and up to a belay ledge (there is a peg 5m up the small corner of Bats' Belfry.)
2. 20m 5b Traverse across and up to small ledges on the left, under the bulge guarding the hanging corner. Gain a big flat hold with a long reach and pull up over the bulge into the corner. Climb the corner by the left wall and exit out left at the top to small ledges with a peg belay.

3. 10m 4c Traverse away right above the overhangs and mantelshelf onto a block. Continue right round the exposed arete and finish up a small groove.

19   Bats' Belfry   35m   E2 5c ***   (1983)
About 6 metres right of the initial corner of Pterodactyl is a recess with big blocks beside it. Start up the shallow corner in the blunt nose just left of this. Pitches 1 and 2 or 2 and 3 may be combined.
1. 10m 5c Move up into the shallow corner, then go out left and up the wall to Friend placements under bulges. Step left and pull up right over the bulge and so to the belay ledge (peg 3m higher).
2. 15m 5b Go straight up past the belay peg, then hand traverse the break right to a step up into a niche under a roof. Move left and pull up into the hanging corner with small belay ledge above, under the capping roof.
3. 10m 5b Turn the roof on the left, move up and swing left to pull up over the bulge on good holds to gain the mantle-block of Pterodactyl. Climb the wall above directly via the obvious little ledge.

20   Cloisters   35m   VS 4c **   (1980)
The main corner line right of Death Cap is characterised by a hanging square-cut slab and capping roofs. The line is gained by a traverse from the right, starting from a higher ledge of the grass bank, where a short wall leads up to another grass ledge.
1. 15m Climb the short wall to the grass ledge and move left to the base of a prominent corner (Ugly Bugs Ball). Traverse round the left edge to another ledge and belay beside a short corner crack.
2. 20m 4c Move round left into the main corner, then go up left across the slab. Climb the overhang above to an exposed perch and finish up a short steep groove (just right of the final groove of Pterodactyl).
Direct Start: 15m   HVS 5a
The original start is harder and more serious. Start under the grey lower wall below the main corner beside some big blocks, at a recessed overhung corner. Climb the corner to swing left and pull over the bulge to a ledge. Climb the left-hand of twin corners and step right to the belay beside the corner crack.

21   Cloisters Right-Hand   20m   VS 4c *   (1983)
Instead of climbing out left up the hanging slab, go straight up the back of the corner, then traverse out right below the capping roofs to gain a ledge on top of a great block. Continue by stepping out right to finish up the top groove of Ugly Bugs Ball.

22   Bugs' Boogie   30m   E1 5b *   (1983)
The wall and overhang right of Cloisters. The first pitch is poor and may be avoided via Cloisters traverse.
1. 10m 5a Start at the boulders of Cloisters Direct start. Climb the overhanging groove above the right side of the boulders to exit left onto a ledge. Climb the right-hand of twin corners to the belay ledge of Cloisters beside a corner crack.

2. 20m 5b Step up right and go up the wall to good holds on top of the obvious rock boss under the bulge. Step onto the boss and pull up over the bulge leftwards to take a steep crack on good holds to a ledge on top of the block. Step out right to finish up the top groove of Ugly Bugs' Ball. Strenuous.

23 Buggeroo 20m E2 6a * (1983)

This takes the left arete of Ugly Bugs' Ball corner direct. Climb the short wall to traverse left and belay on the ledge under the corner. This start is as for Cloisters. Climb the initial bulge of the arete, making hard moves to gain a standing position above the overhang. Move up the arete to a small ledge, then take the crack on the left to a ledge. Finish up the top groove of Ugly Bugs' Ball.

24 Ugly Bugs' Ball 20m VS 4c ** (1979)

Start as for Cloisters on the higher ledge, where a short wall leads up onto another grass ledge on the face. The route takes the vertical 10m corner at the left end of this ledge, and like Cloisters, is not as hard as it looks. Climb the corner moving out left at the top. Move up right on top of a pedestal. Traverse across left and finish up the obvious groove.

25 Rattus Norvegicus 20m HVS 5a (1979)

This takes a hanging groove right of Ugly Bugs' Ball. Gain the grass ledge as for Cloisters. Climb the awkward bulging wall some 6m right of the vertical corner of Ugly Bugs' Ball, then go up right to finish up the groove.

26 Thunderbolt Crack 10m Hard Severe (1980)

Recent rockfall has left this route in a dangerous condition; not recommended. Start up the lower rocks of the Descent Route and climb up left over a bulge to gain a crack.

27 The Descent Route 20m Very Difficult

Rockfall has left this route in an unpleasant state, but it is still a feasible descent. In ascent, from where the grass bank peters out, climb rightwards up blocky steps to a 3m wall leading to a splintered pedestal. Finish up the obvious chimney crack. The chimney is the right end of a choked-up crevice running behind the cliff, towards the crack of Batty Bat. So all the routes lie on a single sizeable flake, perhaps doomed someday to fall into the bay.

28 Stratosfear 85m E2 5c ** (1981)

A spectacular high-level traverse of the Right Wall. The highlight is a sensational crossing from the eyrie of Death Cap, over the great wall of Prehistoric Monster. The climbing is not technical apart from one well protected move round the Cloisters Slab.
1. 15m Cloisters, pitch 1.
2. 25m 5c Climb left up the green slab to runners at the top. Move down the arete and make a hard move into the hanging corner of Bats' Belfry. Continue left round another edge, past a doubtful block, into the top part of the hanging

corner of Pterodactyl. Move out left and traverse across to the eyrie belay of Death Cap.
3. 35m 5a Step across left onto a little arete, then make a very exposed horizontal traverse left to ledges. Go left along the ledges to the final corner of Mysterious Journey. Swing down the bulge below, then reverse the shelf system of Mysterious Journey (fulmars in summer) to the perfect belay on top of the rib.
4. 10m 4b Climb left round the arete, then go across and up into the final notch of Earnsheugh Ridge.

THE FAR WALL

This is the north-west facing wall of Earnsheugh Bay. It looks most repulsive and is largely overhanging. An exploratory route has been made up a stepped corner crack which separates the main overhanging bastion from a lesser wall on the left. The main bastion is divided from the Left Wall of the main cliff by a vertical green shute which usually pours water. Access is by a dangerous scramble to the seaward side of the lesser wall, or by abseil from stakes straight down it.

Ghastly Crack   20m   VS 4c   (1981)
The corner crack is slimy, grassy and rotten, but a fine natural line.

THE PINK BAND CLIFF   *(Map Ref 944 980)*

This crag is at the southern tip of Earnsheugh Bay. Scramble down the shoulder of the headland and climb down the side of a prominent chimney with a spike at the top, joining the chimney halfway down (Very Difficult).

Spike Chimney   20m   Very Difficult   (1981)
Climb the chimney direct.

Frontier Rib   20m   Mild VS 4b *   (1983)
The right rib of the chimney. Climb straight up to ledges, then move up right and continue straight up to the top.

The Pink Band   25m   Hard Severe   (1983)
The obvious fault leading right and up, skirting the most impressive part of the wall. The final nose and bulges can be turned on the left. Spoiled by bird effluent all year round.

THE RED BAND CLIFF   *(Map Ref 945 978)*

This crag is situated on the next headland south of Earnsheugh Bay, beyond a small inlet. The cliff is steep, about 20m high and of good sound rock. A visit is not recommended in the nesting season as it throngs with kittiwakes, although some of the routes are still possible. It is usual to abseil in, the best point being the wall near the north tip, where Spider comes up. There is a good rock pavement below the cliff but the southern end is tidal. In contrast to Earnsheugh, the cliff is fissured from the base upwards. There are two caves which are interconnected by a cleavage inside the cliff. Access to and from the cliff is possible using a remarkable vault-like passage (often slimy) running south from inside the mouth of the southerly cave. This is not a good escape route in rain since reaching the clifftop from the southern gulch is tricky when wet. It is possible to traverse round the south extremity of the crag at low tide. There is also a higher traverse line at VS 4c.

The routes are described from north to south.

Phallus Chimney   20m   Severe   (1977)
The obvious green chimney at the north end gives a chossy climb.

Bovver Fly   20m   E1 5b *   (1983)
Start below the phallus to the left of the Chimney. Go directly over the roof above into a big niche. Traverse left onto the arete and continue to the top.

Hover Fly   20m   VS 4c   (1982)
The wall near the north end has a prominent roof. Climb the right end of a bulge, then turn the roof on the right to finish up the slabby wall.

Spider   20m   VS 4c *   (1975)
Go up the left side of the bulge to turn the roof on the left. Finish up the obvious corner in the red rock.

Arachnid   20m   E1 5b *   (1982)
A good eliminate up the overhanging crack. Go directly up a bulge and finish up the left-trending crack line to easier rock.

Strainer   20m   VS 4c   (1975)
The obvious left-slanting fault line gives awkward climbing, starting from an old iron spike at the undercut base. There is a variation finish on the right wall.

Colander Wall   20m   E2 5b   (1983)
Climb Strainer for 3m, then traverse left across an undercut slab and go up to a sloping ledge. Climb the obvious crack above and move left round a nose. Climb the bulging wall above to pull onto the upper ramp of Strainer.

The Prison   25m   E3 5c *   (1985)
The big roof-capped corner left of Strainer. Climb the initial bulge and corner, then traverse right under the roof via a shelf (intimidating) to pull out onto small ledges. Move left under a bulge, then pull up the continuation corner in the red band. Climb this and go up to step right to the top. The nests at the end of the roof need removing by abseil, but those on the traverse can be avoided.

Shawangunks Wall   25m   E2 5b **   (1983)
This climbs the steep undercut wall. Again, an abseil or two may be needed to
clear off nests. Swing up the left side of the cave to a recess under the capping
roof. Pull out left and go up to better holds. Move up the wall, then traverse the
faults left and up to a prominent resting niche. Move up the wall right of the niche
to the red band. Step left and pull up right onto a big foothold on the red band.
Finish steeply straight up.

The Great Green Thing   25m   VS 4c **   (1975)
The obvious right-curving fault forming the left border of the wall gives an unusual
route, well worthwhile despite its name. Climb the fault and swing up left over the
red band to a ledge. Finish up and right under roofs.

Fauntleroy's Fault   25m   VS 4c   (1982)
The fault line left of Great Green Thing. Start up near the left side of the broad
rib, then swing up left onto the edge and ledges. Take the break in the red band
above and go up a wall to a ledge under a big block. Surmount this and go up
walls to the top.

Chicken Licken   25m   Hard Severe   (1982)
Round the face well left of the previous route is a small groove in the red band.
Climb up to this groove, then traverse right across a steep wall and move up to
ledges. Finish easily up left.

Kentucky Fried Chicken   20m   E1 5c   (1988)
Right of Fertiliser is a corner in the red band which is usually wet. This route
crosses the red band 2 metres right of this. Start in a small cave below and well
right of the wet corner. Climb up into the back of the cave and traverse out left
to a ledge. Go diagonally right until at a point of no return. Climb the red band
and the short wall above to ledges. Finish up easy corners.

Fertiliser   25m   VS 4c   (1982)
Above and right of the southerly cave is the prominent groove of Scrutiniser. This
contrived route takes a line right of this. Climb up ledges to the red band. Move
up right, then make a tricky move up left. Return back up right and go up a red
slab to swing up right onto a ledge. Finish straight up or out right.

Scrutiniser   25m   VS 4c   (1978)
The obvious groove line right of the cave. Climb the wall right of the cave, go up
right and take a small groove in the red band. Finish straight up the fault line.

BOGLESHEUGH   *(Map Ref 944 977)*

South of the Red Band cliff is a fairly long inlet with a steep vegetated south wall. Boglesheugh is the next impressive wall to the south, characterised by a drastically undercut slab at its top left end, with a curving red band below. This cliff is in the Earnsheugh mould and similar remarks apply. While at first glance it may inspire shudders, on closer scrutiny it provides climbing of great character. Like Earnsheugh, the cliff is north-facing, dark and gloomy. It is very sheltered but this can be a drawback since green algae often make the lower walls repulsively greasy; a favourable breeze seems necessary for dry conditions. Unfortunately nature is doing its best to reclaim the place and the routes seem to sprout weeds in a remarkably short time after cleaning. Together with its reputation for slime and gloom, this seems likely to deter the trendy modern climber, who risks a severe dimming of the lycra tights. Unless the routes get more traffic, re-cleaning by abseil may be necessary in certain places. All this is a pity because the routes are good.

Descent is by a simple scramble down the grassy ridge to the north. There is a tidal pool under the wall, which affects some of the routes. At the bottom right is a mysterious and creepy little cave. A disgusting pool near the entrance discourages exploration.

The red band is plastered with kittiwakes in the nesting season. Herring gulls, fulmars and kittiwakes are present on other parts of the cliff but they are rarely troublesome. There are guillemots and razorbills at the left end of the ledge above the red band, but climbers are unlikely to disturb them due to the kittiwake deterrent below.

There are belay stakes on the grassy clifftop, although these become hard to find in late summer. When greasy, it is usually possible to salvage a visit by abseiling down the hanging corner of Freaker's Ball. Half a dozen good pitches are quickly accessible in this way.

The climbs are described from right to left.

1   Petrified Forest   45m   E3 5c **

The hanging corner and bulges right of Wrat Wraith. Start at the foot of the blunt rib left of the cave.

1. 25m 5c Climb up left to a jug, then go straight up to a resting place under a bulge. Move up right round the edge and go up left (2 peg runners) to the base of the corner. Climb the corner to exit left onto the edge. Climb straight up the thin quartz crack and go up right onto the big slab. Belay as for Wrat Wraith at a peg.

2. 20m 5c Climb bulging rock right of the belay to pull up onto big blocks (peg runner on the left). Climb the bulge above direct, or if rested, traverse right to a shoogly block on the lip and gain jugs up on the right to surmount the bulge (peg runner above). Move up right to good holds and pull leftwards up the next overhang, then go over another bulge onto the final wall. Arms allowing, climb this moving up right.

2   Wrat Wraith   35m   E1 5a **   (1982)
The most prominent of several vertical quartz bands right of the big roofed corner
at the right end of the wall gives an impressive and serious route. The start is
possible when greasy. Start at a vivid green roofed corner about 10 metres left
of the cave mouth.
1. 10m 4c Climb the corner for 5m, then hand traverse left onto the face and go
straight up to a ledge to belay beside standing blocks under the quartz band.
2. 25m 5a Climb the band, surmounting an overhang at the top. Continue
directly up the bulging wall above in the same line to a perch with good runners.
Continue directly up the quartz band on big doubtful jugs over the bulge above
and finish out right past a dubious flake. Poor protection.

3   Cobra Corner   40m   E3 6a ***   (1982)
This route takes the general line of the big roofed corner, using the less
pronounced quartz band left of the Wrat Wraith, and taking an improbable direct
line through the roof. The exit move from the roof (the crux) may need cleaning.
This could easily be done while climbing Stone Lizard. Start on top of the
left-hand of several big boulders.
1. 30m 6a Pull up the bulge into the obvious crack and go up right to join Wrat
Wraith. Follow this to the ledge beside the standing blocks. Climb the quartz
band on the left side of the blocks up into the corner and follow this to a big
vibrating block under the roofs. Move left up the overhanging inset wall above to
reach a good handrail. Swing left along this and pull over the top to emerge onto
the easy slab of Stone Lizard.
2. 10m 4c Finish up the headwall of Stone Lizard.

4   Stone Lizard   40m   E3 5c **   (1982)
This is the original route on the crag, taking a fine natural line up the big slab.
The preliminary wall is the crux. Start at a small undercut corner under a big
jutting oval roof, the Lizard's Head.
1. 10m 5c Climb the small corner and the wall above up the left side of the
Lizard's Head. Awkwardly gain a big hold on the lip of the jutting roof above and
pull up over into the crack; strenuous and sensational. Exit right onto a belay
ledge under the slab. An alternative is to hand traverse the Lizard's Head;
harder.
2. 30m 5a Climb the wall near the right end of the ledge and follow holds straight
up and slightly left to a steepening in the slab. Climb up and right along under
bulges to an easy slab above the big jutting prow of the Cobra. Go left up the
slab to a grass ledge left of a chossy chimney. Possible belay. Climb the wall
above, swinging up left onto a block and continue to the top.

The following two routes climb up into the right-angled corner which forms the
right-hand boundary of the hanging slab. They are common in their central
section. The obnoxious wet platform of watercress is avoided by a left traverse.

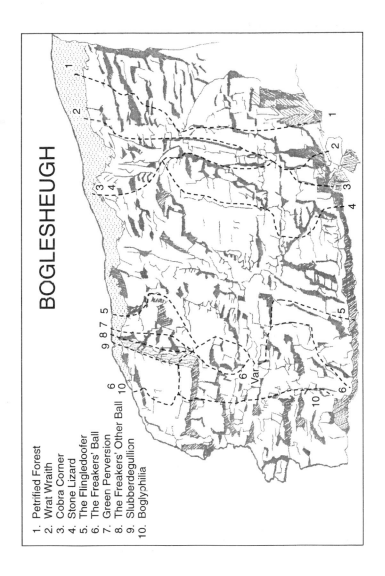

BOGLESHEUGH

1. Petrified Forest
2. Wrat Wraith
3. Cobra Corner
4. Stone Lizard
5. The Flingledoofer
6. The Freakers' Ball
7. Green Perversion
8. The Freakers' Other Ball
9. Slubberdegullion
10. Boglyphilia

5 The Flingledoofer 55m E1 5b **   (1982)
This starts by a thin crack in the wall left of the much more obvious Freakers'
Crack and takes the right slab of the corner above.
1. 10m 4b Gain the platform under the red band either by climbing diagonally
right up a wall (low tide) or by traversing in from the right just above the pool and
up a groove. Often greasy.
2. 10m 5b Follow a traverse line right to the thin crack, then climb it to a ledge.
Move right along the ledge to a peg belay.
3. 20m 5b Move up to shattered ledges and traverse the ledges left for 10m (peg
runner). Climb the big bulge on jugs (peg runner). Pull over another bulge with a
long reach for a good jug and go up past a big hanging block on its right side to
the corner with comfortable belay.
4. 15m 4c Move diagonally right across the slab and go up near the edge to its
top. Finish up the grooves above.

6 The Freakers' Ball 50m E1 5b ***   (1982)
A spectacular line venturing out onto the hanging corner by a wild hand traverse
left out of the hanging corner. Start up the left-hand of the two obvious cracks in
the wall right of the red band, starting by the edge of the tidal pool (problematical
at high tide).
1. 10m 5b Swing up the bulge (often greasy) into the crack and climb it to a ledge
and peg belay. Alternatively, before the belay, traverse down left under roofs,
on the lip of the main roof, to a thin crack leading to a belay below the bulge on
pitch 3 of Flingledoofer (E2 5b and very exciting).
2. 20m 5b Flingledoofer, pitch 3.
3. 20m 5a Hand traverse left out of the corner to the undercut slab using a good
flake crack. Step up and traverse horizontally left until halfway along the slab,
where a line of holds leads to the top. Thought is required to protect the second.

The following three pitches give more direct finishes from the hanging corner.

7 Green Perversion 10m E3 6a *   (1986)
This climbs the roof above the belay in the hanging corner. Step right and go
straight up the slab to climb the roof direct, aiming for holds on the left. Well
protected.

8 The Freakers' Other Ball 10m HVS 5a **   (1986)
Climb the obvious shallow groove springing up from the Freakers' hand traverse
(on the right side of the arete).

9 Slubberdegullion 15m E1 5b ***   (1988)
Climb the superbly situated arete direct after the Freakers' hand traverse.

10 Boglyphilia 45m E3 5c ***   (1986)
This route climbs the main roof direct, to join Freakers' Ball in the centre of the
slab. It starts up the red band in the lower wall. A low tide is required to start

direct, but at all but the highest tide it is possible to traverse in from the foot of Flingledoofer and belay on the platform beside the red band. The main pitch can also be gained by abseil down the hanging corner and bulge of Freakers' to the halfway ledge.

1. 20m 5b Climb the obvious crack to the red band. Climb this direct up a bulging section, then go straight up to the halfway ledge and a peg belay. (It is possible to climb past the nests on this pitch without much bother.)

2. 25m 5c Step left from the belay and pull leftwards awkwardly over the overhang (peg runner) to a resting place. Climb the wall and roof direct (Friend $3\frac{1}{2}$ or 4, or Hex 11 desirable) to gain the traverse line of Freakers' (optional belay). Finish as for Freakers'. Well protected.

Just south of Boglesheugh is a big scooped out overhanging wall which has been dubbed The Orchestra Cave. There are also some walls south again. A Very Difficult chimney can be descended for access. There are more walls south of this before the major inlet of Kay Hole is reached.

FINDON NESS

KAY HOLE

Kay Hole is the spectacular chasm-like inlet at the north side of the headland of Findon Ness. The fearful south wall is about 45m high and holds the distinction of being the most ghastly of all the Findon cliffs. Unlike the others, this crag is as bad as it looks, the main face being not only loose and scaling but also lacking in protection cracks.

A route has been made towards the left end where the rock is better and the cliff not so fierce. Access is by a scramble down Findon Ness at the eastern end of the inlet. Traverse in along the wall by a ledge system for about 30 metres. The route takes the first obvious big slab running the height of the cliff, characterised by a sentry box on its right side.

The Glider   25m   Hard Severe   (1981)
Climb into the sentry box and traverse left into the corner, or gain this point directly. Go up the corner to a small ledge. Traverse right across the slab below an overhang, then climb the obvious hanging corner (the left wall is rather brittle throughout).

The access traverse for The Glider can be continued (Severe) on quite good red rock right into the back of the inlet, where a big wet recess gives the following route:

Kay Hole Fall   35m   IV/V ***
This fine icefall is known to have been in climbable condition in at least three winters during the 1980s. Access is by abseil down the overhanging gully (stake required).

THE GREY WALL

The steep drab 30m wall immediately south of the tip of Findon Ness forms a dry little bay with overhangs at the back. Access is simple. The best of the rock round to the left is similar to that at Berrymuir Head, but in the main it needs careful handling. The routes are described from right to left.

Boulders Route   35m   VS 4c *   (1980)

This is the original route, taking a line of diagonal cracks into the prominent overhung scoop, near the top right side of the wall, from where a traverse left past poised boulders leads to a finish up the left corner of the scoop. Start by stepping off a fallen boulder below the middle of the wall and climbing a 6m corner and a further shattered corner to join the diagonal crack.

Grave Doubts   30m   E3 5b *   (1982)

The thin central crack line gives a fine but scary and poorly protected climb; a serious lead. Start 10 metres left of the boulder of the previous route at some quartz below and left of a roof. Climb a little gangway and go up the left side of the flake formation above (this is the right side of a big vague scoop) to a thin crack line. Climb this to a little overlap and pull over right onto a little slab under a steep wall. Move up left over dubious flakes and climb up to a bulge where a thin flake crack runs up the headwall (nut runner at the bottom). Climb the crack to the top.

Gronk   30m   HVS 5a   (1982)

The obvious slabby corner line leading up to overhangs near the left side of the wall. Start 5 metres left of Grave Doubts just below the left rib of the big vague scoop. Pull up left onto the rib and go straight up to slabbier rocks. Now take the general line of the slabby slanting diedre above to the overhangs at the top. Surmount the overhang and finish out rightwards.

South Arete   20m   VS 4c   (1979)

South of the Grey Wall are some more motley rocks. This route takes the prominent edge of the far buttress. Climb a groove and follow the edge as closely as possible.

South Groove   15m   Very Difficult

The large open corner right of South Arete.

Armed Conflict   25m   E4 5c *   (1988)

Round to the right of South Groove is a gently overhanging wall. Start at the foot of a ramp in the middle of the wall. Go up the ramp to a ledge, then traverse left to obvious twin cracks. Go up these and traverse diagonally right up the crack to finish.

Downies to Newtonhill

This 5km stretch of coastline offers fine climbing at four main venues. These are Downies, Floor's Craig, Craig Stirling and Newtonhill. Additionally, several smaller crags provide sport. Each area holds its own particular attractions. The climbs of Craig Stirling, mostly poised over deep water and with a fairly serious feel, contrast with the smaller and sunnier aspect of Newtonhill. Downies has many bold and some unlikely-looking lines on looming walls, while Floor's Craig has an outcrop-like layout, tucked away on a quiet promontory. All share similar strenuous climbing, almost always on steep or very steep rock. Lower grade climbs are fairly few and beginners will find the scope very limited, with the rock less reliable than the more popular areas nearer Aberdeen. The only exception is Floor's Craig which, whilst steep and a bit awkward to find at first acquaintance, does have a lot to offer the VS climber. Other lower grade gems are more dispersed.

The rock is predominantly a contorted schistose type, almost always steep and set down in many curling layers, some friable but often running to good juggy holds and pockets. Many climbs rely on pockets for protection and progress. The cliffs are fairly free from vegetation and are generally fast to dry. Nesting seabirds are also fairly rare, favouring instead the platforms and ledges beneath the cliffs. This can present an odious hazard, especially at Downies, particularly for the hapless belayer. A pleasant contrast are the house martins which nest below the overhangs of Newtonhill. Puffins may also be seen in large numbers, nesting on the cliff tops of Downies.

DOWNIES

The little village of Downies and its attendant cliffs, some 9km (5½ miles) south of Aberdeen, are reached by leaving the A92 dual carriageway at any one of the entrances to Portlethen and heading for Portlethen Academy, which is on the south-east side of the town. From beside the school, a minor road signposted to Downies leads to the village, where cars should be parked sensibly. There are shops in Portlethen but none in Downies.

The climbing areas of Downies are in two distinct sections, both of which offer steep good quality climbing which is little affected by nesting seabirds and only partially tidal. Closest to the village are the Knaps, a collection of hump-backed, grassy hillocks which drop away to steep walls. These lie at the end of the rough track which runs seawards from the village.

A few hundred metres to the south, and separated from the Knaps by the picturesque bay of Downies Haven, is the promontory of Berrymuir Head. The climbing here is generally on a more impressive scale than the Knaps and it tends to catch more sun.

THE KNAPS
Although exposed rock abounds here, much of it is of doubtful quality and climbing has been confined to the furthest seaward of the Knaps (The Gorilla's Head) and the squat sea-stack on its north side. These are reached by following a path out along the top of the main grassy ridge, The Camel's Back, which then drops down right and twists back to a rocky neck which joins the Camel's Back to the Gorilla's Head. Below the neck is a fine, natural howff.

THE GORILLA'S HEAD
This Knap resembles the head of a Gorilla from at least two angles. Two walls provide climbing, the east-facing Cave Wall, and the North Wall. There are a couple of *in situ* stakes near the top of the Head for belaying.

The Cave Wall is reached by scrambling from the neck around the grassy south side of the Head to reach a slabby shelf which runs below the length of the wall. For most of its length the wall overhangs ominously and is split by two fierce cracks, one springing from a dry cave.

Cath's Catharsis   10m   Severe   (1981)
The undercut hanging corner, bounding the face on the left.

Monkey   10m   E2 5c   (1981)
Start right of Catharsis and climb direct the shorter less prominent crack line left of the obvious Animal crack. Avoid the left exit.

Animal   10m   E3 5c **   (1981)
The ferocious and intimidating crack in the centre of the wall. Belay stakes are in place at the top.

Animosity   15m   E4 5c *   (1993)
This takes the wall right of Animal. Start at a thin crack and hand traverse right. Climb up to a jutting flake and continue to a horizontal crack with good Friend placements. Hand traverse right to a big jug, then make a succession of three hard and quite serious moves to reach a flake crack. Exit out left to the top of Animal.

The following five routes can be affected by birds in the bay of Zinjanthropus.

Gentleman Jim   6m   E2 5b *   (1981)
Enter the leaning crack above the cave from the right and jam up into the bay above. Finish as for Banana Crack.

Banana Crack   15m   E1 5b *   (1981)
The thin overhanging crack right of Gentleman Jim is strenuous but on good holds. Finish by the leaning corner above.

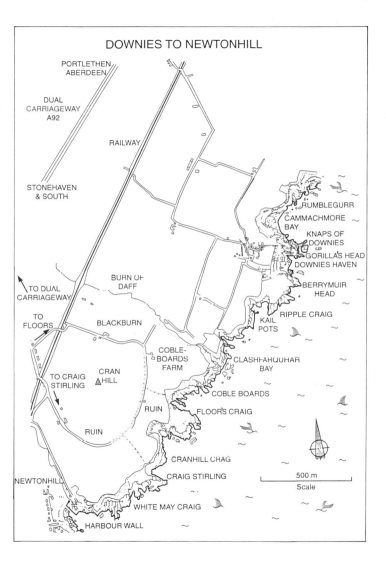

DOWNIES TO NEWTONHILL

PORTLETHEN
ABERDEEN

DUAL
CARRIAGEWAY
A92

RAILWAY

STONEHAVEN
& SOUTH

RUMBLEGURR

CAMMACHMORE
BAY

KNAPS OF
DOWNIES

GORILLA'S HEAD

DOWNIES HAVEN

BERRYMUIR
HEAD

BURN OF
DAFF

TO DUAL
CARRIAGEWAY

RIPPLE CRAIG

TO
FLOORS

BLACKBURN

KAIL
POTS

COBLE-
BOARDS
FARM

CLASHFARQUHAR
BAY

CRAN
HILL

TO CRAIG
STIRLING

COBLE BOARDS

RUIN

FLOOR'S CRAIG

RUIN

CRANHILL CRAG

CRAIG STIRLING

NEWTONHILL

500 m

Scale

WHITE MAY CRAIG

HARBOUR WALL

Lazy Daze   6m   E1 5a   (1983)
The twin crack just left of Banana Crack, finishing up the last bit of Gentleman Jim.

Right of Banana Crack, the angle eases where the Cave and North walls meet.

Zinjanthropus   15m   Very Difficult *   (1981)
The pioneer route of the area. Climb a green slab which separates the two walls, then traverse left along a shelf to an undercut bay. Go up another green slab by its right side, then make a delicate traverse to an exposed position on the left edge. Climb this to finish.

Java Man   15m   Mild Severe   (1981)
Go rightwards up the first slab of Zinjanthropus to a recess. Swing right round the arete, then go straight up to finish by a protruding block.

The North Wall is steep with numerous bulges. Access is a problem at high tide, otherwise it is easily reached from the small inlet on the north side of the rocky neck.

Funky Gibbon   10m   HVS 4c *   (1981)
A good value route going through the series of overhangs at the right end of the wall. Climb a recessed corner below and left of the first overhang to a roof. Swing up right onto a hanging, cracked slab. Both roofs above are taken directly to reach a short corner and belay ledge which leads around to easy ground.

Howler Monkey   20m   HVS 5a *   (1987)
Climb the chimney just left of Funky Gibbon and pull out left to traverse the lip of the yellow slab. Climb the slab exiting up left to a ledge. Traverse across right and up to Funky Gibbon.

THE STACK
This is the squat stack opposite the north wall of the Gorilla's Head. It is reached from the rocky neck but it is cut off at high tide. The rock is generally sound and there are climbs on all its faces. Birds nesting on the top of the stack can be a difficulty in season.

Starting on the South Wall, there are two obvious weaknesses which start from a raised shelf. Both can be used for descent, but abseil may seem a better idea.

Splashway   10m   Very Difficult   (1981)
Trend left up the obvious edge overlooking a tidal pool, past some poor rock at the top.

Quick Lay   6m   VS 4c   (1981)
Climb the obvious undercut layback corner, started from the right end of the shelf.

Downside Upwindies   10m   E4 6b *   (1987)
Right of Quick Lay are three crack lines. This route takes the central crack and
shares a protection peg with the following climb. Climb the crack to the second
small pod and move right to a big hold and the peg. Go back left to the crack and
go up to an obvious jug. Finish straight up.

Upside Downwindies   10m   E3 5c *   (1987)
Starting beneath the rightmost crack line, go up left to clip the peg and back right
to finish via the short hanging corner.

Spiffing   10m   HVS 5b   (1983)
This climbs the overhanging East Wall of the Stack, round left from Black
Napkins. Climb to a ledge, then go up the overhanging wall to the next ledge,
and so to top.

Smegmatoid   10m   E1 5b   (1987)
The arete left of Spiffing, starting from the same ledge.

The Sea Wall is the best feature of the Stack, and holds some braw wee routes.

Black Napkins   10m   VS 4c **   (1981)
The hanging corner near the left end of the wall, starting from a raised platform
and finishing by a short wall.

Cream Doughnut   10m   E1 5b *   (1983)
This is the central crack line, bulging in the middle. An easier groove then leads
to the top.

The Grand Wazoo   10m   HVS 4c **   (1981)
Start as for Cream Doughnut, then follow the obvious hand traverse right to the
arete (strenuous). Swing round and finish up the groove above (The Greener).

Gateaux of Delirium   10m   E2 5b *   (1987)
Climb the bulge and wall above the Grand Wazoo traverse, starting up that route.

White Serviette   10m   HVS 5b   (1983)
A direct ascent of the right-hand arete, joining Grand Wazoo at the end of its
traverse.

The following climbs are on the Westerly Wall.

Scab and Matter Custard   6m   E3 6a *   (1987)
Climb the thin crack and bulge just right of the White Serviette arete. Move up
right on final moves to join The Greener.

Snot and Bogey Pie   5m   E1 5b   (1987)
The bulging wall to the right, starting up the left side of a small cleft.

The Greener   15m   Hard Severe   (1981)
A slabby shelf runs up left above overhangs. Start from a big block at the right
end of the overhangs. Climb onto the wall and move up to an edge on the right
to pull onto the shelf. Follow this up left to gain and finish up a groove on the left
edge.

Grazoopkins   30m   HVS 4c **   (1982)
The entertaining and sustained girdle of the west, sea and east walls is at its best
when the base is awash (outgoing tide preferable). Short pitches will avoid rope
drag.
1. 10m 4b Climb the Greener to the end of the shelf.
2. 10m 4c Move down and swing around left to gain the end of the Grand
Wazoo. Follow its hand traverse across the wall. Continue traversing under a
bulge and swing up into the corner of Black Napkins.
3. 10m 4c Climb the wall above, trending left on good holds to a small ledge
around the arete. Continue left along ledges until the top bulge can be overcome.
The last part is common to Spiffing.

BERRYMUIR HEAD   *(Map Ref 927 948)*

The headland, forming the south side of Downies Haven, provides the location
for some of the more gymnastic climbing on this stretch of coast. By contrast, it
also offers a few engaging lower grade climbs on particularly good rock. The
main cliffs are on the east-facing side, at the base of which is a huge slabby area
which itself rises to form small cliffs above the sea on the east and north sides.
The slabby area and its cliffs are known as Nippet Rocks. Direct hits are common
during nesting time and few routes are free of the winged devils and their pukey
offspring. However, a good day can be had in the nesting season if one is
selective.
    From the grassy headland top the position of the main cliffs, which are hard
to see from above, may be ascertained by locating a deep ravine which cuts back
from the cliff top, Boulder Gully. This is roughly the centre point of the cliffs.

Descent
The slabby area of Nippet Rocks may be reached by descending easy ground
at the southerly end of the cliffs and cutting back along the base. However, this
is only practical at low tide. The more commonly used descent approaches the
cliffs from their northern end, by way of a grass-topped crumbling ridge which
cuts back at a narrow sloping shelf leading down onto the slabby area. This
descent feels insecure and care is required as a fall from the ridge would be very
serious.
    Three big walls form the main stretch of cliff. From north to south, these are:
The Barrier Wall, with its belt of huge roofs and a prominent undercut arete

defining the left end; The Central Wall, which meets the former at the arete; and the Gully Wall, which is split from the Central Wall by the deep chasm of Boulder Gully. The Sea Nose is a smaller, tidal prow on the end of the Gully Wall.

THE BARRIER WALL

This is the long wall left of the descent shelf. Its main features are a big diagonal ramp rising left across the centre. The underside of this ramp forms a belt of huge roofs. The ramp is a favourite venue of gulls at nesting time, while the odd family of fulmars enjoy lurking where least expected!

1   Bilious Chokes   15m   VS 4c   (1982)
The right end of Barrier Wall has some atrocious rock. This route climbs the best of it. Start directly below a short corner at the top of the wall and some 10 metres left of the descent shelf. Go up to a diagonal protection crack, then trend up right to a big horizontal fault. Go straight up, then out right and up, right of the corner to finish.

2   The Flyover   30m   HVS 4c   (1981)
This one takes the worst of the bad rock! It was the first route to breach this wall and probably has not been followed in its entirety since. It follows the ramp above the roofs after climbing a rotten, green overhanging chimney, right of the lower roofs. Traverse left awkwardly round a rib and onto the slab-ramp where it is possible to belay some way up. Where the ramp peters out, follow either of two exposed horizontal fault lines to a ledge system beyond. Finish straight up by the first break in the upper wall.

3   Roof-Roof   30m   E4 6a **   (1982)
The biggest roof crack on the coast, above the slab-ramp of Flyover, is often damp. Start 6 metres left of a big boulder on the shelf which runs across the wall. Gain a small shelf and go up a crack to step right to the 3½m roof. Jam out to reach Flyover. A direct finish follows a well protected crack in poor rock, followed by vertical soil above (5b).

4   The Paranormal   20m   E3 5c ***   (1982)
Good climbing with an outrageous dangly bit. Below the main roof is an obvious horizontal break which comes out and left around a protruding block as an obvious hand rail. This is the sensational but reasonable *raison d'être* of the route. Start at a vague open corner and move up the right side, then cross the corner (crux) to pull over a bulge to a resting place. Move left and up to good holds at the start of the hand rail. Follow the rail round to ledges. Finish by the obvious break above.

5   Coco the Clown   20m   E2 5c **   (1981)
Another rib tickler. Left of Paranormal is an undercut corner leading to a roof, below Paranormal's hand traverse. Pull over into the corner and go up to the roof. Using the crack below the roof, go out left around the roof into the short crack above and up to ledges. Finish through the obvious break above.

6 Little Strawberry went into the Sea 25m E1 5c * (1981)
This takes a right-slanting diagonal line on the undercut wall left of Coco the
Clown. Start at the undercut shallow corner at the base of Erseless Arete. Pull
awkwardly into the corner (crux) and traverse around the arete to a ledge. Move
up and follow the right-slanting line of flakes up the wall, then go straight up to a
ledge. Finish by Erseless or Flyover.

THE CENTRAL WALL
This south-facing wall looms over the slabby area below, and offers only one
reasonable weakness right of centre. The wall is split at mid-height by ledges,
above which few of the routes bother to find an independent finish.

7 Erseless Arete 25m HVS 5a * (1978)
The undercut arete at the right end. The initial traverse to the arete is the crux.
Starting some 3m left of the arete, pull up to a good flake and go right to reach
the edge, with a long reach mid-way. Climb the groove above, then go up to a
ledge on the Barrier Wall. Possible belay. Go right along the ledge, then climb
the wall above to traverse back left below the overlap to a break and a good
finishing crack.

8 Bumless Wall 10m E1 5b * (1984)
Climb the wall above the initial traverse of Erseless Arete, passing a jutting nose
on its left side.

9 The Notch 20m Hard Severe (1978)
This takes the obvious break in the wall. Go into a recessed corner crack and
follow it to ledges. Finish by a groove in the huge upper notch.

10 Frog Face 10m E3 6a (1984)
Climb the bulging wall right of the Nighthawk crack to join Nighthawk on the
sloping shelves below the ledge; strenuous.

11 Nighthawk 25m E2 5c * (1981)
The hanging crack line on the overhanging wall left of the Notch. Go up to and
climb the crack until possible to palm out right on sloping holds to a ledge above.
Make an awkward move onto the upper wall and climb it, avoiding an overhanging prow on the right.

12 Nighthawk Direct 10m E3 5c ** (1984)
As for Nighthawk, but stay with the crack to the ledge.

13 The X-Crack 10m E3 5c ** (1984)
Climb the left-slanting crack line left of Nighthawk. Step left and climb the wall
(pockets for small Friends) to a sloping finish on the shelf.

BERRYMUIR HEAD (DOWNIES)

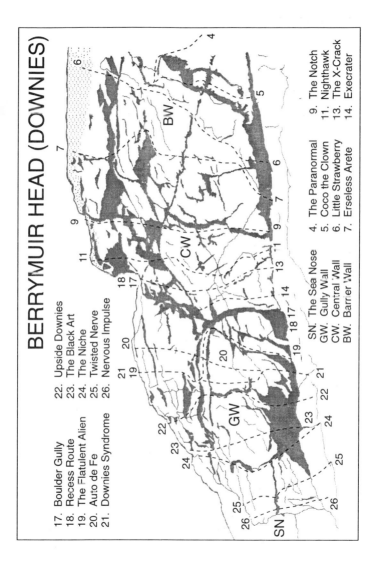

17. Boulder Gully
18. Recess Route
19. The Flatulent Alien
20. Auto de Fe
21. Downies Syndrome

22. Upside Downies
23. The Black Art
24. The Niche
25. Twisted Nerve
26. Nervous Impulse

4. The Paranormal
6. Coco the Clown
6. Little Strawberry
7. Erseless Arete

9. The Notch
11. Nighthawk
13. The X-Crack
14. Execrater

SN. The Sea Nose
GW. Gully Wall
CW. Central Wall
BW. Barrier Wall

14   Execrater   10m   E3 5c *   (1984)
This approximates to the left aspect of the X-cracks formation and uses the blunt left rib. Strenuous. Starting some 3 metres right of Plod's Playpiece, climb the open wall to a break and good Friend. Swing left and move up round the rib to the ledge above (break down left of ledge for Friends). Finish directly up the bulging wall above on good holds.
Left-Hand Start: 6a   (1986)
A boulder problem, taking the right-curving flake line right of Plod's Playpiece.

15   Plod's Playpiece   20m   VS 5b   (1982)
The undercut left arete. Starting on the right, climb on sloping holds to the edge. Now climb the arete on its slabby left side; straightforward but poorly protected.

The right wall of Boulder Gully is undercut and leans back to easy slabs in its upper half.

16   Nyaff's Overhang   20m   E1 6a   (1982)
An athletic problem. Starting mid-way along the undercut wall, gain an obvious hold by a jump, long reach or leg-up and swing up to reach sloping holds above, leading to the easy slab.

17   Boulder Gully   30m   Mild VS 4b   (1978)
An interesting expedition after a heatwave, but repulsive at any other time with some entertaining guano climbing involved. A great capping roof forces an exit right over slabs. The guano may freeze up in a good winter!

THE GULLY WALL
This big tapering wall, running from Boulder Gully to the sea, gives probably the boldest and some of the best climbing at Downies. The left-hand routes are affected by the tide.

18   Recess Route   30m   VS 4c   (1978)
The obvious groove on the left side of the gully. The bulging section is most easily climbed out on the left face but it can be taken directly. The final vegetated wall is avoided by an escape over jammed boulders and up the slabs of Boulder Gully. Birds are rarely a problem on any of the following routes, however their north-easterly aspect can keep them damp; look for a breeze.

19   The Flatulent Alien   35m   HVS 4c **   (1981)
This one's a gas! Near the mouth of the gully and above a pool is a right-trending groove leading to twin horizontal faults. Climb the groove, with a detour out right at three-quarters height, to a stance and possible belay. Traverse left along the faults to a corner and climb its right wall to a ledge. A short wall leads to the top. The initial groove is slow to dry and poorly protected. Protection in the upper corner is fairly absent too.

20   Auto de Fe   20m   E4 5c **   (1986)
A bold effort with everything there but protection. It takes a vague crack line directly up the big wall left of the start of Flatulent Alien, crossing a bulging section by going left (Friend 2), or right to gain the twin faults. Climb the wall above the faults direct to a long ledge.

21   Downies Syndrome   20m   E4 6a **   (1984)
Another fine though unlikely-looking climb. Start as for Auto de Fe to the first bulging section, then traverse left to good holds in a vague scoop. Pull straight up the bulging wall above to small ledges at the foot of the Flatulent corner. Finish as for that route. Difficult to protect.

22   Upside Downies   20m   E5 6b **   (1982)
Well left of Downies Syndrome is a fiercely undercut bottomless groove. Climb the groove, strenuous and technical (small wires), to a thin crack which snakes up the wall above; protection is hard to arrange. Exit left from the top of the crack. An unsatisfactory but easier alternative is to traverse 2 metres right from the top of the groove and forge straight up to finish up the top corner of Flatulent Alien.

23   The Black Art   15m   E3 6a **   (1984)
The wall left of Upside Downies. Step up using the initial holds in the crack of the Niche, but go straight up the bulge to a jug (nut placement beside previous finger hold; no runners above). Pull up the wall above the jug and move up left to a diagonal crack line. Go right up this and straight over the final bulge. A wee gem.

24   The Niche   15m   VS 4c ***   (1978)
Another gem, steep and well protected. Climb the obvious left-trending crack, then go up to the niche and finish up right.

25   Twisted Nerve   10m   HVS 5b **   (1978)
Another fine little climb with good protection and a one move crux. Starting left of the Niche, climb the wall directly or via a rest perch on the left edge.

26   Nervous Impulse   10m   E1 5b   (1984)
The edge left of Twisted Nerve gives fingery climbing to the optional rest perch of Twisted Nerve. Continue straight over the bulge to the top.

THE SEA NOSE
This is the narrow tidal wall at the south end of the Gully Wall.

Quick Draw McGraw   10m   E1 5b *   (1981)
The obvious crack splitting the Sea Nose is strenuous but on good holds, with a rest ledge on the right at half-height.

Bobalouie   15m   E4 6a **   (1992)
This is the line left of Quick Draw McGraw; low tide is required. Climb a crack
line leftwards to a shelf (Rock 7 behind hidden jug above), then go diagonally
right to climb a hanging corner.

NIPPET ROCKS

The slabby area forming the tip of Berrymuir Head gives climbing on two faces,
both above the sea. On the eastern side is The Flatface, a slabby wall giving
delicate climbing on sound rock, which is reached by descending an easy ramp
just north of the face, and traversing under some overhangs to below the wall.
Access is problematical at high tide. An amusing Very Difficult problem cuts
through the overhangs above the traverse.

Flatface Original   10m   Hard Severe *   (1981)
From a narrow shelf at the end of the traverse, pull over a bulge to gain the slabby
wall. Follow a good hand rail up right to the edge and go up to finish.

Flatface Direct   10m   Hard Severe *   (1981)
Pull over same bulge as for Original, then go straight up.

Mega Direct   20m   Mild VS 4b *   (1981)
From the same shelf, continue traversing left for some 8 metres, then climb
directly to the highest point of the face.

Cosmic Codpiece   15m   VS 4c *   (1981)
An entertaining left to right traverse. From the south end of the face, descend an
easy ramp to gain the wall at mid-height. The route rises initially, then continues
at two-thirds height to the handrail of Flatface Original, which is followed to its
end.

   On the north-facing section of Nippet rocks, overlooking Downies Haven, is
an overhanging arete (unclimbed) easily spied from above. The arete is set
between two corners which are reached by a diagonal descent down some
cracks near the westward end of the face (about Very Difficult).

Pseudo Corner   10m   Severe   (1981)
The first corner is scrappy and barely worth the effort. A dirty section at
two-thirds height is avoided out right.

Skulking Corner   10m   Mild Severe   (1981)
An improvement. Gain the bottom of this diagonal corner crack by moving
around below the overhanging arete.

FLOOR'S CRAIG   *(Map Ref 922 940)*

This small promontory, some 11km (7 miles) south of Aberdeen, offers some enjoyable climbing on steep compact walls, mostly with large ledges at the bottom. It is probably the best area south of Cove for the novice. Protection is adequate. A revival of interest in the place over the past few years has added several higher standard climbs. It can be hard to find but is well worth the trouble. Birds are few and far between in most years.

Access

Leave the A92 dual carriageway at a single track road, signposted East Cammachmore. This turn-off is easily missed but is some 3km (2 miles) south of Portlethen and preceded by a sign for Cammachmore (when approaching from Aberdeen). Follow the single track road for a few hundred metres, passing some cottages, until an inconspicuous farm track leads left from beside a cottage. Take the track, crossing a railway bridge, forking right then passing between a cottage and outbuildings, to its end at a farm. Permission to park here should be sought in order to continue the good relations presently enjoyed.

To reach the cliffs, follow a continuation of the track southwards, then head seawards along the edge of a field just before a ruined steading is reached. Follow the bottom of the field south for some 50 metres, passing a large bay which contains a curious Half Dome-shaped cliff, then head out onto the promontory by the edge of another small field. The Half Dome cliff is pretty rotten and only one route has been climbed: **The Crack of Dome** (Severe) takes an unpleasant crack towards the seaward end and requires an abseil descent.

Alternatively, and possibly better, approach from Craig Stirling to the south, round the coast, parking as for that area to reach the promontory.

The cliffs of Floor's Craig lie on the seaward face of the promontory, and are bounded on the south by a narrow inlet. A short way north of the inlet is a large recess cutting back into the clifftop.

Descent

At low tide all the climbs may be reached by way of the south descent, an easy ramp sloping down from the cliff top to the narrow inlet. A short corner then leads down to a large platform which runs below the cliff as far as the recess. Beyond this a series of ledges continue beneath the cliff, separated from the recess by a short wall. At high tide this short wall becomes awkward to cross. To avoid a soaking, the routes beyond the recess may be gained by the north descent. This is an easy ramp, a few metres along the cliff top from the recess. All routes beyond the recess are described by way of this descent.

CLIMBS APPROACHED FROM THE SOUTH DESCENT

The wall on the opposite side of the inlet holds a few routes, while at the back of the inlet is an obvious crumbling pinnacle:

The Pan-Galactic Mealie Pudding   12m   HVS 4c   (1981)
Like a mini-Spigolo (of the Cove variety), this climb takes the seaward face on less than perfect rock. The only decent belay on top is a downward-pointing flake on the north (right) side. Descent is by the rotten chimney on the left and is best safeguarded.

The Solar Sausage Supper   12m   VS 4c   (1986)
Well left of Pan-Galactic is an obvious left-slanting diagonal fault, started up a rib right of a shallow cave.

Celestial Scampi   12m   VS 4c   (1986)
Climb the wall right of Solar Sausage Supper to an obvious protection crack. Traverse right to an edge, then climb this to a chossy finish.

Interstellar Onion Bradie   8m   HVS 5a *   (1986)
A worthwhile climb which starts from the left end of the ledges. Climb a steep wall to a tiny, left-trending ramp. Reach over to a good right-trending crack, which leads to the top.

Right of the south descent is a steep slabby wall with a prominent S-shaped crack.

East Wind   10m   HVS 5a   (1981)
Dubious rock and poor protection. Start at the foot of the S-shaped crack and go up to a small ledge. Climb a short flake-groove to another small ledge and finish up the wall above.

South Paw   10m   Mild VS 4b   (1980)
Climb up to the middle of the S-shaped crack on sloping holds, then follow the crack to the top.

Kinhaken   10m   VS 4c   (1980)
This is the first obvious line round on the seaward face. Go up an easy corner to surmount an awkward bulge, then continue to the top.

Lonsdale Belt   10m   E3 5b   (1993)
Traverse the highly exposed horizontal break from the top of Kinhaken to finish at the top of Blockbuster.

Space Rats, Red Hole, Cove (Climbers, Neil Morrison and Dave Gillan)

Italian Stallion   10m   E2 5c *   (1987)
Start below Kinhaken and climb cracks diagonally rightwards to a ledge. Climb
the thin crack line up the bulging headwall to finish by a deep crack where the
angle eases.

Blockbuster   10m   HVS 5b *   (1980)
This climbs the next obvious feature some 10 metres right of Kinhaken, an
overhanging corner crack with the crux at the top.

   Further right from Blockbuster is another overhanging corner-groove. The
following three routes start left of this.

Raging Bull   10m   E2 5b **   (1987)
A fine sustained and strenuous pitch which is not technically hard and almost
entirely protected by Friends in horizontal slots. Start a few metres left of the
corner. Follow a line of jugs up the wall, at first slightly right then left into a short
hanging corner. Traverse right from the top of the corner using a wafer-thin
handrail to finish by the top crack of Sprunt's route.

The Boxer   10m   E2 5c *   (1987)
A steep line between Sprunt's Route and Raging Bull. Start at the foot of Raging
Bull and work up and right to a thin crack which leads to a ledge. Finish as for
Sprunt's Route.

Sprunt's Route   10m   E2 5c *   (1981)
This follows a line breaking through the bulging wall, just left of Coup De Grace.
Strenuous.

Coup de Grace   10m   E2 5c **   (1980)
The prominent overhanging corner-groove gives a sustained climb.

   Further right is an impressive overhanging arete, The Pugilist.

The Manassa Mauler   15m   E4 6a ***   (1988)
A splendid encounter on the ferocious-looking wall left of Pugilist. Climb the
groove of Pugilist to a peg. Step left and make a long reach for a jug (peg). Make
another long reach and go slightly right to a final peg (RP placements below peg).
Move up, then go left to the arete to pull over the final bulge to an easier finish.

The Pugilist   15m   E4 6a ***   (1987)
Gripping stuff on the overhanging arete, with good holds and adequate protection with one preplaced peg. Starting left of the prow, fingery moves lead to a
good horizontal break. Climb a groove on the left and swing right at its top to
below a bulge. Climb this to a small ledge below the final wall.

Pugilist, Floor's Craig (Climber, Alastair Robertson)

Sair Fecht   15m   E3 6a **   (1987)
This climbs the right side of the Pugilist arete to join Cestus. Climb directly to peg runner at 6m (Pugilist peg also available). Climb straight up (Friend 1½) to swing left onto the resting ledge of Pugilist. Finish up right as for Cestus.

Cestus   15m   E4 6a **   (1987)
The obvious fault in the middle of the wall right of Sair Fecht gives a serious lead. Scramble up ledges to belay in the corner of the recess. Climb up and traverse out into the middle of the wall (reasonable blade peg and poor Rock 6), then move across to the ledge of Pugilist. From right end of the ledge go up the wall to finish. A bit redundant since the addition of Sair Fecht.

Route Minor   6m   VS 5a   (1984)
Climb the bulging cracks at the back left of the recess.

Shuffle   8m   Mild VS 4b   (1980)
Climb the scooped wall above a big greasy block at the back of the recess, right of Route Minor.

Black Hope   10m   E1 5a   (1987)
The black wall right of Shuffle is often wet. Finish straight up to join the exit of Uppercut (escapable into Shuffle).

Uppercut   10m   HVS 5a *   (1979)
The steep crack just left of the obvious chimney is also often wet.

Jap's Eye Chimney   10m   Severe   (1981)
The obvious chimney. Climb up and onto a great jammed block. The Jap's Eye is a narrow slit, up behind another big block, which is passable by skinny types. Those of greater girth must swing out right. A short wall leads to the top.

Cold Turkey   10m   VS 4c **   (1981)
Starting some 4 metres right of Jap's Eye Chimney, climb vague cracks until a traverse left can be made into a shallow recess. Follow a handrail up right and over a bulge to finish.
Direct Start: 5b *   (1982)
Climb a thin crack to reach the recess more directly.

Bantam Wall   10m   Hard Severe *   (1980)
The right-trending line up the wall right of Cold Turkey is strenuous to start.

CLIMBS APPROACHED FROM THE NORTH DESCENT
The following climbs are on the wall above and stretching out right from the north descent ramp.

Eric the Maladjusted Mollusc   7m   Severe   (1981)
This crack line starts from about halfway down the ramp. Climb it direct with an awkward finish.

The Slug   10m   Difficult   (1980)
The obvious corner, further down the ramp.

Slug Arete   10m   VS 4c   (1981)
This is the left arete of The Slug.

Filler In   10m   Very Difficult   (1981)
This takes the easiest way up the face between One Below the Belt and The Slug, starting at the left end of the recessed break of One Below.

One Below the Belt   10m   VS 4c *   (1979)
A good climb going up the wall above ledges at the foot of the ramp. Climb a very steep wall on good holds to a horizontal break. Pull over a bulge leftwards to an easier finish.

Traversing left from the foot of the ramp, with a short descent *en route*, a prominent arete with two overhanging cracks to its left is reached.

Punchline   10m   VS 4c *   (1981)
The line on the wall right of the arete provides a good climb despite being escapable. Start directly up a black bulge and finish out right.

Right Hook   10m   HVS 5a   (1981)
The strenuous arete is started by a hand traverse from the left.

Right Jab   10m   HVS 5a   (1979)
The right-hand of the two overhanging cracks.

Left Jab   10m   VS 4c   (1980)
The left-hand crack is also strenuous.

Left Hook   10m   Very Difficult   (1981)
This is the arete left of the Jab Cracks (the right edge of Bantam Wall). Climb left up a wall onto a ledge on the arete. Surmount a short overhanging crack, then climb a short wall to the top.

North of this section of cliff is a deep chimney, easily identified from above.

The Thrapple   20m   Hard Severe   (1980)
Gain the foot of the chimney by descending a dirty face just north and making an exposed traverse on jugs back across a steep wall. The chimney gives a good climb when dry, but it is slimy and repulsive when wet.

COBLE BOARDS   *(Map Ref 923 943)*

This unassuming little crag offers several good routes and one real classic. It lies on the headland north of Floor's Craig and faces north-east, so it can be damp. Although lying north of Floor's Craig, it is described in this sequence for ease of access.

Access
Park as for Floor's Craig but head for the coast in a more easterly direction, arriving some 100 metres south of a stream. A large pile of boulders set back from the headland is a useful landmark. Descend steep grass north of the crag to rocky shelves and large boulders beneath the steeply overhanging crag. An overhanging left arete and a large roof with a flake crack identify the crag. The routes are described from left to right.

Chunky's Edge   20m   E2 5c *   (1990)
The wildly overhanging roofed left edge of the wall requires a low tide. Start from boulders below a black slot in the bulge. Climb through the slot, then go over twin bulges to squat beneath the main roof. Cross this rightwards, then go up the wall to finish. Escapable before the main roof.

Trapped   15m   E1 5a   (1990)
Climb directly into a square-cut alcove, swing out right, then finish leftwards up the headwall.

Of Mice and Men   15m   E2 5c   (1990)
Start directly below obvious jam crack in the detached-looking block. Ascend directly until beneath the block, move left avoiding the block, then climb easier ground bearing right to the top. The foolhardy can jam the crack.

Jihad   15m   E4 6a ***   (1990)
The stunning diagonal flake crack is well protected with Friends. Climb an initial bulge to a ledge. Muscle over a bulge into the crack line, and follow it to easy ground. A quality route.

Exiled Emir   15m   E2 6a *   (1990)
This is the thin crack high on the backwall, well right of the other routes. Climb the lower wall rightwards, traverse left to the crack and head for the top. Difficulty is dependent on digit size.

Just south of Coble Boards is a narrow inlet with a steep north-facing orange wall on its south side.

Fuzzy Stone   12m   HVS 5a *
Start up the obvious crack. Traverse right along a horizontal break to a recess and finish up a steep groove. Peculiar rock.

The overhanging corner right of the previous route provides a fairly chossy experience (HVS 5a).

CRAIG STIRLING   *(Map Ref 919 936)*

The striking promontory of Craig Stirling, some 13km (8 miles) south of Aberdeen, offers a fine concentration of upper grade climbs on generally excellent rock. The lines are bold, unrelentingly steep and are mostly poised above deep water. Freedom from nesting seabirds makes it possible to climb here throughout the summer.

Also in the vicinity is Cranhill Crag (the long rotten-looking wall on the north side of Craig Stirling) and Rotter's Rock (the small block-like headland on the south side). The crags' sheltered aspect can lead to lingering dampness and as with many of the crags a favourable breeze is recommended. The E3 leader will have a field day here.

Access

For Craig Stirling, leave the A92 at the single track road taken for Floor's Craig (see Floor's Craig access and map). Continue along the single track road, passing the track for Floor's Craig, and cross a railway bridge. Beyond the bridge, the road veers down right and a farm track leads off left (cars should be left here). Follow the track which passes a couple of houses to its end at a field a few hundred metres beyond a ruined building. Head seawards across the field to its foot, then turn right and go along the bottom for a short way until the narrow promontory of Craig Stirling can be seen running out to sea. From Craig Stirling, the cliffs of Cranhill Crag and Rotter's Rock are easily seen.

Descent

The cliffs of Craig Stirling are split into two distinct sections, a west buttress and an east buttress, both of which are north-east facing. The buttresses are situated on either side of a dry inlet containing a huge fallen block, about two-thirds of the way along the promontory. Access to climbs on both buttresses is by way of this inlet, the floor of which is reached by descending an easy groove on its far side.

Both buttresses drop into the sea, although there are small ledges below some of the climbs. High seas can sweep the lower quarters of the cliffs making access difficult. Most of the climbs may be gained by abseil if necessary. A couple of entertaining jamming problems exist on the fallen block.

THE WEST BUTTRESS

This is the more extensive of the two buttresses. Starting from the back of the inlet as a series of slabby shelves, it steepens to form the fine corner of Free Fall, immediately behind the fallen block. Right of this, the wall overhangs and here are the exacting lines of Yahoochie and Running Wild. The right wall is bounded by the arete of the Electric Chair. Beyond the arete and heading landwards, the buttress is unrelentingly steep, often overhanging, for some 25m to a slight easing in the huge undercut corner of Jack Sprat. Right of this is an impressive bottomless wall, which is in turn bounded on the right by the obvious corner of Green Vomit. Beyond this, the buttress extends another 15 metres or so, terminating in a fierce overhanging (unclimbed) arete.

Free Fall   20m   VS 4c   (1973)
An entertaining but disappointing climb. Climb the fine corner crack to a platform. Ignoring the obvious escape, climb the severely overhanging crack above either direct (HVS) or via a very awkwardly gained ledge up on the left. An escape can be made along the ledge.

Yippiekaiae   20m   E3 5c *   (1993)
Climb the corner of Free Fall to the ledge, then take the overhanging crack line up and right to join the top of Yertezoot.

Yahoochie   20m   E5 6a ***   (1982)
Start up Free Fall for a couple of metres, then follow an obvious ramp right and up to two pegs. Climb the wall above the pegs and move left to a semi-rest at jugs (assorted nut runners; the protection would be significantly improved by placing the Rock 4 in Yertezoot). Move back right and climb the overhanging pocketed wall to a sloping hold (crux). Another hard move gains the break above. Traverse left into a short corner and continue to the top.

Yertezoot   20m   E5 6b **   (1987)
The obvious left-hand finish to Yahoochie. Climb Yahoochie to the nut placements above the pegs. A good Rock 4 can be placed in a flake to the left, awkwardly. Climb straight up from the flake to reach jugs (crux) where a Rock 5 (or Friend 2) can be placed, strenuously. Finish straight up (Friend 2) or swing left at top.

Yassassin   20m   E6 6b   (1993)
An eliminate with some excellent climbing up the Yahoochie Wall. Start just right of Free Fall. Climb a little boulder problem past a pocket to the ramp of Yahoochie. Continue up the wall just right of the corner to a horizontal break (possible escape). Make a long reach to a good pocket in the brown streak above, and cross over to the shake-out jugs common to Yahoochie and Yertezoot. Forge straight up the brown streak to the final corner of Yahoochie.

Running Wild   20m   E5 6b ***   (1985)
A well-named route taking the crack in the lower wall right of Yahoochie, and the arete direct. Climb the crack on good slots, then make hard moves up to a horizontal break. Swing right and up to a resting place on Electric Chair. Climb the overhanging arete direct to the perch of Electric Chair (Friend runner). Finish up the final wall, easiest on the right, as for Electric Chair.

The Electric Chair   20m   E2 5b *   (1981)
The arete gives a scary and serious route, with some dubious rock and protection, climbed mainly on the right side. From the platform behind the block, swing

up right onto a small ledge on the edge. Gain a higher ledge, then go up near the edge to a horizontal break and good runners. Go directly into a shallow groove right of the edge; at its top grovel left onto an exposed perch. Pull up the final wall on its right to finish.

At low tide, small ledges below the seaward face of the west buttress may be gained by traversing around under the arete. At high tide they can be gained with difficulty from the small ledge of the arete at about VS 4c. They may also be reached by abseil.

Electric Blue   20m   E1 5a **   (1978)
The first obvious line on the seaward face gives good climbing despite dubious rock at the top. From the ledges, move left into a slanting groove just right of the arete. Climb it to ledges at mid-height. The leaning wall above is climbed by the left of two corner-grooves, and the final wall is climbed direct or by swinging out left (both strenuous).

Nob Goblin   20m   E2 5b *   (1981)
This takes the wall and bulges between the more obvious lines of Electric Blue and Omnivore. Quite serious on its lower half. From the ledges, follow a line of holds straight up to stand on a good hold at 5m (just left of a thin right-curving crack). Go up left (crux) to leave the smooth wall and gain an easier groove, which leads to ledges at mid-height (common to Electric Blue). Move up the right-hand of the two leaning corner grooves and swing up right, out of the corner, over a bulge on good holds. Cross an overlap then go directly to the top, crossing another overlap.

Omnivore   25m   E1 5a **   (1978)
This is the prominent groove line right of Nob Goblin, with tricky route finding on the poorly protected lower wall. Start as for Nob Goblin to reach the good hold, then traverse away right in the general line of the curving crack to better holds below an arching overhang, not far left of a big platform. Trend left up and across to the Electric Blue ledges. Go up right to the base of the groove at the left extremity of a yellow hanging slab, then climb the groove to the top.

From the right end of the ledge system, a short Severe crack leads up to a prominent platform about 5m above the ledge. The following three climbs start from this platform. Omnivore can also be started from here.

Greedy Pig   20m   E3 5c **   (1982)
This climbs the bulging wall directly above the platform. Climb the obvious corner up and round right to a loose block. Go straight up to undercuts, then move left to big jugs which lead onto the slab above. Move up right to a small borehole, then swing left and up to a good hand traverse crack. Go left along this, then climb the wall above. Good value.

Lean Meat   25m   E3 5c **   (1979)
This takes the sensational overhanging flake crack right of the platform. Climb the flake out rightwards to the arete. Go up the slabby right wall to ledges, and finish by the obvious grassy exit.

Jack Sprat   35m   E2 5c *   (1982)
The big slabby corner in the centre of the buttress is straightforward but a fine and difficult traverse is required to reach it. From the platform, climb rightwards down a shelf system to its end. Now traverse right across the wall using pockets and slots, then step up right onto an obvious foothold and traverse round right to ledges. Finish up the corner, moving left at the top to join Lean Meat.

Green Vomit   25m   VS 4c   (1978)
The name says it all. The big green corner right again was originally top roped and probably never since repeated. Abseil required for any takers.

Between the Devil and the Deep Blue Sea   40m   E4 6a ***   (1991)
Abseil down Green Vomit and walk along the ledges eastwards (low tide required) to belay beneath a massive roofed corner.
1. 15m 5c Climb a small left-facing corner and traverse left under the roof round the arete to belay on a slab by ledges on the right side of the Jack Sprat Corner.
2. 25m 6a Traverse right on a shelf under the overhangs to reach a boss of rock and good protection. Make hard moves over the roof on pockets, then climb the superb bold wall above (5a) to ledges. Scramble off right.

Bone Machine   30m   E5 6b ***   (1993)
Just right of the start of the previous route is an obvious corner crack in the black rock. Climb the corner over a small overhang to a bridging rest. Traverse left under the overhang to the base of a hanging corner (Friend 2½ on the left, RP3 in the corner). Climb the corner (crux), then make more hard moves exiting out left. Continue up the slabby arete to ledges and finish on the right as for the previous climb. Superb, well protected technical climbing.

At the very right-hand end of west buttress is a fierce overhanging arete, just left of which is a fine crack line. Descend at lowish tide by abseil from a stake at the top, with anchors well back. Both this and the preceding route are on a dank north-facing wall and require a northerly breeze for dry conditions.

When the North Wind Blows   15m   E4 6a **   (1993)
Excellent, sustained and pumpy climbing up the fine crack. Take a Friend 3½. Rather than continue up the loose rock at the top, it is probably better to clip into the abseil rope, lower off and climb either of the preceding two routes.

Searcher   30m   E2 5b *   (1985)
This takes an obvious traverse line around the west buttress. Starting as for Yahoochie, traverse round past the pegs and around the arete to gain the

mid-height ledges. Go across as for Omnivore and go up onto the yellow hanging slab. Traverse the slab to finish at the top of Lean Meat. The yellow slab would benefit from some cleaning.

Western Girdle   40m   E3 5c   (1993)
Abseil down Green Vomit, climb the first pitch of Between the Devil and the Deep Blue Sea, then reverse the crux traverse of Jack Sprat. Climb down the "Severe" crack leading into Greedy Pig and Lean Meat and continue round to the barnacled ledges below Electric Blue.

THE EAST BUTTRESS
The main attractions of the east buttress are a great roofed corner, which gives the classic climb of Grand Diedre, and its impressive barrel-shaped right wall. The buttress is girdled by starting from the inlet; this girdle can be used to gain a small platform below Grand Diedre and its adjoining walls. At the back of the inlet, though not strictly part of the east buttress, is a black slab which forms a corner with the overhanging back wall.

Walter's Way   10m   Very Difficult   (1982)
This takes the slab corner with a delicate move at two-thirds height. Often greasy.

Panic In Detroit   10m   E3 5c   (1993)
A poor route. Climb the first step of Walter's Way, then move right and climb the wall direct to the top.

Cracked Actor   10m   E3 5c *   (1989)
Climb cracks up the centre of the overhanging back wall.

Aladdin Sane   10m   E4 6a   (1993)
This worthwhile route takes the vague crack line right of Cracked Actor, the true angle of which can be seen from the top of Free Fall. Climb easy rock up and right and lean across to a crack in the undercut wall. Climb up to a quartz pocket and continue past a peg runner to a horizontal break. More hard moves lead to the top.

Petite Diedre   20m   Very Difficult *
Left of the descent groove is a fine corner, which gives a good climb despite some dubious rock. Traverse into the corner and climb it to its top. Follow ledges up and left to the top.

Eastern Girdle   45m   Hard Severe *   (1973)
An interesting excursion with some exposure. Start traversing as for Petite Diedre. When below the corner, descend a few metres, then move left and go round beneath a big roof. Go diagonally down left and step round an edge onto the platform below Grand Diedre. Two ways are available from here:

Either, climb Grand Diedre for 10m to a horizontal break on the left wall. Traverse the break to turn the arete and follow the fault across a steep wall to reach a slabby area.
Or, descend from the platform and cross a short wall just above the high tide mark. Climb a fine flake crack to gain the slabby area. The best finish lies directly up the wall above.

The following climbs start from the platform below Grand Diedre. The convex right wall offers some testing climbing.

Depth Charge   25m   E1 5a **   (1978)
This takes the right edge of the wall after advancing across the obvious traverse line. Bold and steep. Climb a short wall to a crack (Clockwork Rat) and traverse away out until near the right arete. Forge up the wall above to a welcome ledge. Finish up an obvious corner crack. An easier but inferior way to the ledge is to continue the traverse around the right arete and climb a scrappy wall above.
Direct Start: 5m   E3 5c   (1993)
A bold variation. Start 3m down and right of the normal way. Climb the overhanging arete, then the wall just right of a left-facing corner to join the normal route.

Sea Cat   15m   E3 5b **   (1980)
The thin cracks up the wall are taken by Clockwork Rat. Sea Cat follows a line of good holds, always to the right of the cracks, then climbs the upper wall to the right. Start along Depth Charge then go straight up and right until moves up left lead to good holds and a resting place in the middle of the wall where the angle eases. A line of holds leads up then right to the top.

Clockwork Rat   15m   E3 5c **   (1982)
A direct line. Go straight up the first crack, then transfer right and climb the second to the resting place of Sea Cat. Head straight up the middle of the wall above, in a thin and contrived manner on small holds to a big flat hold, thence to the top.

A combination of the lower crack of Clockwork Rat and the upper wall of Sea Cat is often climbed and perhaps provides the best way up the wall.

Grand Diedre   20m   HVS 5a ***   (1973)
A steep and well protected classic, following the fine roofed corner. The moves around the roof present the crux. Often damp.

The narrow wall left of the corner is steep and capped by roofs. Two climbs take this wall, starting from the platform.

Transvestite Bat   20m   HVS 5a *   (1982)
This climbs the wall and takes a short hanging corner through the roofs. From the bottom of Grand Diedre, move left up a short slab and over an overhang to

a point below a smaller overhang. Step left and pull over this and up to the break of the Girdle. Climb directly up into the hanging corner, then go up to step right onto an edge, finishing up a crack. A 5b start goes up the obvious groove.

Wet Pussy   20m   F4 5c **   (1982)
The left arete gives bold climbing on the lower half. Climb up left onto the edge and step up to where protection can be arranged in a small horizontal crack. Pull up left over the bulging edge, then climb the wall to the girdle break. The arete leads to the top via a crack.

From below Wet Pussy, a short left traverse just above the high tide mark reaches another platform below a fine crack line. This may be more easily reached by traversing in from the eastern end and descending a short corner on iron spikes.

Walrus   15m   HVS 5a **   (1978)
This takes the fine crack above the platform. Climb a shallow recess to the bulge and awkwardly gain the crack above. Take this to the top. A fine route.

ROTTER'S ROCK
The blocky headland immediately south of Craig Stirling has some minor routes.

Powerfinger   10m   E3 5c   (1983)
A line up the right side of the overhanging north wall. Climb the wall trending slightly left to a break at 6m. Traverse right along the break to better holds and thence the top. Brittle rock.

Strain Don't Train   10m   VS 4c   (1983)
Start near the left end of the north wall. Go up on good holds and move out left to a platform on the edge. Climb out left onto the east wall and go up to finish.

Nautilus   10m   E1 5b   (1984)
Climb the previous route to the platform. Pull out right over a large block and climb the wall above to a break. Strenuous moves up and left lead to the top.

The Sandbagger   10m   E1 5c   (1983)
The east wall may be climbed by an indifferent Hard Severe route. Sandbagger is the short bulging crack near the left end, gained direct up the leaning lower wall.

Slow Motion   10m   Very Severe 4c   (1983)
The south wall is slabby and faces a pair of squat pinnacles. Climb the vague central cracks.

The left side of the wall gives a route at Very Difficult. The thin crack line on the right is HVS.

CRANHILL CRAG
This is the extensive rotten-looking and neglected wall on the north side of Craig Stirling. The rock is better than it appears when viewed from Craig Stirling, but it has only three climbs. The cliff lies above a huge slabby area and is unaffected by high seas. To approach the climbs, it is possible to climb down Birders Route, but better to rope down the shorter north end of the cliff.

Birder's Route   30m   Very Difficult
The twisting shelf system near the centre of the cliff was probably first descended by egg collectors. Start at the right end of a sloping undercut shelf and follow it, then a further series of shelves, up left to a short corner. Climb the corner (exposed) to reach more shelves leading up right to the top.

Time Warp   30m   HVS 5a *   (1978)
Some 60 metres left of Birder's Route is a corner with prominent quartz bands high up. Start close to a point where a lower wall drops away below. Climb a deceptively bulging wall on the right and traverse left to a slot which leads to a platform on the left (optional belay). Go out right and up to finish (exposed).

Hexlax   30m   Hard Severe   (1978)
Around 30 metres left of Time Warp is an easing in the cliff with a prominent bay high up. This route takes the easiest way into the bay by walls and ledges to make an exit out right.

NEWTONHILL

The village of Newtonhill, 14km (9 miles) south of Aberdeen on the A92, sits high above a picturesque natural harbour, the north side of which runs out as a small headland forming some fine steep walls. A low tunnel pierces the headland near its tip, the Needle's Eye. The climbing is situated on two walls either side of the Eye: The Harbour Wall and Back Door Wall. The climbing is steep and strenuous on both walls. The Harbour Wall can be great on a sunny winter's day. Birds are not a problem here.

Access
Approach as for Craig Stirling but continue down to park under the railway viaduct. A rough track leads to the beach. Alternatively drive into Newtonhill village, go down Skateraw Road to a car park, then follow steps to the beach. At low tide the climbs may be reached by scrambling along from the harbour, passing a big cave on the way.

At other than low tide, the cliffs may be approached from above by descending a short shelf (not obvious) some 30 metres north of the small headland. This way leads to Back Door Wall. At ebbing tide, the Harbour Wall may be reached through the eye. At high tide, some of the Harbour Wall climbs can be gained by traversing around the tip.

THE HARBOUR WALL   *(Map Ref 916 935)*

This fine south-facing wall overlooks the bay. The climbs are described from left to right.

The Snirgler   15m   Hard Sovoro   (1977)
The pillar between the big cave and a shallow cave to the right. Start on the left and climb to a ledge. Go up and around the edge to reach and climb a short steep wall, followed by a grassy finish.

Skeletor   15m   HVS 5a   (1986)
Climb the right side of the pillar, starting at the left side of the cave. Join The Snirgler to finish.

Sidewinder   15m   VS   (1975)
Climb the left-slanting crack on the right of the shallow cave. From a bulge near the top traverse out right on poor rock until the top can be reached.

Desederio   15m   E4 6a **   (1991)
Climb the crack and roof in the golden wall just right of Sidewinder. The final wall is climbed slanting right

The Great Escape   15m   HVS 5a **   (1977)
This finds a way around the great roofed alcove after overcoming the bulging undercut wall below. Pull over the bulge just left of the 'Eye' and go up to below the roof. Take the obvious traverse line left and make a seemingly unlikely move round the bulging arete to gain a steep groove. Climb this to the top.
Direct Start: 10m   HVS 5a   (1980)
Climb a bulge directly beneath the upper groove, then move right to the alcove.

The Wooden Horse   15m   E2 5c   (1980)
A direct eliminate of The Great Escape. Begin up its Direct Start, then move out left to climb a bigger bulge to join The Great Escape at its finishing groove.

Usurper   15m   E5 6a   (1983)
This neglected climb takes a direct line through The Great Escape roof. Climb The Great Escape to the alcove and pull out under the roof to a horizontal break (Friend runner). Move out to reach a small V-notch (crucial Rock 1) and climb directly over the lip to easy ground.

Exit Stage Right   15m   E2 5b   (1981)
This goes out around the right side of the roof from the alcove.

Tigger   15m   E1 5b **   (1977)
Above the 'Eye' is a gun-shaped roof set between twin crack lines. Tigger takes the left-hand crack. Start up the chimney above the 'Eye' or swing up the bulge on the left. Climb the crack and move up right over the roof to finish.

Hired Gun   15m   E3 5c   (1985)
Start under the 'Gun'. Go up the shallow corner to the 'trigger' and exit into a
roofed alcove. Climb the awkward bulging wall above (side runner available in
Tigger).

Cheetah   15m   HVS 5a *   (1977)
Climb the right-hand corner crack, starting up the chimney or the corner to the
right.

El-D   15m   E2 5b **   (1983)
Starting right of the 'Eye', go directly up the centre of the wall right of Cheetah.

At high tide it is still possible to gain the preceding four climbs by a horizontal
traverse from the right.

Pooh's Arete   15m   E2 5b *   (1982)
The fairly obvious blunt arete at the right end of Harbour Wall. After a hard start
up the right side, swing out left onto Harbour Wall, then go up via a horizontal
break to the top.

Bottleneck Chimney   10m   Very Difficult
Climb the bulging chimney at the tip which divides the Harbour and Back Door
Walls.

A series of short awkward walls left of the chimney may be climbed at Very
Difficult.

BACK DOOR WALL

This steep and juggy wall gives some strong arm climbing. The right margin of
the wall is defined by the scaling North Chimney.

Bizarre Buttress   10m   Mild VS 4c   (1978)
North of North Chimney is an obvious prow. Start by dodgy rock plates on the
right.

The groove immediately left of Bizarre Buttress can be climbed at HVS.

Wish You Were Here   10m   E2 5b   (1983)
A direct way up Bizarre Buttress. Climb the overhanging arete direct by brittle
plates to good holds on the left side. Swing right onto a flake and finish up the
top crack of the normal route. The start is serious.

North Chimney   10m   Very Difficult
Well worth avoiding.

Flying Circus   10m   HVS 5a *   (1981)
From the base of North Chimney, climb the wall above directly to a fine finish
over the split bulge above.

Snoopy   10m   VS 4c *   (1976)
From the same start as Flying Circus, work up left into the obvious hanging
corner to finish at a pull onto a quartz ledge.

Daka Daka Daka   10m   HVS 5a   (1985)
Climb the undercut wall left of Snoopy to cross that route and finish by the bulge
of Flying Circus.

Acapulco   10m   E1 5b **   (1977)
One of Newtonhill's finest. Starting right of the 'Eye', swing up left over the
leaning undercut wall and get into a short roof-capped corner. Go out left onto
a hanging edge and climb into a short groove. Continue up the wall above to a
ledge to finish. Small Friends are useful.
Left-Hand Start: 6m   HVS 5a **   (1982)
Starting left of the 'Eye', go up and right to reach the corner.

The Red Baron   10m   HVS 5a **   (1976)
Starting left of the 'Eye', climb a bulge, then move right to right-trending cracks
which lead to the ledge common to Acapulco.

The Groan   10m   HVS 5a *   (1978)
This goes up the left side of the wall, starting at a big bulge on the left. Swing up
and right and go up the wall to gain an upper ledge by hand traversing left. Climb
a short wall to finish.

Van Riftoften   10m   E1 5b   (1985)
Climb directly over a bulge to gain a shallow roofed corner left of The Groan.
Climb it to a sloping ledge, then finish up a short wall.

DYKE'S CLIFF   *(Map Ref 914 934)*

This recently developed crag offers some good short steep routes and is suitable
for bouldering. It lies on the south side of Newtonhill Bay and faces north-east.
To reach it, turn off the dual carriageway into Newtonhill. Follow the road down
over the railway and turn right at the Bakers (Skateraw Road). There is a car
park at the foot of the road. Descend the steep grassy ridge directly below the
car park to reach the flat grassy cliff top with *in situ* belay stakes. Descend easily
at the north or south end of the crag. All the routes were climbed in 1990; they
are described from left to right.

Whale Nation   10m   HVS 5a *
Go up to climb a left-slanting crack to a horizontal break. Move right and climb the left-slanting line to finish on the left edge of the wall.

MacSpace Cadet   10m   E3 6a
An eliminate which climbs directly to the left end of a cleaned ledge in a depression.

Bad Medicine Waltz   10m   E2 5b *
The crack line leading to the centre of the cleaned ledge.

The Caucasian Chalk Circle   10m   E1 5b
A little further right, climb direct to the top and swing left onto the ledge.

Exasperation   10m   E2 5b *
The central crack line.

Rock Torbet   10m   E2 5b
Start just right of a thin crack and climb to a vague crack line. Move up to a slanting break, then reach up to a horizontal slot and continue over the capping bulge.

Nanaimo   10m   E2 5c *
Start left of the pool and climb a vague crack line to some spiky jugs at the slanting break. Make a hard move up right to a juggy finish.

Flipper   10m   E1 5b
At the right end of the crag are three parallel cracks. Start just left of the pool and make a rising traverse to reach and climb the left-hand crack.

The Granite Kipper   10m   E1 5a
The middle crack, starting right of the pool, has dodgy rock and poor protection.

Fisherman's Blues   10m   VS 5a
The best of the three cracks. Climb a corner and the obvious left-slanting crack.

Skateraw Road   15m   E2 5b
The obvious diagonal break. Start up Fisherman's Blues, then continue on the break until forced up to the horizontal slot on Rock Torbet. Move left into the little V-corner.

About 100 metres south of Dyke's Cliff are two routes, set well back from the sea, approached by easy rock between them. **The Enemy Within** (HVS 5b *) takes the very obvious south-east facing crack. The wide north-east facing crack 30 metres south of The Enemy Within gives a short VS 4c.

Newtonhill to Muchalls

These are the most southerly of the Aberdeen sea-cliffs. Only two areas have been discovered that are worth climbing on, the John's Heugh cliffs and the Muchalls cliffs. Initial exploration seems to have taken place around the turn of the century, although nothing was recorded. Limited activity took place in the early 1980s, but many new routes were found in 1988. With the exception of Brown Crag, the rock in this section is poorer than the cliffs further north. There is still a fair amount of scope for exploration.

JOHN'S HEUGH CLIFFS

This is the first climbing area encountered south of Newtonhill, with a choice of four separate and contrasting cliffs. The best of these is undoubtedly Brown Crag. From Aberdeen follow the dual carriageway south, turn in to Newtonhill, take the first right, then go left down a dirt track. If approaching from the south take the Newtonhill slip road; the dirt track is then the first right. Follow the dirt track as far as the Mains of Monduff farm where limited parking is available on the broad grass verge opposite the farm house. Cars can go no further and care must be taken not to block the field gate. Please consult the farmer if in doubt. On the return journey, the track divides with the right-hand fork leading towards Newtonhill. Follow this and the village is soon entered. This way allows much easier access back onto the dual carriageway.
  Walk through the farm buildings and follow the track towards the sea to a railway bridge. This bridge is the common departure point for the four cliffs, of which the most northerly is described first.

JOHN'S HEUGH   *(Map Ref 912 926)*

The rock of this large north-facing cliff is similar to Downies although the quality is poorer. The cliff only receives sun early in the day, so it can be damp. Nesting birds are also a problem during the summer. The rock platform below the cliff is not completely tidal so access only becomes tricky if there is a swell running. Once over the bridge turn left and go over a gate. Follow the fence on the right to its end and keep going towards the sea, eventually arriving at the head of a large bay. The crag is on the right and faces north. Walk right along the top of the cliff to gain easy descent ledges which are followed to sea-level. Walk back left along a wide rock platform to view the cliff.

The Hunchback   12m   VS 4c   (1983)
This climbs up to bulges on the left side of the overhanging wall, then escapes out left. Climb the lower wall to a ledge and continue up the obvious flake to escape left along the constricted slab.

Pump Junkie   20m   E4 5c   (1990)
The leftmost crack line on the main crag. Belay on a ledge 5m up. Climb the
right-facing corner, pull over the overhang and thug it to the top. Some dubious
rock.

Jaded Ledge Lizard   25m   E4 5c *   (1989)
The obvious overhanging crack line up the centre of the wall right of the
Hunchback. Start just right of the cave and climb the short wall to ledges. Follow
the quartz-blotched crack above, surmounting a roof, to a horizontal break. Step
left and climb the wall left of the crack until it can be regained. Finish up the crack
and its continuation to reach the top. A meaty little number.

Where Seagulls Dare   20m   E4 6a *   (1989)
This route follows the smooth black wall at the right side of the cliff, below a
grassy ledge. Climb a small sharp rib, which leads to a ledge. Traverse some
way left to a resting place, then continue up right using a broken crack to a peg
runner. Reach past this (crux) and climb the wall above to a niche. Traverse left
to the arete and step onto a big sloping belay ledge. Either abseil or finish up a
gruesome pitch. Often wet.

BROWN CRAG   *(Map Ref 911 925)*

The cliff faces south-east and is a sun trap, drying very quickly after showers. It
is not tidal although the routes are affected by high seas. The rock is excellent,
with a profusion of positive holds. Friends are essential for protection. Nesting
birds are not a problem here, but routes to the right of the main wall are affected.
    From the bridge turn right and go down to a gate. Cross this and head straight
towards the sea. After crossing the fence at the bottom of the field, descend the
grassy slope to a flat platform on top of the cliff. Round to the right of the cliff
(almost facing it) is a tricky ramp. Descent is possible by climbing most of the
way down this, dropping down to a ledge system and cutting back towards the
platform at the base of the cliff (Very Difficult). Because this is so awkward,
abseiling is probably best, at least on first acquaintance. There is a useful thread
for belays and abseils located centrally above the cliff.

The Truant   10m   E3 6a   (1991)
The line left of Muhammed Wira Bin Jamel.

Muhammed Wira Bin Jamel   10m   E2 5c **   (1989)
Climb the obvious line directly up the impending wall, just left of The Grail.

The Grail   10m   VS 5a *   (1988)
Climb the obvious overhanging corner at the left end of the cliff.

Black Mass   10m   E1 5c *   (1988)
Climb the flake 2 metres right of the corner to small ledges and finish up the short
wall above.

Pinch of Salt   15m   E5 6b *   (1988)
Climb the wall a few metres right of the black streak all the way to the top. The initial wall is the crux and is both fingery and vicious.

Rock Lobster   15m   E3 5c **   (1988)
Climb Incontinence Crack for a few metres, step left, then go up slightly left to a rest. Finish straight up. Protection improves with height.

Incontinence Crack   15m   HVS 5a *   (1988)
This is the obvious crack which is usually wet near the top. Finish up the wall and arete above. The wet streak can be avoided on the left wall at the same grade.

Nappy Rash   15m   E1 5b   (1988)
Right of the top section of Incontinence Crack is a small grey roof. Start below this and climb straight up to it. Surmount the roof directly and finish as for Z Bend.

Z Bend   15m   Mild VS 4b   (1983)
From underneath Incontinence Crack make a rising right traverse to a small ledge. Return up left and finish up a small corner (often wet).

Clean Round the Bend   15m   HVS 5a   (1988)
Z Bend traverses left underneath a diagonal crack in the brown headwall. Start below and just right of this. Climb up the wall to join Z Bend and continue to the base of the crack. Climb it, move right to a jug, and mantelshelf to finish. A good eliminate.

Domestos   20m   E1 5b *   (1988)
Start below the brown left-facing corner at half-height. Climb directly up to the corner, and finish up a shallow left-facing corner above.

Weakling's Wall   20m   E2 5b   (1988)
Right of Domestos is a cracked wall with a roof at half-height. Climb directly to the roof, pull through, then finish up the wall above.

Davidson's Delight   20m   E1 5a *   (1988)
At the right end of the cliff is an obvious arete. Climb the wall just left of the arete to a ledge. Finish up the easier arete above. Good, well protected climbing.

The Under Toad   12m   HVS 5a   (1989)
Round the edge to the right of Davidson's Delight is a small hanging corner. This route climbs the next corner to the right to a ledge at half-height. Finish up the obvious right-slanting crack in the steep headwall.

I.G.Y.   15m   VS 5a   (1989)
Four metres right of the last route is another corner. Climb this for 2m, move right, and climb the right-slanting wide crack. Continue up the wall above to the top.

CLOCHINDARE CRAGS

There are two quite sunny cliffs here divided by a large tidal inlet. The rock is very friable in places and the cliffs are tidal. Although nesting birds are not present on all the lines, they can be a problem.

From the bridge turn right and go over the gate. Walk south for about 200 metres, then turn and walk towards the sea. There is a large dry inlet below the point where the drystone dyke turns 90 degrees towards the sea. Descend grassy slopes on the south side of the dry inlet to reach sea-level. At the mouth of the inlet on its north side is Yellow Crag. On the opposite side of the inlet, hidden from all sides, is Drab Crag.

YELLOW CRAG   *(Map Ref 907 923)*

There is only one route on this sunny, south-facing cliff. Although it appears worthwhile on first acquaintance, horrible yellow lichen covers the rock.

The Secret Policeman's Other Ball   12m   E2 5c   (1983)
This route lies on the shorter brown wall closest to the sea. Climb the centre of the wall about 5 metres left of the seaward arete by broken cracks to a small platform and belay. To descend it is best to scramble down to the left.

DRAB CRAG   *(Map Ref 907 922)*

The cliff faces out to sea and access is by ledges leading south about 5m up. There is an abseil stake in place on top of the cliff which is worth locating before descending. The first obvious feature is a large overhung niche with an over-hanging left wall and a slabby right wall.

Wasp Slab   10m   Difficult *   (1983)
Climb up into the niche and exit rightwards.

The Secret Policeman's Ball   10m   HVS 5a *   (1983)
The obvious arete left of Wasp Slab. Start in the centre of the slab at an obvious thin crack. Climb this until a line of holds leads out to the finishing arete.

The Vomiting Parrot   20m   Hard Severe   (1983)
Climb the obvious corner left of Policeman's Ball, exiting left onto a ledge. Finish up right across a slab. Friable rock.

Soft Touch   20m   E1 5a   (1983)
Climb the crumbly-looking wall 2 metres left of Vomiting Parrot directly, starting up a small corner-ramp. Finish up an obvious black niche.

Billy Liar   20m   HVS 5a *   (1983)
This is the first crack line left of Soft Touch. Climb it directly exiting right under the final roof.

DOONIE POINT   *(Map Ref 904 909)*

This is the small headland about 1km south of Muchalls village. Although the scenery is gaunt and lovely, there is very little climbing in the immediate vicinity of Muchalls, due to rotten rock. Of particular interest is the big cavern-like archway below the houses.

The climbing is on the seaward side of a ridge, pierced by two natural arches, easily seen and best approached from the highest part of the headland. The rock is quite sound although friable patches will be encountered. Tidal variations do not affect the cliff but a big swell will make climbing impossible. Some of the routes are used by nesting gulls.

Access

The best approach is by a cliff top path from the village, passing a 10m stack down on the shore. This has been climbed, but it is loose and not recommended. South of the stack, on top of the hill, is a small group of buildings (the Mill of Muchalls). Go past these, cross a stream, and follow the path for a few hundred metres to a grassy headland. This is easily identified by three wartime concrete blocks which bar the pathway out onto its brow. It is possible to drive down to the Mill of Muchalls directly from the dual carriageway, but access problems with the locals have been encountered.

Descend on the right side of the headland to gain a shallow wet gully. This leads down easily to broken ground below the cliff. There are two routes on the steep south-facing gable end of the ridge.

Bran Flake   10m   Hard Severe 4b   (1982)
A good climb taking a direct line. Climb the centre of the steep lower wall and continue to the top via a dubious flake.

Dev's Dilemma   10m   Hard Severe 4a   (1982)
Climb a steep groove at the right end of the lower wall and move right, round the arete, to a ledge. Climb the corner crack above to finish.

The Dirty Arch Deacon   10m   Very Difficult   (1982)
Climb the obvious right-slanting groove on the left of the seaward arch, as seen from Dev's Dilemma.

Arc de Triomphe   10m   Hard Severe 4a   (1982)
Start as for the previous route and traverse right above the arch to gain the central crack. Finish up this.

Lucy   10m   Difficult *   (1982)
Climb the slab on the right side of the arch to the top.

Hang Fire   10m   VS 4c *   (1982)
On the north-facing side of the seaward arch is a short leaning corner above an
overhanging wall. Climb the wall to the corner and finish up it, moving right and
up to the top.

A Walk on the Wide Side   12m   Hard Severe 4b   (1982)
On the northernmost wall is a crack line rising from left to right. Follow this to a
niche, step left, and go straight up to finish.

CASTLE ROCK OF MUCHALLS
This big offshore rock lies south of Doonie Point.

North Face   30m   VS
Cross boulders to reach base of rock, traverse left at sea-level onto the north
face. Climb an easy right-rising ramp, then follow an open left-facing groove to
a desperately loose finish. A 20m free abseil down the landward face from a
block just south of the summit is the best descent.

Fame and Fortune Traverse   80m   Severe   (1991)
A clockwise sea-level girdle of the stack on excellent rock.

CASTLE WALL   (Map Ref 899 903)
Opposite Castle Rock and slightly to its north, a narrow steep grassy ridge runs
inland. Its seaward end stops abruptly above a platform in a steep triangular 25m
wall, characterised by a centrally positioned cave at its foot. The following two
routes give exhilaratingly steep climbing on rough bubbly rock, the reliability of
which will improve with traffic. There is some limited scope for further routes.
    The best descent is to scramble down the slabs and lower corner on the left
side of the crag. Continuing along the crest of the ridge is best reserved for those
of alpine persuasion! One can either approach by walking along the coast south
from Muchalls, or alternatively directly from the A92 using the farm bridge across
the railway line (Map Ref 897 904).

The Ramparts   25m   E1 5a   (1991)
An excellent and sustained route. Start 5 metres left of the cave and climb
directly up to a horizontal break level with the cave roof. Move left to gain a
right-slanting crack, follow this for 5m and move left again to a second right-
trending fault. Move up then right (crux) into a niche, and finish using an unlikely
series of holds on the impending headwall.

Portcullis   25m   HVS 5a   (1991)
Start just right of the cave and climb the steep wall above for 10m on excellent
holds. Move up and left into the central depression and finish up the loose
right-facing corner above.

Collieston to Whinnyfold

The sleepy picturesque village of Collieston marks the start of the northern climbing grounds, 30km (18 miles) up the coast from Aberdeen. The harboured village was once a veritable den of smugglers in the 18th century. Smuggling was a profession in which all the coastal dwellers seem to have willingly engaged. Fishing, smuggling and plundering of wrecks being three allied occupations. Nowadays the area offers very pleasant climbing in the low to middle grades on sound metamorphic rock. The area is virtually bird-free.

Access

Turn off the A92 and follow the A975 to a crossroads 3km (2 miles) beyond Newburgh, then turn right onto the B9003 signposted to Collieston. Follow this until just beyond the church where a road on the left leads down to a large car park. This is just north of the harbour and forms the northern boundary of the village. An unusual 1989 sculpture entitled 'Flotsam and Jetsam' is at the end of the car park, created by a Frenchman and described by some locals as being reminiscent of 'a giant tattie masher'.

Beside the sculpture is a little inlet which provides an entertaining preamble to the climbs further north. One route is described but others have been climbed.

Crab's Wall   10m   Difficult   (1949)
Climb the wall to the north side of the little inlet, traversing across right and up on excellent holds. Access problems at high tide. A climb of historic importance in that it was Tom Patey's first ever new route, which he reached from his home in Ellon by bicycle. A small beginning that was to lead to international mountaineering renown.

SMUGGLER'S CLIFF   *(Map Ref 043 287)*

This is the fairly large cliff about 200 metres north of the car park. There is a tidal cave at the base of the main sea-facing wall while a better known cave, Cave Arthur, lies up the slope of the inlet bounding the cliff on the south. In one of the creeks just north of Collieston is a pool called by the fishermen St Catherine's Dub where tradition has always affirmed that the *Santa Caterina*, one of the galleons of the Spanish Armada, was wrecked in 1588.

Scurvy   12m   VS 4c
The cliff forms a south wall where it angles into the inlet of Cave Arthur. This route takes a prominent hanging corner crack near the seaward end. The rock is appalling in places.

The following routes lie on the wall north of the nose of the cliff and the tidal cave. The starts can be reached by crossing the tidal channel going round under the nose to a cave, or by reversing Lookout (Difficult). Both need a low tide.

A third possibility is to abseil. A wooden fence post at the top of the cliff provides a useful belay. The routes are described from left to right. Left of Castaway are two crack lines.

Animal Magnetism   20m   E5 6b **   (1991)
The left-hand crack line. Climb an unprotected arete and use a sidepull to reach up right and clip a peg runner over the roof (quite serious). Relax and crank out the crux moves to a horizontal break. Continue to the top.

Pornograffiti   20m   E3 5c   (1991)
Start up Castaway until established over roof. Step left and continue direct with tricky bulges high up.

Castaway   15m   E2 5b **   (1987)
Right of the cave mouth is an obvious roof. Climb the roof and wall above, gaining the lip of the roof from the left, swinging freely out and up on good holds. An excellent and improbable route, previously aided.

Robinson Crusoe   15m   VS 4c
Climb the hanging chimney at the right end of the roof to a sloping ledge on the left. Climb as directly as possible to the top.

Contrabandeer   15m   HVS 5a *   (1987)
Start at the obvious corner in the centre of the bulging wall and climb up to an overhang, move left and follow the steep quartz streaked headwall on good holds.

Swagbag   15m   HVS 5a **   (1989)
Start as for the previous route, climb the corner and surmount the overhang. Finish directly and steeply on sound holds. A good route, well protected with Friends in horizontal breaks.

Block and Tackle   12m   VS 4c
Starting right of the previous routes, climb diagonally right to a shallow chimney on the skyline. The chimney can also be gained directly with no change of grade.

Lookout   10m   Difficult
This takes a steep line of jugs out right to the edge of the cliff.

There is further potential for routes on the cliff, a big rising girdle, finishing over the roof of the cave being an interesting prospect.

THE GRAIP   *(Map Ref 044 288)*

This is the big shingle bay just north of Smuggler's Cliff, where a fine crag scored by numerous grooves and cracks runs out seawards on the north side. The Graip offers excellent climbing in the lower grades in a pleasant setting. The crag faces south and dries quickly. Apart from some yellow lichen the rock is good, and birds are not a problem (although some nest on the top). Most of the routes described were probably climbed in the 1950s although details are a little vague.

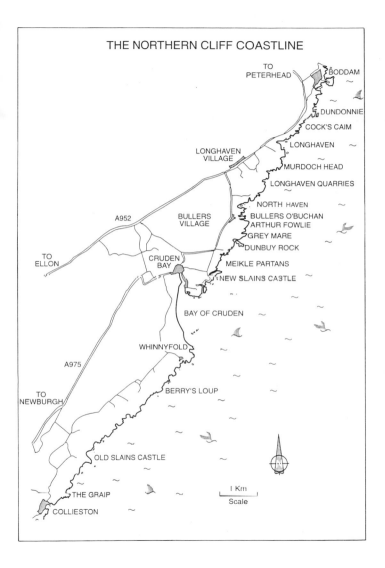

THE NORTHERN CLIFF COASTLINE

TO
PETERHEAD

BODDAM

DUNDONNIE

COCK'S CAIM

LONGHAVEN
VILLAGE

LONGHAVEN

MURDOCH HEAD

LONGHAVEN QUARRIES

A952

BULLERS
VILLAGE

NORTH HAVEN

BULLERS O'BUCHAN

ARTHUR FOWLIE

GREY MARE

DUNBUY ROCK

TO
ELLON

CRUDEN
BAY

MEIKLE PARTANS

NEW SLAINS CASTLE

BAY OF CRUDEN

WHINNYFOLD

A975

BERRY'S LOUP

TO
NEWBURGH

OLD SLAINS CASTLE

THE GRAIP

COLLIESTON

1 Km

Scale

The main part of the crag stands proud from the flanks and is marked by distinct clean-cut corners. The steep left-hand section has probably been climbed, but is of poorer rock. The routes are described from left to right.

Doorway   15m   E2 5b   (1990)
The leftmost route, 7 metres left of the obvious Bogus Corner. Climb a thin crack up to break in the overhang, exit left on good holds to a ledge, then finish up the right-hand crack.

Bogus Corner   12m   Severe
The leftmost of the obvious corner lines right of a smooth section of wall. Useless rusty old pegs are still in place.

Graip and Pillage   15m   Mild VS 4b   (1985)
Climb the hanging subsidiary corner left of Slain's Corner, starting as for that route.

Slain's Corner   15m   E2 5c **   (1984)
The next big corner running the full height of the cliff gives an excellent technical route, sustained and well protected.

The Sensual World   15m   E3 5c *   (1990)
This is based on the hanging corner right of Slain's Corner. Start up Slain's Corner, then go right onto a hanging arete. Continue up the arete over bulges until it is possible to bridge up between the hanging corner and the arete.

The Graip Vine   15m   VS 4c *
Just left of the next main corner is an obvious crack line. Climb this and keep to the left arete to finish.

Spanish Corner   15m   VS 4c **
Climb the main corner, then go left under a roof.

Elbow Groove   15m   Hard Severe
The next obvious clean-cut corner.

Knee Trembler   15m   Hard Severe **
There are two obvious breaks up the steep wall right of Elbow Groove. Start up a bulge, then go up and slightly right past small overlaps.

Bone Shaker   15m   Hard Severe *
The right-hand break. Start up a bulging groove on the right side of a nose, then go up cracks to the top.

The Phantom Graipist   15m   VS 4c *   (1985)
This climbs the wall right of Bone Shaker. Start up a crack, move right to the edge and finish up this.

Crick in the Neck   15m   Severe *
The next fine corner, exiting right at the small final roof.

Graips of Wrath   15m   Hard Severe *
Start as Crick in the Neck. Move out right under a small roof and climb the fine wall above. The crux is at the top.

Bunches of Fives   15m   Hard Severe **
Start up a fine corner-crack left of the far arete, then go straight up.

Far Edge   10m   Very Difficult *
Climb the arete starting up on a ledge to the right.

Faraway Chimney   10m   Difficult
The small right-facing corner bounding the main wall provides a useful descent at high tide for routes on the east side.

Crack Variant   10m   Severe
The crack immediately left of the corner alongside the arete.

Sea-Level Traverse   90m   Difficult **
The traverse of the cliff just above the high tide mark is excellent. For maximum enjoyment start at the seaward end with a high tide and frisky sea. As with most sea-level traverses, holding the 100 metres swimming badge is an advantage.

   A traverse of the cliff has been done at half-height. It is best started at the seaward end and follows horizontal cracks. A rather unsatisfactory HVS 5a.

OLD CASTLE

Old Castle is a small scattering of houses around the Old Castle of Slains, one corner of which is all that still stands. The Castle was blown up in 1594 when James VI marched into the north after the Battle of Glenlivet to reduce the powerful Earls of Huntly and Errol to obedience after their support of a Catholic rebellion. New Slains Castle was built as its replacement in 1664 in its present site just north of Cruden Bay. There is a cannon beside Old Slains Castle believed to have been recovered from the Spanish ship *Santa Catarina*.

Access
Follow the B9003 as for Collieston, then just before the church take the road on the left signposted Whinnyfold. After about 2km (1 mile) take the farm road on the right. Follow this past the farm and go left down a narrow track to the headland of the Castle. Care is required not to cause an obstruction with parked cars.

   The only crag of note at Old Castle is a curious rock separated from the mainland by a boulder beach below the Castle. Access is cut off at high tide. The rock is unusual and sound-looking holds sometimes come away. Birds are also a problem, with the top of the crag usually a mass of gulls. The rock at the top of the face is very loose and there are no suitable belays.

For descent, there is a handy corner-ramp towards the southern end of the broken seaward side (Very Difficult). At higher tide this is unsuitable. There is a dirty mouldering zigzag descent at the landward end. Not surprisingly the area has never gained popularity.

Old Castle Chimney   12m   Very Difficult   (1975)
This is the most prominent chimney-crack in the middle of the main face.

Carrion Laughing   12m   VS 4c *   (1983)
This takes the second clean crack line right of Old Castle Chimney. Go up to and climb the fine crack to a ledge. From a higher ledge finish over a bulge.

Morte d' Arthur   12m   VS 4c   (1983)
Start some 3 metres left of the obvious corner towards the right side of the face (Burnt off Corner). Climb a steep wall and cracks to move left round a bulge and gain a groove leading to the top.

Burnt off Corner   12m   E1 5b *   (1975)
The obvious corner provides a good steep pitch, hard to protect at the bottom.

WHINNYFOLD

Whinnyfold (pronounced locally as 'Finnyfaul') is the next fishing village north of Old Castle. It is perched out on the clifftop overlooking the Skares, a notorious reef upon which many a gallant ship has foundered.

To reach the village follow the A975 just short of Cruden Bay to the signposted road on the right, 1km beyond the prominent isolated church. Follow this road to the first turn-off on the left, signposted Whinnyfold.

BERRY'S LOUP

This is the prominent stack about 1km south of the village. It is a wild and little frequented area, but those making the effort should be rewarded in some way. Berry's Loup refers to the small gap between the stack and parent cliff. Louping on to the stack from the cliff provides an entertaining adventure, although thought is required for getting back up or down to the bottom. The stack can be approached from its north side across easy-angled slabs which are exposed to waves at high tide or in rough seas. The walls facing the stack have obvious possibilities but are heavily birded and messy for much of the year.

Hell's Hole   12m   VS *
At the start of the slabs leading round to the stack is a small cave, at the back of which is a chimney leading to the cliff top. An amusing and unique climb.

The following two routes are on the seaward (east) wall of the stack, starting on the huge platform which can be reached by scrambling from the base of the stack. To descend, it is possible to abseil back down the route or down the gap between stack and cliff. A third option is to climb across the gap onto the parent cliff and so to the top

The Berrys   10m   HVS 5a   (1986)
Climb up the centre of the east wall of the stack. Trend right, then go straight up. Strenuous.

Cyndi Louper   10m   VS 4c   (1986)
Climb the south-east arete, moving left at the top to finish.

SILKIE'S CLIFF
This cliff is on the opposite side (north) of the small inlet from the descent to Berry's Loup Stack. Descent is via Forlorn Chimney or by abseil. The rock is metamorphic; northwards from here the rock changes to pink Longhaven granite. Silkie's Cliff is also badly affected by birds. The best time to visit is around March, when the winter storms have given the face a good clean.

Seal's Show   20m   VS 4b
The cliff has a distinct left arete. Climb up left round this onto the face above the small lagoon. Climb up left to break over the upper bulge.

Reach for the Sky   12m   HVS 5a **
The big left-facing corner line right of the previous route. The headwall is strenuous and exposed.

Flying Crack   12m   VS 4c *
The prominent crack line left of the obvious Forlorn Chimney gives a good route.

Forlorn Chimney   12m   Difficult
The chimney in the middle of the cliff leading to the prominent notch; this is also a handy descent.

Wilse's Gander   12m   Severe *   (1986)
Climb the hanging corner right of Forlorn Chimney.

Wire Nest Corner   12m   Mild Severe
The prominent corner towards the right side of the cliff.

Silk Cut   12m   VS 5a   (1986)
Climb the crack in the right wall of Wire Nest Corner.

Cruden Bay to North Haven

Relatively small and broken crags run north from Cruden Bay to Fulmar Wall and Meikle Partans, which are the first important climbing grounds. Little of note has been discovered, as much of the rock is brittle and poor. The scenery is very fine, with the ruin of New Slain's Castle providing a familiar landmark on its lonely headland. It was here that Bram Stoker wrote *Dracula*; to visit on a wild day one can see why.

SLAIN'S CASTLE

The castle is perched on the brink of the crags on a headland known as The Bow. There are two interesting local curios here, just north of the castle. At the mouth of the Longhaven (a very long and narrow inlet almost isolating the headland), is a tower of shaley rock, The Sugar Loaf, which is still unclimbed. Near the far end of the promontory is a fragile double rock archway, The Twa E'en. Further still is another small archway with an interesting and fierce short wall beyond it. Heading up towards Fulmar Wall only one route has been recorded on a small wall 200 metres south of Fulmar Wall, above a wide rocky shelf with large rounded boulders.

In Flight Entertainment   8m   E2 5c   (1989)
Start in the middle of the red wall and move right to the arete, standing on a spike. Move up and left below a wide crack in the overhang, then finish straight up on jugs. The rock is poor.

FULMAR WALL TO DUNBUY ROCK

This is one of the best stretches on the coast for either the beginner or a first visit, with several friendly and open crags on excellent granite. There is a prominent bend and parking area about 2km (1 mile) north of the village of Cruden Bay on the A975. From here, a track leads east to an overgrown level disused tip which overlooks an inlet on the south, the Twa Havens. The track is not marked on the O.S. map. Fulmar Wall lies to the south-east, Meikle Partans below and east of the level area and the other areas are to the north along a path.

FULMAR WALL   *(Map Ref 105 368)*

This excellent cliff has a large number of routes at a variety of grades. The cliff catches a lot of sunshine and is sheltered from big swells by Bowfart's Ridge. It is virtually bird-free in the nesting season and only the north end of the cliff is tidal. The only real disadvantage is an exposed and slightly awkward descent which is guaranteed to put off the novice.

From the open area at the end of the track, go south-east down into a little col, where a path leads onto the headland. Descend a small gully at the south-east of the headland for about 8m until it is possible to go left (facing out) across a bad step and down a V-groove to the foot of the wall. Alternatively, at low tide, descend south from the col and skirt the shoreline to reach the cliff. The wall runs away north-east gaining in height.

Pulsar   10m   VS 4c   (1984)
Climb the obvious leaning black groove above the foot of the descent groove.

Male Menopause   10m   HVS 4c   (1984)
Immediately right is a large slab. Climb its left arete, starting at the break.

The following three routes all use a solitary peg as the only real protection.

Quark   10m   E2 5a *   (1984)
Start below the peg and surmount an awkward bulge with a subsidiary overlap. Move up to the break and, after clipping the peg, traverse left to climb up left of an overlap to the top.

The Excited Atom   10m   E1 5b *   (1983)
Follow Quark over the bulge. Gain the narrow ledge, then climb direct to the top passing the peg runner to its left.

Particle Accelerator   10m   E2 5b   (1984)
Right again is a vague groove leading to a shallow corner. Pull over the bulge onto the slab, then climb to the base of the shallow corner. Clip the peg, then climb the shield of rock right of the corner.

Neutrino   10m   VS 4c   (1975)
Launch awkwardly onto the slab beneath a short right-facing corner. Climb the corner, then finish up the left side of a jutting roof.

Last of the Summer Wine   10m   E2 6a *   (1983)
Right of Neutrino there are two conspicuous thin crack lines. This is the left-hand crack, taken on its left to finish easily right of the jutting nose.

Norah Batty   10m   E3 6a   (1984)
Climb the right-hand crack with difficulty onto the easy ground common with the previous route.

Compo   12m   E4 5c   (1984)
The bulging wall direct right of Norah Batty. Start up an overhanging crack, then go straight up to finish at a pointed block. Serious.

The Knacker's Yard   20m   E2 5c *   (1988)
A line left of and parallel to Knacker's Crack, taking the exciting finger crack left of its top section. Start right of Compo and climb up and right to a black groove (often wet), then cross it to gain the easy ramp. The overhanging finger crack provides a superb finale.

Knacker's Crack   20m   E1 5b **   (1975)
An obvious shelf runs up left across the wall (Ledge Route). This climb takes the fierce crack line which crosses the shelf and develops into a chimney-crack. A belay can be taken on the shelf if desired. Despite its escapability, this is a route of distinct character, and both halves are hard and strenuous.

Knackered   10m   E3 5c   (1991)
Right of the lower section of Knacker's Crack is a short hanging corner. Gain this from the left and climb it to belay on the shelf.

Ledge Route   35m   Very Difficult   (1986)
Climb indefinite rocks in the centre of the wall to the shelf. Go away left up the shelf to an awkward finish.

Oh Well   20m   Hard Severe   (1969)
This goes up the yellow cracked left-slanting ramp in the upper part of the wall, starting up indefinite rock. It is possible to start further left and take in a small triangular roof at half-height with no change in grade.

Oh Well Part Two   20m   HVS 5a   (1982)
The twin line right of Oh Well.

Bird's Nest Route   20m   Severe *   (1967)
Follow a vague recessed fault directly up the wall to finish by an obvious V-scoop. Deviations are required to avoid steeper sections.

Intrusion   20m   Mild VS 4b **   (1969)
Right of Bird's Nest Route the wall bulges out. Climb the line of a quartz band to a big flake, then proceed steeply to the ledge above. Step right and go over a bulge to finish left by an awkward overhung shelf.

Albatross   20m   Severe **   (1969)
Start up a steep scoop right of Intrusion and finish directly up a steep wall on big jugs.

The Weight   20m   Hard Severe ***   (1970)
A real classic up very steep rock in a fine position. Climb an awkward black bulge at the right end of the cliff, then go up over two more bulges to finish straight up the wall on huge jugs.

The Weight, Fulmar Wall (Climber, Duncan Sutherland)

Billy the Kid   20m   HVS 5b **   (1973)
Start up The Weight and move up right to an obvious tongue-like flake. Climb the
shallow hanging corner (crux) to finish up a final steep corner.

The Cowboy   20m   E2 5c *   (1990)
Climb Billy the Kid to the block, then traverse right, feet on the lip of the roof, to
pull into a groove (crux). Move right into another groove. Climb this, exit left, then
move slightly right and finish up a steep intimidating wall just right of Billy the Kid.

The Shaft   20m   VS 4c   (1971)
A good line going up the hanging cleft between the Beak and Shadow Slab. Gain
the cleft awkwardly from the steep rocks to the right and climb it to the top.

Girdle Traverse   60m   VS 4c   (1969)
Take the easiest line from left to right, reversing the upper part of Ledge Route
to start and finishing by the steep corner of Billy the Kid.

SHADOW SLAB
The right arete of Fulmar Wall is The Beak, and around the corner from this is
Shadow Slab. Low tide is required to traverse round from Fulmar Wall. The slab
is climbable at most points.

Left Out Route   20m   Hard Severe   (1982)
This is the neglected slabby corner between the slabs proper and the shaft. The
start is awkward.

Left Edge Route   20m   Very Difficult   (1969)
Go up the edge of the slabs right of Left Out Route.

Route One   25m   Very Difficult *   (1969)
Go up just right of Left Edge to finish by an obvious break in the upper overlap.

Route Two   35m   Very Difficult   (1969)
Traverse right just above sea-level for 12 metres, then climb a line of cracks
going up and right. Rather loose and grassy at the top.

FLUTED BUTTRESS
This is the steep buttress facing south on the west side of the descent to Fulmar
Wall. The rock is poorer than elsewhere at Meikle Partans. It has only one route
discounting its easy left ridge.

Jammy Piece   10m   VS 4c   (1975)
The buttress is defined on the right by a narrow beaky rib. Follow the bulging
crack tucked into the left side of the rib. Continue up by a flake on the left to finish
by a short crack.

*Brian Sprunt (leading) and Charlie Macleod on the first ascent of Yahoochie,
Craig Stirling, in 1982*

The ridge that shelters Fulmar Wall from the full force of the sea is Bowfart's Ridge. A past guidebook noted that its crest "gives an interesting romp over a small tower to the seaward end". And, "on the south-east side of the ridge a pleasant traverse can be had just above the high water mark, some 60 metres long of Mild Severe standard". Whilst one or two routes have been done more recently on fine rock on this face, they are escapable and unsatisfactory.

MEIKLE PARTANS   *(Map Ref 106 369)*

Situated below and east of the level area at the end of the approach track, Meikle Partans faces straight out to sea and is easily reached round its northern end where a short scrambling descent leads onto a ramp below the first few routes. The climbs are described from north to south.

1   Boardman's Crack   10m   E2 5b   (1983)
The first little crack line reached from the north gives a strenuous climb.

2   Epistrophe   10m   VS 4c *   (1968)
A fine little route going up the first steep buttress. Swing up an awkward overhanging crack and move straight up to finish by an awkward bulge. There is an easier start on the right and an alternative finish on the left.

3   The Bridge   10m   Mild VS 4b *   (1968)
Left of the previous route is a big overhang. Climb a hard bulging wall to reach the corner left of the overhang. Climb the corner to exit out to an easy shelf.

4   Left-hand Variation: VS 4c
Continue up the small hanging corner above. Another alternative is to traverse right along the lip of the overhang from the corner to climb a crack in the arete to the top (VS 4c).

5   Dungo   10m   Hard Severe   (1971)
Climb awkwardly up the vague scarred fault left of The Bridge.

6   Slanting Crack   10m   Moderate   (1967)
The obvious crack on the easier rocks left of Dungo. The start is awkward; the right-hand groove gives a harder finish (Difficult).

There are five routes squeezed onto the fine vertical wall left of Slanting Crack.

7   The Band of Hope   10m   HVS 5a *   (1968)
A well-known little problem, now overshadowed by Strawclutcher's Wall, which takes the line of a quartz band at the right side of the wall. Pull over a bulge just right of the band, then follow it to finish up an easier bulge. Precarious, with awkward protection.

MEIKLE PARTANS

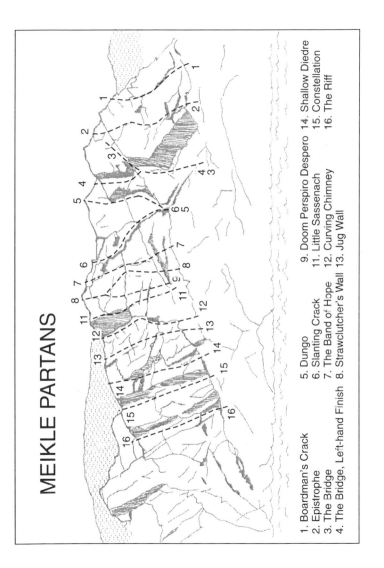

1. Boardman's Crack
2. Epistrophe
3. The Bridge
4. The Bridge, Left-hand Finish
5. Dungo
6. Slanting Crack
7. The Band of Hope
8. Strawclutcher's Wall
9. Doom Perspiro Despero
11. Little Sassenach
12. Curving Chimney
13. Jug Wall
14. Shallow Diedre
15. Constellation
16. The Riff

8   Strawclutcher's Wall   10m   E1 5b *   (1978)
Climb directly up the wall left of Band of Hope to a large flake. Make a hard move
up and left to reach a slanting crack. Traverse left and go up to the obvious finish.

9   Doom Perspiro Despero   10m   E4 6c   (1984)
A direct line up the wall left of Strawclutcher's. Climb the wall past a finger pocket
to the break of Flaky Traverse (runners). Make a long reach for a tiny finger hold
up on the left and use this to reach the next break and so to the top. Nasty.

10   Flaky Traverse   10m   VS 4c   (1971)
This traverses across the wall from left to right. Climb up on good holds near the
left edge. Traverse right using a thin horizontal crack to gain the band below the
top bulge.

11   Little Sassenach   10m   E1 5b   (1983)
This climbs the left edge of the wall. Start as for Flaky Traverse but continue
directly up the wall to an obvious flake. Pull out left onto the overhanging wall
and make strenuous moves up and right to gain the top of the flake. Go right and
up to finish.

12   Curving Chimney   10m   Moderate *   (1967)
The fine chimney left of the vertical wall provides a handy descent route.

13   Jug Wall   10m   Moderate *   (1968)
Climb a short crack left of Curving Chimney and the steep wall above on good
holds.

14   Shallow Diedre   10m   VS 4c *   (1971)
The corner left of Jug Wall. The crux is the strenuous bulge.

15   Constellation   15m   Severe *   (1967)
A good line up the deeper corner to the left; reachy at the top.

16   The Riff   12m   Very Difficult   (1967)
The obvious diedre left of Constellation.

Further left is a short Very Difficult groove. From the shelf below The Riff, it is
possible to continue traversing across a steep wall (Difficult) to reach easy ground
overlooking a narrow inlet. The broken wall above has limited interest. At very
low tide it is possible to continue the traverse along the back of the inlet to gain
Shadow Slab on the other side (Difficult). Above and behind the left end of the
main cliff is a small buttress with a thin central crack: **Scum Again** (10m VS 4c)

CRAB'S WALL
This wall of excellent rock some 50 metres north of Epistrophe, facing out to sea,
presents four crack lines, which are (from left to right) VS 5a, HVS 5b, HVS 5b
and VS 4c. Just south of Crab's Wall is a small problem crack, HVS 5c.

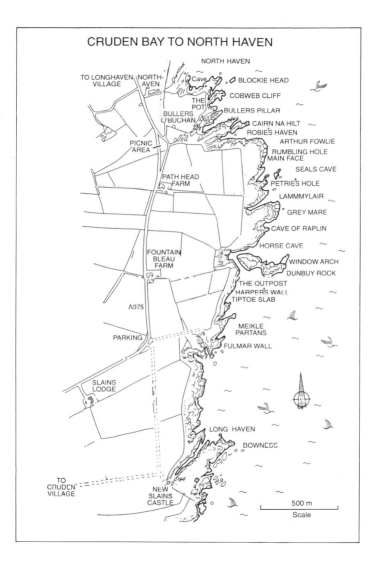

CRUDEN BAY TO NORTH HAVEN

NORTH HAVEN

TO LONGHAVEN — NORTH-AVEN
VILLAGE

Cave — BLOCKIE HEAD

COBWEB CLIFF

THE POT

BULLERS PILLAR

BULLERS
O'BUCHAN

CAIRN NA HILT

ROBIE'S HAVEN

ARTHUR FOWLIE

PICNIC AREA

RUMBLING HOLE
MAIN FACE

SEALS CAVE

PATH HEAD FARM

PETRIE'S HOLE

LAMMMYLAIR

GREY MARE

CAVE OF RAPLIN

HORSE CAVE

FOUNTAIN BLEAU FARM

WINDOW ARCH

DUNBUY ROCK

THE OUTPOST
HARPER'S WALL
TIPTOE SLAB

A975

MEIKLE PARTANS

PARKING

FULMAR WALL

SLAINS LODGE

LONG HAVEN

BOWNESS

TO CRUDEN VILLAGE

NEW SLAINS CASTLE

500 m
Scale

FLAKY BUTTRESS

This is the steep buttress situated on the north side of the small inlet immediately north of Meikle Partans. There are three routes on poor rock.

Blockhead   10m   VS 4c   (1983)
Follow the obvious clean layback crack near the right edge of the buttress.

Waiting for a Train   10m   HVS 4c   (1983)
The best of the routes, following the obvious ramp line in the centre of the face. Surmount the block at the top of the ramp to gain the crack above. Climb this to the top.

A Question of Balance   12m   E1 5c   (1983)
It is questionable whether the route name applies to the difficulty or longevity of the route. A poor route with a hard start, which follows the obvious crack line near the left edge of the buttress. Climb the overhanging right wall of the chimney bordering the buttress on the left, then pull out right into the crack. Follow the loose cracks to the top.

North of Flaky Buttress is a small south-facing trapezoidal wall of good rock. The crack on the left is VS 4b and the centre of the wall is HVS 5b.

TIPTOE SLAB AND HARPER'S WALL

The next two crags lie a couple of hundred metres to the north, beyond a rock spur running out into the sea. Tiptoe Slab is divided from Harper's Wall to its north by a rocky hollow. Both walls face straight out to sea and their tops show up slightly as rocky crests. Finding both cliffs can be difficult on first acquaintance. Approaching from the south a good landmark is the Outpost with the wide ugly crack of Parallax Crack looking south. Harper's Wall lies 100 metres south and Tiptoe Slab 50 metres further south. Both Tiptoe Slab and Harper's Wall are largely free of birds in the nesting season.

TIPTOE SLAB   *(Map Ref 107 372)*

Tiptoe Slab is very steep. The rock is variable but quite dodgy and brittle in places. Generally, it is better towards the left side. Descent can be made on either side and the slab is only affected by the tide in high rough seas. The climbs are described from left to right.

Whimsy   10m   Severe   (1980)
Climb the thinner crack line just left of the much more pronounced line of Tiptoe Crack, starting up a short leaning corner.

Tiptoe Crack   10m   Severe *   (1968)
The obvious left-slanting crack gives good climbing.

Sugar Plum Fairy   13m   Severe *   (1980)
Climb cracks between Tiptoe Crack and Brittle Wall, starting at the foot of Tiptoe
and trending right to follow cracks to the top. The rock and protection are quite
good, unlike Brittle Wall.

Brittle Wall   15m   VS 4c *   (1968)
A direct flaky line up the highest part of the slab, with a prominent flake in the
centre. A serious lead with unreliable rock and protection, and small holds.

Snap, Crackle and Pop   15m   HVS 4c   (1980)
A badly protected eliminate up the face between Brittle Wall and Chinese Dance.
Start up Chinese Dance, then climb straight up the wall starting up the flakes
right of Brittle Wall.

The Chinese Dance   15m   VS 4c   (1980)
The obvious little right-bounding corner of the slab. Cross over the slab by the
diagonal crack to gain the base of the corner (easy escape right) Climb the
corner.

HARPER'S WALL   *(Map Ref 107 373)*

This is an attractive steep wall with good rock and quite a variety of climbing. The
base of the wall is undercut, so all the routes are quite hard to start. The routes
are accessible except at a very high tide or during a rough south-easterly swell.
The left-hand part of the crag is a superb 10m cracked wall. The routes are
described from left to right; they can be approached from either the south or
(more usually) the north end. Access is described in the Tiptoe Slab introduction,
above.

1   Riesenwand   6m   HVS 5a   (1984)
The line up the centre left of the steep wall left of White Ape.

2   White Ape   8m   HVS 5a   (1979)
The leftmost of the obvious cracks up the wall is strenuous with a bold start.

3   Free Spirit   10m   E3 5c **   (1981)
The next crack right of White Ape is strenuous and difficult to start but quickly
relents at an obvious horizontal break (possible escape). The route finishes up
the technical wall more or less directly.

4   Silent Partner   10m   E2 5b **   (1981)
The next crack right of Free Spirit. Make a very strenuous move over the initial
bulge, belt in a runner, then make a few moves right into the main crack system
and climb it to the top.

5   One, Two, Three Go   10m   HVS 5a **   (1979)
The fine steep groove right of Silent Partner, just left of the obvious break of
Kevin's Fault, gives an excellent pitch with the usual primitive delights of the
bottomless start. Dwarfs may have to adopt a flying leap.

6   Urban Gorilla   13m   E3 5c **   (1984)
Start up the left-hand start of Kevin's Fault, then swing left to a big pocket on the
lip of the roof. Hand traverse left along a flake, pull up and continue up the wall
to gain Kevin's Fault. A bold and strenuous undertaking.

7   Kevin's Fault   20m   HVS 5a   (1969/1979)
The obvious diagonal break slanting up left. Start up the right-hand gangway, or
the corner on the left (E1 5b).

8   Rock Mushroom   15m   E1 5b   (1979)
Start up the diagonal gangway, then move up the right wall to join a left-slanting
crack line.

9   Ché   15m   E2 5c *   (1987)
This climb is based on the obvious curving crack on the upper wall between Rock
Mushroom and Renegade. Climb the corner of Kevin's Fault to the ramp. Cross
the ramp, follow Rock Mushroom to where it goes left, then climb straight up a
crack (easier on right) to a ledge. Climb the curving crack, pulling out right to
finish.

10   Making Windows   15m   E6 6b **   (1992)
Climb the obvious crack below Renegade's upper wall (crucial RPs), finishing
right from the final pocket to reach ledges on Renegade.

11   Renegade   20m   VS 4c **   (1969)
A fine steep climb up the highest part of the wall. Start at the right end and skirt
the initial bulge by scrambling up right and taking a steep flake traverse left. Move
up to a prominent halfway ledge, then finish straight up the bulging wall above.

12   Walkabout   20m   VS 4c   (1969)
Start along the traverse of Renegade, then climb the centre of the fine wall
above. There is a more direct start up a little corner below the traverse at 5b.

13   Orangutang   35m   HVS 5a, 4c   (1985)
A girdle of the wall. Go up White Ape to the ledge, then continue right at the same
height to belay on the ramp of Kevin's Fault. Go right to the ledge of Renegade
and finish up the right-curving overlap.

HARPER'S WALL

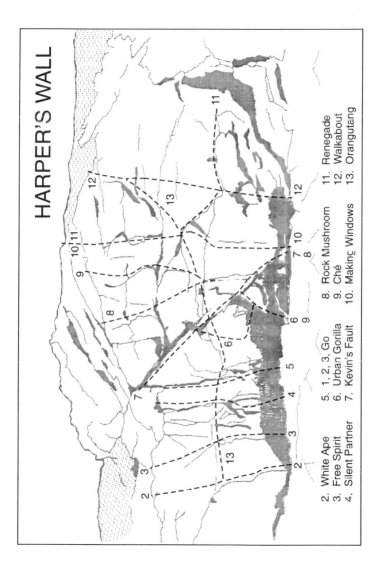

2. White Ape
3. Free Spirit
4. Silent Partner

5. 1, 2, 3, Go
6. Urban Gorilla
7. Kevin's Fault

8. Rock Mushroom
9. Ché
10. Making Windows

11. Renegade
12. Walkabout
13. Orangutang

THE OUTPOST

This is the prominent jutting buttress about 100 metres north of Harper's Wall, overlooking the mouth of the Dunbuy Channel. The rock needs careful handling in places. The best access is by a scramble down just north of Harper's Wall.

Parallax Crack   20m   E3 5c **   (1981)
The challenging line up the big ugly crack on the impressive overhanging south face of the buttress gives a very strenuous undertaking. Start by a small rib just left of the crack. Climb a bulge and follow the crack up and right to a final struggle up the wide section.

Outrider   25m   E2 5b   (1980)
The line of cracks over a bulge right of Parallax Crack. Climb cracks over a small bulge to an awkward niche under the main bulge. Pull out right and follow the crack to a platform. Move up right to climb final short wall by a crack.

Hot Rats   30m   VS 4c *   (1982)
The wall just round the edge of the buttress provides a good steep route which is not accessible at high tide. Starting right of the arete, climb trending slightly right until, a short traverse at a break leads left onto the arete. Go straight up to a ledge, gain a higher ledge, then finish up the short wall crack of Outrider.

It is possible to climb the buttress right of Hot Rats without much technical difficulty, but this cannot be recommended as the rock is very poor. It is possible to traverse the tall wall overlooking the Dunbuy Channel (165m Very Difficult) to reach the boulder beach used for access to Dunbuy Rock.

DUNBUY ROCK   *(Map Ref 103 372)*

Dunbuy, with its gigantic natural window, is one of the most spectacular landmarks on the coast. A sanctuary for sea birds, its extensive grassy top is covered with a thick cushion of guano. The rock is cut off from the mainland by a channel some 30m wide at its narrowest point. This means that it is seldom visited, but for climbers with a boat, dinghy or whatever, a day's visit makes for an entertaining and adventurous outing. In summer, the place is a screeching madhouse of birds. The pebble beach opposite the west end of the rock is reached by descending a grassy trough. There is a fixed bolt on the landing rocks at the western tip of the rock to which a lifeline across the narrowest point of the channel can be fixed. It should be mentioned that currents sweeping through the channel are sometimes very strong.

On landing, the crumbling flanks of the Rock are avoided by traversing round to the northern side where easier slopes lead to the flat top. A vegetatious buttress provides the first opportunity. Nothing of great significance has been climbed on Dunbuy but there is a very impressive wall on the north-west side of the arch.

THE WESTERN MASS

This has only a couple of climbs. The best wall lies on the Window and is reached from the east side.

Pioneers' Traverse   30m   VS   (1973)
The first promising wall on the north side has an obvious traverse line below overhangs, climbed from east to west. The line is unrepeated and the grade uncertain. Overlooking the window further on is a clean undercut slab.

The Hanging Slab   20m   Severe   (1975)
The slab is reached by climbing down the western side. Climb it by the obvious groove.

THE EASTERN MASS

The rock is generally superior on this part of Dunbuy. The whole mass can be traversed not high above sea-level. This is interesting, if largely easy, and familiarises the climber with the layout of the place.

Eastern Circuit   600m   Severe
The best start is perhaps the north-east tip. Go south and find a way along under a series of overhanging walls and shelves and across escape slabs (descent route) to a platform in the gulch of the Window. Cross the great eastern slab, passing through the Window (tricky) to gain ledges on the other side. Continue easily under steep walls to easy slopes on the north.

There are three routes on the eastern rocks to the north of the complex overhanging walls and shelves section.

PIRATE'S BUTTRESS

This is the most northerly buttress, the overhanging back wall of a tiny inlet.

Jolly Rogerer   20m   HVS 5a *   (1981)
The obvious traverse line left below the upper roof gives a good little route with a fine hand traverse. Move left down a shelf to a corner. Climb this, then take the exposed traverse away left and continue up to the top.

The remaining two climbs lie south of Pirate's Buttress.

Far East Crack   13m   VS 4c   (1972)
A line of twin cracks taking the obvious break in the next rock mass south of Pirate's.

North Sea Buttress   20m   Severe   (1972)
The ill-defined leaning buttress south of the previous route can be climbed by moving onto its slabby right edge.

The overhanging walls to the south can be breached at several points by slanting shelves of various standards, which are interesting and on excellent rock but very short. The slabs between the walls and the Window are straightforward, giving a good descent route for the Window climbs. The rock needs care at the top.

THE WINDOW CLIMBS

Jelly Fish   40m   VS 4c **   (1975)
The left side of the great south-east slab gives an excellent climb on small holds, but it is serious for its grade with little protection. Starting from below the arch at a platform, climb up left until overlooking the northerly Arch Corner. Move up to the arch, then finish by the southerly corner in a superb situation. To make a safe belay an extra rope is needed to reach rocks on the far side of the arch.

Arch Corner   20m   Severe   (1975)
The slab on the north east side of the arch can be reached by traversing the south-east slab or else from the northern side. Follow the corner below the arch, moving out left at the top. This top part is very grassy, forcing tedious insecure detours especially if damp.

Hand Rail Slab   40m   Difficult   (1980)
The slabs left of Arch Corner. Gain the line of a flake crack running up left, follow this and go up slabby rock which degenerates to grass.

Dunbuy Diedre   45m   VS 4b *   (1972)
The wall opposite the south-east slab is in general very steep. This route takes the main break of the big diedre, a striking feature from the mainland. This whole section is thronged with kittiwakes in summer and the nest residue is slow to wash away. Climb down to the base of the diedre (low tide is required but it looks possible to traverse in slightly higher). Climb the corner to finish awkwardly on the exposed left wall.

The wall left of the diedre is very steep with an odd knobbly formation lacking in lines or cracks (heavily nested). The fine wall just right of the diedre should give a good pitch with better climbing than the diedre. Right again a curving flake crack offers a surprisingly easy way up such a steep wall.

The Bender   35m   VS 4b   (1975)
The flake is steep but only Severe. The climb finishes as for the Diedre, this being the crux.

SEAFARERS' WALL

This is a steep wall on the eastern mass north of the north-east slab of the window. The climbs are described from left to right. The slanting groove on the left is taken by Varmint; no details are available.

Vagitus   20m   E2 5a *   (1982)
This takes the obvious flake formation up the rather blank-looking central wall, left of twin slanting cracks. It is seriously unprotected and messy.

Valgus   15m   Very Difficult   (1982)
Climb the obvious right-slanting shelf system right of the thin slanting cracks.

GREYMARE SLABS   *(Map Ref 112 375)*

No recorded routes have been made on the cliffs between the boulder beach and the headland of Greymare. Set in the middle is the gulch of the Horse Cave, and immediately north of the beach is the Cave of Dunbuy. The rock north of Horse Cave is superb but easy, terminating on the easy slabs of the Back of Raplin. In contrast, the walls to the south are fierce and loose. Smooth walls around the Horse Cave have stopped traversing attempts. The quarried rocks overlooking the small inlet just south of Greymare offer little continuous climbing. The impressive shaft in the back of the inlet forms a tall and narrow inner chamber — the Cave of Raplin.

Greymare Slabs presents the most attractive sweep of slabs on the north-east coast, providing very enjoyable climbing in the lower grades. The rock is exceptionally rough and moderate in angle. The slabs are clear of birds all the year round. The cliff faces east, straight out to sea, on the peninsula north of Dunbuy Rock about 1km south of the hamlet of Bullers of Buchan.

Access
Either continue round the coast from Meikle Partans onto the headland north of Dunbuy, or approach from the Bullers of Buchan (slightly faster). The coastguard hut marked on the O.S. map was demolished in a recent storm. From the headland, the top of the slabs can be seen as a rocky crest. It is best to leave rucksacs near the north end.

The climbs mainly take crack lines, but harder artificial variants can be made between the routes described. Freak waves come very high here in rough seas and the slabs dip straight into the water — no place for a slip. There are three distinct slabs, the main central one being defined by the big diedres of Amen Corner to the north and Groovin' High to the south. The northern slab is broken and useful for descent, although beginners may prefer to abseil.

1   Klacktovededstene   160m   Difficult *   (1967)
This girdle of the three slabs, following an obvious natural line, provides a good introduction. Climb down a huge V-notch at the north end of the cliff until a traverse following a line of jugs leads south. A descending fault leads to the base of Amen Corner (45m). Continue along the fault across the main slab to the foot of the great diedre of Groovin' High. Here a steep tower (The Aiguille du Trou) is partly separated from the slab by a gaping crevasse. Climb the tower by its seaward side, or, in high seas, by the green chimney behind. Leave the tower

by a short shelf on the abutting vertical wall to gain the third slab. Go diagonally left up this to finish up a detached flake on the skyline. A harder and lower finish can be made by traversing past the Aiguille along under a steep wall to a final awkward swing off the cliff down the terminal overhang (Hard Severe). A finish can then be made by Gobbledygook or Ledgeway if desired.

2   Amen Corner   30m   Difficult *   (1967)
This clean-cut diedre is an excellent beginners' route and a quick way of descent for the experienced (potentially even quicker for the inexperienced).

   On the main slab between Amen Corner and Groovin' High, there are five climbs following the most continuous crack lines.

3   Ornithology   30m   Difficult **   (1967)
Left of the rib overlooking Amen Corner are twin crack lines slanting up slightly right and converging below the final wall. Climb either of these cracks and surmount the bulge of the wall above, then easier rock to the top.

4   Ostrichism   30m   Difficult *
Climb the left-slanting crack between the twin cracks of Ornithology and the prominent quartz crack of Airegin. The easiest way up the final wall lies on the left.

5   Airegin   30m   Difficult **   (1967)
The most pronounced line up the slab, a quartz crack running up the centre, forms a ladder of quartz which joins Ostrichism below the top wall.

6   Straight-No-Chaser   30m   Severe *   (1967)
The faint crack left of Airegin is delicate, especially if climbed direct.

7   Oleo   30m   Hard Severe *   (1967)
The next crack to the left, close to Groovin' High.

8   Groovin' High   35m   Severe **   (1967)
The classic corner-crack of the great diedre provides a popular climb. Climb the corner above the expectant mouth of the crevasse, encountering a layback crack at the top. From the recess escape is possible but the steep fault on the left provides a good finish. This climb can be damp when the others are dry.

9   Nagless Crack   25m   E3 6a *   (1983)
A vicious climb taking the obvious groove in the overhanging left wall of Groovin' High. Start below the layback section of Groovin' High. Climb a crack steeply to enter the groove which is followed more easily to the top.

GREYMARE SLABS

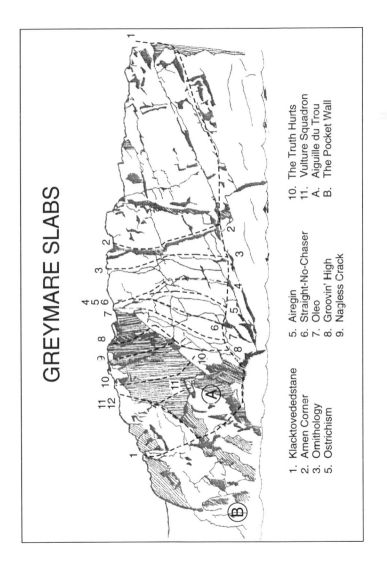

1. Klacktovededstane
2. Amen Corner
3. Ornithology
5. Ostrichism

5. Airegin
6. Straight-No-Chaser
7. Oleo
8. Groovin' High
9. Nagless Crack

10. The Truth Hurts
11. Vulture Squadron
A. Aiguille du Trou
B. The Pocket Wall

10   The Truth Hurts   20m   E5 6b ***   (1985)
This takes the centre of the steep wall of lovely golden rock left of Nagless Crack.
Start below and slightly right of twin cracks. Follow the obvious line to reach these
cracks which lead to the top. Unremittingly strenuous with no rests.

11   Vulture Squadron   20m   E2 5c **   (1985)
At the bottom left of the wall is a left-curving crack line. Start immediately above
the crevasse below Groovin' High. The crack overhangs at first and then is
delicate. After this section escape is possible but the best awaits. Take the
shallow continuation corner just right of the arete to finish steeply.

12   Ginhouse   35m   Severe *   (1967)
The exposed edge of the third slab, overlooking Groovin' High. Climb the Aiguille
du Trou by its seaward side or, less pleasantly, by the green chimney. A short
shelf leads onto the slab. Climb thinly up the slab (best and easiest close to the
edge) to finish up the impending nose direct on good holds in a fine situation.

The Aiguille du Trou has some short problems on its north side. A slanting
groove on the left is HVS 5a whilst the slab right of this is also 5a, with a lurch
across the crevasse to start.

THE POCKET WALL
A steep short wall of lovely pink rock can be reached by continuing the traverse
round below the Aiguille du Trou and the third slab just above the high tide mark.
The routes are well worth the visit and are described from right to left.

Dare   10m   E1 5a *   (1985)
The line of thin flakes curving left at the right-hand side of the wall, finishing at a
vast flake jug. Bold.

Pocket Wall   10m   E1 5b *   (1980)
Climb the wall left of Dare steeply, starting beside a small rock pocket.

Golden Handshake   10m   E4 6b **   (1993)
Climb the fine groove between Haricot Wall and Pocket Wall, with an HB6 runner
in the right-hand crack.

Haricot   10m   HVS *   (1980)
The obvious peapod groove on the left side of the wall.

Whispering Wind   10m   E2 5c   (1985)
The arete left of Haricot.

THE SOUTHERN ROCKS

This face is reached by a simple scramble down to sea-level from the top of the slabs.

Ledgeway 35m Difficult

Start up the obvious fault near sea-level and move up right onto a broad ledge. Go along this onto the slabs to finish at the flake of Klacktovededstene.

Gobbledygook 25m Severe

Start up the fault of Ledgeway and move up left to a bulging crack. Jam up this to an exit left, or finish up Klacktovededstene flake.

THE NORTHERN ROCKS

The rocks leading along towards the deep inlet of Lammylair are characterised by chimneys and aretes dropping straight into the sea. This makes access difficult. At the mouth of the inlet lies the first route.

Three Steps 30m Severe (1985)

Start at the foot of the V-notch descended by Klacktovededstene. Ascend the seaward edge north of the gully on large holds to a ledge. The steep wall above is taken in the middle (hard) or by the left-hand crack (easier). Climb the final wall direct on good holds, avoiding the easier alternative to the right.

The Iron Mare 40m VS 4b * (1975)

This is the first elegant swooping arete (the most easterly). From the vicinity of the descent notch of Klacktovededstene, slant down moderate rock to the base of the chimney alongside. Step across the gulch and swing onto the vertical lower tower. Climb the impending wall to a fine platform and finish up the arete (which is quite straightforward).

The Chute 40m Hard Severe * (1976)

This is the chimney on the left (east) side of the arete. The overhang can be turned on the right but is best climbed direct. An enjoyable pitch.

Doos Chimney 25m Severe (1980)

Climb the hidden chimney tucked behind the Iron Mare arete direct. It can be reached by climbing diagonally down from the top of the tower of Iron Mare, or (more difficult) by a traverse round below the impending nose of the tower. (A variant of Iron Mare goes up the side of the nose hereabouts.)

Sidekick 20m Severe (1980)

A trifling corner crack on the slabby face right of Doos Chimney. This is on the left flank of the wedge buttress used to start traversing into Lammylair. Both Sidekick and Doos Chimney are probably accessible from the wedge buttress side.

LAMMYLAIR

This is the deep and spectacular inlet just north of Greymare and south of Seals' Caves. Much of the rock is unsuited for climbing but some worthwhile routes have been picked out. The head of the inlet is encircled by repulsive walls and so far no traverse has been pushed right into the back. It contains a cave, a pile of big boulders, and some rubbish dumped from above. The north wall is slabby and broken but contains five climbs. The south wall is more dramatic. It is steepest and cleanest in the centre where there is an arching cave, the home of a band of shags.

THE NORTH SIDE

Descent is made by an easy pavement of slab overlooking the mouth of the inlet. Even at high tide it is possible to traverse in and along to the outpost of a great pinnacle flake. Beyond the cliff overhangs.

THE PAVEMENT SLAB

This is the small slab at the foot of the descent. It has three minor climbs.

The Schism   20m   Difficult *   (1978)
A good line taking the obvious crack splitting the slab.

Quirk   15m   Difficult   (1978)
Climb a crack right of the Schism. Move right along a flake crack, go up a short bulging wall and traverse off right.

Quibble   15m   Very Difficult   (1978)
Climb the left edge on small holds.

The cliff between this slab and the pinnacle-flake is dominated by a big broken slab. The rock is by no means perfect.

Lammylair Slab   45m   Hard Severe   (1978)
Work leftwards up the slab and go up a groove to an obvious bulging nose. Climb this on the right to finish left by a deep crack below the final overhanging wall. Pegs were needed for belaying at the top on first ascent.

Jinky Grooves   30m   Mild Severe   (1978)
Right of the big slab is a jagged buttress with an obvious line of grooves. Climb the twisting grooves to finish up a loose but straightforward headwall.

THE SHAG'S CAVE FACE

This south wall of Lammylair provides some good climbing, notably on the remarkable traverse over the Shag's Cave. Two or three good vertical lines remain unclimbed, but for such an impressive face the scope is disappointingly limited and the upper slabs need gardening. Kittiwakes in summer and a dark atmosphere seem to have kept people away.

Lammylair Traverse   170m   VS 4c *   (1980)
This is a sea-level traverse finishing diagonally up the face right of Shag's Cave.
It is also the access route for the other climbs here. Low tide is required to
negotiate the cave, but not for access. Start down an obvious slab (Very Difficult)
on the wedge-shaped buttress over towards Greymare and traverse into the inlet
on excellent moderate rock. Continue along a steeper wall and traverse into the Shag's Cave.
Traverse the slabby cave floor, slimy if wet. Make an awkward move at sea-level
at the far side (greasy) to gain the far walls. Work rightwards up these by walls
and shelves to gain the top by grassy slabs. It may be possible to push the
traverse into the back of the inlet.

Phalacrocorax   30m   Severe   (1980)
Not far short of the Shag's Cave an obvious crack curves up rightwards. Climb
this to a ledge. Go left along the ledge to climb a little corner slanting up right,
then work up to a belay platform.

Shangri-La   150m   HVS 5a **   (1980)
The rising traverse over the Shag's Cave gives superb situations. From the
Phalacrocorax crack follow a hand traverse rightwards and go under a roof to
gain tiny ledges on the wall close to the cave. A slabby belt of rock runs along
between the lip of the cave and overhangs above. Follow this away right to gain
a big slabby shelf at the far side. The hardest part is near the end where
strenuous exposed moves are made just above the cave lip. From the belay shelf
it is possible to traverse off onto easy grass but a direct finish is worthwhile. Gain
shelves above the belay and move up left onto the exposed wall. Follow a
gardened line up left to a ledge 6m below the top, beside a steep nose of rock.
   Unfortunately many of the holds and ledges support kittiwake nests and the
face is sheltered from storms. The crux area will probably always require cleaning
by abseil (from the belay at the top of the direct finish). The escape back along
Lammylair Traverse is about Mild Severe.

SEALS' CAVES

This is the stretch of cliffs between Lammylair and the headland of Arthur Fowlie
to the north. There are three consecutive little inlets leading into impressive sea
caves, the North and South Seals', and Petrie's Hole, the most southerly. The
main face runs north from North Seals' Cave. There seems a strong likelihood
that the narrow South Cave and Petrie's Hole are interconnected.

PETRIE'S HOLE

This little inlet has no climbs of any significance but is worth a visit. To reach the
north side, scramble down easy rocks on the north side just south of the South
Cave. It is possible to traverse in from the seaward end of the gulch to the top of
a big pinnacle flake overlooking the cave. Unfortunately it seems impractical to
traverse the cave. There are two obvious chimneys above the traverse. Further
right is a more interesting crack splitting the first wall (VS).

The south side is reached by a scramble down an easy pavement of slabs to the south. This is the Lammylair Descent. An obvious green chimney provides a pleasant romp, best reached by a traverse from the seaward end (Very Difficult).

THE SOUTH CAVE FACE
This broken slabby wall overlooks the second cave on its north side. Reach the bottom by climbing down broken rocks just south of the North Cave. Go down a slabby shelf to near sea-level where a corner runs up leftwards.

Route X   30m   VS 4c   (1974)
Climb the diagonal corner until moves out right are possible. Now work up slabs and walls to the top.

THE MAIN FACE (NORTH SIDE)
This high face is bounded on the south by the great North Cave and on the north by a small hanging quarry. The whole Seals' Caves area is occupied by birds in the nesting season and this face supports a particularly dense community. The cliff largely faces straight out to sea. Access is usually made by abseil down the central fault of Green Groove.

To the south, the cliff swings round into the North Cave and the original route takes the great ramp overlooking the cave.

1   The Crocodile   45m   E2 5b ***   (1971)
A serious and impressive climb, unfortunately out of bounds for much of the year due to nesting birds. If the tide is not low, a short pendulum may be employed to gain the base of a great slab ramp. Climb the slab by the easiest line to a rock scar, which was once the home of a "weird vibrating flake". Gain the shelf above the scar awkwardly, then go up the gently overhanging wall using succeeding shelves to finish up the last part of the corner springing from the cave lip. Great exposure.

2   Maxfield's Route   40m   VS 4c   (1972/85)
Start below a prominent small corner left of Green Groove. Climb up to an overlap and go over it via a thin crack. Step right, surmount a bulge and climb the wall directly to the top.

3   Green Groove   35m   Very Difficult   (1971)
The biggest fault splitting the seaward face is often unpleasantly greasy.

4   Iguana   35m   Very Difficult   (1972)
The obvious groove and crack line right of Green Groove is steep, but has good holds.

5   The Black Cleft   20m   Difficult   (1972)
The obvious fault running up into the quarry is climbed using the rib on the left.

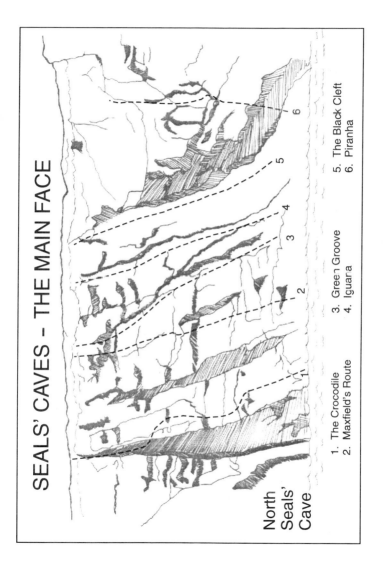

SEALS' CAVES – THE MAIN FACE

North Seals' Cave

1. The Crocodile
2. Maxfield's Route
3. Green Groove
4. Iguara
5. The Black Cleft
6. Piranha

6   Piranha   25m   HVS 5a *   (1972)
A good line taking the hanging corner-crack right of the main bulges and cracks
under the quarry. Climb straight up a big bulging convex wall to gain the crack.
(From here it is possible to traverse away north on excellent rock to gain the
broken slabs south of Arthur Fowlie.) Climb the crack to the top.

ARTHUR FOWLIE   *(Map Ref 113 378)*

This is the headland immediately beyond Seals' Caves. On its north side the sea
invades westwards into the big inlets of Robie's Haven and the Bullers of
Buchan. The headland lies only a few minutes walk from Bullers village, via a
poor path round Robie's Haven. Arthur Fowlie gives a fine view of the Longhaven
cliffs, from where the headland is a striking landmark, ending in a spectacular
overhanging prow. Bold walls of impeccable granite flank this prow to north and
south. Arthur Fowlie offers a bunch of excellent routes, some of which rank with
the best on the coast. Apparently, the name Arthur Fowlie has nothing to do with
a local character but is a corruption of "the headland of the fowls". Unfortunately
for the climber, this is all too true; a motley crew of auks and gulls occupy their
ancestral home from April to August, restricting access to the majority of routes.
After the nesting season, a quick abseil will often be required to clean routes.
Additionally, the North Wall and Prow can be a bit greasy and lichenous.
    The descent lies about 50 metres west of the prow and just east of a small
tidal bay which cuts into the extension of the south wall of Robie's Haven. Steep
grass and a hidden gully (Difficult) lead eastwards down under the north wall.
From here an interesting switchback traverse of about Very Difficult leads along
under the Prow to a platform under the secluded south wall. The cleft of the
Rumbling Hole bars escape to the broken slabs beyond. The traverse is dicey in
rough seas and can be very greasy. A quick alternative for the south wall routes
and the Prow is to rope down the obvious south wall overlaps using a convenient
block.

THE NORTH WALL

This wall sustains a fierce tilt but an obvious ramp provides a remarkably easy
breach. The routes are described from Reprieve northwards.

1   Reprieve   30m   Very Difficult *   (1969)
Climb the straightforward left-slanting ramp to the crux exit up a short wall near
the top of the Prow.

2   The Gallows   20m   E2 6a   (1978)
The parallel shelf poised above and right of Reprieve. The shelf is easy but a
vicious overhanging wall must be climbed to reach it. This is climbed at a thin
crack, moving out right and swinging back left.
Direct Finish: 5m   E3 6a   (1986)
From the small perch continue straight up the gently overhanging wall above.
More in keeping with the lower part of the route.

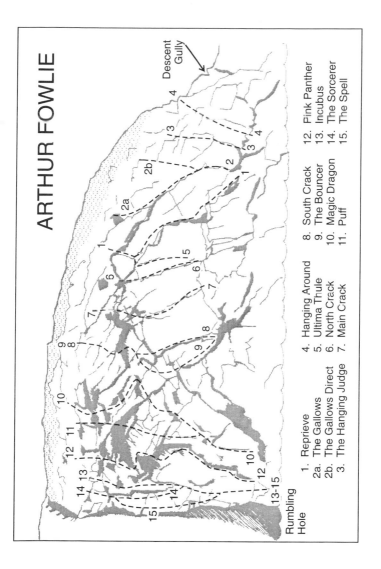

ARTHUR FOWLIE

1. Reprieve
2a. The Gallows
2b. The Gallows Direct
3. The Hanging Judge

4. Hanging Around
5. Ultima Thule
6. North Crack
7. Main Crack

8. South Crack
9. The Bouncer
10. Magic Dragon
11. Puff

12. Pink Panther
13. Incubus
14. The Sorcerer
15. The Spell

Descent Gully

Rumbling Hole

3   The Hanging Judge   12m   E3 6a   (1986)
Climb the obvious corner right of The Gallows. Protection is very awkward to place.

4   Hanging Around   10m   E4 6a *   (1986)
An obvious line up the overhanging wall some 5 metres right of The Hanging Judge. A serious little number.

THE PROW
There are several thin crack lines running up the impressive "inverted slab" of the Prow. This was once exclusively aid territory but recently some very impressive free ascents have been made. Two pedestals, 10m above the sea and separated by a green cleft, provide comfortable stances for bored belayers. The first three cracks start from the northern pedestal.

5   Ultima Thule   15m   E5 6b ***   (1987)
The thin flake crack just right of North Crack, starting at the same point, but finishing out right onto the last bit of Reprieve. Go up right to gain and climb the crack. Gear is very strenuous to place (heavily yo-yoed on the only ascent to date). The exit is often wet and needs to be dry.

6   North Crack   20m   E3 6a *   (1972/1979)
The first emphatic crack line reached from the north. Originally aided, it provides a fine strenuous climb, technical near the bottom. An abseil may be necessary to clean off a kittiwake nest.

7   Main Crack   20m   E5 6a ***   (1987)
A remorseless route in a stunning position. It is best to belay on a ledge down left. Follow the left-slanting cracks all the way, starting from North Crack's pedestal. Protection is good and there is a rest leaning into the corner at two-thirds height. The technical crux is near the bottom and the exit ledge will usually need cleaning by abseil.

8   South Crack   20m   A1 and VS   (1972)
A thin crack line starts from the north side of the southerly pedestal, above the gulch. The crack leads off the overhang some 6m up whence free climbing leads up into a big niche. Break left up the headwall to the top. A free ascent is within the realms of possibility.

9   The Bouncer   20m   E2 5c **   (1978)
The short, fierce wide crack left of South Crack. Climb the unusual crack to a shelf, then exit out left onto ledges near Magic Dragon. Trend right to the edge of the wall and into a big niche, then break left up the wall to the top. The last section is common to South Crack.

THE SOUTH WALL

This is steep, compact and attractive, but in rough seas the cliff base may be awash. Removal of kittiwake nests by abseil will usually be necessary.

10   Magic Dragon   35m   Hard Severe ***   (1971)
An exhilarating route taking the easiest way up the wall. Climb up on jugs right of the blunt nose of the wall and make an awkward move up right to gain a steep crack line leading up rightwards. Exit left onto a ledge (possible belay) and thread the overlapping slabs above, trending right then left. Above the steep wall it is possible to veer left over the slabs and finish through the bulges as for Pink Panther; sensational but VS.
Direct Start: 8m   HVS 5a *
Climb the steep wall right of the usual start on good holds. Strenuous.

11   Puff   25m   E2 6a   (1985)
An eliminate. Climb Magic Dragon for 6m then move left into a thin crack. Climb this (crux) to move left to the arete near the top. Finish easily up the overlaps left of Magic Dragon.

The following four routes offer fine climbing but nest material seriously affects all of them.

12   Pink Panther   35m   E2 5c **   (1975/1978)
Left of the Dragon are two big corner lines. This is the smooth roof-topped right-hand corner. Climb the corner then step right to small ledges. Climb the precarious wall above to gain the slab under the roof (peg runner.) Traverse left over the slab and swing up left onto a shelf. Ignore the line up left and return back right to make a hard move onto the upper slab. Step up to a flake on the wall above, then move left to climb directly through a break in the roofs to the top.

13   Incubus   30m   E1 5b **   (1978)
The thin hanging corner between Pink Panther and Sorcerer. Start up the slab of Sorcerer, move right into the base of the corner, then climb it to a ledge. Climb left up a water-washed wall (the old finish of Pink Panther), then straight to the top. A better finish is to move right through the roofs.

14   The Sorcerer   35m   E1 5b **   (1976)
The big left-hand diedre is not technically sustained and provides very enjoyable climbing on beautiful rock. Start up a slab and climb the steep section up the back of the corner (crux) to better holds.

15   The Spell   30m   E3 6a *   (1984)
Start up the slab of Sorcerer then move up left into the obvious corner. Pull up
this to gain a break which leads round left (crux) and up to an awkward perch
overlooking the Rumbling Hole. Pull up and move out right onto slabbier rock.
Finish as for Sorcerer. It looks quite possible to finish up the edge but it is badly
nested. An abseil may be needed to clean the perch area.

The Rumbling Hole   35m   VS 4c *   (1978)
This is the south bounding cleft of Arthur Fowlie, a drowned chimney cutting back
into the cliff as an eerie shaft for an unknown distance. It forms a boulder-choked
rent running back along the cliff top, through which geysers of spray spout in
stormy weather. If these boulders could be excavated, a unique subterranean
climb could be made. The ascent of the lum mouth yields a less problematical
expedition. The cleft has been traversed unroped at exceptionally low tide.
Otherwise rope moves are required on the greasy south wall to gain the mouth
of the shaft. The chimney is climbed back and foot and then by wriggling back in
the cleft. An easier open chimney leads to the top. If climbed free at very low tide
the approach traverse is technically the hardest part of the climb.

Between Arthur Fowlie and the Red Walls of Robie's Haven is a wet recessed
area.

Pariah Crack   25m   E2 5b   (1987)
This route takes the obvious corner crack in the buttress right of the wet area.
Start up slabs on the right, move left and up to ledges (nested), then climb the
crack and finish up a blocky wall on the right (dodgy). Stake belays.

THE BULLERS OF BUCHAN

This area includes all the tortuous coastline between North Haven and the
headland of Arthur Fowlie. As a climbing ground Bullers was shunned until 1975.
Characterised by rotten, sombre, grass-festooned walls, it compares badly with
the crags nearby. Nevertheless, worthwhile climbing has been found on the
cleaner and sounder walls, amid some quite impressive scenery. It has failed to
gain favour with the modern rock climber but can offer adventurous days out for
those jaded by other venues.

Bullers of Buchan village is a small cluster of cottages tucked at the back of
the main inlet, just off the A975. There is a car park beside the road, Bullers being
a listed tourist attraction which offers not only spectacular cliff scenery but a
thriving bird population. This does have its down side as curious tourists gawk
at the struggling climber vainly trying to retain his cool.

Although the cliffs are readily accessible, all the climbs require traverses to
reach them; it is best to visit at low tide. With tidal dangers and much loose rock,
Bullers is very unsuitable for the inexperienced. Route exits are sometimes
grassy and belayless. More stakes need placing, but a stance well back is the
usual alternative.

ROBIE'S HAVEN

This is the big inlet south of the main Bullers inlet. The south side, the Red Walls, provides the best climbing at Bullers. This big cliff faces north and suffers from a lack of sunshine. On the other hand it is usually very sheltered and the approach traverse is possible at high tide if the sea is not rough. The rock is unusual but quite good with sharp holds. There are birds in the nesting season but few on the routes. There are stakes in place at the top. The narrow ridge running out along the north side of the inlet provides a very good viewpoint. It is pierced by a big archway and runs out to a rounded tower, Cairn-Na-Hilt. The tower is not hard, mostly easily climbed on the north, but the rock is rotten. A pleasant traverse can be made round the tower and the east wall of the arch. The west wall is smooth and no traverse has been recorded. The flanks of the ridge are mostly vile but there is a clean arete and slab amid the tottering rubbish facing the Red Walls. The easy grass descent down into the inlet is obvious.

Baskers' Arete   30m   Severe   (1976)
The arete on the north side of Robie's Haven, which is difficult to reach at high tide. Traverse round to ledges under the blunt nose of the arete, then climb cracks just to the right and go up to a belay ledge. Go up and left onto the knife edge to finish directly by the obvious break. There is a variation start on the right. The chimney line left of the arete is worthless.

9   Sea-Level Traverse   210m   Mild VS 4c   (1975)
This is quite interesting with excellent rock. There are optional finishing points, but it can be continued via the Arthur Fowlie traverse and a finish up a route on the South Wall. This gives some 350m of enjoyable climbing although much of it is easy. The crux pitch is only practical at low tide.
     Pass along under the unclimbed Blue Wall to reach the Red Walls. Set between the bases of two big diedres is a short barrier wall; cross this directly (Severe) and go along easier rocks to cross a little gulch (tidal). Beyond the cliffs drop into the sea. Starting at low tide level, climb the overhanging wall on good holds to reach a rock boss of rock, then go left to a belay. Continue round to a small bay at the end of the Red Walls. The rocks beyond are sometimes slippery. Pass along under multi-hued green walls to reach the descent gully of Arthur Fowlie.

1   Octopus' Garden   35m   VS 4b   (1975)
The first section of the Red Walls is a fine steep wall with broken rock above. This, the original route, follows the curving boundary rib to the right, then veers left up the broken face. Climb the rib and groove to ledges and go up by a big dubious flake. Work up and left to belay at another big flake. Go up the vague fault above to a grassy exit.

2   Squiddly-Diddly   13m   HVS 5a *   (1980)
The thin crack line right of Robie's Crack. Start up slightly left and then slightly right to the first ledge of Octopus' Garden. Sustained and steep for the grade.

3   Robie's Crack   30m   HVS 5a **   (1977)
This fine route takes the obvious forking crack which splits the wall. Climb the crack, staying in the main line, then go directly up walls to the belay flake.

4   Main Street   30m   HVS 4c **   (1979)
The left edge of the wall is a fine arete which forms the right side of the big diedre of Deputy Dawg. This route takes the arete on its right side, joining the true edge higher up. Start just left of Robie's Crack and climb steeply up leftwards on peculiar grey holds over a bulge. Go up and turn a bulging section on the right to cross back left and gain the arete proper. This leads to the big belay flake of Octopus' Garden. Protection is pretty sparse.

5   Road Runner   30m   VS 4c **   (1980)
A more direct ascent of the arete, turning the bulging part on the left. Start directly under the arete and go up through a break in a bulge. Go on up to turn a bulge on the left side of the arete then go straight up the edge as for Main Street. Protection could be better.

6   Deputy Dawg   30m   HVS 5a **   (1977)
The first and smaller of the two diedres. Climb the corner, surmounting a difficult bulge near the top. Finish up Road Runner.

7   Muckle Corner   35m   E3 5c *   (1989)
The main corner left of Deputy Dawg. The top leaning corner is the crux. A very doubtful block dictates a left traverse here to climb thin cracks near the arete and rejoin the corner at the top. Spoiled by nesting material.

GOBLET BUTTRESS
This is the buttress overlooking the little gulch. The gulch is tidal but alternative access is via rappel from stakes.

8   Bash Street   35m   VS 4c *   (1980)
Climb a prominent crack up the middle of the lower neck and go directly up to gain a shelf. Traverse right and follow a ramp up left until it peters out. Launch out left onto the wall and gain a ledge on the left. Gain the top of the flake above and follow small corners to the top. Beware of fulmars and loose rock.

THE POT
This well-known local feature is the big basin north of the houses. It appears to have been formed by the collapse of a huge cavern, and is a spectacular place in a storm, with the sea rushing in through a great arch. Traverse of the arch walls is problematical while the inner walls are sheer and repulsive. A narrow ridge runs round the outer face culminating in a grass-topped pillar. The base of this is reached by traversing the seaward face (the north side of the main Bullers inlet). There is one good HVS on the pillar.

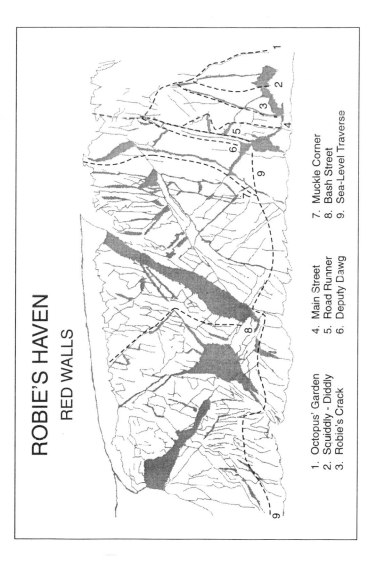

ROBIE'S HAVEN
RED WALLS

1. Octopus' Garden
2. Squiddly - Diddly
3. Robie's Crack
4. Main Street
5. Road Runner
6. Deputy Dawg
7. Muckle Corner
8. Bash Street
9. Sea-Level Traverse

THE BULLERS PILLAR

The traverse is easy but has a unique little start. A path leads down to the pebble beach below the cottages. Go down into the Smugglers' Cave and through a tunnel to ledges on the seaward face. Backing up is necessary at all but lowest tide (at high tide the tunnel becomes that pot-holers' delight, a water-filled sump. It can be avoided by crossing the Severe seaward wall but this is loose and lichenous). Easy climbing leads to the pillar, which presents an impressive south wall and is packed with kittiwakes in the nesting season. There are no stakes on top.

Sugary Slit   30m   VS 4c   (1975)
The obvious crack flanking the south wall on the left. Climb the crack to ledges. The continuation looks nasty, so traverse left onto a broken arete and up this to the top.

Big Bully   20m   HVS 5a *   (1980)
The fine south wall. Start under some stepped roofs. Climb out right and go up the face to traverse left to a resting perch on the edge. Go steeply up right to finish by a little corner (obvious from the ground).

Pillar Edge   30m   Very Difficult   (1975)
The right edge is disappointing, being loose and grassy in the broken upper half.

THE COBWEB CLIFF

On the other side of the Pot entrance from Bullers Pillar there is a broken buttress. North again across a little inlet lies another small headland with an imposing red wall on its south side, well seen face on from around the Pot. This, the Cobweb Cliff, is rarely visited. On the flat grassy tops of both this headland and Blockie Head, can be seen overgrown traces of earth ramparts, said to be remnants of look-outs used around the time of Canute's Danish invasion in the 11th century.

Abseil down a grassy shute on the north side, using a convenient iron ring on the narrow neck. Alternatively, go down zigzag shelves on the extreme tip; this is not difficult once located, but it is loose and exposed. Traverse round to the wall, negotiating a shallow cave to gain the slab apron under the wall (which is a potential trap at high tide). The wall is plastered with kittiwakes in summer.

Spider's Corner   35m   HVS 5a *   (1976)
The obvious line left of centre is steep and strenuous and littered with kittiwake nests. Start up a bulging arete just right of the initial crack, then go up to climb a steep brittle corner. Finish up the deep crack, exiting left near the top.

BLOCKIE HEAD

This is the headland north of the Cobweb headland, across the little inlet of Dunnythagert. It forms the south wall of the major bay of North Haven. Blockie

Head's chief point of interest is a narrow sea cave gouged right through the headland. The cliffs are high and largely uninviting but sound rock at sea-level allows a traverse of unusual character, threading the mysterious sea cave. The climb is serious and easy to get trapped on. There are no real escapes.

Goblin's Traverse   200m   VS 4c *   (1976)
Start from the boulder beach of North Haven. Cross the base of a horrible arete to reach a secluded corner. Traverse through the Green Arch beyond to flat rocks. Continue around the corner to a barrier wall. Cross this by going up left and down a groove. Swing down an awkward overhang beyond to gain the rocks alongside the cave gulch. Jump the sea-filled gap (Lawrie's Leap) to gain the rocks on the other side; committing. Swing into the cave on flakes just above the sea and go along shelves until possible to transfer to a belay ledge on the opposite wall. The boulders below only show at low tide. Climb diagonally down and boulder-hop to the dog-leg and the back door of the cave. It is also possible to continue past the cave entrance and through another big scooped cave at the tip of the headland and on round to the back door. This is also only practical at low tide. This second cave is threaded by a hidden hole leading onto the south side. Just north of the hole is an arete forming the prow of the headland, which gives a handy exit to the top

Blockhead Arete   25m   Moderate   (1974)
Start up an easy shelf avoiding the vertical lower part of the arete. Finish up blocks on the crest in a nice situation. This finish is recommended and allows investigation of both caves. Alternatively, from the back door, continue round the back of Dunnythagert and under a green bulbous bastion to finish up easy zigzag shelves on the tip of the Cobweb headland (The Cobweb Descent). Logically, this traverse continues round to the Cobweb Cliff where further progress looks unlikely. Spider's Corner gives a demanding finish.

NORTH HAVEN

This large bay lies in the heart of the climbing grounds and is the dominant inlet of the area. The name Longhaven cliffs is not particularly appropriate since Longhaven itself lies away north of Murdoch Head. Although offering little in the way of climbing, North Haven is a very peaceful and pleasant place. The bay is divided in two by a big shark's fin stack, which can be reached at low tide and has sound rock at the seaward end, though the summit section is dangerously loose and best left alone. The north wall of the bay has been traversed for most of its length at about Severe standard. Offshore there are more rocks, most notably "The Old Ship".

North Haven to Longhaven Quarries

This is a complex area with many old quarries, the re-working of which has thankfully been successfully limited. Although 90% of the rock in these decaying citadels is useless for climbing purposes, they provide an atmospheric backdrop to climbing on the sea-cliffs hereabouts.

The quality of the pink granite in this section is very mixed, the rock varying from magnificent at Rob's Butt, Red Wall and the eastward face of Scimitar Ridge (left of The Great Diedre), to the consistency of granulated sugar in some of the quarries. On the rest of the cliffs the rock is generally solid. As with the many of the sections north of Aberdeen, most of the cliffs in this area are prime nesting grounds and as such useless to the climber for much of the summer.

Many of the cliffs require abseil descents, some of which feel quite serious. However, approaches of this kind have an advantage in that a high percentage of the routes will require cleaning beforehand. If the ropes are left in place and jumars used, the risk is considerably reduced. In fact these methods will enable the climber to explore sections of cliff which would otherwise be unapproachable and which add greatly to the enjoyment of the area.

Access

There are two access tracks, the main one leading to the recently re-worked quarry being the usual choice. This track leaves the A952 a couple of hundred metres past Longhaven Village (26 miles from Aberdeen) at a house called Granite Lodge. Follow the track, taking the right-hand alternatives, to park near the quarry office. There is a better track which starts about 100 metres south of Granite Cottage, opposite a side road on the left, which leads to the same point. Cross the fence and walk rightwards past a deep quarry and down to the recently quarried area. Thread your way through the mountainous piles of boulders; the old main Longhaven Quarries lie beyond the left corner of the worked zone. The Red Wall is directly seawards on a small headland beyond the zone, and the Alligator, Walrus Ridge, etc., lie to the south, around the area of the big Perdonlie Inlet.

The alternative track gives easier access to the climbs in the vicinity of Perdonlie, but the use of this track is dependent upon the goodwill of the farmer. The track leads off at Whiteshin Farm on the A975, midway between the Bullers of Buchan Village and its junction with the A952. Beyond the farm a small sawmill is passed and a small bridge crossed from where the track leads to the head of Perdonlie Inlet. The track now continues to the quarry zone (although it is not passable by car). Park at the head of Perdonlie just after a "No Dumping" sign and just before the Longhaven Quarries Wildlife Preserve sign. From here the Hellgate Cliff and Alligator Ridge lie just east of Perdonlie whilst Walrus Ridge is the buttress forming the seaward extremity of the west side.

Stoneface, Round Tower (Climber, Niall Ritchie)

PERDONLIE INLET

This prominent deep inlet is characterised by an impressive west wall stretching the full length of the inlet. Generally the rock is very steep, vegetated and rather loose. It is doubtful if there is any scope for good modern lines. However, the rock is much better around sea-level and for the full height of the southern end alongside Walrus Ridge.

Sea-Level Traverse   120m   Very Difficult *   (1968)
Scramble down a grass slope on the north-east corner of the inlet to the rubbish at the bottom, underneath the overhanging back wall. Start traversing along an obvious shelf and keep going, never more than 7m above the high water mark, to reach a broad dipping shelf at the end of the wall. From here easy climbing leads round into a narrow inlet where a deep cave blocks direct access to Walrus Ridge.

Perdonlie Edge   45m   Very Difficult   (1968)
This is the easiest way of reaching the top after the Sea-Level Traverse. From the dipping shelf climb straight up into a long indefinite groove and follow this to an obvious tooth of rock. From here, climb the wall above to easy ground below the final overhangs. Turn these on the left via a delicate slab and a big heave.

Perdonlie Crack   45m   Severe *   (1973)
At the end of the dipping shelf is a steep 12m wall of perfect rock. Climb a crack near the left edge to a ledge. Continue straight up (or climb up left and up a steep groove, better). Both variations lead to the delicate slab of Perdonlie Edge. Either finish by that route or break through the overhangs on the right, via an obvious awkward niche (VS).

Zwango   60m   VS 4c *   (1969)
This is a continuation of the Sea-Level Traverse, which links it to the North-East Ridge of Walrus Ridge. It takes a fine natural line in an impressive position. Easy ledges lead round from the dipping shelf into the gulch. From the furthest ledge follow a ramp, which develops into an obvious crack, to a comfortable recess (30m). Go up the right edge of the slabby face for 7m and traverse a horizontal fault crossing the whole face. If the fault is choked with nests it is possible to cross the slabby face directly by a thin crack to regain the fault later on (HVS 5a). Descend to the chimney crack splitting the roof of the cave. Continue down easy rock and follow a ramp up left onto the North East Ridge, approximately 20m below the gendarmes.

Greater Perdonlie Traverse   300m   VS 4c **   (1969)
A combination of the Sea-Level Traverse, Zwango and then reversing North-East Ridge and Tennent's Girdle, where The Plug gives a fine finish if desired. A very enjoyable outing, although not sustained.

Dougie Dinwoodie on the first ascent of Tyrant Crack, Round Tower, in 1978

WALRUS RIDGE

The proper local name for this feature is the Bink of Whiteshin. There are several routes on this buttress but by far the best expedition is to gain it via the Greater Perdonlie Traverse. Tennent's Girdle is not recommended in high seas. Although the rock on the quarried side of the ridge is poor and the seaward side is birded, this is a good cliff for the adventurous.

Access

Walrus Ridge is separated from another small buttress, Rob's Butt, by a large quarry dipping down into the sea (Rob's Butt is the first climbing crag north of North Haven). The climbs on both features are gained from the quarry floor. Descend to the first notch on Walrus Ridge (iron spike) and then work down right by grassy ledges and a smooth groove (Moderate) to reach the quarry floor. The climbing is at the mouth of the dry inlet, Walrus Ridge to the left and Rob's Butt on the right.

Ordinary Route   75m   Difficult   (1950s)

A good choice when high seas prevent access to the other routes. Start from the sea end of the quarry floor. Climb the steep slab which is thrown down from the ridge to the quarry floor near its right edge (friable) for 30m to a ledge. Trend right up the slab to reach the crest which is followed over a gendarme back to the top.

Tennent's Girdle and North-East Ridge   90m   Severe   (1950s)

An interesting scenic tour but the climbing is very scrappy. The only Severe pitch may be abseiled, lowering the standard to Difficult. Start as for Walrus Ridge but instead traverse right to reach a promontory below the overhanging nose of the ridge. Cross a deep inlet by a Severe 10m descent and continue traversing low down to reach the foot of the North-East Ridge. Climb the ridge turning the gendarme at the top on the right, and finish along the crest of the main ridge.

The Plug   30m   VS 4c *   (1960s)

From the back of the deep inlet of Tennent's Girdle a fine chimney-corner slants left to join the Ordinary Route. Climb the crack throughout, starting from beyond the 10m descent on the girdle.

Aivik   30m   VS 4c   (1979)

This is on the steep rock right of The Plug. Climb the fault right of twin overhanging cracks to a large ledge. Continue up the groove above (**Gendarme Groove** Mild VS 4b, gained from ledges on the right) to the gap between the gendarmes on the ridge crest, or, traverse left up a slab then zigzag up and climb the crest to the summit gendarme.

ROB'S BUTT

On the sunny south-west wall of the Walrus Quarry is a wastepipe, sometimes used for the disposal of whisky effluent (beware!). The pipe ends a few feet

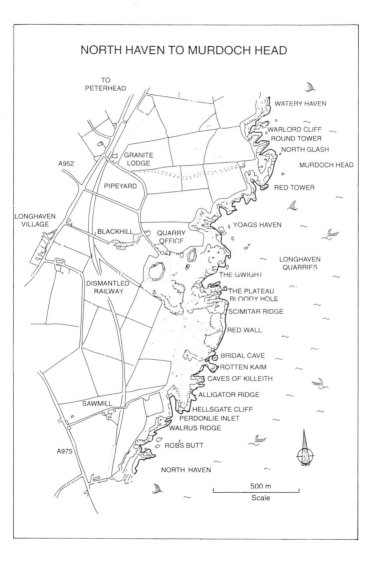

NORTH HAVEN TO MURDOCH HEAD

TO
PETERHEAD

WATERY HAVEN

WARLORD CLIFF
ROUND TOWER
NORTH GLASH

MURDOCH HEAD

GRANITE
LODGE

A952

RED TOWER

PIPEYARD

LONGHAVEN
VILLAGE

BLACKHILL

QUARRY
OFFICE

YOAGS HAVEN

LONGHAVEN
QUARRIES

THE GWIGHT

DISMANTLED
RAILWAY

THE PLATEAU
BLOODY HOLE

SCIMITAR RIDGE

RED WALL

BRIDAL CAVE
ROTTEN KAIM
CAVES OF KILLEITH

ALLIGATOR RIDGE

SAWMILL

HELLSGATE CLIFF
PERDONLIE INLET
WALRUS RIDGE

ROB'S BUTT

A975

NORTH HAVEN

500 m
Scale

above the sea and the seaward wall immediately south gives the following excellent routes on superb rock. Unfortunately, rough seas would preclude any climbing here (with the possible exception of White Lightning) and during the nesting season the wall is badly nested. Access is described in the Walrus Ridge section.

Whisky Galore   25m   HVS 5a **   (1973)
Some 12m left of the end of the pipe and hidden round a corner is a thin crack, splitting a steep wall, above a sea-washed platform. Climb this to a ledge and then continue by the deeper crack directly above until easier ground is reached.

Frolic Variation   30m   HVS 5a *   (1976)
At high tide the start of Whisky Galore is inaccessible, in which case this is an entertaining alternative. At the left of the end of the whisky pipe a steep crack runs diagonally left. Climb this to a hidden ledge, then traverse left to join Whisky Galore.

White Lightning   10m   E1 5c   (1979)
This is the thin technical crack just right of Frolic Variation. Belay in the large niche (old unsafe peg; it is better to climb down to the right, as you face the cliff).

Bell's Groove   30m   VS 4b   (1976)
From the platform beneath Whisky Galore traverse up left to gain a groove on the edge of the buttress. Follow the groove for a few feet, pull out right, then climb the slab to an easy rake. Finish over the cracked bulge and slab above.

THE HELLGATE CLIFF AND ALLIGATOR RIDGE

The Hellgate Cliff lies just across Perdonlie from Walrus Ridge; Alligator Ridge is the next feature immediately north. These cliffs could not differ more in character. The former is steep, forbidding and a potentially serious place to climb. The latter has easier-angled rock for the most part and the climbing is much more light-hearted.

Access
This is common to both cliffs and lies between them, although one of the Hellgate routes (The Beast), is gained from the Perdonlie side of the inlet. Park as for access to Perdonlie. To locate the descent accurately it is best to follow the east side of Perdonlie to the boulder-strewn cliff edge at the south end. From here walk back north-east for about 12m, overlooking the obvious sheer walls of the aptly named Green Void, and passing the prominent chimneys of Hellgate and Kincorth.

About 6m north-east of the top of Kincorth Chimney, an easy-angled ramp, The Gangway, slants down north towards Alligator Ridge. This juts out at right angles from the coastline, and is easily identified by the huge notch cut into it by rock-fall. The slabby area at the bottom of The Gangway is known as the Slidegate (although this map name may in fact refer to the Ridge itself). The Hellgate Cliff routes are reached by an easy traverse south from the bottom of the Gangway.

HELLGATE CLIFF

This cliff is split into pillars by two big chimneys, the left-hand of which gives the cliff its name and is a prominent landmark from Arthur Fowlie. Left again is the breath-catching little box inlet containing Green Void. Kittiwakes rule this cliff in summer, although the chimneys are largely unaffected. After the nesting season the nests may disappear quite quickly since big waves batter the cliff in rough weather. Unlike Alligator, even a moderate swell may rule out climbing here. The quality of the rock varies but is generally quite reasonable. The routes are described from right to left.

Kincorth Chimney 20m Severe   (1950s)
This is the first of the prominent chimneys.

Isostase 20m Mild VS 4b   (1973)
The rib between the two chimneys. Take the centre of the rib to below a large overhang, then move left into a groove overlooking Hellgate Chimney. Follow this to the top.
Direct Finish: Mild VS 4b   (1985)
Once established in the groove, move back right above an obvious bulge and climb the centre of the pillar to the top.

Hellgate Chimney 20m Mild VS 4b *   (1950s)
The great left-hand cleft, more impressive than its neighbour.

Pearly Gates 20m VS 4b   (1975)
Climb the badly protected right edge of the pillar, left of Hellgate Chimney.

The Left Hand of Darkness 20m E2 6a **   (1980)
This is the crack line in the centre of the pillar and was one of the first routes in the North-East to be graded 6a. Protection is excellent and a long reach is helpful. Finish up the arete on the right after the crack ends. Cleaning by abseil is probably necessary except during the spring.

The following routes are situated in the little box inlet to the left. Although access is possible by traversing from under Left Hand of Darkness, this is not recommended as it is tricky and often quite green. The preferred means of approach is by abseil from a belay located centrally above the Left Hand of Darkness pillar, well back from the top. Abseil down the pillar to a small ledge, where the drop on the left becomes immediately apparent; secure the rope again here. Continue the descent to the ragged recess of Green Void (about 20m in total). Ideally, the abseil rope should be left in place and jumars are also quite handy. The opportunity to brush the climbs while descending should also be taken.

Right of Way   20m   HVS 4c   (1985)
Start from the initial ledge of Green Void. Go diagonally right to the arete, move up, then traverse right to finish up the final arete of Left Hand of Darkness; fine situations but very poor protection. In the absence of an abseil rope this is the easiest escape from the inlet.

Green Void   15m   E2 5b **   (1980)
This route takes the left wall of the pillar. Belay in an obvious ragged recess. Climb the recess and the wall immediately above, moving left at the top.

Pretty Vacant   15m   E3 5c   (1985)
The big corner left of Green Void, starting from its belay niche. Climb the corner to join and finish up The Beast. (The continuation corner is very loose.)

The next route is gained by a scramble down some precarious and sugary rocks on the Perdonlie side of the cliff, to reach a platform on the west side of the inlet.

The Beast   25m   E4 6a *   (1982)
This is an unusual and exacting line taking the obvious chimney and traverse line on the back wall of the inlet. From the platform traverse right to the chimney and cross it to a shelf on the other side. Move up the edge and surmount the bulge above (crux) until it is possible to step right and up to a handrail. Traverse right across the back wall of the inlet (much easier) to gain a final slanting corner. Move up and right to gain the top holds of Green Void. A serious line on which bad rope drag is unavoidable. It is unfortunately frequently nested and very awkward to clean by abseil.

ALLIGATOR RIDGE
Alligator Ridge is composed of variable rock and has a sunny aspect. The crest of the ridge is horizontal and offers a superb situation where the slabby north face drops straight into the sea alongside a formidable wall. Seabirds are not much of a problem during the breeding season. Climbing should be possible here in all but the roughest seas, with the exception of the north wall which is rather dank and more prone to hostile waves.

The following climbs are on the wall alongside the Gangway.

Seapod   12m   E1 5b **   (1975)
On the back wall, above the base of the ramp, is a smooth tapering chimney topped by a steep wall. Climb the chimney, break out left onto the wall, then finish straight up. Sustained climbing on steep rock.

Slim Jim   12m   E1 5a   (1980)
Climb the narrow groove between Black Wall and Seapod. Continue straight up
the wall above to the top.

Black Wall   12m   HVS 5a   (1975)
Start in a short corner left of Seapod and climb the black-streaked wall to the
top.

Green Wall   10m   E1 5b   (1980)
Just left of Black Wall is a short V-groove at the top of the cliff. Climb a bulge and
enter the groove (sometimes green and slimy) by swinging in from the left.

The following routes are all to the right of Seapod.

Under 40s Only   12m   HVS 5a   (1986)
Start at the bottom of Seapod. Climb up a crack trending rightwards, then go
straight up the steep wall above.

Encore   12m   E1 5b   (1989)
Five metres right of Seapod are two short overhanging cracks. Pull into the
left-hand crack, go up to a ledge, then finish up the thin crack in the wall above.

Stretch   20m   Severe   (1967)
Pull into the right-hand crack and climb more easily up the wall above, finishing
just left of a projecting nose of rock (prominent from the gangway). Alternatively,
gain the upper section by a more delicate ramp leading right from the foot of
Seapod (Hard Severe).

Rhino   20m   Difficult   (1950s)
Climb a steep little crack 2m right of Stretch to a large ledge, then go up and left
to finish by climbing round to the right of the projecting nose.

Stratapax   12m   HVS 5a   (1986)
Start right of Rhino. Climb the bulge from a groove on the right to gain a sloping
ledge. Move up and over an overlap, and go slightly right to an overhanging
crack, which is climbed strenuously to the top.

Oboe   20m   Difficult   (1950s)
Climb the initial rampart by a deep crack right of Rhino. Move left and follow
slabby ledges rightwards to gain a deep recess in the middle of the wall formed
by the intersection of two chimneys. Finish by either chimney.

SOUTH WALL OF ALLIGATOR RIDGE
A rockfall in the early 1980s towards the seaward end of the ridge removed one
of the best Alligator routes, the wide crack of Man Eater, and also left a rather
ugly gap. The northerly aspect of this crack, Norseman, also disappeared and

the old route, Ridge Walk, is now impossible. From the ridge crest a Severe wall bars access to the top; this finish is common to all the climbs on the ridge proper.

Alligator Crawl   30m   Severe *   (1950s)
The trade route on the cliff (Patey's tribute to Fats Waller, the climb being smooth and in the groove). Climb the corner crack up the angle between the ridge and the Back Wall. From the neck of the ridge either continue up the corner directly (Mild VS 4c on poor rock) or, more in keeping with the standard of the lower pitch, climb two slightly converging cracks about 3m right of the corner.

There are three other variations from the vicinity of the neck:

Sellar's Sortie   10m   Mild VS 4b   (1950s)
From the neck traverse right by a delicate ledge with considerable exposure, then climb a steep arete to the top.

Lovat's Escape   12m   Mild VS 4b   (1950s)
About 4m below the neck make an awkward leftward pull out of Alligator Crawl to gain an overhung recess with a V-shaped floor. A steep climb out of the recess joins Oboe at the top.

Snapper   10m   E1 5b   (1979)
This is the steep leaning crack on the wall between Lovat's Escape and the direct finish to Alligator Crawl. Strenuous and well-named; a horrible problem.

Right of the Crawl, several crack lines up the slab provide enjoyable climbing.

Parted Jaws   20m   Mild VS 4b **   (1950s)
The first obvious crack right of the Crawl, with an awkward overhung start. After this the climbing is much easier.

Slippery Sam   20m   VS 4c   (1983)
Start in a small corner right of Parted Jaws and just left of the much more obvious crack line of Viper's Drag. Follow the thin crack for 10m to a small overlap. Take either of the two cracks above to finish.

Viper's Drag   20m   Severe **   (1950s)
An excellent crack climb in the centre of the face. If the start is taken directly it is VS 4c.

V-Climb   20m   Very Difficult   (1950s)
Start just right of Viper's Drag and finish at the prominent notch on the ridge. The last few feet are the crux.

The Milky Bar Kid   20m   HVS 5a   (1983)
The vague crack up the slab right of V-Climb. Go up the crack just left of the rockfall directly, then finish up the awkward headwall.

NORTH WALL OF ALLIGATOR RIDGE

This face is steep, forbidding and very greasy. Below lie smooth hollows and a big cave where the water boils impressively in a big swell. Large unclimbed cliffs extend northwards up the coast; Toltec is the only route so far to have breached this formidable fortress. The rock on the north face is thought to be reasonably sound. The rockfall already mentioned, besides removing Norseman, has made Alligator slab problematical.

Slithy   15m   HVS 5a   (1975)
Where the slab joins the main cliff there is a smooth corner, undercut at the bottom. It is best approached by abseiling down the climb. A magnificent situation which is often slimy and awkward to approach. Now serious and committing.

The Toltec   35m   E1 5a   (1975)
This route climbs the impressive wall just north of Alligator Ridge. It starts from a squat pinnacle below the wall which drops straight into the sea. To reach this pinnacle descend a watercourse at the north-east end of the wall, cut into the wall along slabs, then rope down onto the pinnacle. (It is wise to leave a rope in place.) From the top of the pinnacle, climb the obvious steep corner crack to reach a niche on the right. Pull up and move right to climb a big notch. Go up stepped slabs to finish up a nasty disintegrating wall. An impressive and serious route, although an escape can be had along the abseil slabs at mid-height.

Romp   75m   HVS 5a   (1975)
This traverse line, running north from the watercourse, gives a good approach to The Naked Edge. Descend the watercourse to mid-height, where an obvious traverse easily north to the edge of the cliff. Descend almost to sea-level, then traverse to below a short wall and the descent to the start of The Naked Edge.

The Naked Edge   25m   Hard Severe   (1975)
Some 400 metres south of the Red Wall and 100 metres east of Perdonlie Inlet is a narrow inlet, the south wall of which ends in a sharp ridge with a prominent peak. The Naked Edge is the seaward edge of the peak. The start is reached via the neck between the cliff and the peak, then down an obvious chimney on the south side of the peak. Climb the edge directly. The green groove on the right is Very Difficult.

Between Alligator Ridge and the Red Wall Quarry there are no recorded routes. However closer inspection may reveal some worthwhile climbing for those willing to explore. There is a small promontory north of The Naked Edge known as the Rotten Kaim. This can be reached by a small abseil from belays well back. Immediately to the south is one of the most impressive caverns on the coast — The Caves of Killeith. This can be entered by slippery slabs after scrambling down from the neck of the Kaim and is well worth a visit.

THE RED WALL QUARRY

This big quarry, which opens out to the sea, lies a few hundred metres north of Alligator Ridge. It is bounded on the left by the Red Wall and on the right by the Bridal Cave, which sends a shaft right up through the cliff. It is smelly, slimy and filled with nesting shags. It looks problematical to free climb into the cave mouth but the south-facing aperture can be reached from above by a scramble. Not much has been done here due to the disconcerting nature of the rock. Apart from the two routes described, some other scrappy little pitches have been climbed near Stepped Ridge.

Access
This is via a grassy shelf at the back of the quarry (not too obvious from above), that slants down to the south-west corner of the quarry. This is also the access for the Red Wall, the crest of which can be seen at the north corner of the quarry.

D-B Arete   35m   Severe   (1950s)
This is the prominent arete at the far south end of the quarry, close to the Bridal Cave. Climb to a ledge, then go straight up a deep crack right of a groove. Go up the arete and traverse left just below the top. The name is abbreviated from Digestive Biscuits, an indication of the quality of the rock.

Rough Diamond   12m   E1 5b   (1980)
The obvious corner at the back of the quarry, almost directly underneath the top of the access ramp. Climb the corner (old pegs) to a big ledge. The wall above looks perilous, so rope back down from a peg. (This has been in place since the first ascent, so beware!)

THE RED WALL

This is one of the most impressive cliffs on the coast. It is a triangular 45m wall facing straight out to sea. The top forms a narrow headland which is sandwiched between the Red Wall Quarry and the Main Longhaven Quarry to the north. There is a plaque in memory of two young climbers tragically killed on the wall. The cliff can only be viewed properly from a boat. In rough seas, waves have on occasion been seen breaking over the top of the wall. The rock is in places magnificent but unfortunately the cliff is a favoured nesting site for all species of seabirds, and any climbers venturing here during the nesting season would be wasting their time. Even after this period the nests can linger a long time on the easier routes. Escape is difficult in the event of rain.

Access
From the recently quarried zone, head seawards along an older track, passing 50 metres right of an obvious concrete block. This leads to the head of the Red Wall Quarry from where the Stepped Ridge, the southern edge of the wall, can be seen. It is a short walk from the floor of the quarry to the start of the Stepped

Ridge. The upper part of the wall is split by several right-slanting faults which give fine climbing in the lower grades. Below them a superb 25m wall provides harder climbing. Access for climbs on this section is via the Red Wall Traverse (Hard Severe) or by abseil from the Dais, straight down the wall to ledges 10m up. This is recommended if the base is awash in heavy seas, but a rope should be left in place. All the routes on the lower wall join the traverse lines of Diagonal Crack, Phaff or The Groak, but a couple of more direct finishes have been made up the steep headwall. The routes are described from left to right:

1 Stepped Ridge 60m Difficult   (1950)
A scrappy route, but a good introduction to the cliff for inexperienced parties as the pitches are short and not exposed. However, access is difficult. A quick descent route for the experienced.
1. 20m Climb a short pitch to the left, or scramble up the nose of the ridge to beneath a short inset corner.
2. 20m Climb this corner to gain the ridge crest on the left. Follow this past an awkward short wall to a recess.
3. 20m Finish easily to the left or climb an exposed groove on the right.

2 Diagonal Shelf 65m Very Difficult   (1951)
1. 20m Stepped Ridge, pitch 1.
2. 30m Climb the short inset corner of Stepped Ridge, then continue up the obvious shelf above to belay under the top wall.
3. 15m Climb up into a recess with a V-shaped floor and finish straight up over a large jammed chockstone, avoiding an escape right.

3 Diagonal Crack 70m Very Difficult ***   (1951)
This is one of the best routes of its grade on the Aberdeen coast, but it is very serious for such a low technical grade so care is required. Follow the first pitch of Stepped Ridge onto the broad backbone of the ridge.
1. 20m Move across a slab to the right to reach a right-slanting crack below overhangs. Follow this to a large platform, the Dais.
2. 30m Continue up the crack past an awkward mantelshelf to a stance and belays just below the top. Finish up and right, or traverse left and go up past a prominent flake (exposed, Severe). Belay well back. Escapes are possible onto Diagonal Shelf.

4 Phaff 75m Severe ***   (1966)
This is another serious and exposed line which is even more impressive than Diagonal Crack.
1. 45m Follow Diagonal Crack to the Dais, then move round a corner and traverse right to a ledge.
2. 15m Move up to the roof and traverse below it to reach ledges at the far end.
3. 15m Either finish straight up the broken groove or move right and finish up the left side of a prominent gendarme.

There are two hard finishes up the steep headwall above Phaff which can be either climbed independently, starting from Phaff, or as convenient finishes for any of the routes that climb up to join Phaff from the Red Wall Traverse.

20   The Arrow   10m   E3 6b   (1983)
Climb the obvious thin crack up the wall, just left of the Phaff roof, to join the upper reaches of Diagonal Crack.

21   The Bow   15m   E2 5c *   (1983)
This finishes over the Phaff roof. Climb up and along the Phaff hand traverse, then pull over the roof to gain a small slanting corner. Move up this and the crack above, exiting right near the top.

Red Wall Traverse   75m   Hard Severe   (1952)
This gives access to all the routes situated on the wall below and right of Phaff.
1. 25m Contour round Stepped Ridge and go along rounded slabby ledges about 10m above the sea. These peter out after 20m at a small cave. Swing down the bulge below on good holds to reach a slab (or swing down slightly earlier and descend a VS finger crack). Continue more easily to belay in an obvious recess (Pooh Corner).
2. 50m Climb round the corner and go easily northwards on big ledges to the end of the Red Wall opposite Scimitar Ridge. Further progress is barred by the gulch of the Cave of Stein.

The following routes start from varying points along the Traverse. However, by far the best approach is to abseil from above Pooh Pooh (the Dais); quicker and safer. There are also abseil points further right along Phaff which can be used for access to Red Cloud and the routes right of it. The leftmost routes usually stay pretty clean.

5   Ain't Nogood   12m   E1 5b   (1987)
Start at the base of Pooh Corner. Traverse left across the slab to the skyline arete and finish straight up. This avoids the main challenge.

6   Pooh Corner   15m   HVS 5b **   (1975)
Above the obvious recess a fine steep corner leads to a roof. From here, traverse left to easy ledges on Diagonal Crack.

7   Pooh Pooh   15m   E2 5c ***   (1985)
The direct finish to Pooh Corner. From the roof move up right to gain the corner continuation, and climb this to reach the Dais; a classic.

8   Subline   20m   E3 5c ***   (1975)
This superb route on perfect rock takes the thin crack in the right wall of Pooh Corner. Well protected.

LONGHAVEN
THE RED WALL

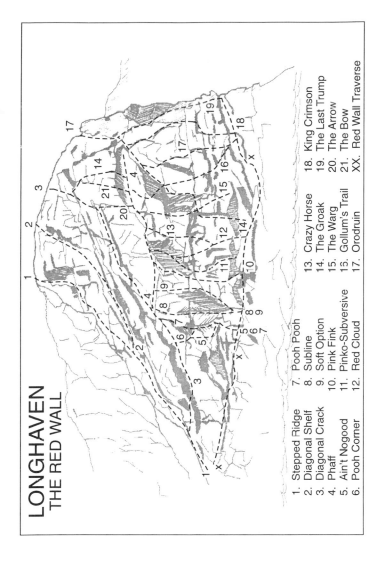

1. Stepped Ridge
2. Diagonal Shelf
3. Diagonal Crack
4. Phaff
5. Ain't Nogood
6. Pooh Corner
7. Pooh Pooh
8. Subline
9. Soft Option
10. Pink Fink
11. Pinko-Subversive
12. Red Cloud
13. Crazy Horse
14. The Groak
15. The Warg
15. Gollum's Trail
17. Orodruin
18. King Crimson
19. The Last Trump
20. The Arrow
21. The Bow
XX. Red Wall Traverse

9   Soft Option   20m   Hard Severe **   (1975)
When combined with Phaff this provides a very fine outing. Climb up to the foot of the Subline crack either by steps on the left or by a corner directly below it. Traverse right into a groove which slants up right to a ledge. Climb the groove above, stepping left, and go up to join Phaff at the start of the long traverse.

All of the following routes are badly affected by nesting birds and unless there has been a big storm, they will need to be cleaned by abseil. This can be done from the Phaff traverse for the first few routes.

10   Pink Fink   20m   E1 5b   (1983)
This climbs the wall round right from Soft Option, starting from just across the last awkward gap on Red Wall Traverse. The start is awkward and unprotected. Step left over the gap to pull up into a flake crack. Go straight up the wall to the flat ledge of Soft Option, then climb the right rib via its right wall to reach Phaff.

11   Pinko-Subversive   20m   E1 5b *   (1983)
The steep flake line just right of the gap.
1. 15m 5b Start up the leftmost of several little corners, then move left and up onto a small flat shelf. Climb straight up the flake line above to bigger holds and so to a good flat belay ledge (common to Red Cloud).
2. 5m 4b Climb the scoop above to gain the Phaff traverse.

12   Red Cloud   20m   HVS 5a **   (1983)
Takes a line just right of Pinko-Subversive, turning the central roof where it is a mere bulge at its left end. Just right of Pinko-Subversive is another shallow corner; Red Cloud climbs the next corner to the right.
1. 15m 5a Climb the corner on good holds then move up left to a bulge. Pull left over this to gain the belay ledge common with Pinko-Subversive.
2. 5m 4b Pinko-Subversive, pitch 2.

13   Crazy Horse   20m   E2 5b *   (1983)
Climb Red Cloud to the rest, then move right and surmount the central overhang at a prominent shield of rock underneath the bulge. Continue straight up to belay on Phaff. A strenuous pitch.

14   The Groak   30m   Hard Severe *   (1973)
This route starts up the obvious left-facing corner on the lower wall right of Red Cloud, leading to the right end of the central roof.
1. 20m Climb the corner then traverse right under an open groove to gain a bigger one which leads straight up into a diagonal fault line under overhangs.
2. 10m Climb the slanting crack to ledges at the end of the Phaff traverse.

15   The Warg   20m   HVS 5a *   (1983)
Climb the corner just right of The Groak past a bulge (crux). Step left and go up
the shallow groove above the initial corner of The Groak to step right at the
bulges above. Surmount the bulge, move up left, and go up to the belay ledge
under the rise in the Phaff traverse. The last part of the following route gives the
easiest finish.

16   Gollum's Trail   35m   HVS 5a *   (1983)
Start up a break in the roof midway between The Warg and the big right-facing
corners of Orodruin.
1. 20m 5a Start up on the right and move up left and through the break to a
perfect flake crack. Climb this to a platform, then go left up the rib and across to
belay under bulges on the line of The Groak.
2. 15m 5a Climb the overhang above and go up the wall to the Phaff hand
traverse under the overhangs. Move along the traverse and surmount the roof
just right of the little slanting corner of The Bow (5b) or more easily a little to the
right (5a). Climb up into the corner above which leads to the top.

17   Orodruin   30m   Mild VS 4b   (1972)
Climb the prominent system of north facing grooves and corners left of the north
edge of the Red Wall, finishing up the diagonal crack of The Groak.

18   King Crimson   30m   Mild VS 4c *   (1975)
Start just right of Orodruin and climb up into a small roofed corner at 5m.
Traverse 2 metres right, surmount the roof, then follow an indefinite line of
grooves up and left to the end of the traverse on Phaff.

19   The Last Trump   30m   Mild VS 4b   (1952)
Climb the right edge of the wall for 25m, then make an awkward pull into a
V-notch. Continue up to join Phaff just left of the gendarme.

LONGHAVEN QUARRIES

The original quarrying has left this as one of the most spectacular and tortuous
parts of the North-East coast. The area has many diverse expeditions covering
some spectacular rock scenery and should offer something to titillate even the
most jaded of mountaineering palates. On the north side, the amphitheatre is
enclosed by the Plateau, a great isolated mass which is connected to the
mainland by a jagged ridge, and which has a great archway at its seaward end
— The Hawk's Nest. Munich Buttress is the bold overhanging buttress jutting out
from the Plateau's south flank.

The Scimitar (called the Stein on some maps) is the great saw-toothed ridge,
parallel to the main coastline and cut off from it by the hole of the main quarry. It
is separated from the Plateau by the long inlet of the Bloody Hole. On the

headland immediately south of the Scimitar is the Red Wall, already described. Access between the two is barred by the inlet of the Blue Lagoon (alias the Cave of Stein).

Access
The big inlet beyond the north-east extremity of the newly quarried zone is known as The Gwight. The great amphitheatre of Longhaven Quarries is quickly reached by following an old grassy track (from the newly quarried zone), down the southern margin of this inlet. This passes Munich Buttress before it stops on the grassy top of an old spoil heap.

THE PLATEAU
The four routes described here, and the Munich Buttress climbs, are set well back from the sea, although in exceptionally rough weather spray may carry to them. They also have the advantage of a sunny aspect and freedom from broody seabirds. There are no obvious abseil points on top of The Plateau so the descent route, Hanging Blocks Climb, is worth locating beforehand.

The Ridge Route   45m   Difficult   (1950)
The ridge running out to the plateau gives easy climbing to a gendarme, the Monkey. Just beyond is an awkward descent down a crack to a col. Above, piled blocks lead to the grassy top of The Plateau.

Monkey Direct   15m   Hard Severe 4b   (1950)
This route climbs the steep corner crack on the south side of the ridge, going straight up to the notch just left of The Monkey.

Apeshit   12m   E4 6a   (1986)
The thin crack in the smooth overhanging wall left of Hanging Blocks Route. A grotty problem aptly named.

Hanging Blocks Climb   12m   Difficult   (1950)
This gains the col between The Monkey and the main mass of The Plateau from the south side, starting not far left of Munich Buttress. Climb rightwards up a slab, then up cracks to a higher ledge. Traverse left, then pull up left with a couple of awkward moves to reach the col. This is the usual line of descent from The Plateau.

MUNICH BUTTRESS
This bold oblong buttress, left of the track at the head of the Bloody Hole, has a number of excellent routes on reasonable rock and is justifiably popular. Originally it held only one peg route (hence the name).

The American Route   20m   E2 5c ***   (1975)
Climb the central crack directly to a ledge below a huge rectangular block. Thin
moves rightwards across the wall, then up, lead to a small ledge. From here go
up to a large platform and climb either of the short corners above to easier
ground.
Direct Finish: 6m   E3 6b *   (1984)
The old aid finish up the right side of the block. This should become the usual
finish for Nazi Swine. A stiff little number.
Jammy Dodger Finish: 6m   E2 6a **   (1982)
From the ledge below the rectangular block step left and climb the crack up the
left side of the block to gain the big ledge. Climbed with either difficulty or ease,
depending on your interpretation of the name.

Monkey Puzzle   25m   E3 5c **   (1982)
This route climbs the left edge of the buttress. Take care to avoid rope drag.
Climb a flake crack (poor rock) round the left edge of the buttress, then pull up
right onto the edge to gain a shelf leading right to a rest under Jammy Dodger.
Follow the hand traverse line left round the edge and up into a wide crack. Move
up this and hand traverse right, back round the edge, to pull up onto a shelf. Move
up left and finish up the edge.

African Face   20m   E5 6b *   (1990)
An eliminate. Start up the left-hand start to American Route and follow it to near
its top to a good flat hold (runners). Traverse out left via a hard move to gain the
ledge of Monkey Puzzle. Step up as for Monkey Puzzle, then go straight up using
a horizontal break (Friend 0) and technical moves to slap for the ledge. Finish as
for Monkey Puzzle.

Nazi Swine   20m   E4 6b   (1983)
This is the free version of the old aid start. Climb the thin crack to the right of The
American Route as far as the halfway resting ledge. Finish as for American
Route. The obvious link of this and the old aid finish still awaits an ascent.

Russian Arete   20m   E2 5c   (1985)
The right edge of Munich Buttress. Start on a small ledge just left of Little Black
Book. Climb the wall just right of the arete to join and finish up American Route
just after its crux.

Azerbaijani   25m   E5 6b ***   (1991)
Climb the crux of Russian Arete, then move right and climb the centre of the wall
to the top (3 peg runners).

Little Black Book   20m   E2 5b   (1979)
The steep black corner right of Munich Buttress gives a technical bridging
exercise on crumbly rock, best avoided until you've done everything else.

Third Time Lucky   20m   E1 5b   (1986)
The obvious rib right of Little Black Book. Start up an obvious slanting crack and
swing onto the arete after 10m. Climb this to the top.

The slanting grassy shelf right of Munich Buttress is only Moderate but is loose,
dirty and exposed. Not recommended.

THE BLOODY WALL

This is the extensive face right of Munich Buttress, overlooking the Bloody Hole.
Although not the most attractive of cliffs, this is one of the biggest walls on the
coast and a couple of good routes have been added since the last guide. It is
south-facing, quite sunny and most routes should be possible even in rough
seas. All the routes here were done on sight so the occasional loose hold will be
encountered. The rock is of the same quality as Munich Buttress but more nests
are present. There are no belays on the Plateau at the top of this wall so it is best
to walk well back and take a seat.

Access
Scramble down the steep gravely slope below Munich Buttress to reach the
boulder beach at the bottom. Care should be taken as the slope is quite unstable.
From the beach, scramble to the foot of the routes, which are described from left
to right.

Excalibur   35m   E1 5a   (1982)
Climb over a prominent, upward-pointing fang into a groove, which leads to a big
ledge on the right. Go up and left into a jam crack formed behind the huge block.
Climb this until it is possible to straddle the pointed top. (It is unwise to use this
as a runner as its stability is dubious.) Gain the wall above and go left until the
slab ramp above can be gained. A belay is available in the short chimney just
below the summit.

The Great White   45m   E3 5c   (1983)
This route takes the twin cracks and shallow chimneys about 10 metres right of
Excalibur.
1. 25m 5c Climb the cracks to a precarious ledge, then go up the chimney to its
deceptively overhanging top. From there make for good holds high on the left
which lead to a large ledge. Climb the flake on the right to a belay on a small
ledge.
2. 20m 5a Climb the crack on the left and then move left to gain the grassy slab
to finish.

Captain Blood   45m   E2 5b *   (1985)
Right of The Great White are two large corner lines. This is the left-hand one.
1. 20m 5b Start at the base of the corner at a big block with a lesser swivelling
block on top. From the top left end of the block, pull up over a bulge. Step left,
then up and back right to gain a ledge and belay.

2. 25m 5b Climb on top of a block to the right and pull up to a small ledge. Climb straight up the crack line above to a good platform. Step right and finish up a rib and groove, trending right. Protection is good, but the rock should be handled with care in places.

Bloody Hell   45m   E3 5c **   (1987)
The main corner line on the wall right of Captain Blood.
1. 25m 5c Belay as for Captain Blood. Climb up and go directly up a bulging wall to the base of the corner. Climb the corner exiting right to a good belay.
2. 20m 5b Move up slightly left to climb the corner above with a bulge at the top, then finish directly up cracks right of Captain Blood.

The Bloody Traverse   120m   HVS 5a   (early 1980s)
Traverse the base of the wall at sea-level to the pillar alongside the tunnel. From here climb diagonally right, then diagonally left to the crest of the Plateau.

THE HAWK'S NEST
There are a few routes here around the big gothic arch, all requiring an abseil descent. Down-climbing is a complicated and exposed Severe (part of which is the last pitch of Brooker's Boomerang) and should not be attempted on first acquaintance. The routes are without exception badly affected by nests and rough seas can make belaying problematical. The rock is superb in places and in general the routes are well protected. A serious place to climb.

Access
There are two methods, neither easy. The first involves gaining the top of The Plateau and walking seawards, crossing an exposed ridge, to where it ends. Down to the left (facing the sea) is a deep V-notch which provides good anchor points (Brooker's Boomerang finishes here). A double abseil straight down the cliff ends at the small belay ledge of Jonathan Livingstone Seagull, directly underneath the arch. To gain the Hawk's Nest, abseil for about 15m and do a short pendulum rightwards to gain ledges (junction with Brooker's Boomerang). Secure the ropes here and continue down to the top of the arch.
    The second access route involves climbing most of Brooker's Boomerang to the ledges and abseiling from there. The route from the arch to join Brooker's Boomerang is Severe and difficult to locate from above. Once on the Hawk's Nest the easiest descent is on the seaward face (Difficult) and a Severe traverse left towards the arch, along a horizontal crack and down, leads to Pumping Velvet. Alternatively, abseil from the top of the arch. From under Pumping Velvet there is a good view of Jonathan Livingstone Seagull.

Jonathan Livingstone Seagull   35m   E1 5c **   (1985)
The soaring corner crack on the south side of the arch. Start on a small ledge directly under the arch and just above the sea. Climb up to the roof of the arch and traverse left (crux) to gain the crack. Follow the line to easier ground. A great route only spoiled by the difficult access.

Let's Go Drinking   30m   E2 5c   (1985)
The left rib of the previous route. Belay on the same level but 4m to the left. Climb
the rib to a huge block. From its top, pull right on to the rib (crux) and go up to a
belay.

The Winds of War   35m   HVS 5b *   (1985)
The chimney line round to the left of Let's Go Drinking. Belay about the same
point as the previous route.
1. 25m 5b Traverse left and climb the chimney to finish up a chimney-groove
curving left. A sustained pitch.
2. 10m 4c Climb up the cracked pink wall to the top.

Yikes Dikes   15m   HVS 5a *   (1986)
Climb the obvious finger crack starting from the top of the arch, immediately right
of Jonathan Livingstone Seagull.

Ying   8m   Severe 4a   (1986)
This and the next route starts across the Arch. Starting at sea-level climb the
wide crack on the seaward wall of The Hawk's Nest. Short but superb rock.

Pumping Velvet   20m   E1 5c   (1986)
On the right-hand side of the arch are two roof-capped corners. This route takes
the right-hand corner, exiting right at the roof. It is best to belay near the top of
The Hawk's Nest.

   The other corners to the right have also been climbed (Very Difficult to
Severe).

THE PLATEAU — NORTH FACE
The north face is reached by descending into The Gwight, whence a fine tunnel
penetrating the main mass of The Plateau can be seen. There are also two
pinnacles hereabouts, the Longhaven Aiguilles. This face is much grassier than
elsewhere on The Plateau.

Herbivore   40m   VS 4c   (1978)
This climb follows the steep slabby arete, left of the large vegetated diedre, which
leads to the neck between The Monkey and The Plateau. Starting at the foot of
the diedre, follow the arete first on its right, then the left, to an overhang. A peg
was used to reach the roof where a traverse left leads to cracks and the top.
Needs gardening.

Brooker's Boomerang   100m   Mild Severe **   (1956)
This is a fine girdle along the north face. Start from the pile of blocks jammed
between the first aiguille and the main face. The first 10m to a more distant
jammed block is traditionally climbed with hands on one wall and feet on the

other. From here climb the face for 10m and continue traversing leftwards until parallel grassy cracks are reached which slant up to a slabby platform on the seaward ridge of The Plateau (abseil point for the Hawk's Nest). Follow this ridge to the top. A more difficult variation (VS) starts at about the high tide mark and climbs an obvious groove, then traverses left to the jammed block.

The north face has been climbed direct from the jammed block, but the route is spoiled by masses of turf on the upper slabs (Severe).

Gwight Traverse   VS 4c   (1976)
The wall opposite Brooker's Boomerang on the north side of The Gwight has been traversed around the headland into the next cove. Climbing near sea-level, two good pitches were encountered on the steep clean buttress at the seaward end.

THE QUARRIES

The next climbs lie in Longhaven Quarries proper. They are reached by descending the talus slope at the end of the track and lie well back from the sea.

Horseback Ridge   55m   Moderate   (1950)
The ridge bisects the quarry and links the main clifftop to the centre of Scimitar Ridge. Several variations of no great merit are possible between Moderate and Very Difficult.

Telegraph Road   20m   E2 5b   (1989)
This is the obvious cleaned crack line on the landward side of Scimitar Ridge immediately opposite the talus slope. Bold climbing on slightly crumbling rock.

Lochan Buttress   8m   Very Difficult   (1950s)
The short buttress behind the pool at the extreme north end of Scimitar Ridge, started from the notch overlooking The Bloody Hole.

Rush   6m   E1 5c   (1988)
Below and right of the notch by Lochan buttress is a short steep wall. Climb the leftmost thin crack.

Levitator   8m   E3 6b *   (1983)
This route takes the obvious thin crack line on the smooth slabby face of Lochan Buttress, overlooking the pool. Difficulties ease after 5m.

Stuka   8m   HVS 5a   (1983)
The obvious corner left of Levitator, made easier by a rockfall. Dubious rock.

Scimitar Ridge Traverse   150m   Difficult **   (1940s)
Highly recommended fun for beginners, this route provides a good scenic tour
for those wishing to orientate themselves with the area. Start at the extreme north
end of the ridge beside the pool near Levitator. Traverse into obvious twin cracks
and climb them to broken ground. Follow the easy crest to the upper of two large
platforms. There are three alternatives:
(a) The edge of the slab on the right (Very Difficult).
(b) The overhanging groove in the centre of the wall (Jerry's Diversion, VS).
(c) Step round left (exposed) and climb an inset corner to the ridge crest
(Difficult). Traverse the crest southwards and descend via a stone refuge, or by
abseil from iron spikes. A final slab is descended using more spikes (tricky).

Descent into the Main Quarry:
From the lowest point on Horseback Ridge a series of iron pegs allow a
convenient descent down a corner into the quarry (Very Difficult).

INLAND WALL OF SCIMITAR RIDGE
The following climbs start from the Main Quarry Floor:

Hallelujah Staircase   60m   VS 4c   (1951)
An old classic providing surprisingly reasonable climbing in dry weather, despite
its abominable appearance. Slow drying. From the south-west corner of the
quarry gain a huge isolated block. Go up the chimney behind and left of the block,
then traverse delicately left to attain the next ledge. Surmount a short steep wall
to another ledge and surmount the final overhang (where combined tactics were
traditionally used).

A high girdle, **The Necklace** (VS), linking Horseback Ridge and Hallelujah
Staircase has been made. It finished with an abseil into the Staircase, but the
route is not recommended. Just to the left of the descent there are two short
rather uninspiring routes, **Virgo** and **Thisinura**.

MORRISON'S SLABS
This is the slabby quarry face of Scimitar Ridge, which extends from Horseback
Ridge to the south end of the face. These slabs were named after Charlie
Morrison, who died abroad. The climbs are not particularly good.

Route 1   15m   Mild Severe   (1950s)
Start at the foot of the slabs just left of the descent into the quarry. Climb a thin
hairline crack to the terrace below overhangs.

Route 2   20m   Difficult   (1950s)
This is near the right edge of the slabs where they border on a gutter. Start at a
large block and move left a few feet, then back right towards the crest. Climb
past the red overhangs on the right to join Scimitar Ridge.

Red Slab   30m   Hard Severe   (1960s)
Starts between Route 2 and Slab and Layback. Climb straight up the slab and
cross the overlap at an obvious break. Move right to a scoop, then go up cracks.

Slab and Layback   25m   Mild Severe   (1955)
The route begins directly below and finishes up a prominent crack at the right
end of the slabs.

Lagoon Edge   15m   Difficult   (1950s)
Descend to a ledge above The Blue Lagoon and climb the edge of Scimitar
Ridge by an obvious groove to finish at the stone refuge. Usually quite green and
nasty.

SEAWARD WALL OF SCIMITAR RIDGE
This neglected area of excellent rock now provides many fine routes. Most
require abseil descents and almost all are affected to some extent by nesting
birds. If the sea is rough the routes left of The Great Diedre become water-
washed.

   To reach the climbs at the north end of the cliff, traverse from the large ledges
on Scimitar Ridge to an iron ring located on the seaward side. There is an
awkward descent here (Hard Severe), but it is much easier to abseil.

Windy Corner   25m   Very Difficult   (1950s)
Traverse northwards along a thin ledge across a steep wall to a lofty exposed
corner which is climbed back to the ridge crest. (This corner overlooks the inlet
of the Bloody Hole).

Do Androids Dream of Electric Sheep?   20m   HVS 5a *   (1983)
Start at the base of an obvious crack below where Windy Ledge turns the
corner. Climb the crack to the traverse ledge and follow the crack continuation
to a ramp which leads to the top.

Eliminate the 'Droid   20m   E1 5c   (1985)
Climb the slab between the previous route and Under-Exposure for a move
(direct is 6a). From the ledge climb up directly, just left of some tufts of grass.

Under Exposure   15m   E1 5b   (1983)
This route climbs the left end of the Windy Corner wall just before it becomes
broken, then continues up the slabby wall above. Start at a very small indistinct
corner. Climb up to a horizontal break, then continue to the ledge. Climb the slab
to a wide crack which is followed to a ramp. Finish up this.

Stormwatch   20m   E1 5b   (1987)
The obvious wide corner crack left of the Android slab.

The Long Traverse   100m   Moderate   (1950s)
This is an access line only, following a system of ledges south along the base of
Scimitar Ridge. It is useful to reach the following five climbs. (This is a favourite
haunt for squads of auks in the nesting season, and as such should be avoided.)

The Great Diedre   25m   VS 4c   (1950s)
At the south end of The Long Traverse a crack slants down to a gully ending in
the sea. A blank wall prevents further progress and the groove of The Great
Diedre offers an obvious line to the ridge crest. Climb it directly, avoiding an
escape right where the groove develops into a cleft at mid-height.

Gemini   30m   Mild VS 4b *   (1966)
Start 10 metres right of The Great Diedre. Go diagonally left to a ledge, then hand
traverse right into a corner. Higher up this, mantelshelf right onto a large ledge.
Go up the corner and over the top sensationally to finish easily onto the ridge
crest.

Loony Tunes   12m   E1 5a   (1983)
The obvious right-trending ramp starting 12 metres right of The Great Diedre.

Riders on the Storm   20m   E2 5c **   (1984)
This is the right-hand of the two vague cracks running up the rib left of The Great
Diedre. Launch over a gap and climb straight up the vague crack line on the left
side of a subsidiary rib. Finish straight up a bulge, then follow the shallow
continuation groove.

End Game   20m   E3 5c **   (1984)
The left-hand crack line. Start as for Riders on the Storm, then make a hard move
to the left end of the shelf. Climb the obvious line to the top.

The following routes at the south end of the wall are gained by abseil from
large ledges at the south end of Scimitar Ridge. These ledges can be gained
either from the Main Quarry floor or by following Scimitar Ridge. The third and
quickest access is by gaining the Horseback Ridge and climbing up it seawards,
towards Scimitar Ridge, for about 10m. A large grassy narrowing ledge system
now leads off rightwards to join the main ridge. An easy short descent leads to
the large ledges (Moderate). A large iron ring on these ledges is the usual abseil
point for the routes here, the big groove of Pea Pod being located almost
immediately below it. It is probably worth using this approach to reach Riders on
the Storm and End Games, especially after the nesting season, as they will need
brushing.

Flight from Poseidon   20m   E3 6a *   (1984)
Start at the foot of Pea Pod. Climb the obvious line up right onto the edge, then
climb a thin crack to the top. It is possible to escape onto End Game on the upper
section.

Pea Pod   25m   HVS 5b **   (1975)
Climb the obvious flared groove 10 metres left of The Great Diedre. Well protected and quite sustained.

The following four routes are all serious and their lower sections climb very smooth marble-like rock.

Squid Vicious   20m   E6 6b *   (1986)
The thin blind crack left of Pea Pod, finishing up a prominent small corner. Belay at the foot of Pea Pod and traverse left to the base of the crack. Climb the crack (Rock 1 at 5m) to a ledge. The prominent corner provides a tricky finish. Both crux sections are poorly protected and a fall from the first will result in a salty bath, so it is best done at high tide with a calm sea.

Squid Pro Quo   20m   E6 6b **   (1990)
Belay at the base of Pea Pod. Follow Octopussy to where it breaks out left across the slab. From here, climb up to a poor peg. Continue up the faint blind crack (just to the right) to a horizontal break (crux). Move right to the ledge of Squid Vicious and finish up this.

Octopussy   20m   E5 6b **   (1985)
Takes the centre of the big slab left of Squid Vicious, belaying at the foot of that route. Some thought is needed in placing protection to avoid rope drag. Traverse across left, via small ledges, until directly under a shallow corner. Go up to a small flake. Step up again and levitate leftwards to gratefully grab a prominent jug in the middle of the slab. Go up this and slightly right to finish up the crack in the headwall. (It is possible to finish up the slab to the left of this at about 5b.)

Gies a Squid   20m   E6 6b **   (1990)
Belay at the base of Sea-Sprout. Traverse right and climb the blunt arete (the left edge of the Octopussy slab) to an obvious deep pocket (Friend). Move up left and continue straight up to a large jug. Swing right on to the slab and finish up Octopussy left-hand finish.

Sea-Sprout   25m   VS   (1984)
Climb a parallel groove feature right of Sea-Scoop to join it after 8m. Follow Sea-Scoop on to a large slab ramp and finish independently by one of several lines leading off the ramp.

Sea-Scoop   25m   VS 4c *   (1977)
Follows the groove at the back of the large recess just south of Pea Pod. Gain the route by a traverse (5b) from Pea Pod or by abseil.

Murdoch Head

Murdoch Head, or Murdo Head as it is sometimes called, lies about 2km north of Longhaven Quarries, and is the most prominent headland in the vicinity. The Red Tower is an obvious feature when seen from the coastline to the south. The Red Tower and Round Tower areas offer one of the best areas on the coast with excellent rock and a high concentration of routes. However, the majority of these routes are in the higher grades. The headland is wild and unspoilt, apart from old quarrying. Being a reasonable distance from the road and the ravages of modern quarrying, it has a pleasing air of seclusion.

Between Murdoch Head and Longhaven Quarries to the south the coastline is spectacular enough but apart from some entertaining sea-level traversing it is generally too loose and vegetated to be of interest. The climbing at Murdoch Head extends for about 500 metres from the Little Red Tower at the very south end northwards past the loftier Red and Round Towers to a small headland containing the Warlord Cliff. Both the Red Tower and Round Tower are only partly affected by nesting seabirds and a number of routes (particularly the harder ones) are unaffected.

Access
Approach as for the Longhaven Quarries to the car park beside the quarry office. Walk back along the track to a prominent bend where a gate leads down into the fields. Cut at first diagonally across the fields, down through several gates to a coastal path near the shallow quarry which runs parallel to the coast and almost cuts off the headland. Turn north for 100 metres for the Round Tower and the Warlord Peninsula beyond, or make for an obvious ruined building if heading for the Red Tower area. If crops are growing in the fields they should obviously not be trampled on. The headland can also be reached by following the coast northwards from the quarry office. This may be preferable since the farmer has been known to object to people crossing the fields.

THE RED TOWER AREA   *(Map Ref 122 396)*

Descend southwards from the ruined building to cross an arch and gain the grassless Escarpment with an inclined top dipping south into the sea. The east wall of the Escarpment is a spectacular face of beautiful clean granite which has been developed in recent years into one of the premier cliffs of the coast. From the foot of this face, a short neck links the Red Tower to the Escarpment. The rocks and tunnels under the descent archway provide an interesting diversion and a few routes. The majority of routes are severely affected by rough seas. To reach the south wall of the Escarpment and the Corkscrew Wall, follow the dipping strata of the Escarpment down towards the sea at its south-west end. For the Corkscrew Wall cut back right into a sheltered alcove.

THE CORKSCREW WALL

This wall is underneath the approach to the Escarpment in the aforementioned tunnels. It lies in a sheltered alcove, with a tunnel at its back, at the west end of the south wall. Their sheltered nature can lead to lingering damp, so sunshine and a breeze are recommended. The short corner at the left end of the wall provides a short Severe.

The Shining   12m   E3 5c **   (1988)
The main overhanging corner line provides a brutal little route. Climb the corner to a semi-rest below the overhang. Move left and use a thin crack to surmount the overhang.

Roamin' in the Gloamin'   12m   E3 5c *   (1987)
The flake crack right of The Shining. The line struggles for independence from its right-hand neighbour at the start. Swing out left at the top.

Rumpy Pumpy   10m   E2 5b   (1987)
The obvious recessed line just left of the tunnel. Climb up past a boss of rock, then up the overhanging wall on good holds, stepping out right.

THE SOUTH WALL OF THE ESCARPMENT

On reaching the sea go east.

Parallel Chimneys   15m   Difficult *   (1950s)
Traditionally, this is the descent of one chimney on the south wall and re-emergence using another nearby. The more seaward of the two is longer and narrower and it is best to descend the shorter landward one. Enjoyable short variants have been made in the vicinity of Parallel Chimneys.

Innocuous Cracks   20m   VS 4c *   (1976)
This is the crack line right of the seaward chimney.

THE LOWER EAST WALL OF THE ESCARPMENT

This impressive wall contains a number of excellent routes. The wall is characterised by a pothole in its centre at one-third height (gained by Hole-in-the-Wall) and the right-angled corner of Jungle Book on the right. Access to the wall can be via a traverse from the foot of the south wall involving a tricky (HVS 5b) couple of moves along a flat narrow seaweedy ledge. More usually, abseil to the foot of the routes. A hanging belay can be taken on the ledge below Mowgli, but the problems of rope drag for some of the routes often dictate a hanging belay below the line, with attendant rope problems.

Mowgli   20m   E3 6b **   (1983)
A well-hidden route climbing the groove on the edge between the south and east walls. Belay on the square-cut ledge, climb the groove until it fades, step left and continue more easily to finish to the arete.

Shere Khan   20m   E6 6c ***   (1988)
The thin twin cracks on the left of the wall, left of Hole-in-the-Wall, at present
sport four peg runners. Climb the wall to the first of the pegs. A sustained and
technical wobble up the twin cracks leads to a jug just right of the fourth peg.
Move up to a junction with Hole-in-the-Wall and follow this to the top.

Hole-in-the-Wall   20m   E5 6b ***   (1985)
A superb route taking the most amenable line up a tremendous piece of rock.
Gain the hole directly by some thin moves; runners can be arranged in and above
the hole and can involve a tied down skyhook if it takes your fancy. The crux
follows, moving left and palming up the edge to a jug. Finish by the obvious line
above.

Bagheera   20m   E6 6c **   (1987)
Yet another stunning route, starting from a hanging belay at the foot of Hole-in-
the-Wall, then climbing the wall to its right. Traverse right and go up the right side
of a thin crack line to clip a peg runner in a horizontal crack with difficulty. Move
up left from here to a good layback hold (Rock 4 at the top, RP3 above the
overlap on the left). Go left under the overlap and up to a HB3 placement. A high
palm on the edge of the little corner running up here allows a move across right
to undercuts (crux). Go up right to a hole (Friend 1) and pull up to better holds
(Rock 5 or 6). Finish more easily.

Jungle Book   25m   E1 5b **   (1978)
The big corner followed all the way. A worthwhile and interesting first pitch takes
the traverse round from the south wall. However, if the sea is too rough, abseil
in.

Fred Flintstone   25m   HVS 4b *   (1985)
Starting from the foot of Jungle Book, climb the wall on the right to gain the arete.
Follow this past a junction with Neanderthal Man to finish up a shallow corner.
Poorly protected in the upper half.

UPPER EAST WALL
The following routes are approached via Abseil Route on the North Wall or more
commonly by an abseil straight down the wall into the neck between the
Escarpment and the Red Tower.

Neanderthal Man   25m   E2 5b **   (1978)
The bold face of beautiful granite on the left. Climb out leftwards from the neck
to some flake runners. Moves up and left lead to a smooth rounded groove which
is followed to its top. Regain the centre of the wall by a right traverse, then move
up towards the left end of a large ledge. (The puny will scuttle up here for a
breather.) Move up left into an obvious small corner to finish. A fine sustained
route, although not the purest of lines.

Piltdown Connection   25m   E3 5c **   (1985)
Essentially Neanderthal Man direct, this enjoyable route finds an alternative way
up the same stretch of rock. From the flakes on the original route, make a couple
of moves directly up the wall, then veer slightly left to gain the finishing corner.

Plutonic Verses   20m   E4 6a **   (1991)
The wall between Piltdown Connection and Waltzinblack. Move out left from the
Neck as for Waltzinblack. Where this moves right, climb straight up the wall past
a small ledge and two thin flakes (runners to the right in Waltzinblack). Continue
directly and boldly to a left-slanting flake crack. Climb to ledges, then move up
and left for a short detour to the Neanderthal Man corner. Move back right onto
the wall to finish.

Waltzinblack   25m   E4 5c **   (1983)
The groove and wall just left of Tarzan Wall. Move out left from the neck as for
Neanderthal Man, then climb up and right to gain the groove and some crucial
RP runners. Enter the groove and proceed to a horizontal break; the choice is
now open to fiddle in a small wire or dash boldly leftwards to a large ledge. Finish
by the obvious deep crack.

Tarzan Wall   20m   Hard Severe **   (1950s)
A steep and fairly intimidating climb for its grade. taking a crack-groove at the
right side of the wall. Follow the crack from the neck to the crux at two-thirds
height. Large holds lead out right to finish up the edge.

THE NORTH WALL
This overlooks the small inlet out on the north side of the Escarpment. The face
is slabby and shadowed and tends to be greasy and mossy. Access to the routes
is by abseil or down-climbing. The first route is useful for access to the neck when
dry.

Abseil Route   20m   Difficult   (1950s)
This is the most prominent crack line on the face, about 5 metres in from the
edge of the wall. It is sustained on big and sometimes doubtful-looking holds. A
lot of variation is possible.

Pancake Crack   20m   Difficult   (1980)
The crack right of Abseil Route has rather brittle rock.

Pink Edge   20m   Difficult   (1980)
Traverse left from Abseil Route to climb cracks overlooking Tarzan Wall.

THE RED TOWER
The relative difficulty of approach to this thumb-like Tower, by abseil or down-
climbing, adds an extra dimension to the climbing here and makes it well worth
the visit for the expedition.

North-West Corner   10m   Very Difficult   (1950)
From the neck, cross a short slippery slab to the left and from the apex of this
pull up over the bulge on good holds. Sometimes slimy and unpleasant.

West Wall   8m   HVS 5b
The short crack.

South-West Corner   10m   Very Difficult   (1950s)
The corner to the right provides a better way to the top of the Tower and a good
descent, although abseiling may be preferred.

South Wall   12m   VS 4c *   (1976)
The obvious crack splitting the bulge of the south wall, very strenuous. Move
right and finish by a steep grove.

Sea Traverse   25m   Hard Severe   (1950s)
Traverse the south wall close to the sea to reach the platform on the east side.
The final bit round the edge is awkward and requires a fairly calm sea.

South-East Corner   10m   Severe   (1950s)
Follows naturally upon the previous traverse. Climb an easy ledge on the east
wall to gain an exposed ledge halfway up the South-East Corner. Climb a steep
crack near the edge of the east wall, avoiding an escape via the final groove of
the South Wall route.

North-East Corner   10m   Severe *
Climb a line of holds near the right edge of the east wall, or start in the centre of
the face and follow a right-slanting crack (VS 4b).

THE LITTLE RED TOWER

This is the small pyramidal Tower some 50 metres south of Murdoch Head at
the southern tip of a long inlet. It is very obvious from the Escarpment. The
approach is either by abseil (anchors are hard to find) or by a scramble down
grass and blocks. Continuing towards the tower, a small jump may be needed
at high tide to cross the neck. A traverse round from the north is the access to
the base of the prominent black corner, maybe problematical in high seas, in
which an abseil down the corner can be taken. The base of the corner is the
start to all 3 routes.

The Seal   8m   Severe   (1990)
The obvious black corner.

Edgeling   20m   VS 4c **   (1990)
The prominent arete which rises straight out of the sea, initially climbed on its
right, then on its left, to finish up a small slab.

Esoteria   10m   E3 6b **   (1990)
The superb east wall of clean granite. Traverse round the edge on good holds,
then move up the centre of the wall to some horizontal slots. Climb directly up
the bulging wall to good holds and the top. (The crux is sequency but no doubt
easier for the tall ... then what's new!)

THE SEA-QUARRIES

The cliffs running north from the Red Tower area have been quarried in the past
and well explored since. There is an interesting traverse finishing up the face
opposite Abseil Route, and a few other worthwhile climbs. In general, the cliffs
lack positive lines. The cliffs are conveniently divided into three parts, north to
south.
1. North Peak and Median Peak. Separated from the Round Tower to the North
by the big inlet of North Glash, and from the main cliffs to the south by a shallow
quarry.
2. Central Buttress and the Arena, the large quarry to its south.
3. The South Buttresses, separated by a shallow quarry. The stone ruin stands
at the top of the South Buttress.

Access to the routes on Central Buttress and Median Peak is by descent into
the quarry below the North Peak. Walk up the seaward side of the inland quarry,
whose mouth faces the Round Tower, and descend with care the ridge overlook
ing North Glash leading out to the North Peak. Six metres down, an easy ledge
goes down into the quarry. On the two peaks and the face of Central Buttress
surrounding the quarry, there are several lines at about Moderate to Difficult in
standard. The rock is poor and details are unnecessary. However, there is good
rock on the seaward side of Median Peak.

Hobnobs   20m   E2 5c   (1990)
A gritty line left of the big slab in the quarry. Follow a corner and slab to the right
of a curving corner above. Climb the corner to small overhang. Pull onto the slab
on the right, then go up to climb a second overhang on the left to easy ground.
Not even remotely recommended.

Django   25m   Severe *   (1967)
This is reached by descent from the quarry to the basin on the south of the
Median Peak. There is a strange hole here going down into a big underground
chasm below the Peak and opening to the sea on the north side. Continue down
the seaward side of the Peak by a sloping shelf to beneath a steep wall. Climb
a superb overhanging wall on good holds and continue directly to the top of the
Peak, avoiding escapes. Many variations are possible on excellent rock.

The Great Traverse   150m   Very Difficult *   (1950s)
An interesting expedition with some good climbing but not as good as North
Glash Traverse. Not recommended in high seas. Starting from the quarry below

North Peak, the climb girdles Central Buttress, with an awkward descent to the Arena. Gain South Buttress via the green slabs (sometimes greasy), then traverse round to the next quarry. On the face opposite the Red Tower is a crack leading diagonally upwards. This is gained by a descending crack and is followed for 30m until a deep cleft cuts back right to the top. The final holds require care, but the last pitch is sensational with superb exposure.

Not So Bad   15m   HVS 5a   (1975)
Above the awkward descent on the girdle of Central Buttress are two thin converging cracks. The rightmost gives this pleasant, delicate problem. The left-hand crack is **Not So Good** (Mild VS) joining the other after 5m.

The South Buttress can be reached via the south side of Central Buttress, where a staircase of broken rocks leads down to the deeper quarry, the Arena (Moderate).

South Buttress Direct   45m   Very Difficult   (1950s)
Follow the Great Traverse onto South Buttress till it is possible to climb straight up the centre of the buttress to a large ledge 5m from the top (much variation possible.) Climb up to a hanging ledge and so to the top.

Left Edge Route   45m   Severe
Follow the Great Traverse until just before it turns the corner, then climb a steep groove to the large fault. Finish up the wall above by a deep crack and a short corner. Many variations are possible on this area of the cliff.

Dandy Corner   30m   Severe *   (1980)
This enjoyable route lies up the big slabby diedre under the finale of the Great Traverse. It is very obvious when viewed from the Red Tower area. Traverse round into the diedre at low tide and climb the corner crack to a horizontal fault. Make an excursion out leftwards to sloping shelves overlooking the inlet. Cut back up right to finish up the top of the diedre (Hard Severe), or easier but not so good, climb up the wall to the left. A finish was made via Great Traverse but an independent finish in the continuation fault might be better.

Bananaman   15m   E3 6a *   (1987)
The angular overhanging corner crack above the base of Dandy Corner (belay on the slab of that route, low tide required). Climb the wall and the overlap by a weird bridge then climb the crack to the top. Only marred by nests over the top, but the exit is not difficult. There is a choice of lines to finish.

NORTH GLASH
The inlet north of the Sea-Quarry Cliffs has a fine traverse along the length of the slabby south wall facing the Round Tower.

North Glash Traverse   125m   Very Difficult ***   (1977)
Start at the mouth of the shallow quarry which cuts across Murdoch Head.
Traverse down to some jumbled blocks at about 5m and gain a descending
crack. Continue down to a horizontal break at 8m which is traversed to a gully.
Gain a ridge on the left and the next gully by a jump or precarious climbing lower
down (often wet). Traverse down cracks to sea-level. The climb now continues
up and over a big cave (serious) then out to the arete which is followed to the
summit of North Peak. With so much traversing and descending both second
and leader should be confident at Very Difficult standard.

A route has been climbed on the land-facing wall of the shallow quarry from
where the North Glash Traverse starts.

Revision   25m   E1 5a   (1991)
The slab just left of a shallow vertical corner is still loose.

THE ROUND TOWER   *(Map Ref 123 397)*

This impressive tower, like a big gritstone buttress perched high above the sea,
has one of the finest concentrations of hard climbs on the coast. There are no
easy climbs and most provide long sustained pitches on solid granite. Approaching up the landward side of the shallow quarry, the crack line of Tyrant Crack
dominates the south wall. Go down the north side of North Glash to a col beneath
the short slabby north side of the Tower (the limit of old quarrying).
Access to climbs on the walls of the Tower is by a fairly easy but rather exposed
and dangerous traverse by grassy ledges round the north side. When damp, this
should be treated with great care. Descend a little ramp and follow the cleanest
rock ledges round to the east side of the Tower. Here, gear can be dumped on
spacious platforms and the routes weighed up. The routes of the south wall are
easily gained from here by a ledge system which circles the Tower and eventually
regains the col, completing a girdle of sorts with some awkward and very exposed
moves along past the base of Tyrant Crack (Hard Severe — 1950s). Unfortunately, most of the climbs on the Tower are messed up with kittiwake nests and
attendant bodily emissions in summer. However, the routes from Tumbling Dice
to Stoneface are always fairly clean.
Descent from the grassy top is via a rather tricky and not too obvious way
close to the north edge overlooking the start of the access traverse (Very Difficult
in ascent). It is exposed and grassy at the top, and abseiling may be preferred.
Start down grassy terrain slanting left (facing out) to gain the edge of the mainland
slab. Step down and across horizontal faults in the slab and so to the bottom.
The routes are described from right to left to the south wall.

1   Tumbling Dice   20m   E1 5b   (1978)
The first major line, following an obvious crack on the slabby north face of the
Tower. At present, the route has been reclaimed by sea grass. The name is
derived from the small dice-like particles of rock which tinkle down from the

climber's holds. Start right of a roof and surmount a bulge. Climb the crack with increasing difficulty, finishing out right near the very top.

2   Atlantis   25m   E3 5c ***   (1979)
This is the fine hanging groove left of Tumbling Dice; absorbing climbing. Start up the blunt rib right of the obvious roofed corner crack of Sun God and left of the lower roof of Tumbling Dice. Gain a strenuous crack which leads to the halfway break. Surmount a bulge into the hanging groove and go up this to finish by the long left-hand crack.

3   Sun God   28m   E5 6b ***   (1982)
The architecture of the Tower is remarkable where it curves round to form the frontal seaward face. The resemblance to a giant human face is striking and the two hardest climbs on the Tower take the left and right sides of this feature. Sun God takes a stunning line out left under the big roof beside Atlantis and up into the right eye of the face, before finishing boldly out on the upper frontal wall.
    Climb the fine corner crack just left of Atlantis and traverse left under the big roof and up into a short roofed corner (the right eye), a useful resting point. Move up round the left edge of the roof above onto the nose at a thin vertical protection crack. Climb straight up to the last of several horizontal cracks, where a fairly crucial nut can be placed with some difficulty. Step up to a flake and pull up to traverse right onto the arete. Climb up here to finish as for Life of Brian, up the arete and out right by a crack. Some fancy ropework is the key to cutting rope drag on the upper wall.

4   Rain God   25m   E6 6b ***   (1987)
This desperate route dissects Sun God. It starts up the obvious crack in the rib to reach the corner on Right Eye then moves out right from the Eye to finish boldly up the slab left of Atlantis. Start as for Stoneface, then climb the crack (RPs) to the Eye. Traverse out right (peg runner) round the rib onto the slab which is climbed direct to finish up the crack as for Sun God (RP2 in the flake on the rib and two RP2s in the horizontal break above). Rope drag is bad on the slab.

5   Stoneface   25m   E4 6a **   (1980/1982)
The obvious crack which starts at the right side of the frontal wall and curves up left past the nose and left eye of the giant face. The right extremity of the frontal wall forms an undercut edge. Gain this direct or by stepping in from the right and move left to the curving crack. Transfer to the vertical crack on the left at 5m and continue to follow the unrelenting curving line to a final pull out left to relatively easy ground right of the obvious corner of Silver Surfer. This whole lower section is strenuous and sustained with no real rests. Move up right to the final thin crack in the headwall. This provides a technical finish. It is possible to split the climb by hand traversing left to belay on The Present above the Silver Surfer corner. The first ascent finished via The Present.

THE ROUND TOWER – MURDOCH HEAD

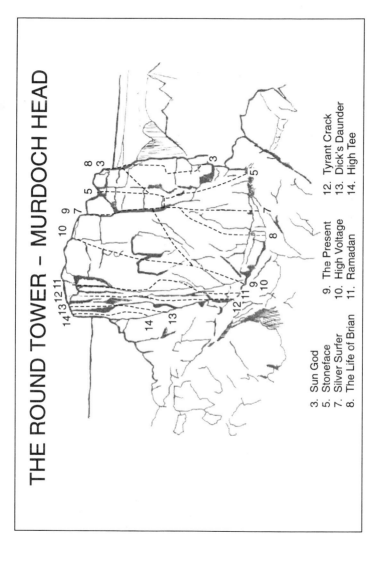

3. Sun God
5. Stoneface
7. Silver Surfer
8. The Life of Brian

9. The Present
10. High Voltage
11. Ramadan

12. Tyrant Crack
13. Dick's Daunder
14. High Tee

6   Facegod   25m   E5 6a **   (1991)
Hybrid but good. Start up the crack left of Stoneface (the direct start), then follow
Stoneface until a hand traverse leads right onto the nose. Continue up Sun God,
but where that route traverses right continue up the black wall on good holds to
finish just left of the arete.

7   Silver Surfer   20m   E3 5c **   (1979)
There is a silvery white streak coming down the middle of the frontal wall. This
fine direct line climbs straight up to the streak then up the left side. The protection
is adequate but strenuous to arrange and a forceful approach is called for. A
small pothole in the rock at two-thirds height is an obvious feature. Above the
steep wall gain an easy slabby corner leading directly to the finishing corner of
The Present. The start is undercut and strenuous.

8   The Life of Brian   30m   E1 5a **   (1980)
This is a counter line to Stoneface, curving right across the frontal wall. Start on
a ledge above and left of Silver Surfer. Follow an obvious ramp curving up and
over Silver Surfer into the easy slabby corner. Rather than finish up The Present,
gain an obvious line of puckered holds and traverse out under the final crack of
Stoneface to the right arete, joining Sun God. Climb the arete to finish by a crack
to the right. Not well protected.

9   The Present   30m   VS 4c *   (1966)
This was the original route breaching the main walls of the Tower. It shares a
common start with High Voltage, about 5m left of the start of Life of Brian. Follow
grooves until not far below an obvious square-cut corner set in the middle of the
wall. Trend right to the fine finishing corner which lies recessed above the slabby
corner of the direct line Silver Surfer. This line is heavily birded in summer and
usually slow to lose its nests.

10   High Voltage   20m   HVS 5a *   (1980)
Begin as for The Present, but continue up the square-cut corner to a small
pedestal on top. Finish straight up by an exciting flake crack in the steep
headwall. It is wise to check that the holds over the top are clean before starting
up this line, which is heavily birded.

11   Ramadan   20m   E1 5b **   (1978)
This is an exciting and wildly exposed route up the edge of the south and frontal
walls. Start up an obvious groove just right of Tyrant Crack strenuously to gain
a weird partly-detached flake just left of the corner of High Voltage. Traverse out
left to the edge and climb this sensationally via a small groove to the top in a
superb position. The first groove is the technical crux but it is possible to start up
The Present, as on the first ascent. This way the grade is perhaps only HVS 5a.

12   Tyrant Crack   20m   E3 6a **   (1978)
The challenging crack dominating the south wall. As for its neighbours, the exposed position hanging over North Glash makes the climbing more impressive here. Hard and strenuous climbing up twin converging cracks leads to the sanctuary of a big spike at 10m. Thereafter the crack is deeper and not so steep.

13   Dick's Daunder   15m   HVS 5a   (1978)
The obvious line left of Tyrant. Start up a small ramp leading up right and go straight up to the top.

14   High Tee   15m   E1 5a   (1983)
The obvious corner crack on the extreme left can be quickly gained from the side of the col.

15   The Underworld   30m   E2 5c   (1987)
The obvious corner system below the south face, spoiled by nests. From the platform below Atlantis, climb down and round to a platform under the overhanging wall. Step left and traverse a slab up left under bulges. Hand traverse out right and surmount the awkward bulge using a jutting projection to gain a ramp. Go up left by a slanting slot to easier slabs, then blocks lead to the grassy neck.

THE WARLORD CLIFF

This is an attractive east-facing triangular wall on the small headland north of the Round Tower, across the inlet. Go round the back of the inlet and walk out to the tip of the headland. The wall is hidden below. The best descent for access is to climb down the north-east edge of the wall (The Warpath, Difficult and exposed). This is not obvious from above but is gained by a short descent down grassy ground. Alternatively abseil (largely free) down the headwall. This is gripping and it is hard to find good anchors. It is also possible to descend a grassy rake from right to left on the Round Tower side (also gripping and not recommended). A further access line is by traversing along the wall of the inlet on the north side of the headland. At low tide this is Very Difficult and gives a pleasant outing when combined with ascent of The Warpath. There are extensive flat rocks under the wall. The routes are described from right to left.

The Warpath   20m   Difficult *
The right edge of the wall, trickiest at the bottom.

Warrior   25m   HVS 5a *   (1977)
The first corner line left of The Warpath. Sustained.

Warlord   25m   E1 5b **   (1977)
A classic. Climb the obvious corner in the middle of the face then traverse out right under a large overlap. Pull round the overlap and continue steeply to the top. Intimidating, but protection is good.

Harmony   25m   E2 5c **   (1993)
A fine line with good rock and protection; high in the grade. Start left of Warlord
at a short chimney. Follow cracks towards the main overhang, then turn this on
the right using underclings. Move up to easier ground, step left into a niche, then
continue via a mantelshelf to the abseil point.

Truce   15m   HVS 5a/b   (1993)
Approach by scrambling about 50 metres left from the foot of the abseil until
below a small buttress of compact rock. Start up a slab, then take the longest
corner in the buttress. The sunny situation is marred by gulls near the bottom.

Skirmish   30m   VS 4c   (1977)
This follows the left-bounding edge of the wall on the slabby face opposite the
Round Tower, with some friable rock. Climb cracks up the slab to finish via a
crack across on the right.

Longhaven to Boddam

Longhaven to Boddam is the most northerly of the granite climbing areas in this guide and is special in that one can generally be assured peace and solitude, climbing in a wild and beautiful setting shared perhaps only with the local lobster fishermen lifting their creels. Those making the effort to come this far north will be rewarded by a choice of quality routes on excellent rock at all standards.

MEACKIE POINT *(Map Ref 124 405)*

Access
About 2km north of Longhaven village on the east side of the A952 stands the solitary Glenugie Cottage. Some 300 metres further on the same side of the road is a derelict cottage with a handy car park at its front. Directly behind the cottage and across the dismantled railway line is a large inlet, the south side of which is Whispering Slabs. Meackie Point is the large headland south of this inlet.

POINT WALL
The wall is at the tip of the headland above a tidal platform and can be approached by scrambling from either the south (which is easier) or by the north. The wall is of superb granite, climbable all year round, being free from birds during the nesting season. It was inexplicably neglected until the mid-1980s.

The routes are described from north to south, the obvious corner of Legend being a useful identifying feature.

The Changeling   15m   E3 6a **   (1985)
The wall and slab at the extreme right end of the cliff immediately right of Legend. Start from the descent ramp on the right at two diagonal cracks. Gain the upper crack, then go left into the centre of the wall. Move up and left, then back right onto the slab. Follow the right edge of the slab, or better and bolder, the left side.

Legend   15m   E2 5c **   (1984)
The obvious corner near the right end of the cliff. The first 6m up to the crux bulge provides strenuous and sustained climbing. Follow the corner to the top.

The Killing Moon   15m   E1 5b **   (1984)
The crack line left of Legend has some technical interest in its lower half. A delightful route.

Trial of Tears   12m   E3 6a **   (1985)
The curving line of flakes left of Killing Moon. Start at the base of that route and follow the flakes to underclings and a finish directly above, avoiding the left arete. This route often has a wet dribble but is still climbable in such conditions and holds on the left arete offer salvation for the weak-willed.

The Water Margin   12m   E1 5a   (1985)

Climb the crack line left of Trial of Tears to a small ledge and shallow corner. The corner can be avoided easily on the left (taken direct it is at least a technical grade harder).

Scurry   25m   HVS 5b   (1977)

Near the centre of the wall a prominent ramp slants up right. Climb a short groove to gain the ramp, then climb it until it is possible to traverse left onto a counter ramp. Climb this to a slab at its end, then finish up and slightly left. A variation start (5a) comes in from the left of Water Margin.

Flurry   20m   HVS 5a **   (1978)

The prominent groove left of Scurry. Start at the foot of Scurry and traverse up left to the foot of the groove. Layback the groove, then break out right and go up the wall on good holds.

Direct Start: 5m   5a   (1986)

Move up into the wide crack below the corner and pull out left onto the ledge.

Impending Doom   25m   E2 5c *   (1984)

Climb the initial groove of Scurry to gain the ramp, then move up and left on flakes to a short crack. From the top of this, move right onto a ramp which trends left to the top.

Direct Start: E3 5c   (1986)

Climb the wide crack of Flurry Direct Start to the ledge under a scoop. Climb directly up the wall just to the right to gain shelves on the normal route.

Fast Reactor   20m   E3 6a *   (1986)

Start just left of the wide crack of Flurry Direct Start. Climb straight up the wall at a flake line to the Flurry ledge. Step right and climb flake cracks up the scoop until it is possible to pull out right and up to a big flake. Swing up left to join Flurry. Contrived, but good climbing.

The Method   20m   E3 6a **   (1986)

A steep line up the face left of Flurry. Start up a little left-slanting ramp, then pull straight up the wall to a shelf. From runners above the top of this, step back down and traverse left using underclings to reach up for holds and the left edge of the wall; junction with the following route.

The Collector   15m   E1 5b *   (1986)

Start on a ledge below and right of a block. Climb steeply up a vague shallow groove to a bulge and swing up right over this to gain a narrow diagonal ramp. Go up this to finish as for Thieves Like Us.

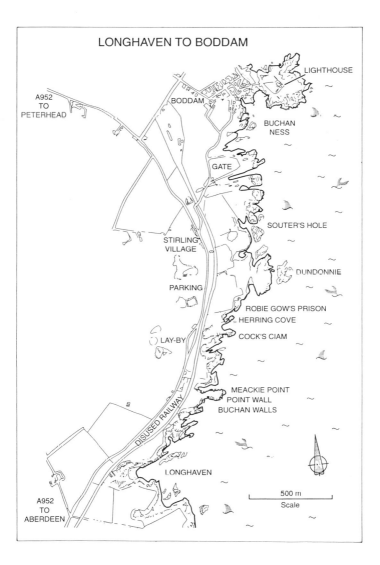

LONGHAVEN TO BODDAM

A952
TO
PETERHEAD

LIGHTHOUSE

BODDAM

BUCHAN
NESS

GATE

SOUTER'S HOLE

STIRLING
VILLAGE

DUNDONNIE

PARKING

ROBIE GOW'S PRISON
HERRING COVE

LAY-BY

COCK'S CIAM

MEACKIE POINT
POINT WALL
BUCHAN WALLS

DISUSED RAILWAY

LONGHAVEN

A952
TO
ABERDEEN

500 m
Scale

Thieves Like Us   15m   HVS 5a *   (1984)
Start from the pointed block at the left extremity of the cliff. Climb a vague groove
to a slabby area under bulges. Traverse out right using undercuts to pull round
onto the seaward face. Now either traverse right to finish up Scurry, or climb the
arete.

Arc of a Diver   35m   E3 5c *   (1988)
This is an exciting left to right girdle of the cliff, sampling the delights of several
of the routes. Start at the left-slanting ramp of The Method, move up then right
onto the ledge of Flurry. Step right, then go up into Impending Doom via its direct
start, cross to Scurry and belay. Traverse the ledge into Water Margin, move
slightly down, then go across Trial of Tears and Killing Moon to Legend. Descend
Legend until moves can be made round to the Changeling, which provides an
exciting finale. It is recommended to have a second who is equally into this sort
of thing.

WHISPERING SLABS
These extensive slabs of fine granite are on the north side of the Meackie Point
headland. However, the area is unfortunately spoiled by the amount of steep
vegetation growing above the decent rock. It has been traversed for 45m at
sea-level (Difficult) from where the top can be reached via the slab and a
prominent left-slanting green groove (45m VS). The rock and vegetation at the
top of the groove is very loose.

BUCHAN WALLS
These are the steep walls on the south-facing side of the inlet 100 metres south
of Meackie Point. They are approached by a traverse from the easy slabs on the
south side of Meackie Point. The walls and access route can best be viewed by
going down over the arete on the south side of the inlet.

Gold Dust   45m   HVS 5a   (1977)
In the centre of the walls is a steep right-sloping ramp. Start 8 metres along a
ledge leading left from the foot of the ramp. Climb the grooves above and the
wall to their left to reach the prominent corner. Climb this until below the
overhang, where a sand-filled crack leads left across an undercut wall. When the
crack runs out, a short wall leads to easy slabs and the top. The cliff is heavily
birded in the nesting season and remains dirty for some time. The rock appears
to be suspect in places.

COCK'S CAIM

The Cock's Caim is a place with considerable character and has a more
mountaineering feel to it. The area saw some of the earliest activity in the
development of sea-cliff climbing in the north-east.

Access
Park as for Meackie Point and walk north along the old railway embankment for 200 metres. Cut across the heathery cliff top towards the unmistakable arete of Cock's Caim. Alternatively, park as for Robie Gow's Prison and walk south.

   The best approach to the main traverse is from the north side to a ridge of quarried granite blocks and then up the short steep grassy north flank. Care is required, and it is not recommended if wet or greasy.

Main Traverse   100m   Moderate
This is the descent to the foot of the other routes. From the flat top of Cock's Caim, walk along then descend to a notch, over the tooth, and down the south face to ledges leading round to the north face.

NORTH FACE

Comet Crack   20m   Difficult   (1950)
The crack between the ridge and the companion rib which culminates at the Tooth.

Tooth Direct   20m   Difficult   (1950)
Climb the rib which leads direct to the Tooth. It is better close to the edge.

Crocks Crack   20m   Very Difficult   (1950)
The obvious narrow layback crack facing left. Finish above the Tooth.

Bottleneck   35m   Severe   (1950)
Start 30 metres along the north face where the cliff juts out to form a bottleneck chimney. Climb the chimney, then move left and continue to the top.

Ring Pull   30m   VS **   (1977)
From the foot of Bottleneck, traverse right to below some roofs on the arete. Climb up and right between the roofs, then go up a crack. A ledge on the left leads to easy slabs and the crest.

   Right of Ring Pull lies a great expanse of unclimbed rock, rough and slabby but unfortunately capped by much vegetation.

SOUTH FACE

An unpleasantly loose cliff, even more unpleasant when heavily birded during the nesting season. A few routes have been climbed but they are marred by loose rock. One route is described.

Cyprus Wall   35m   Mild VS 4b   (1950s)
Traverse from the foot of the ridge below a steep sloping prow to a chimney formed by a basalt intrusion. Climb up right to an awkward pull onto a steep slab which is crossed obliquely right to finish by a corner crack. Poor belay.

HIDDEN INLET

Hidden Inlet is situated at the base of the next headland south of Cock's Caim. At the edge of the cliff top go south-east down a grassy ridge which in turn leads to a grassy slope. Descend the slope at the left edge to the second of two corners which is descended to easy ground. From the grassy ridge the cliff is visible down on the left. An iron stake is in place at the top of the headland to fix a handline if so desired.

The routes, which are on excellent clean rock, face south-east and therefore get a fair amount of sunshine. The cliff is partially tidal and should be climbable all year round. The routes are described from the obvious central corner of Secret Affair.

Secret Affair   12m   HVS 5a **   (1985)
Climb the obvious left-facing corner in the centre of the wall.

The Diddymen   10m   HVS 4c   (1985)
Climb the wall left of Secret Affair, trend slightly left, then go straight up.

Left of the Diddymen are two small cracks, the right-hand is HVS 5b, the left is HVS 5c, the wall between them is E1 5c.

Lonely   12m   E1 5a **   (1985)
This poorly protected route climbs the right arete of the corner of Secret Affair.

Not so Lonely   12m   E2 5c **   (1985)
This climbs the cracks right of the previous route to gain and climb a curving overlap with easy ground above.

Big Diddies   10m   VS 4c *   (1985)
Climb cracks and flakes to the right of Not So Lonely.

Pirelli Wellies   10m   Severe *   (1985)
This route climbs cracks at the right end of the wall.

Opposite the cliff is a wall of black rock which if climbed centrally gives a route of Severe standard.

ROBIE GOW'S PRISON

Access

Some 500 metres north of the Meackie Point car park is another small car park, again on the east side of the road. Turn off the main road opposite the entrance to the old quarry which lies on the west side. From the car park a quaint set of granite steps leads through a gate and down to the disused railway embankment. Cut straight across the field ahead to reach the cliff top where the rocks of

Robie Gow's can be seen. The best descent is to walk north along the rim of the inlet to an easy-angled ramp which leads down to the open sunny area of slabs.

The climbing is on the steep south-facing wall which is split by a shallow chimney. The rock tends to be sugary in places and should be handled with care.

Escape Route   20m   HVS 5a **   (1977)
Start just left of the chimney at the lowest part of the cliff below an obvious roof. Climb up to a sloping ledge below the roof. Move out left under the roof, then follow grooves to the top. A good sustained route.

Two routes have been climbed either side of Escape Route. Both are very close and can be joined to the parent route in places.

Break on Through   20m   HVS 5a   (1985)
Start directly above bright green moss right of Escape Route. Climb an over-hanging flake crack to gain the sloping ledge of Escape Route. Continue up an overhanging crack, then follow the arete to the top.

The Jester   20m   HVS 5a   (1988)
Left of Escape Route at mid-height is a short wall with twin parallel cracks. Climb a groove leading to the cracks and finish up the left arete of Escape Route. Very contrived

Convict's Wall   20m   Hard Severe   (1977)
Left of The Jester the cliff is recessed in its upper half. Climb steep rock (better on the right) to the recess and various finishes.

Right of the chimney, the cliff is shorter but steep and seamed with cracks.

Kinesiology   12m   Hard Severe   (1985)
Climb the bulging wall immediately next to the chimney to a ledge. Move right and climb the obvious corner to finish by the top of the chimney. Belay well back to the fence.

Telekinesis   12m   E3 5c   (1985)
In the centre of this part of the cliff is a striking hanging crack. Climb the wall below the crack, pull over the bulge to its left, then step right into it. Contrived and very unsatisfactory.

Kinetic Control   12m   E2 5c *   (1982)
Climb the short left-facing corner to a point where it is possible to make awkward moves right then left to gain the hanging corner. This leads to the prominent inverted V; finish up this. At the top end of the grade.

Fracture Zone   12m   E1 5b *   (1982)
Right of the previous route an obvious system of cracks runs up through an overhang. Follow these to the top. Strenuous.

HERRING COVE

This is the inlet to the south of Robie Gow's Prison. Access is as for Robie Gow's. From the sunny slabs the beautiful granite sheet of Hidden Treasure Wall can be seen in profile. The following routes are on the main wall and are described from left to right.

Captain Pugwash   20m   E3 6a **   (1985)
This fine route climbs the left arete of the wall all the way to the top.

Hidden Treasure   20m   E2 5c ***   (1982)
Start 3 metres right of the arete. Follow a line of flakes leftwards to reach a horizontal break. Attain a standing position, then climb the thin vertical finger crack strenuously to a ledge. Finish up the short wall above. A classic.

Bloodhunt   15m   E4 6b **   (1985)
The central line on the wall gives a superb route. Start up the initial moves of Hidden Treasure, then follow flakes straight up to the break. Hard moves into and up the parallel cracks lead to the top.

Dwarf Stone   12m   E2 6a *   (1985)
Climb the groove right of Hidden Treasure to ledges, then move left and climb the wall just left of the rightmost thin crack to better holds and the top. Unfortunately it is easy to escape at mid-height.

   Left of the arete of Captain Pugwash lie two rather disappointing routes, both in terms of rock quality and nesting kittiwake debris.

Herring Chimney   25m   VS   (1977)
Immediately left of the arete are two cracks which form a chimney higher up. The two cracks are the crux, the left one being HVS, the right one VS. Escape is possible at mid-height, but the best finish is by the chimney above.

Kipper Wall   50m   VS   (1977)
Traverse left from the arete for about 50 metres, just above sea-level, to a rock platform with a deep crack behind it. From the left end of the platform climb the groove and cracks to where it is possible to traverse horizontally right to a large recess. Follow a left-sloping ramp (some loose rock) to the top.

SOUTER'S HOLE

Access

About 4km (3 miles) north of Longhaven Village is a row of houses called Stirling Village, opposite which a road runs down to Boddam. Follow this road for 300 metres to a track which leads off right. There is a locked gate at the start of the track, beside which cars can be parked providing they do not block access.

Follow the track south-east towards the sea. Where the track swings right parallel to the coast, leave the track on the left at the head of a dry gully. Cut across towards the sea to the next inlet which runs parallel to the coast. This is Chimney Inlet.

CHIMNEY INLET
At the back of Chimney Inlet is a slanting chimney cave.

Chimney Girdle   75m   Very Difficult *
This is a Patey sea-level traverse of the east-facing wall of Chimney Inlet, finishing up the improbable slanting chimney. Three rusty old pegs are still in place. A route of character.

Problem Corner   12m   Hard Severe   (1977)
Climb the obvious right-facing corner on the east-facing side of Chimney inlet.

PROMONTORY WALL
This solid wall of granite on the seaward side of Chimney Inlet faces south, overlooking the channel connecting Souter's Hole to the sea. It is a delightful place which can be climbed on all your round, providing the sea is calm. For sun-worshippers, its aspect allows late evening climbing in the summer months — a place for the connoisseur. The best approach for the routes on the west side is by scrambling down a ramp at the extreme west side of the cliff. This leads to a platform bordering the undercut slab. For the routes on the east side it is possible to downclimb a staircase of jugs on the extreme east side. This leads to a platform beside the rising shelf of the promontory traverse. (Moderate).

The routes are described from west to east.

Promontory Traverse   30m   Severe **   (1977)
Traverse the wall from the landward end via the obvious undercut slab. Beyond the overhanging prow a rising shelf leads to the top. A fine excursion.

Souter Johnnie   10m   E2 6a *   (1989)
Climb the first crack line on the undercut slab to the base of the overhanging wall. Surmount this strenuously to gain the corner above.

Souter's Slab   12m   Mild VS 4b *   (1977)
Starting right of the previous route, follow the next crack line on the slab and climb an overlap to finish directly.

Toe Cap   12m   Mild VS 4b *   (1977)
Right of Souter's Slab is a small shallow chimney with an obvious ledge below it. Climb the shallow chimney, then trend right to finish at the highest point of the cliff. It is best to belay on the obvious ledge.

Tackety Wall   20m   VS 4c   (1977)
Start at the same place as Toe Cap. Climb the cracks above, right of Toe Cap,
then traverse right below the overhangs to easy ground. An escape left is
possible before the traverse right.

Sole Fusion   12m   E1 5b *   (1987)
Start as for Last Groove. Traverse left and climb a scooped groove up and over
a bulge. Continue up the crack to the top. A fine strenuous route.

Soul Mate   15m   E2 5b *   (1992)
A good but escapable climb which takes the overhanging prow. From the belay
at the base of Last Groove, step left across a gap and climb the bulges towards
the arete. Head up to a good flake crack on the left side of the edge, then
continue up the left side before moving right to the final hanging corner.

Last Groove   12m   HVS 5a **   (1977)
On the right side of the overhanging prow lies an obvious groove. Climb a bulge
into a pod-shaped recess. A steep wall above leads to a choice of finish, easier
and more natural on the right but better by the left. An excellent climb.

The short wall of beautiful granite right of Last Groove has been climbed at
E2 5c.

CORBIE'S HOLE

North of Souter's Hole are two prominent inlets receding well back inland, with
the arched remains of Boddam Castle squeezed between. The south inlet is
Corbie's Hole, which offers a number of easy and middle grade routes on its
south-facing walls. These have been unrecorded and left to the individual's keen
sense of exploration. The north inlet is Thief's Loup; this offers little to the climber,
but is interesting from the geological standpoint in that one side is granite, the
other a noticeable seam of basalt. The rock on which Buchan Ness Lighthouse
sits marks the end of the granite cliffs, a coastline of beaches and bays taking
its place.

Moray Area

Not surprisingly, the largely flat Moray plain with its low sandy coastline offers little to the rock climber. The only natural cliffs of any consequence lie on the coast between Burghead and Lossiemouth and large areas of these are formed of very soft sandstone and conglomerate, poorly suited to climbing. However, whilst the scope is limited, the two main areas described offer good climbing in delightful settings. They are largely unspoilt, uncrowded, attractively and conveniently sited and blessed with some of the driest sunniest weather in the whole North-East of Scotland. The climate noticeably improves as you travel west along the Moray Firth towards Inverness, so that all these cliffs, and to a lesser extent those of Banffshire also, are often free of the fog, birds and high seas which are the bane of the Aberdeen coast. Given rain in the west and fog on the east coast, a common combination in the spring season, the Moray Area is a fair bet for a good sunny day with enough attraction to keep most climbers happy.

Cummingston offers a relatively non-serious playground atmosphere with many boulder problems and reasonable landings, whilst Covesea, more recently developed, offers less bouldering and has a more serious atmosphere. The other areas described are of much lesser interest.

CUMMINGSTON   *(Map Ref 130 692)*

The cliffs at Cummingston are composed of a softish sandstone with fluted holds and other wind-eroded features. The climbs are short and steep, even overhanging, often on big flaky holds after a difficult undercut start. The cliffs lie above a tidal beach of sand, gravel or rock, which may provide a good landing, though this is variable from year to year.

The cliff has become popular for strenuous bouldering, but the profusion of big holds leads to many climbs in the lower grades, although protection in the soft rock will always be a worry to the inexperienced. The top of the cliff is composed of sand, originally well bonded by grass but now becoming eroded, particularly on the more popular climbs. Some of the climbs have unpleasant finishes and some are prone to sand on the holds. Belaying at the top is rarely a problem due to belay stakes. The stakes make top roping convenient and more popular than at other crags in the guide. However, it is essential to use a spare rope or long slings to hang over the edge so that the running rope does not cut into the cliff top. The results of failure to do this are sadly obvious.

A further attraction is the site itself. There are a number of caves, associated tunnels and sea-stacks, easily located and admired below mid-tide when the sea retreats completely from the base of the climbs. Many of the climbs are still accessible at high tide. Some undercut sections of the cliff stay dry for bouldering even during rain and the positive nature of the holds and lack of lichen makes climbing tolerable in the wet. The cliffs are also little affected by high seas or nesting birds.

Accessibility and weather make Cummingston the most popular cliff in the guide, although the quality of the climbing does not justify this alone.

Access

Cummingston village lies on the B9040, the coastal road from Burghead to Lossiemouth. From the west, aim for Burghead and turn off the main A96 at the roundabout at the east end of Forres (signposted Findhorn, Burghead, RAF Kinloss, B9011). Later on, ignore the B9011 turn-off to Findhorn and drive through RAF Kinloss on the B9089. About 9km (6 miles) beyond Kinloss, follow the B9089 taking a junction sharp left (just beyond a humpback in the road) to head towards Burghead. Just before Burghead, three big masts are visible on the right and the B9040 turns right on the seaward side of them to reach Cummingston.

From the east (Elgin), take the A941 towards Lossiemouth. This leaves the main A96 from a roundabout on the main road which avoids Elgin centre. Ignore an earlier sign to Lossiemouth, which leaves the main A96 inside Elgin city but nearer Aberdeen. After 800 metres from the roundabout, take the B9012 on the left, signposted to Hopeman and Burghead. Alternatively, if approaching from Aberdeen, avoid Elgin by taking the B9103 to Lossiemouth from just beyond Lhanbryde. At Lossiemouth, follow the B9040 west along the coast to Hopeman and then Cummingston.

For access to the cliffs from Cummingston, look out for a white war memorial with a cross on top. This is roughly in the centre of the village, which is a ribbon settlement along the B9040. Turn towards the sea (north) either just west or 100 metres east of the memorial (on a fast visit, find the memorial and then take the next turning on that side). The turning 100 metres east is a wider road and leads to some new houses. Turn left and then right (or from the other turn-off, right and then left) to reach an unsurfaced car park overlooking the sea. A kiddies' play park and a couple of Portaloos are conveniently at hand for the "married hardman" on a day out with the family.

The Orange Wall is straight out to sea from here, adjacent to the sandy beach, but the more popular areas (The Stacks area and Prophet Walls) are to the left (west). For access to all areas. descend to the old railway line (Kiddies' slide optional). For the Orange Wall, now trend right to the sandy beach where the crag is easily visible on the left. For access to the other more popular areas (except Gutbuster Bay, see below) go to the gravel beach by following the old railway cutting west for about 200 metres until its right wall disappears. Short tracks then lead down to the beach, continuing further left for The Stacks (the big stack is clearly visible) or turning back right where the Prophet Buttress immediately stands out from the gravel and features the three corners, Left, Centre and Right.

ORANGE WALL AREA

This is the eastmost section of cliff, directly out to the shore from the car park. It is a smooth overhanging wall of brittle orange rock, bounded on the right by a blackened cave with bulging walls. The routes here were originally led or soloed,

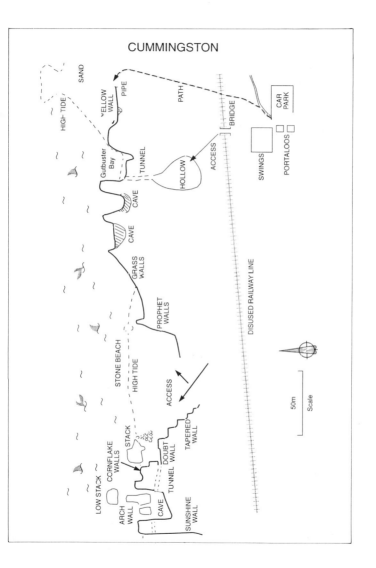

CUMMINGSTON

but top roping is now more common due to poor protection and the snappy nature of the rock (the top edge of the cliff is very sharp and top ropes need padding). Despite this, the profusion of finger flakes makes for unusual and entertaining climbing and a challenge to finger strength.

Orange Peel   6m   E1 5b   (1984)
Climb the wall direct just right of the arete.

Route One   6m   VS 4c   (1978)
Climb the obvious flake to the right of the pipe by layback.

Ginger Snap   6m   HVS 4c   (1984)
The thin crack line immediately right of Route One.

Drainpipe Wall   6m   E2 6b   (1984)
The smooth wall next right.

Thumper   8m   E3 6a   (1984)
The next thin crack line to the right. The crux is at the top and could be protected if the crack was cleaned.

Tangerine Scream   8m   E5 6a   (1984)
The central section of the wall is smooth, overhanging and very fingery. The route takes a line of tiny flakes (skyhook runner). It has been soloed on sight.

Hickory Dickory Dock   8m   E4 6a   (1984)
The crack line left of the obvious line of better holds (Flakey Wall). Protection can be arranged at an incut hold above half-height.

Flakey Wall   8m   E1 5a   (1979)
The more obvious line of right-trending flake holds is a good landmark from which to locate the other routes.

Route Two   8m   E2 5b   (1978)
Right of Flakey Wall an overhang starts which increases in size round to the cave. The route starts at the extreme left of the overhang and trends right to join Skelp.

Skelp   8m   E2 5c   (1983)
Climb direct through the overhang, then go up the wall above.

King Swing   8m   E2 5c   (1983)
An obvious very undercut crack line. Gain the crack from the right, pull out right over the bulge and finish up the crack.

Berserker   10m   E4 6b   (1985)
Start as for King Swing, then traverse right along the bulge to pull up right at a
small vertical seam (crux). Move right into the hanging chimney above the cave
and finish up this. The rock in the cave has a sandy surface which may need
brushing. The wall on the right of the cave has been top roped and is hard.

About 10 metres right of Berserker the cliff descends to sea-level. The first
feature above the beach is a roofed corner (Black Roof) and on its left is a blunt
arete which is the first clean rock to descend to sea-level (Solo Wall).

Solo Wall   10m   Very Difficult   (1979)
Climb the blunt arete.

Black Roof   10m   VS 5a   (1979)
Climb to a niche in the corner below the roof. Step up left on to the facing wall
to finish.

THE GUTBUSTER BAY

Just west of Orange Wall and beyond the last two routes is a large tidal bay,
sometimes with a sandy floor, linked to an inland depression by a through cave.
This cave is a useful point of access above mid-tide. Cross the bridge over the
old railway and trend slightly left into a big depression containing the cave. The
loft (west) wall on the inland side of the cave has been climbed at VS but it is
loose and unpleasant. The cave itself has been chimneyed to exit at the seaward
end but pigeon droppings may deter repeats.
   The left (east) wall of the bay is scrappy but gives a few climbs. The right wall
is overhanging for its short length, but the back wall is one of Cummingston's
best features and is split by five fine lines.

Beastie's Wall   10m   Hard Severe 4a   (1980)
Start near the left side of the left wall by a line of suspiciously hollow flakes. Avoid
the turf above by a short crack on the left.

The Beast   10m   E2 5b   (1984)
Start near the centre of the left wall by a thin crack and flake and continue up the
vertical crack through the roof above. An extra grade has been added for brittle
and sandy rock.

Middle Muddle Groove   10m   Difficult   (1978)
Climb the easier-angled flakes on the right, then traverse right to a depression.
Exit up the groove above.

Middle Muddle Direct   10m   VS 5a   (1978)
Pull over the bulge at a crack a few metres right of the flakes to gain the middle
ledge. Finish up the obvious crack above the start.

Jugular Wall   10m   Hard Severe 4b   (1978)
Right of the last climb is a steep wall. Pull up to a huge jug, continue past a crack
to ledges and climb the steep wall above direct.

Mud, Sweat and Tears   10m   Hard Severe 4b   (1978)
Climb the strenuous chimney at the back surmounting a roof to finish on sand.

Hernia Corner   15m   E2 6a **   (1978)
The first of five splendid lines on the compact back wall takes the bulging crack
and corner on the left. The difficult start is often aided (5a with one aid point).

Null Stretch   15m   E5 6b **   (1989)
Start Just right of Hernia Corner. Make a long reach to a slot above the undercut
start. Gain holds above and move up to the roof (Hex 5 and Rock 5). Make
another long reach to a spike on the right. Gain a standing position, then follow
the arete trending right at the top. A serious route.

Legbuster   20m   E2 6a *   (1978)
Right of the bulging buttress are two wide cracks leading into a bay. Climb the
awkward overhung left crack to the bay. Go up and left on the thin wall to exit;
easier than the crack but more serious. Easier for the tall.

Gutbuster   20m   E2 5c **   (1978)
The right-hand crack is also strenuous and leads to the bay. Go right up the wall
to an exposed arete and a mantelshelf finish. The protection is better than on
Legbuster.

Kneewrecker Chimney   20m   Mild VS 4c **   (1978)
The superb chimney to the right. The very tight chockstone is the crux. The top
section is easier but exposed. An alternative start is to climb on the outside using
a left-hand crack (5a).

The right wall of the bay has several routes. All are poorly protected and were
soloed on the first ascent. Sometimes the landing is sandy. The rock in the top
half of the wall is worrying.

Sea Witch   12m   E3 5b   (1984)
There is a prominent flake-nose left of an obvious overhanging crack (Sandy
Volestrangler). Climb the nose and the fragile wall above.

The Conjurer   12m   E3 6a   (1983)
Climb the wall between the more obvious lines of Sea Witch and Sandy
Volestrangler. Trend right to finish up the crack line of Volestrangler. It was
originally climbed by traversing out right from Sea Witch (technically easier).

Sandy Volestrangler   12m   E3 6b   (1983)
The obvious overhanging crack towards the right side of the high section of wall.
The start is the crux and a foot of sand will drop the technical grade. Forcing your
belayer to lie on the ground will ensure dry feet and/or substitute for the sand.

The Grab   4m   6b   (1984)
Climb the shorter wall direct, right of Sandy Volestrangler and near a short
overhanging crack.

Armstretcher   4m   5c   (1979)
The right end of the shorter overhanging wall containing The Grab. A dynamic
start may be needed if the take-off is bare rock.

   Around the corner on the right (at low tide), is another roof-topped cave. On
its left is an overhanging wall (Dali's Wall); on its right a fine corner (Sidle).

Dali's Wall   12m   Hard Severe 4a   (1978)
Start up the wall left of a slanting overhanging chimney via a bulging start (ignore
an escape up and left), then trend right up the centre of the wall to a poorly
protected finish. Typically Cummingston, huge jugs and a sandy finish.

The Melting Clock   12m   E2 5c   (1984)
The slanting chimney line right of Dali's Wall is horribly sandy; goggles advised.

Sidle   12m   VS 4c   (1978)
This route takes the corner on the right of the cave. Surmount the bulge with
difficulty, then go up the corner to a step right on to the arete. Finish unpleasantly
up grass. The start can be reachy or even dynamic if there is no sand. A fine line
but on sandy-surfaced rock.

THE PROPHET WALLS
Beyond Sidle and another big cave, the rocks become more broken and slant
inland (above high tide mark) for about 100 metres to reach a bay and buttress
just before the cliff-break at the pebble beach. The area can be reached at all
tide levels from the beach. The rock in this section is usually sound and many of
the best hard leads are here.

The Gripper   20m   HVS 5b *   (1979)
At the left side of the overhung bay is a fine corner leading to a roof at the top.
Climb this to a ledge below the roof, which gives an intriguingly awkward finish.

Aesthetic Ape   20m   E3 6a **   (1984)
Approximates to the smooth little hanging corner right of the Gripper and left of
roofs. Climb bulging rock via a pocket to gain holds under the bulging right rib of
the corner. Pull up the rib (crux) to gain the top of a block. Finish up and right.
High in the grade, as protection requires careful arrangement.

Orange Ape   20m   E2 5c *   (1984)
The obvious undercut corner at the back left of the bay.

Bat's Wall   15m   E4 6a **   (1984)
The crack line up the back wall right of the previous route can be started by
gaining a shelf up on the right or direct (harder). A well-protected route, merci-
lessly strenuous with a wicked finish.

Noddy Machine   15m   E2 5b *   (1986)
A sensational route on the overhanging right wall of the bay. Climb a shallow
groove to a ledge with a big vertical flake. Step left and climb the overhanging
wall on big holds to the capping roof. Swing right to gain the arete and a dirty but
easy finish.

Triangular Groove   20m   HVS 5a   (1985)
Immediately round the arete from Noddy Machine is a peapod-shaped groove
with a capping roof. Pull over (a little overgrown) and move right to finish up
Borderline or Border Crossing.

Border Crossing   20m   Hard Severe 4b   (1985)
Climb the shallower groove between Triangular Groove and the big corner of
Borderline. Step right into the upper groove of Borderline, go up a few metres,
then climb the obvious flake up the right wall to finish up the crack of Palmist.

Borderline   15m   VS 4b   (1980)
The big corner tucked into the left side of Prophet buttress provides one of the
best climbs of its grade when clean, but it collects earth readily.

Palmist   15m   E3 6b *   (1984)
The bulge on the left side of Prophet Buttress, just right of Borderline. Gain an
obvious spiky jug with difficulty (direct), where good protection can be arranged.
Gain a standing position on the jug, then go on up a short overhanging crack and
another step to the top. The grade assumes a very good landing.

The Prophet   15m   E2 5c **   (1980)
Start at a small inset corner at the left side of the nose. Climbs its right arete,
then pull into a left-facing corner which leads up to the roof. Surmount the roof
and finish more easily. Low in the grade.

I-Ching   20m   E3 5c *   (1984)
Climb the fine arete left of Left. The runners are too low for comfort.

Left   20m   VS 5a **   (1978)
On the west face of the Prophet Buttress are three corners. This is the left one,
(surprise, surprise).

Centre   20m   Mild VS 4b **   (1978)
As for Left to an overhung flake, then step right and climb the corner directly.
Intimidating rather than difficult.

Right   15m   HVS 5a **   (1978)
Climb the right-hand corner. Recently cleaned, now a fine route with good
protection.

The arete between Centre and Right gives a fine boulder problem, 6a direct,
5c on the right. Descend down Right after 4m.

Spare Rib   15m   HVS 4c *   (1985)
Climb the rib direct right of Right. The crux is unprotected, though below
half-height.

Yoohah   10m   VS 5a   (1984)
The first of two grooves right of Right corner.

Bing-Bong   8m   Severe   (1984)
The second groove, turning a bulge on the left. Tricky grass finish.

Gnib-Gnob   8m   Hard Severe   (1984)
The corner forming the back of the bay at the top of the grass bank, where the
crag changes angle. Beware of fulmars.

A number of short routes and problems have been soloed on the wall above
the grass bank (which provides a good landing). The first two problems were
finished by traversing right into the Weem.

Pigmy Shrew   6m   E1 5c   (1984)
The first defined crack line right of Gnib-Gnob.

Bank Vole   6m   VS 5a   (1984)
The next crack just to the right.

The Weem   10m   Very Difficult   (1984)
The obvious corner and slot right of the previous cracks.

The Wobble   10m   Very Difficult   (1984)
The very shallow left-facing groove right of the Weem. Finish up the wall above.

Thud   10m   HVS 5b   (1984)
The next similar line to the right.

There are four enjoyable problems up the wall right of the previous route, all
5b, ending at a cave where one can walk off right.

THE STACKS AREA

Right of the previous routes is a pebble beach with grassy slopes stretching back to the railway line. Beyond this the cliff restarts with a tapered wall leading down to the main sea-facing wall opposite a large sea stack. A tunnel leads from here into a large cave with a collapsed roof and a further three exits through the cliff. This area of cliff is popular with many easier routes and good bouldering.

THE TAPERED WALL

Apart from the lowest bay containing the Nest, the climbs here are of poorer quality and rather loose.

Slimline Chimney   6m   Severe 4b   (1979)
The short corner-chimney at the top left end of the tapered wall.

Fracture Face   12m   VS 4b   (1987)
Down the bank from Slimline Chimney is a wall with many short cracks. Attempt to find a solid way up here (and fail).

Tall Order   12m   HVS 5b   (1987)
The wall of Fracture Face ends in an arete, climbed direct.

Tom's Wall   12m   Severe
Start at the arete and trend right, finishing up a steep loose chimney.

Graffiti Wall   10m   Very Difficult
The right side of the bay with Tom's Wall is a graffiti-covered slab. Climb the slab up the middle or nearer the right edge.

Pretty Flamingo   6m   E1 5c   (1984)
The next small bay is formed by an obvious clean roofed corner, The Nest. Pretty Flamingo takes the arete left of the Nest, climbed on its right side, to join Graffiti Wall.

Ultra Radical   10m   E4 6b   (1988)
Climbs the middle of the wall (left of the Nest), starting at a thin crack to gain an undercut, then go up the wall above. Starting at the same place but going left to the arete is 6a.

The Nest   10m   E2 6a **   (1982)
A fine little route on good rock, taking the roofed corner. Gaining the nest is the technical crux, leaving it is ....
Left-Hand Start: 6b   (1985)
A good boulder problem, climbing the left wall to grab the sloping perch.
Right-Hand Start: 6a   (1985)
Climb the wall just right of the arete, then snatch left for the perch.

THE DOUBT WALL

This is the long steep wall opposite the largest stack, ending at the tunnel (The Lum).

Doubtless Wall   10m   Severe *   (1979)
At the left end of the wall, a chossy ramp leads to a ledge at two-thirds height. The route climbs the steep wall right of the ramp to gain the ledge, then continues on smaller holds to the top.

The Artful Dodger   12m   HVS 5a *   (1980)
Right of Doubtless Wall is an arete of harder rock. Climb this on its left side to the ledge (no protection but a soft landing). Continue straight up (or traverse off left).

Diedre of Doubt   12m   HVS 5a **
Climb the fine corner directly from the undercut base and finish up the poorly protected smooth corner above. There is a less strenuous start on the right (the start of Double Doubt). The undercut base (low cave) offers a number of fine bum-scraping boulder problems.

Diedre of Double Doubt   12m   E2 5b *   (1982)
Gain and climb the short diedre up and right of Diedre of Doubt and just below the cliff top. Climb strenuously up the centre of the wall, arrange gear awkwardly (only E1 if you trust it) and make the crux move up the small wall to the diedre.

Doubting Thomas   12m   E1 5b   (1987)
Gain and climb the hanging arete right of Double Doubt from directly below. Artificial but good climbing

Staircase Crack   12m   Severe
An unpleasant sandy ledge leads left to an unpleasant right-facing sandy corner.

Green Crack   12m   VS 4c
Gain and follow the prominent crack above the ledge, with a sandy finish. The harder, less obvious crack a few metres right has also been climbed.

Lumside Crack   12m   Severe
Left of the deep chimney above the tunnel entrance (The Lum) is a wide groove. Climb this, or the arete on the right, to a very sandy exit.

The Lum   12m   Very Difficult
The wide chimney above the tunnel. Exit right (very sandy).

Cascade   12m   VS 5a
The Lum's right wall, a steep wrinkled slab, gives a fine technical problem. The finish is very unpleasant. Traversing right and descending is less unpleasant.

THE CORNFLAKE WALLS

Beyond The Lum, the cliff takes a step out towards the sea forming a big arete and preventing access during high tide. Right of the arete, a series of heavily sculptured walls and grooves lead rightwards to a rounded undercut wall left of the next cave entrance.

Snotty Nose   12m   Difficult
The big arete (close to the stack) is loose but still popular.

Pegless Wall   12m   VS 4b   (1985)
An artificial line climbing the narrow bulging wall just right of Snotty Nose and keeping between it and Old Peg Groove (6m to the right). Poorly protected.

Old Peg Groove   12m   VS 4c *
Right of Pegless Wall are two grooves starting at a recess. The route slants left up the left-hand groove, then returns right up the continuation groove. The right-hand groove has also been climbed but is sandy and artificial.

Cornflake Wall   12m   Moderate *
The wall just right of the grooves and left of a left-facing corner has excellent holds but an awkward start for the grade.

Rice Crispie Wall   12m   Difficult *
The steep sculptured wall next right provides an example of verticality without difficulty. Start from a bare rock platform at the base of the cliff and climb directly up a bulging rib. An easier but sandier alternative is to start at the same place as Cornflake Wall and trend right to join the direct line.

The next five routes are in a recessed section left of the obvious rounded undercut wall. The recess is bounded on either side by corners, The Groove on the left and Doddle Diedre on the right. The back wall of the recess contains a more recessed section with an obvious narrow chimney capped by a roof (Blockbuster).

The Groove   12m   Difficult
The shallow right-facing corner. Move on to its juggy left edge at mid-height and finish by a turf cornice.

Bombproof   12m   Severe *
Start at the base of The Groove and climb the overhanging wall on the right on big holds (avoid bridging into The Groove) to a direct finish on cleaned plates.

Blockproof   12m   Mild Severe
Climb the corner at the left side of the deeper recess (2 metres left of Blockbuster chimney). Exit left at the roof to join Bombproof.

Blockbuster   12m   Very Difficult *
Climb the chimney crack to the roof (excellent thread runner). Exit right to stand on a spike on the right arete. Finish obviously as for Doddle Diedre. A harder alternative is to pull direct through the roof on big holds to the left.

Doddle Diedre   12m   Severe **
Climb the fine corner and exit left below the top. Friends are useful (though not essential) for protection.

Stegosaurus   12m   VS 4c **   (1979)
The aptly-named spiky arete between Doddle Diedre and the undercut wall is both exciting and strenuous.

Gibbon   12m   HVS 5c   (1987)
Climb the wall about 2 metres right of Stegosaurus, surmounting a roof at half-height. The dynamic start is harder for the short.

Trapeze   12m   VS 5b **
Above the centre of the wall is a shallow corner. A powerful start leads into the shallow corner and an easier finish

Gorilla   12m   E1 5c   (1978)
The hanging arete at the right end of the undercut wall. The drop in beach level here has restricted this route to gymnasts with wings. The finish is unpleasant.

THE ARCH WALL
The undercut wall ends at the first cave entrance. Further right is a second entrance and between the entrances are two walls, one facing the sea (outer aspect) and one inside the collapsed cave (inner aspect).

Bottomless Chimney   12m   E3 6b   (1978/1983)
Climb the chimney above the first cave entrance, starting on the right wall. The upper half is 5a and can be combined with one of the Soft Option problems to give a HVS route.

   Further out on the right wall of the cave entrance are four fine microroutes, again made much harder by the drop in beach level. Starting cairns ease the difficulty. These and following routes are given technical grades only, being extended boulder problems. Descent is by traversing right and descending Slab and Tickle (Very Difficult). The alternative is to climb the wall above at 5a. Pipefish Wall was the original start (E2 6a). Again, this finish can be combined with one of the Soft Option problems to give a HVS route.

Pipefish Wall   6m   6a *
The overhanging crack set in a shallow corner.

Double Stretch   6m   6a *
A narrow vein of harder rock.

Headbanger   6m   5c *
A bottomless jam-crack.

Jerker   6m   6b
The desperate rounded arete right of Headbanger. Using the initial holds of Headbanger reduces the grade to 6a.

The Soft Option Problems
Due to its disproportionately hard start, Soft Option has been replaced by three fine boulder problems on the undercut wall round the corner and right of Jerker. The first (5b) takes the wall at the first reasonable place right of Jerker, with a jump start for the short. The middle problem (5a) takes a very shallow groove, and problem just right is 5a.

Slab and Tickle   12m   Very Difficult *
The crag changes direction to give a steep, slabby, west-facing wall, then a smooth sea-facing wall leading to the second major cave entrance. From the base of the corner between these two walls (Giraffe Corner), traverse out left to the edge and finish up an easier groove. The start is thin but the finish is easy.

Giraffe Corner   12m   E2 6a   (1984)
The lower corner leads to an obvious bulge (crux) guarding entry into the better-defined upper corner.

Arch Wall   12m   E4 6a   (1988)
The smooth wall right of Giraffe Corner. Start at a vague crack right of the smoothest section of wall. Climb to a runner at 5m, then move up and left to clip a peg runner. Finish straight up. The obvious direct start has not yet been led.

Sandstone Wall   12m   HVS 5a   (1979)
The open crack line right of Arch Wall has an unpleasant finish; Appletiser is a better alternative.

Appletiser   12m   E1 5b *   (1988)
A composite line which avoids the unpleasant finish of Sandstone Wall and the Crunch landing. Start up Sandstone Wall, traverse right into Le Crunch at about half-height and finish up this.

Le Crunch   12m   E4 5c *   (1986)
The blunt overhanging rib to the right of Sandstone Wall forms the left side of the second cave entrance. Climb to a jug in a niche and runners at 8m (bad landing). Move up and left to finish.

The following two routes are inside the cave. A line has been top-roped between them.

Fourth Dimension   10m   E2 5c   (1984)
Gain the crack line on the left side of the inside of the Arch Wall (right of Le Crunch) from the left (or direct; 6a) and finish more easily.

Brain Warp   10m   E2 5c   (1984)
The obvious crack above the minor tunnel, whose outside aspect lies beside Giraffe. Again the start is the crux.

Bullworker   10m   HVS 5a   (1988)
On the right (outside aspect) of the second (westerly) cave entrance is a wall. Start just inside the cave entrance and take the arete direct.

Expanders Crack   10m   VS 4c   (1978)
Trend left up the wall and finish up a crack above an overhang. The start of Bullworker can also be used, transferring right above the overhang.

SUNSHINE WALL
The cliff ends in a west-facing wall which tapers above a grass bank.

Easy Arete   10m   Easy
A scrappy route up the right-hand corner of the seaward face (between Expanders Crack and Sunshine Wall proper).

Sunshine Roof   10m   Hard Severe   (1980)
There is an obvious double roof at the left side of the wall. Climb until under the upper roof, step right to the edge and go back left over the roof. Finish up easy cracks.

Gorse Route   10m   Severe
Climb the crack which springs up from the right side of the lower roof. Start either by moving right under the lower roof or direct up the crack (more strenuous).

Sunshine Groove   8m   Severe   (1978)
Follow the slanting groove just right of the previous route. Start on its right.

Sunshine   8m   HVS 5b   (1980)
The wall on the right is smoother and has two blind cracks. This is the left-hand one; fortunately the landing is soft.

Sunshine Crack   6m   Mild VS 4c   (1978)
The right-hand and more obvious crack. Starting off the grass ledge is cheating.

Sunshine Extra   6m   Hard Severe 4b   (1985)
Another similar crack line, passing just left of the Sunshine Recess.

Sunshine Recess   4m   Severe   (1986)
Climb the obvious small recess, surmounting the roof directly.

Central Face Low Level Traverse   5c **   (1979)
Start in the first cave entrance. Traverse out left to the arete of Gorilla, cross the
Trapeze wall above the bulge (good holds), then continue left at low level to the
crux crossing of the Lum. Easier ground then leads to a strenuous crossing of
Artful Dodger and a finish down Doubtless Wall.

THE STACK
Originally called the East Tower, this is the largest of the stacks and lies opposite
the Doubt Wall. It is cut off by the highest tides, but normally the top is accessible.
Descent is either by abseil or by descending Back Passage, a chimney-corner
on the east side (Moderate). The routes are described anti-clockwise from the
left side of the landward face (rightwards).

Captain Birdseye   12m   E1 5b *   (1985)
Climb the left edge of the wall to a niche and finish directly up the bulge and
groove above.

Fingers Wall   12m   E3 5b   (1983)
Start immediately right of Captain Birdseye. Climb to an obvious small square
ledge, then move across right to thin cracks which slant up slightly right (ground
fall potential). Go up these and finish directly up a "platey" but well protected wall.
Direct Start: 6a
Climb a direct line up the centre of the wall.

Flying Buttress, Left Side   10m   Very Difficult
Start at the top right of the sloping shelf. Climb the corner to a ledge, then go up
a short wall to the top.

Flying Buttress, Right Side   12m   Difficult
The opposite side of the same corner crack.

Flying Groove   12m   VS 4c *   (1979)
Right again is another groove, difficult to climb elegantly.

The Prow   12m   E5 6a **   (1987)
The big overhanging prow on the east side. Climb out on massive holds, then go
up the left edge to gain and pass the lip (unprotected). The original ascent
reached the lip further right (6b). There are several runners (mostly big Friends)
but the placements are poor.

Cutty Sark   12m   Severe   (1985)
On the seaward side of the Prow is a large inset corner (Back Passage). Start
left of the corner and trend left up the edge of the Prow, then go straight up the
wall to an unpleasant finish.

East Side Story   12m   Very Difficult
Climb the wall left of Back Passage, passing right of a grass ledge.

Back Passage   12m   Moderate
The deep cracked corner is a useful descent route.

Dirty Old Man   12m   Very Difficult
Climb easy-angled lichenous cracks up the wall right of Back Passage.

Sunset Song   12m   Hard Severe 4b   (1985)
Inset in the north-east arete of the stack is an attractive curved groove of good
clean rock. Climb the groove and finish directly over the little bulge above.

Footloose   12m   Mild VS 4b   (1985)
Climb the right edge of the north wall of the stack for a few metres, or more direct
if you dare, then pull over left and climb to a ledge. Finish leftwards over an
awkward bulge.

Blocky   12m   Very Difficult   (1985)
Climb an obvious fault just right of the start of Footloose to the right end of the
ledge and finish up the corner above.

Butchers Broom   12m   Mild VS 4b   (1985)
Climb cleaned cracks up the left edge of the west wall. Light people can turn the
awkward bulge more easily by using spikes on the left arete.

Shadow Flake   10m   HVS 5a   (1985)
Climb the west wall to an obvious small flake. Pull up past the flake (reachy) and
finish out rightwards.

Coach Bolt Crack   10m   VS 4c
There are two steep cracks at the right side of the wall. This is the left one.

Huggy Bear   12m   VS 4c   (1988)
Climb the right-hand steep crack, using some holds on the south-west arete.

Girdle Traverse   4c/5b *
The traverse is greatly improved at high tide, and 5b if the base of Fingers Wall
is included. Clockwise is the best direction.

THE SENTINEL STACK

There is a smaller stack west of the large one and a further two about 100 metres west of the end of the cliff at Sunshine Wall. The better of the two is the nearer and is split by a central tunnel.

The Pedestal   4c *

Walk through the tunnel, mount the pedestal and pull over the overhang on huge jugs. A fine boulder problem, offering an introduction to heel hooking. The grade is nominal.

Jutting Flake Crack   Hard Severe 4b

On the south-east corner of the stack.

Ramp Route   Severe *

On the east face, near the right end, is a diagonal ramp; follow it past a jutting flake, then go straight up on large holds.

PRIMROSE BAY   *(Map Ref 149 702)*

This beautiful little bay, lying a short distance east of Hopeman, is a popular local picnic spot so parking on a sunny Sunday afternoon can be a problem. There is not much worthwhile climbing here, but what there is gives good entertainment. The charm promised by the bay's name is not belied by its actual appearance, a delightful spot approached in summer through a blaze of yellow gorse.

Access

From the junction of the B9012 and the B9040 just east of Hopeman Village take a rough track north for 400 metres to park by a gate on the right. Cross the gate and walk 200 metres east along the track, then cut left down a rough path through the gorse into the sheltered bay beneath.

Most of the rock in this area is not very good, but the small buttress above the sea on the west side of the bay offers a number of obvious climbs of varying standards on good rock. The imposing 15m smooth wall of soft sandstone to its left (bounded on its right by a prominent undercut corner) has seen the (unsuccessful!) attentions of a phantom bolter but remains a rather doubtful prospect for the free climber. East of the small sandy beach is a 15m slab with good rock and plentiful holds. There are no defined lines since the slab is climbable anywhere at about Moderate to Difficult, but at least three independent routes are possible. Protection is limited but stakes allow convenient top-roping for youngsters or non-athletic novices.

COVESEA   *(Map Ref 176 708)*

Extensive 12m sandstone cliffs stretch east for 3km from Primrose Bay, eventually dwindling into the vast sandy beaches of Silver Sands around the Covesea Skerries Lighthouse. Some exploration has been made in this fascinatingly

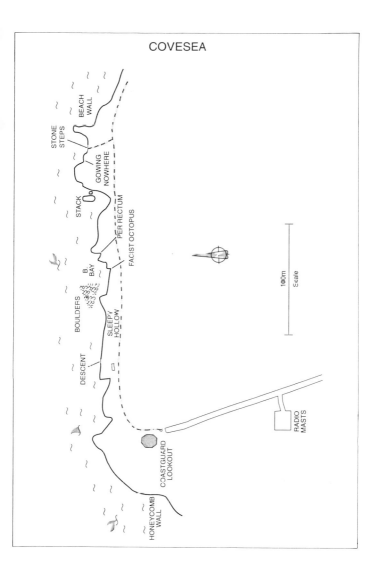

COVESEA

BEACH WALL

STONE STEPS

GOWING NOWHERE

STACK

PER RECTUM

FACIST OCTOPUS

B. BAY

BOULDERS

SLEEPY HOLLOW

DESCENT

COASTGUARD LOOKOUT

HONEYCOMB WALL

RADIO MASTS

100m

Scale

unspoilt area but though there seem to be many exciting possibilities, sound rock is not extensive.

The localised climbing area described here offers well defined lines with technically interesting features and sometimes good protection (Friends required) providing enjoyable leads. Being less sea-washed and less popular than Cummingston, the rock is not as clean nor as reliable. Soloing is risky and the bouldering inferior.

Access

Approaching from the east (Lossiemouth) on the B9040, pass the Covesea Skerries Lighthouse. A small rectangular wood is soon seen on the approaching crest (also there is a farm complex, Wester Covesea). Go beyond the wood to a larger wood, also on the right (north) of the road. Park on the verge before a locked gate on the narrow tarmac road leading to the coast immediately before this wood. This is 3km beyond Covesea Skerries Lighthouse and 1km past the farm complex. Follow the tarmac road to the two 15m radio masts, then take a rough track down to the coast and an octagonal lookout station.

Approaching from the west (Cummingston and Hopeman) continue along the B9040 for about 3km past the Duffus turn, where a break in the woods on the left (north) side and the small tarmac road leads to the coast (easily missed).

Looking out to sea from the coastguard lookout station, the best area (Boulders Bay) is to the right. The Stack Bay is further right while Honeycomb Wall is close on the left. The sections are described in this order.

BOULDERS BAY

From the lookout station, follow a path down steps, then along the coast eastwards for 50 metres until some bare rock shows on the path. On the left, beside some square boulders on the cliff top, descend a short narrow chimney, at present with a fixed rope and stepladder to the west end of a stony beach. The main section of crag is 100 metres east, but to the west are the first two routes. Going east from the descent, the cliff soon becomes its full height at an arete, beyond which is a sculptured wall ending in a roofed recess. Left of this is a large pile of grassy boulders.

The sculptured wall and the arete itself offer a number of lines but reality is disappointing and the rock is poorer and dirtier than appearances would suggest. One unattractive line has been climbed, the wide crack and wall towards the right of this face (**The Land of Nod**, HVS 4c).

The main crag stretches from here to a small promontory. At the back of the promontory is a low cave. Right of this is a smooth wall with a roofed corner (Fascist Octopus) near the cave and two crack lines (Domino Effect and Sandanista) at the right end next to the biggest pile of boulders.

Fifty metres west of the descent chimney, just before the tidal caves on the way to Honeycomb Wall, there are two steep corners with ledges at two-thirds height.

Off the Leash   15m   VS 4b   (1990)
Climb the left-hand corner.

Juggernaut   15m   HVS 5a   (1990)
Climb the right-hand corner. The start is awkward and undercut.

Past Imperfect   12m   HVS 5a *   (1985)
Climb the right-facing corner at the left end of the sculptured wall and right of the piled boulders.

Sleepy Hollow   12m   E1 5a   (1985)
A hanging corner just left of Past Imperfect and at the right end of a roof. Climb the speckled wall (poor protection), then move left into the hanging corner.

Private Dancer   12m   E3 5c   (1986)
Round the arete to the right of Sandanista is a thin crack leading into a hanging corner.

The following three routes have unprotected but easier runouts in their upper halves.

Sandanista   12m   E2 5c *   (1985)
Climb the right-hand of two crack lines towards the right side of the main wall. Belay peg 10 metres back.

The Domino Effect   12m   E2 5c **   (1985)
The left-hand crack line, with a finish at the same point, is sustained and strenuous but well-protected.

Squadrone Muerte   15m   E3 5c   (1986)
Start on a boulder and climb the corners up right of Banana Republic, then go up the wall direct; poorly protected with some loose holds. There is a belay stake 30 metres back.

Banana Republic   15m   E1 5b **   (1985)
The route climbs the roof about 8 metres right of the big roofed corner of Fascist Octopus. Start on top of a pointed block and climb up into a corner. Pull over the roof and climb a crack.

Fascist Octopus   15m   E5 6b **   (1986)
The big roofed corner at the back left of the bay. Start on top of a boulder right of the main corner. Step on to the wall and move up left into the corner (the lower corner is often wet). Go up to the roof (peg runner), then move across left to pull up over the roof (long reach) and move up to a good flat ledge. Finish up the corner.

Bottle Dungeon   15m   E4 6a *   (1986)
Climb the corner running up above the cave left of Fascist Octopus, starting up the right arete of the cave.

Dancing in the Dark   15m   E2 5c **   (1985)
Start up the undercut left arete of the inner cave, then move left to climb the crack
line which rises above the left side of the cave's upper slot.

Urban Gorilla   15m   E3 5c **   (1990)
Climb the roof right of Roof Crack directly, where the lip is formed by an obvious
flat-topped block, starting up the left arete of the outer cave. Continue to the
same finish as Dancing in the Dark.

Roof Crack   15m   E6 6c **   (1989)
An obvious roof crack and its upper continuation is for thugs only.

Girsie Crack   12m   VS 4c   (1988)
A set of steep grassy cracks just left of the above.

Annie Hall   12m   HVS 5a **   (1987)
The crack line immediately right of the arete of Orphan Annie is well protected.

Orphan Annie   12m   E2 5b   (1986)
The prominent arete is a fine line, but artificial and poorly protected (graded for
runners in Annie Hall, E3 without).

Thatcher's Crack   12m   Mild VS 4b *   (1986)
Climb the crack in the wall right of Per Rectum. Well protected.

Per Rectum   12m   VS 4c *   (1985)
Start in an overhung bay 10 metres left of Orphan Annie and go up through a
hole formed by a jammed block. Finish up the exciting arete on the right, starting
on its left side (the route can be reduced in grade and quality by finishing up the
steep wall on the left, or easily up the corner).

THE STACK BAY

The next bay east of Boulders Bay contains a stack. The stack of Gow's Castle
lies in a large bay to the east. The cliff line is continuous between the two bays
and access between the two is cut off above half tide. At high tide make a short
abseil off a large wooden fence post, the nearest of a fence which comes down
to the coast. At the west end of the bay is a step-roofed recess with a low cave.
The first four routes take the buttress right (west) of the cave, the other side of
the headland of Per Rectum.

Protection Racket   12m   E1 5b *   (1988)
This lies on the seaward face of the right-hand buttress, starting 3 metres right
of Celebrate the Bullet. Climb a wide crack to the grass ledge. Go up to the
obvious roof and pull through at a short crack, then go straight up on good holds.
At high tide the grass ledge can be reached by descending the top corner of Per
Rectum (Very Difficult).

Celebrate the Bullet   12m   HVS 5a *   (1985)
Pull strenuously into a short groove, then follow a left-trending crack to a bulge.
Climb this into a corner which is followed to the top.

Synthetic Pathway   15m   E1 5a *   (1988)
Start as for Celebrate the Bullet, then traverse along the lip of the roof to the left
arete. Climb up into a cave, then pull out right and finish direct.

Creepie Crawlie   12m   HVS 5b   (1986)
Start just right of the cave arch. Climb the hanging corner crack to a ledge. Finish
up more broken rock.

Between the cave and the left hand buttress are three routes which give good
climbing when dry but suffer from seepage.

Slyme Cryme   10m   E4 6a   (1986)
A serious route taking the arete forming the left arch of the cave on its right, then
a thin crack.

Paul Tax   10m   E3 6a *   (1990)
The obvious central line on the wall. A bulge leads into a shallow right-facing
corner. Climb this and go over the small roof at the top (crux) to more amenable
finishing cracks.

Back and Foot Disease   10m   HVS 5a   (1990)
The wall bounded on the left by a chimney capped by a huge block is well
protected and easier for the tall.

The Vertical Smile   10m   VS 4c   (1985)
The obvious crack line on the left-hand buttress, beyond which the cliff bends
round into a more recessed part of the bay.

Crack-a-Gow-Gow   10m   Mild VS 4c *   (1986)
The crack line on the west-facing wall of the Stack. Descend immediately
rightwards.

The Gowp   15m   E1 5a *   (1988)
This breaches the undercut wall facing the Stack on its east side. Start by the
lowest big block in the gully bed and gain an obvious hold 3m up. Move up right
to a large sloping ledge, then follow a line of shallow scoops leftwards up the
wall.

The Growl   12m   E2 5b *   (1990)
On the wall to the left, immediately below the large boulder, is a thin crack with
an undercut base. Climb the crack, trending right near the top to finish.

Battle of the Bulge　10m　HVS 5a　(1987)

Ten metres to the left is a cave set in a recessed corner. This is the bulging crack on its right wall, at the right end of the cave.

Legover Wall　10m　E1 5c　(1987)

The thin crack on the wall immediately left of the cave and 6 metres left of Battle of the Bulge.

Horny Beast　10m　E1 5c　(1987)

Three metres left of Legover Wall is a wide crack breaking through a roof at half-height. Climb straight up and over the roof at this crack.

STONE STEPS AREA

The previous routes are set in the west side of a small headland which can be walked round at mid-tide. The seaward point of the headland can be climbed at Very Difficult. Beyond (east) the headland is a small bay with stone steps, a descent at all tides. Between the steps and the headland is an obvious chimney-crack line, the following route.

Gowing Nowhere　12m　VS 4c *　(1986)

Climb the chimney-crack, as elegantly as dared.

BEACH WALL

Round the next small headland, on the west side of a bigger open bay (this bay has Gow's Castle on its east side) is a vertical east-facing wall.

The Beachboys　10m　HVS 5a　(1986)

Climb the wall, keeping away from the right arete except at the top. Easy to escape.

Reach or Beach　10m　E1 5b　(1986)

Climb up to a rusty peg, then traverse right to a small right-facing corner at half-height (or climb the wall direct to the corner). Climb the corner and finish straight up.

HONEYCOMB WALL

This is a west-facing wall which angles up above vegetation at the east end of a stony beach and 50 metres west of the coastguard lookout. From the seaward side of the lookout, a small path leads west through gorse. A belay stake above the cliff is almost immediately visible. There are two smaller stakes, often hidden by vegetation, on its uphill side for belays above the upper end of the cliff. Abseil from the stake is the easiest access and at high tide the only access. At three-quarters tide, one can walk another 100 metres west until above the next bay. Follow a short vague path and descend some old sculptured steps in a rock flake. Walk back to Honeycomb Wall. At high tide there is a 3 metre gap which could be waded in an emergency. At mid to low tide one can walk along the beach from Boulders Bay.

The rock is flaky and brittle and the protection often poor, usually shallow Friend placements. The stakes make top-roping attractive, particularly as the climbing is sustained and fingery and the wall dries quickly.

The Sandman   10m   E4 6a   (1986)
Climb a thin pocketed crack about 2 metres left of the top end of the wall (an unpleasant corner).

Invisible Sun   10m   E3 5c   (1988)
Climb near a thin vein just left and barely separate from the previous route.

The Sandbagger   10m   E2 5b   (1986)
Climb the wall between Invisible Sun and Cat's Claws, trending slightly left, then go right to finish at a small triangular slot on the cliff-top.

Cat's Claws   10m   E2 5c   (1986)
Climb a cluster of short cracks, finishing on the left at a short crack on the cliff-top.

Drone Warfare   10m   E2 5a   (1986)
Left of Cat's Claws there is a wedge formation of two hairline veins of harder sandstone which meet 2½m below the cliff-top. Climb the right-hand vein to the apex, then finish slightly rightwards up a small scoop. Minimal protection.

Shear Fear   12m   E3 5c   (1986)
Climb the left-hand vein. Just below its top, move slightly left and finish up another blocky scoop.

Primal Scream   12m   E5 6a   (1986)
Left of Shear Fear are two obvious rock scars. Climb the wall passing just right of these, to reach a right-trending ramp. More serious than technical.

Primitive Thoughts about Modern Girls   15m   E1 5b   (1986)
Climb a bulging wall to a small ledge. Move right and up to a small ledge. Move right along this to a big ramp which leads up right to the top, finishing above Primal Scream.

Banff Area

At first sight, the extensive and often massive cliffs of Banffshire would seem to offer the rock climber a much happier hunting ground than the lowly Moray coast. However, large areas of shale, conglomerate and slate dominate. Exploration to date has so far produced only three locations worthy of record, at the Horse's Head near Buckie, Mull Cleave near Macduff, and Logie Head at Cullen. Of these, the latter is the most recent discovery and the most significant.

The previous guide recorded a number of climbs scattered along the coast, particularly on the attractive and complex series of walls and ridges just east of Tarlair near Macduff. Further exploration has revealed that these routes are either short boulder problems or scrappy scrambles, often on indifferent rock. Given the wealth of high class climbing available on the nearby Buchan coast, they are not worthy of systematic record. However, these cliffs cover such a huge area that it is conceivable that intensive exploration will uncover a few more hidden jewels. The cliffs offer coastal scenery of overwhelming magnificence, totally unspoilt, and enjoying milder weather than the more popular Buchan and Aberdeen cliffs. This helps to compensate for their large areas of unhelpful grass, shale, conglomerate and slate. The haar is less of a problem, and when south-easterlies create damp and cold around Aberdeen, the Banff area is a welcome venue.

LOGIE HEAD   *(Map Ref 528 682)*

This attractive cliff is composed of a number of steep smooth walls, similar to the greywacke cliffs of the south of Scotland coasts, soft enough to have been eroded into good fingerholds and thin cracks but hard enough to be trustworthy for climbing and runner placements. The rock is not perfect, though better than Cummingston, and the thinnest flakes and occasional blocks must be treated with care; plentiful runners remove most of the doubts. The quality of the rock is generally predictable; the more sculptured the features, the poorer the quality, while the seaward end (Star Face) is close to impeccable.

The walls are impressively steep, while the cracks produce good lines and reassuring protection. The steepness, yet regularity of incut holds provides the best climbs in the middle grades and powerful arms are not needed, though finger strength is an advantage. The rock dries quickly and stays dry during blustery showers from the west. Even in the wet the rock is less slippery than most and might tempt the enthusiast. Most of the routes are accessible at all tide levels and nesting seabirds are rarely a problem.

The situation and approach are most attractive, using the unofficial coastal path from Cullen to Findlater, with the Findlater end being particularly beautiful and unspoilt; the main climbing section faces this way. The town of Cullen is a holiday resort from a past era, still popular but slightly quaint in its lack of commercialisation and characterised by The Tea Cozy, the popular tea room opposite the small main square. Findlater Castle is a remarkable ruin set into the cliff and a pleasant visit can be made on a day interrupted by rain. A curiosity of the coastal path is a section of steps next to the crag, built by local stonemason Tony Hetherington, who took a six-month vow of silence to complete a monumental task and who leaves a legacy in keeping with the atmosphere of the place.

Access
1. The commonest approach is from Cullen Caravan Park. Entering Cullen from the east by the A98, turn right at the sign to the Caravan Park. This is just beyond the Community Centre, which is on the right at the top of the steep hill forming the town's main street. From the west, the turning is signposted to the left about 150 metres beyond the town square. Park 450 metres further on at a tarmac car park beside the site entrance. Walk east round the site beside a football pitch to gain a track leading northwards to a wide, open grassy bay. Logie Head is the obvious rocky headland forming the east side of the bay. The Pinnacle is clearly visible on the approach but other climbing sections are hidden. A good path leads round eastwards and crosses the neck of the final rocky crest of the headland to gain a smaller rocky bay on the far side. The main east face of the ridge faces across the bay. Allow about 20 minutes.

   This approach can also be gained directly along the coast from Cullen harbour by a rough track, passable for cars with a high clearance and potentially saving 10 minutes.
2. A slightly longer but much more attractive approach starts at the car park for Findlater Castle and Sunnyside Beach. Turn north (towards the sea) off the A98 at a point 3km (2 miles) east from the Cullen 'out-of-town' signs and take the only tarmac minor road hereabouts. Follow this minor road north and then east until a signposted farm road (patched tarmac) leads north to the car park in the farmyard at Barnyards of Findlater. From the farm, follow the signposted track straight down to the sea and a clifftop view of Findlater Castle (ignore the track on the left which peters out in fields). From here follow a path left and down to Sunnyside Beach, then go west along the back of the beach to the furthest point seen along the coast. From this small headland, the main climbing area is unmistakable about 250 metres away. Allow about 30 minutes.

Layout
Logie Head ends in a long ridge jutting out to sea. The east side of the ridge is a virtually continuous rock face while the west (Cullen) side is grassier with occasional rock walls. The seaward end of the ridge is split into two by an odd gully hidden from view except from the crest.

   The east face is composed of four distinctive 10m walls, Embankments One and Two, separated by a chossy ramp (used for access to the crest), a short section of sculptured chimneys near high tide mark and The Tidal Zone (Cullen Crack Area) on the seaward end of the east arm of the ridge. The Star Zone appears as a seaward continuity of these walls, but is actually the east face of the other arm of the ridge and is continuous with the hidden Gully Wall. The west face is more broken with the best walls at the seaward end. Elsewhere in this area the rock would seem to be too loose to offer any extended climbing.

EMBANKMENT ONE

This is the most popular section of cliff, being sheltered from westerly winds, catching a lot of sun and being away from the sea and associated dampness. The rock is sound apart from occasional flaky or blocky holds and the routes are well protected. Descent is just to the left of the climbs, scrambling down a ramp and short wall to the base of the slope.

The embankment is characterised by a diagonal break which rises up to the left. Two short routes finish on the break just before it reaches the top of the cliff (at a fading, white rockfall scar). There are some very short deep cracks between these and the descent on the left.

Mousehole   5m   Severe 4b
The thin crack on the left side of a short smooth wall is technical but well protected.

Sea Mouse   6m   Hard Severe 4b   (1982)
Just right of Mousehole is a steep little wall below the right end of the rockfall scar. Climb its centre on improving fingery holds. Try to avoid stepping right near the top.

The next four routes finish by the three crack lines above the top left part of the diagonal break.

Bladder Wrack   10m   Severe 4b   (1982)
Climb a tricky crack straight up to and finish by the wide leftmost upper crack.

Sea Urchin   10m   Hard Severe 4b   (1982)
Climb the more obvious break in the wall just right of Bladder Wrack and follow the second upper crack from the left.

Sea Link   10m   Very Difficult *
A composite of the previous two routes makes a worthwhile easier climb. Climb the initial break of Sea Urchin to the diagonal break. Step left below the bulge and finish up the top wide crack of Bladder Wrack.

Poacher   10m   Mild VS 4b **   (1982)
A fine pitch, sustained and well protected. Start just left of where the diagonal break meets the ground. Climb the wall to the break. Pull through the bulge by a short diagonal crack, then go up the main crack leftwards to the top. It is the same standard to go right above the diagonal crack to join the finish of Cullenary Delight.

Cullenary Delight   10m   VS 5a ***   (1982)
Another fine pitch up the vague crack line on the right, with some technical moves up and left at mid-height where the crack is less defined. Where the

diagonal break meets the ground, the ramp that divides Embankments One and Two slopes up right. Start at the base of the diagonal break where there is a small flaky recess at head height. Climb past the recess into the left-slanting crack line which is followed to the top.

Easy Over   10m   E1 5b   (1988)
Very artificial, but a fine series of well protected moves for the blinkered. Climb the short crack starting about just right of Cullenary Delight. Continue straight up the wall above to reach a finishing crack.

Sunnyside Up   10m   HVS 5a **   (1984)
Climb the short crack, as for Easy Over, then move right into a well defined crack and finish up this.

Sunnyside Direct   10m   E1 5c *   (1984)
The well defined upper crack of Sunnyside Up has a thin lower continuation. Climb this without bridging left into the ordinary start (or do so at 5b) and finish as before.

Fisherman's Tail   10m   Hard Severe   (1982)
Climb the more broken wall right of the Sunnyside crack, starting right of a defined crack.

   Right of Fisherman's Tail and above the big ramp is a steep wall split into top and bottom halves by a diagonal crack. There are two thin vertical cracks in its smooth lower half.

Sandy Crack   8m   E1 5b *   (1984)
Climb the left-hand thin crack and its short continuation.

No Hands Crack   8m   E1 5b **   (1984)
Climb the right-hand crack to a niche. Finish by the crack above the niche.

Doc's Crack   6m   HVS 5b *   (1984)
Start 3m higher up the ramp. Climb left across the lower wall to reach and follow the prominent crack right of the final crack of No Hands Crack.

The Central Belt   30m   E1 5b **   (1986)
A rising traverse rightwards across the whole wall, following the obvious line. Start at Bladder Wrack and traverse with feet in the fault (apart from a short section just before Fisherman's Tail) to finish up cracks in the upper wall right of Doc's Crack (these can be climbed independently at HVS).

EMBANKMENT TWO
The rock on this section of wall right of Embankment One and below the ramp is not as good as on Embankment One, although still acceptable.

That is the Question   8m   HVS 5a   (1985)
The overhang and crack on the left side of the wall but right of a narrow chimney (which is Very Difficult).

On the Beach   10m   HVS 5a   (1986)
The obvious left-slanting crack is Dave's Dilemma. This route pulls over the initial roof at a deep crack just right of That is the Question, then goes rightwards up the thin cracks above to cross Dave's Dilemma at a wider pod near the top. Finish up thin cracks on the right.

Dave's Dilemma   10m   E1 5b *   (1982)
The obvious left-slanting crack.

Holy Ground   12m   E2 5c **   (1985)
The twin right-curving cracks right of Dave's Dilemma and left of Crow's Crack. Start up Dave's Dilemma and use a thin crack just to its right to gain a standing position in the obvious hole. Step right using another hole and move up the twin cracks to swing left on reaching better holds. Finish obviously.

Crow's Crack   12m   HVS 4c   (1985)
The wide crack on the right of the wall is loose in places.

THE TIDAL ZONE

Right of Embankment Two are several deeply eroded and sculptured chimneys. These give unusual climbs but have not been detailed because the rock is worryingly soft (Very Difficult to Severe). Beyond this section is a wall with a prominent straight crack (Cullen Crack) and bounded on the left by a right-facing chimney corner (The Clam). At middle tide levels, the climbs are best approached from the seaward end after descending by the gully.

The Clam   12m   Difficult   (1982)
The chimney-corner gives an entertaining wriggle, unfortunately marred by pigeon droppings, to the crest of the ridge, arriving at the start of the gully descent.

Cullen Chimney   12m   Severe   (1984)
The narrow well defined chimney line between the Clam and Cullen Crack.

Bouillabaisse   12m   HVS 5a   (1986)
An artificial line climbing directly up the wall between Cullen Chimney and Cullen Crack. Near the top, move right into the last few metres of Cullen Crack.

Cullen Crack   12m   Mild VS 4b **   (1982)
The straight wide crack is more accommodating than it looks.

The Skunk   12m   Very Difficult   (1989)
The sculptured chimney right of Cullen Crack has an obvious jammed block, avoided on the right. Exit left under the capping overhangs.

The Skink   12m   Mild Severe   (1984)
Climb the rightmost crack on this face to a platform on Findlater Rib. Finish up the rib by a corner on the right.

Findlater Rib   12m   Very Difficult   (1982)
The right end of this face forms a stepped rib which is the end of the shorter eastern arm of the main ridge. Gain the rib easily from the foot of the descent gully. Start up the crest and finish by corners on the right.

GULLY WALL

This refers to the left wall (in descent) of the gully. It is composed of (a) a gloomy slab shadowed by the opposite right arm of the ridge and (b) The Star Zone, a seaward continuation beyond the confines of the gully. The gloomy slab is best reached by following the ridge crest (usually reached by climbing the ramp between Embankments One and Two, but more safely by reversing the descent from Embankment One) and descending the gully. The gloomy slab is slow to dry on still days but does get the sun in the middle of the day. The first climb (Sea Snake) is on the right wall of the gully near its base. The remainder are on the left wall, described from top to bottom.

Sea Snake   10m   E2 5b   (1983)
The overhanging crack line on the right near the foot of the gully is strenuous, but a soft touch at the grade.

The Shrimp   5m   Very Difficult   (1982)
The little corner bounding the left edge of the gloomy slab, near the top of the gully.

The Angry Anchovy   8m   VS 4c   (1982)
Climb the wall immediately right of The Shrimp.

Callous Crayfish   8m   VS 5a   (1982)
This is the first thin crack with a problematical start.

Daisy Link   10m   5c   (1982)
A boulder problem. The next blind crack right of Crayfish peters out. Climb it to the break, then finish up (or reverse) one of the adjacent cracks.

Daisy Cutter   10m   HVS 5b *   (1982)
The better-defined crack right of the previous route gives a pleasant climb with a hard start.

Sea Pink   12m   VS 4c **   (1982)
The fine obvious crack right of Daisy Cutter gives an excellent route.

Sea Anemone   12m   E1 5b ***   (1982)
Start on top of the huge wedged block at the foot of the gully and take the faint
crack line veering slightly left up the right end of the slab. A superb sustained
pitch with good protection.

Greenpeace   12m   Mild Severe   (1982)
Takes the green chimney-crack separating the slab section from the clean walls
to the right (Star Zone) and starting from the obvious wedged block at the base
of the gully.

Greenvoe   12m   Mild Severe   (1985)
This could be classed as a right-hand variation to Greenpeace. Start at a rock
pool below the wedged block and climb a stepped groove up left to a ledge above
the jammed block. Follow the right-hand crack of the Greenpeace chimney to
finish up the last section of that route.

STAR ZONE

This open sunny wall has the best rock at Logie. It is continuous with the left gully
wall. Below the wall is a rock platform which is submerged only at high tide. At
mid-tide the wall is best approached down the gully itself (an awkward scramble).
At low tide it is most easily approached along the base of the east wall. An
entertaining approach can also be made by the West Face, then through the
Black Hole. An abseil rope is the best option when several routes are planned.

Higg's Boson   12m   HVS 5b   (1993)
Start at the foot of Anti-Matter, and climb the tapering pillar on the left without
touching the cracks on either side. Rather eliminate, but good climbing.

Anti-Matter   12m   Hard Severe   (1982)
Right of the Greenpeace chimney is an obvious hole in the ridge (the Black Hole).
Start at the rock pool below the wedged block. Climb to the Black Hole, then take
the groove and flakes on the left.

The White Dwarf   12m   VS 4c   (1986)
The wall between Anti-Matter and Brittle Star and above the Black Hole. Climb
Anti-Matter to above the Black Hole, then pull right onto the wall at a crack. Go
up the crack, then go right when it ends to finish direct.

Brittle Star   12m   Hard Severe *   (1982)
A worthwhile route despite some doubtful rock. Start at the rock pool below the
wedged block, as for Anti-Matter. Take the obvious ramp up and right, passing
the Black Hole.

Variation: E1 5b   (1993)
Start up the slabs right of the pool and join the normal route above the Black Hole
at the diagonal overlap. Swing left on to the foot of the shield on the left and climb
steeply to join the upper section of The White Dwarf.

Black Hole   15m   Difficult *   (1982)
An odd excursion. Start a few metres right of Brittle Star and climb a short corner
and flakes to gain the hole. Go through the hole to easy ground on the west side
of the ridge and climb a slanting groove above to the ridge crest.

Moray Eel   10m   Mild VS 4b **   (1982)
Start in the centre of the fine wall right of Brittle Star and climb a line of flakes up
and left to gain and climb the obvious steep crack finishing at the top of the ramp
on Brittle Star.

Rising Star   10m   HVS 5b ***   (1982)
Start as for Moray Eel and climb straight up to gain and climb the thin crack in
the centre of the upper part of the wall. A delightful route.

Western Star   10m   E2 5c **   (1993)
Climb directly to the foot of the fine wall which divides Rising Star from Fallen
Star. Climb this directly to an obvious crack at the top, without touching either of
the other routes. Slightly eliminate, but good delicate climbing

Fallen Star   10m   VS 4c ***   (1982)
A wee classic. Start just left of the edge of the wall. Climb up left to a flake and
then follow a right-slanting crack to finish in a fine position at the top of the arete.

Fading Star   10m   HVS 5a **   (1982)
An eliminate up the right edge of the wall, artificial but very enjoyable. Climb the
edge near the arete forming the end of the wall to a pocket at 3m. Step up left
towards the crack of Fallen Star, then move back right to gain a small ledge on
the arete. Continue up the edge to finish.
Variation: E2 6a **   (1993)
Even more eliminate, but even better. Start at the exact foot of the arete and
climb it direct, keeping the right hand on or round the arete the whole way.

Dark Star   10m   E1 5b ***   (1982)
The left branch of the ridge ends in a steep, narrow, black wall facing north and
dropping straight into the sea. This is split by two parallel cracks. Make a hard
move up the left-hand crack to a jug. Swing right and finish up the right-hand
crack. A fine line in a good situation.

Southern Cross   12m   E2 5b *   (1988)
A counter diagonal to Dark Star. Start round on the west face and take a low
diagonal crack leading out left to the crest. Traverse left (crossing Dark Star) and
finish sensationally up the left-hand crack.

Northern Logic   10m   HVS 5a *   (1988)
Start up the crack on the west face (as for Southern Cross), then take the right crack of Dark Star throughout.

WEST FACE

This face of the ridge is lower and more broken than the east face, but where there is rock showing it is clean and of good quality. A few enjoyable problems are scattered along its length. The climbs are easily gained by scrambling along the crest and down left near the start of the descent gully.

The Cull   8m   E1 5b **   (1982)
At the far north end of the face is this ferocious leaning crack, started by stepping off a rock pedestal.

Lone Star   8m   Hard Severe   (1982)
Right of The Cull is the obvious hole of Black Hole piercing the ridge. Lone Star climbs up the bulging wall to its right (minor variations possible), starting by stepping off a triangular pedestal.

Little Green Man   6m   Difficult   (1982)
Right of Lone Star is a defined crack which stops at a smooth wall below the top. Right again and just left of an obvious chimney (the rear side of Greenpeace chimney) is a juggy crack, the line of the route.

Polaris   15m   Very Difficult   (1986)
A curiosity route little affected when wet. Ropes are of marginal advantage to the leader. About 3 metres out from the west face is a deep long slot (not the one immediately under the west face). Scramble down inside at the landward end, which is near (west of) the start of the descent gully, to reach the base, full of water at high tide. Chimney upwards at the highest point, exiting just on the seaward side of a big chockstone.

Beside the top of the descent gully, on the west side of the ridge, a grassy ramp descends diagonally down towards the land. This is close to the start of Polaris. The short walls above this ramp give some reasonable diversion.

Buckies   5m   Very Difficult   (1982)
The left-hand of two slightly mossy short corners above the ramp.

Cockles   6m   Very Difficult   (1982)
The more interesting right-hand corner.

Mussels   8m   VS 4b *   (1982)
Round the corner to the right of the above corners is a short steep clean wall facing west. Climb its left side strenuously.

Black Pearl   5m   Mild Severe   (1982)
About 12 metres right of Mussels is a short right-angled corner crack, gained by an easy scramble round from the foot of the ramp to the base of a shorter rock ramp which goes down to high tide mark. Trivial but pleasant.

Limpet Flakes   8m   HVS 5a   (1989)
Right of Black Pearl is a short impending wall. Climb the obvious central crack line using a block to start. Some brittle rock.

PATH WALL
This is a steep narrow wall of rock overlooking the path at the back of the dry inlet just to the west of the ridge, near some concrete steps. It is split by three thin cracks and is very obvious on the right, on the approach from Cullen, just before the main crag is reached.

Pathetique   3m   Severe   (1982)
The short left-hand crack gives a pleasant boulder problem.

Pathology   8m   HVS 5b *   (1982)
The central crack gives a fine strenuous problem with excellent protection.

Apathy   8m   E2 6a *   (1987)
The thin crack immediately left of Garden Path.

The Garden Path   10m   Hard Severe   (1982)
The groove on the right of the wall is a good line, but rather dirty and unsound.

THE PINNACLE
This area lies on the west face of the attractive pinnacle north of the Path Wall. The face is hidden and has to be approached by cutting down and west from the Path Wall, until underneath the wall. At very high tide the base of the routes is affected. All of the lines are obvious and offer fine climbing. Descent is to the right as one views the cliff.

Remembrance Sunday   25m   E2 5b *   (1990)
The left-hand thin crack and shallow corner has a difficult move up above break at one-third height and sustained climbing above.

Fianchetto   15m   HVS 5b *   (1990)
Start up the parallel crack line, then head for a Y-shaped crack at the top with an awkward move at the junction with Remembrance Sunday.

Endgame   15m   E1 5b   (1990)
Join together the short sections of crack midway between Fianchetto and Material Advantage. There is an obvious cracked thread on a pancake of rock at half-height. Good climbing but escapable to the right.

Material Advantage   15m   HVS 5a *   (1990)
The next line right gives steep climbing on good holds.

Hanging Pawn   15m   HVS 5a   (1990)
Climb straight up through the zigzag crack line.

Mating Net   16m   E1 5b   (1990)
The rightmost line, climbing the obvious jam crack, is graded for stepping in at
2m. Strenuous moves lead up right, then go back left at the top of the crack. The
rather artificial start adds perhaps a technical grade.

THE HORSE'S HEAD   *(Map Ref 475 684)*

Midway between the villages of Findochty and Portknockie and just west of
Tronach Head, a spectacular rocky crest known as the Horse's Head runs out
seawards for some 30 metres from the cliff top before plunging seawards in a
sheer 35m rocky nose. The east face of the ridge is grassy but the very steep
west face and the seaward nose are of clean though very variable rock. The west
face curves round westwards into a repulsive overhanging red wall sheltering an
attractive amphitheatre with a sloping grassy floor and a grand view of the
climbing arena.

Access
Park beside the prominent isolated cemetery midway between Portknockie and
Findochty on the A942 and walk north across the disused railway line to the
obvious marker pole above the cliff top. The ridge runs out northwards immediately below the pole. Descend eastwards down a grassy shelf with an embryo
path into a bay on the right, looking out. Gain the west side of the ridge by a weird
narrow tunnel, the Hole, which pierces the ridge and comes out at the grassy
floored amphitheatre. Right of the tunnel entrance is a distinctive tidal arch not
to be confused with the tunnel itself.

The only route to date takes an obvious overhung recess and groove left of
the tunnel. It is a fine route on fairly good rock and justifies a visit. On the
impressive seaward nose to the left are some imposing groove lines. However,
the rock is variable at the bottom, deteriorating to rubble on the ridge crest itself
and all exploration so far has found discretion very much the better part of valour.

Tombstone   30m   VS 4c *
A worthwhile route gaining the obvious overhung recess in the west wall of the
ridge and finishing up a fine groove curving round to the right of the overhang.
Start some way left of the tunnel and climb broken rock to a bulge, surmounted
on the right to gain a recess. Follow the slab and groove on the right to the neck
of the ridge. Peg belay in place on right.

If loose rock is not your scene, further exploration may be avoided by a
diversion to the caves and stacks between here and Findochty.

MULL CLEAVE

The coast between MacDuff and Rosehearty is continuously rocky, rising at Troup Head and Pennan Head to the highest cliffs in the whole North-East of Scotland. It has been only intermittently explored and Mull Cleave is the only major climbing location yet discovered.

Situated due north of the Mill of Melrose, a short distance east of Macduff, Mull Cleave is a spectacular rock blade whose smooth west wall rises steeply above a platform dipping into the sea, covered at high tide. This wall gives four climbs and the short wall above broken rock on the landward side gives some worthwhile short problems. The rock on the west face is clean and sound; some of the shorter landward problems are a little loose at the top.

Access

Follow the B9031 eastwards off the main A98 for about 2km (1 mile) towards Gardenstown, until a road leads off left down to the Mill of Melrose. Park here (please do not block access) and cross a gate just east of the Mill. Walk north and westwards round the edge of the fields, following a fence to the cliff top, which is followed eastwards to the stack. Gain the stack by scrambling down a grassy trough on the headland opposite. Traverse easily round the south, landward, margin of the stack to reach the west wall. The short landward walls are gained by a steep dirty scramble. Descent is by abseil or by reversing Jamcrack. Belays are very difficult to find on top. Birds are a problem in the nesting season, with the summit area inhabited by some thuggish gulls.

WEST FACE

This steep, open, rectangular face of good rock has scope for further routes.

Hammerhead   25m   E1 5a   (1979)
A sustained pitch up the left edge of the wall. Start directly below the edge of the wall. Climb easy cracks up and left to the large ledge below the seaward arete. Step right below a bulge to gain a niche, then pull left over the bulge and follow cracks directly to a peg belay at the top.

Shark's Back   25m   E1 5b *
The original route taking a central line. Near the centre of the wall is a band of bulges with a slot at its right-hand side. Climb through the bulge left of the slot to gain the left-hand of two parallel cracks. Follow the crack to a tricky finish above the diagonal fault.

Loan Shark   25m   E1 5b *   (1988)
Starting between Shark's Back and Cleavage, go through the slot in the bulge, then follow a curving line up and right to join the final moves of Cleavage.

Cleavage   25m   Mild VS 4b **   (1979)
Climb the obvious crack up the right edge of the wall directly. A good route at a reasonable standard with excellent protection.

THE LANDWARD WALLS

A short steep wall of mainly sound rock tops the broken ledges of grass and rock forming the east side of the blade.

The Snout   10m   VS 4c *   (1979)
An attractive problem spectacularly situated on the south arete of the blade. Scramble to a large platform below the steep upper nose. Pull into a groove on the right edge and then swing diagonally left across the wall to gain the left edge and the last few metres of Cleavage.

The Clasper   8m   Severe   (1979)
In the middle of the east wall is a prominent deep crack. This route steps off a pinnacle just left of this crack to gain and climb the right-hand of two short corners.

Jam Crack   8m   Severe   (1979)
The prominent deep crack in the centre of the wall is probably the easiest route of descent from the crest of the blade.

Shagreen   10m   VS 4c   (1979)
Climb a thin crack in the wall right of Jam Crack, finishing rightwards.

Spiracle   10m   Mild Severe   (1979)
Follow the curving corner at the right end of the wall to finish up the last few metres of the seaward arete.

Less than 800 metres east of Mull Cleave can be found the Scalpel, a sharp ridge recognisable by its clean slatey west face. This may give some worthwhile climbing and can be gained by a steep grassy scramble down the main cliffs to the beach.

About 2km west of Mill of Melrose, and 400 metres east of the swimming pool at Tarlair, lies the Bay of Cullen. There is a buttress here, known as the Black Tower, which rears up from the beach path, facing a small pinnacle known as the Tooth. This promises some reasonable climbing but is disappointing close up.

Moving east, the next township is Gardenstown. The Dalradian slate of Macduff prevails here too, but in big grassy headlands — More Head to the west, and Troup Head on the east. East of Troup the cliff scenery becomes more dramatically sheer, but the rock is conglomerate and hopeless for climbing. Hell's Lum, a natural tunnel through the cliffs, is worth a visit.

East of Pennan, the grassy conglomerate cliffs are over 120m high. The scale and verticality is breathtaking, but climbing doesn't bear thinking about. Further east, towards Rosehearty, the rock reverts to Dalradian slate. Some climbing might be worthwhile around Quarry Head.

The Deeside Crags

Moving away from the coast, this chapter describes the climbing to be found in the Dee valley.

CLACH NA BEINN   *(Map Ref 616 866)*

The vast majority of the hills in lower Deeside are of the rounded, heather-clad sort and very much lacking in rock outcrops. Clach na Beinn is one of the most notable exceptions, sporting an austere, wart-like summit tor, reminiscent of those in the Cairngorms. It is one of the North-East's most striking landmarks. Over the centuries its salient position has been accounted for by a number of varied explanations. However, the most local and infinitely most romantic legend was set to verse by the Rev. Joseph Knowles of Birse in the mid-18th century. As he informs us, the stone formerly lay low in the plain and its present position is entirely due to a domestic quarrel between the Devil and his wife. "Have at you now, you Beldame" roared the Fiend, And hurled the rock through the resounding skies; Dreadful it fell, and crushed his breathless fiend, And there entombed Her Hellish Highness lies.

Todays local climbers hold no truck with yesterdays explanations and believe the only devils to watch out for are more physical than mythical and lurk in Clach na Beinn's jam cracks, waiting to ambush the unwary. There are enjoyable routes of all grades on the tor, usually following well protected crack lines (a good selection of Friends is recommended), which vary in height from 10 to 30m. As such, Clach na Beinn provides an excellent opportunity to master the intricate skills of jamming Another, and rather unusual, facet of the climbing here is the presence of a number of gullies which, although upon first introduction may seem to represent a botanist's Eden, provide interesting excursions in their own right. Indeed, considering how popular the hill is with weekend walkers, it supports an impressive variety of flora and fauna; in the 19th century sea eagles used to nest on the tor.

The exceptionally rough granite is generally sound although booming flakes may be occasionally encountered. Due to its exposed south-easterly aspect the cliff is a sun trap and will dry quickly after showers. However, on a cold windy day climbing here can be virtually impossible.

During the writing of this guide a lot of old climbing information has been unearthed. As a result, the original names of the older routes have been preferred with the sole exception of Cairngorm Club Crack.

Access

The tor forms the highest part of Clach na Beinn at 580m and lies up the attractively wooded Glen Dye, an offshoot of Feughside, some 12km (7 miles) south of Banchory on the B974, Cairn o' Mount road. For the quickest approach from Aberdeen, follow the A943 (South Deeside Road) as far as the Bridge of

Feugh. Once over the bridge, turn left up Feughside, and follow the B974 for 4km (2½ miles) to Strachan. Turn left again here, still on the B974, and follow the road for 9km (5½ miles) to reach the shortest access track (this is on the right, immediately after a sharp bend and there are some derelict looking cottages further on, on the left). This track should not be confused with the one into Glen Dye Lodge which is a little further down the brae, closer to the river. Cars should be parked as close to the start of the forestry track as possible and care is required not to cause any obstruction.

Follow the track through the wood for a few minutes until the objective becomes clear. Turn left down the hill (through a gate) and cross a burn. Now turn right and follow the track to the lower edge of the prominent isolated wood beneath the hill. Turn right here and follow a path uphill, beside the right edge of the wood. At the top of the wood the path veers left. Follow this (marshy in places) and its continuation which goes up the hill towards the tor (allow 1 hour). On the return journey, it is best to retrace the line of ascent, as the more direct descent going diagonally left down the hillside from the top of the wood has recently been interrupted by a new plantation surrounded by electric fencing. Although a stile has been provided across the fence, the ploughed hillside is now very rough going and should be avoided.

For visiting climbers from the south, the quickest, and indeed the most panoramic approach of all is by the B974, turning left off the dual-carriageway just after the northern exit for Brechin. Follow the road through Edzell and Fettercairn and cross The Clatterin' Brig to reach the steepest part of The Mounth. As the summit is crested (the cairn on the left dates from around 2000 BC), the tor is seen in stark relief, totally dominating the surrounding countryside. From here a further 10 minutes driving leads to the new Bridge of Dye (the old bridge on the left was recently retired after 300 years service) and the approach track is just further on at the top of the hill, on the left immediately before a bend.

The grassy bay beside Cairngorm Club Crack is the usual recovery and gearing-up point and is also the finest part of the tor. No.2 Gully is the obvious cleft towards the left side of the bay and is a useful reference point, the routes being described in two sections. Firstly, the climbs are described going right from the gully, then left.

No.2 Gully   12m   Very Difficult   (1919)
After the dirty initial bulge, this can be climbed by exiting out right by cracks below the top, or by stepping right at the very top. Not a particularly pleasant route.

Viper Cracks   12m   HVS 5a   (1980)
Near the mouth of the gully and on its right wall is a thin crack. Climb this to a junction with Python cracks which is then followed to the top.

Python Cracks   12m   Very Difficult *   (c.1948)
The first crack line on the open face right of the gully is usually started via No.1 Chimney. A slightly harder alternative start is available on the left or, the crack can be approached directly (4c).

No.1 Chimney   12m   Very Difficult ***   (1948)
The fine central fault which starts as a crack and widens into a chimney higher up. Elegant climbing.

Cairngorm Club Crack   12m   Severe **   (1901)
The classic chimney crack in the back corner of the bay which is all a bit of a struggle. Originally named No.1 Gully.

Man Eater   10m   HVS 5a *   (1978)
The left-hand of the trio of fierce cracks, right of Cairngorm Club Crack. There is an alternative start via Cairngorm Club Crack which may be unsporting, but is eminently more sensible.

Gnasher   10m   E1 5b **   (1978)
The central crack which requires a forceful approach and a high pain threshold.

Rough Rider   10m   HVS 5a **   (1978)
The right-hand crack. A big knob proves helpful on this route which is the easiest of the cracks.

Twinkletoes   10m   E1 5b **   (1981)
The thin parallel cracks right of Rough Rider, starting at the right edge of the bay Step up left to follow the cracks awkwardly and finish up by a big flake. Sustained.

Erk   10m   E3 5b **   (1982)
This fine climb up the face of the right bounding rib of the bay is sustained and badly protected, with ground fall potential. Climb up and left by a crack to the centre of the rib. Go up near the right edge using a pocket, then step left and up to a final flake.

Yikes   10m   VS 4c *   (1982)
The obvious layback flake, high on the right side of the rib. Start up Stuffer, then move left and go up to the flake. Follow this to the top.

Stuffer   12m   Hard Severe 4b   (1982)
Climb the corner-crack round the right side of the Erk rib to reach broken ground. A choice of easier finishes leads to the top.

Micro Rib   12m   Mild VS 4b   (1982)
The obvious little rib right of Stuffer has a choice of finishes up the more broken ground above.

Micro Line   12m   Very Difficult   (1925)
The obvious corner right of Micro Rib with a helpful jam crack on the right wall. A bit dirty.

Flip Flop   10m   HVS 5b   (1982)
Gain a sloping ledge on the wall right of Micro Line using a fragile flake. Step left
and climb the wall directly to the top.

Keepy Uppy   12m   HVS 5c   (1982)
This climbs the right hand rib indirectly. Start up Fissure Feugh for a move, then
go up left and round the rib to gain the sloping ledge of Flip Flop. Finish straight
up.

Fissure Feugh   10m   Mild VS 4b *   (1982)
The obvious last jam crack before the rocks peter out.

The rest of the routes are described going left from No.2 Gully:

Snotty Wotty   15m   VS 5a   (1986)
Start at the foot of No.2 Gully at a large block. Climb the obvious corner with
some vegetation to a roof. Turn the roof on the right and climb the steep wall
above, via a small bulge, to the top.

Twilight Zone   15m   VS 4c *   (1981)
The obvious clean cracks on the left wall of No.2 Gully, just below the arete of
Silver Rib.

Silver Rib   15m   E2 5b *   (1981)
The clean cut rib to the left of No.2 Gully. Start up a small corner on the right
side of the rib and exit out left onto the face. Move up into a shallow groove and
make hard moves up left onto the edge. Move up right to easier ground.
Escapable.

Square Chimney   15m   Very Difficult *   (1948)
The chimney right of Silver Rib, stepping right at the top.

Sgoiltean na Lamhan Fuilteach   15m   E1 5b **   (1989)
Start as for Bolero and climb up to a prominent hollow flake on the right. Move
right to the arete and climb a finger crack which leads to a small ledge. Continue
straight up the crack and groove to eventually gain the arete. Finish up this.

Bolero   15m   VS 4c **   (1981)
Climb the central cracks in the broad face left of Square Chimney, starting just
right of a boulder.

Blawearie's Secret   20m   HVS 5a   (1989)
This route climbs the obvious left-facing corner between Bolero and Central
Gully. Move up from the left to gain the base of the corner and follow it to the
roof. Pull over this and move up left to finish up a jam crack.

Central Gully   25m   Very Difficult   (1925)
The obvious grassy fault in the middle of the wall has loose rock and lush vegetation. A fine traditional route.

Flypaper   25m   VS 4c   (1981)
Start up a grassy groove on the right side of the big rib left of Central Gully. Climb up onto a right-slanting slab and follow this to pull up over a bulge. Follow cracks to the top. Very scrappy.

Bogendreip Buttress   25m   VS 5a ***   (1981)
One of the best routes on Clach na Beinn , taking the central rib-like buttress direct. Climb cracks left of the crest and go up to a ledge on the crest. Move up onto slabs below an obvious notch in the rib. Pull through the notch and finish moving left and up. There is a harder alternative finish on the right.

Crack o' the Mearns   25m   VS 4c ***   (1981)
The obvious crack system on the left side of Bogendreip Buttress. Climb the clean crack running up the left flank of the rib (right of a big corner) and climb the main crack up slightly right to the top.

Solus's na h-Uamhan   20m   Severe **   (1989)
This is the once vegetated gully to the left of Crack o' the Mearns. Climb up the corner just left of the clean crack and move left to the gully proper after a few metres. Continue up via a through-route behind the chockstone at the top.

Hell's Bells   20m   E1 5c *   (1989)
This route climbs the crack line to the left of Solus's na h-Uamhan. Start directly below the gully and climb straight up for 3m. Step left to a huge jug in the middle of the slab and move left again to the crack. Climb this and trend right to a ledge. Continue straight up until forced left onto a slab. Move up right and then finish straight up a groove.

Hell Cat   20m   VS 5a   (1989)
Start in the shallow green-looking chimney to the left of Hell's Bells. Climb this and pull out left. Continue straight up to easier ground which leads to a final deep crack. Finish up this.

Window Gully   25m   Hard Severe 4b   (1948)
This is the next big gully to the left, of which the lower half is dirty. The best and cleanest finish uses a combination of the final wide crack and a subsidiary crack system on the right. Escape is possible up chossy ground further right again

Cave Crack   20m   Hard Severe 4a *   (Pre-1907)
The wide crack just left of Grasshopper Gully, passing to the right of a small cave at two-thirds height, provides good climbing.

THE SLABS

The slabs towards the left side of the crag are about 30m high but become broken at about 20m, where routes converge. A fair amount of variation is possible in this area and the routes are described from left to right.

Platform Climb   20m   Difficult **   (1947)

The sharp rib bounding the left-hand side of the slabs is broken at mid-height but provides enjoyable, airy climbing. Climb the crest throughout.

Outside Left   35m   Difficult   (1948)

Starting at the lowest point of the face, climb the left side via shallow corners and flakes.

Inside Left   35m   Very Difficult   (1948)

The line of flakes just right of the previous route.

Striker   35m   Hard Severe 4a *

Start just left of an embedded boulder. Climb directly up the slab using small flakes to a more broken area. Continue up and right along a slender ramp under bulges, to pull over onto slabs with ledges above. A good direct line.

Inside Right   35m   Hard Severe

Start at the embedded boulder 8 metres right of the lowest point of the slabs. Climb up an obvious flake to below another flake at 8m. Step left and go up to where a small right-slanting corner forms the left side of a pink slab. Climb this corner to easier ground.

Pink Slab Variation   12m   Hard Severe

Climb Inside Right for 5m, then go right and up flakes to traverse left over the pink slab, using a rotten flake. Finish as for Inside Right.

Outside Right   30m   VS 4c   (1989)

Start at the rightmost boulders. Climb up a pink-spotted flake and follow the obvious right-slanting groove to make a hard stride right to grab a flake. Move up to easier ground, then move right to climb the right edge to a ledge with a small cave. Continue up the crack above to reach the platform and finish as for the other routes. A route that would benefit from liberal application of weed killer.

THE WESTERN SECTOR

There are some trifling climbs round left from the slabs. The area of the south-eastern gully is useful as a descent route. The climbs are described from the final left-hand rib.

Outline   20m   Hard Severe *   (1981)
The last rib just left of a grassy groove. Start at the right side of the rib beside the
groove. Climb the rib up and right to return left under an overhang. Pull over the
bulge to easy rocks. Artificial but good.

Eagle Buttress   20m   Difficult   (1948)
The obvious chimney-groove has an awkward first section and easy slabs
above.

Flakesville   20m   Severe
Climb the layback flakes just right of the chimney.

Flakemania   20m   Very Difficult
Climb the next, and more continuous, line of flakes to the right.

South-Eastern Gully   30m   Moderate   (1919)
Start up the shallow, grassy groove just to the left of Shrew Rib. Where the rock
noticeably steepens, move left across a small slab to a wide grassy continuation.
Scramble to the top.

Vimy Ridge   30m   VS 4c *   (1989)
Follow South-Eastern Gully to the small slab. Pull straight into the hanging
groove above and climb this to the top.

There are a few boulder problems on the short back side of the tor, from where
a bleak wilderness of peat hags stretches towards Mount Battock and Mount
Keen. Short problems also exist on the smaller tors nearby, some dating from
the 1920s and 30s.

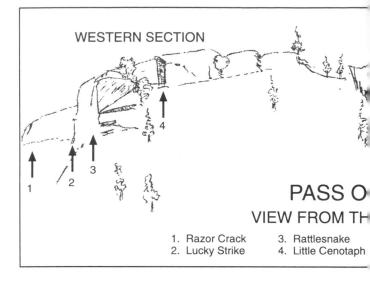

WESTERN SECTION

PASS O
VIEW FROM TH

1. Razor Crack
2. Lucky Strike
3. Rattlesnake
4. Little Cenotaph

UPPER DEESIDE

The crags of Upper Deeside were initially viewed as retreats for climbers washed out of the hills and off the mountain crags. However, "The Pass" (Creag an t-Seabhaig) has been increasingly used in its own right and now ranks as one of the North-East's premier outcrops. Unfortunately the down side of this has been increased litter and erosion of the paths. In contrast the other crags described all offer a far greater degree of solitude.

The Cadha Dubh received a face lift in the late 1980s, whilst the Pannanich cliffs and Cambus o' May quarries emerged from the mists of time. For better or worse, massive cleaning operations and removal of vegetation were used to achieve this. At present, it is difficult to tell whether they will ever be popular or if nature will reclaim them.

THE PASS OF BALLATER   *(Map Ref 367 971)*

These south-facing cliffs, known as Creag an t-Seabhaig, have a delightfully sunny aspect and provide good routes of all grades on clean solid granite, although the odd crumbly patch of rock will be encountered. Excellent protection can be found on most of the routes and micro-nuts are particularly useful on the harder climbs. The cliff dries very quickly after light rain, especially the Western Tiers, and it is usually possible to climb here from March through to December.

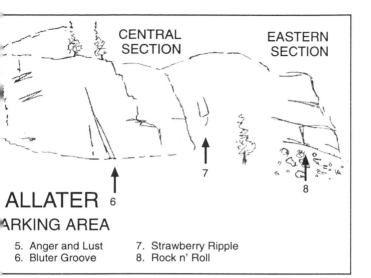

CENTRAL SECTION

EASTERN SECTION

ALLATER 6

ARKING AREA

5. Anger and Lust
6. Bluter Groove
7. Strawberry Ripple
8. Rock n' Roll

The cliff is a great place to climb and it plays host to a wide variety of wildlife. There is a very active and noisy colony of jackdaws and slow worms can occasionally be spotted basking in the sun. Numerous and varied raptors frequently hunt in the area and there are many large ant colonies above the cliffs.

Access
The cliff is easily located on the north side of the B972 (5 minutes by car from Ballater). A recently-constructed car park lies below the central section.

The cliffs are divided into three sections, the western and central areas are clearly visible from the car park, while the smaller eastern section is largely hidden by trees. The western section is divided into two tiers. The upper tier, above a broad terrace, has the easily recognisable features of Smith's Arete and Little Cenotaph located centrally. The lower tier, below the terrace, has a huge slab on the right, bounded on its left by an impressive wall distinguished by a vertical quartz seam running up its right edge.

The central section, which is above and just right of the gate, is characterised by two fine obvious lines. In the centre of the cliff is the obvious corner of Bluter Groove, whilst on the left (gully) wall is the impressive capped corner of Anger and Lust.

The eastern section is composed of shorter cliffs and is more secluded. This lack of height in no way detracts from the climbing and there are some excellent problems here.

WESTERN SECTION: UPPER TIER

The routes are described as being left or right of Little Cenotaph, which is located roughly in the centre of the tier.

1   Little Cenotaph   8m   HVS 5b **   (1975)
A popular route which is distinctly easier for the taller. Climb the obvious right-angled corner by a variety of contortions to a ledge on the right. Finish up the shallow corner on the left. If the upper corner is avoided, the grade is lowered to 5a.

2   Dod's Dead Cat   12m   E2 5c *   (1986)
Climb Little Cenotaph to a horizontal break, then traverse left to Smith's Arete and finish up this. A hybrid, but good.

3   Smith's Arete   10m   E5 6a ***   (1983)
This is the striking arete left of Little Cenotaph. Climb the edge to an accommodating horizontal break at two-thirds height, which provides a welcome rest and runners. Finish directly up the slab above.

4   Peel's Wall   10m   E4 6a ***   (1977)
The fine wall to the left of Smith's is a popular test piece. Gain an undercut flake and proceed with long reaches to the horizontal break. Move straight up until an awkward long reach to a narrow ledge allows a committing move up and right to be made. A quick jibber up the short slabby wall leads to the top.

5   Fingerwrecker   10m   HVS 5c *   (1979)
Two metres left of Peel's Wall is an obvious thin crack. Climb this (no cheating from boulders) and gain a scoop. Finish by Original Route. An aptly named route.

6   Wrecker's Traverse   15m   E2 5c *   (1984)
A must for lateral thinkers which crosses some unlikely territory. Follow Fingerwrecker to the scoop. Move up right and dash across Peel's Wall via the obvious break, to attain a standing position on Smith's Arete. Finish up this.

7   Original Route   10m   VS 5a *   (1971)
About 2 metres left of Fingerwrecker is a corner. Gain this awkwardly and continue up right to a ledge. Finish by deep cracks above.

8   Right-Hand Crack   10m   HVS 5a   (1975)
The obvious crack to the left of Original Route has a dirty finish.

Silent Spring, Pass of Ballater (Climber, Dave George)

9   Left-Hand Crack   10m   VS 4c   (1975)
The crack line left again is continually interesting.

10   Cheap Trick   10m   E4 6b *   (1984)
Climb the short crack left of Left-Hand Crack to the break, then go directly up the wall above.

11   Janus   10m   E4 6a *   (1990)
Start up Cheap Trick, then move left into the crack and follow this with hard moves to the top. A direct start is possible up the wall below the crack using an obvious side pull. This is more serious and artificial (E4 6c).

12   The Joke   10m   E2 6a   (1985)
Start just right of a boulder just right of a tree-filled scoop 5 metres left of Cheap Trick. Climb the wall going slightly left, then right (possible high side runner on trees to the left).

The following climbs are on the right hand side of the upper tier. There is an easy descent right (when facing the cliff) from the top of Little Cenotaph, down a diagonal ramp.

13   Pink Wall   8m   VS 5a *   (1972)
This gives sustained but well protected climbing up the middle of the right wall of Little Cenotaph. An eliminate is possible, keeping just right of Pink Wall (HVS 5a).

14   Green Laughter   8m   HVS 5b   (1982)
Halfway down the descent an obvious ledge leads out right. Climb the groove above the end of this ledge.

15   Flibbertigibbet   10m   VS 4c   (1982)
Climb the obvious hanging slab 3 metres right of Green Laughter, starting from 3m the descent ramp. It is easier if the hanging slab is gained from the right.

16   Green Wall   8m   HVS 5a   (1982)
This is the steep wall 2 metres right of the descent ramp. Climb to a horizontal break and go straight up the wall above, exiting right to a grotty finish.

17   Swine Before Pearls   10m   VS 4c   (1982)
Climb the arete left of Jackdaw Groove, finishing out left just below the top.

18   Jackdaw Groove   10m   HVS 4c   (1971)
This slim elegant corner is the first major feature right of Green Wall. It is sustained with poor protection and bad rock.

Cold Rage, Pass of Ballater   (Climber, Derek Austin)

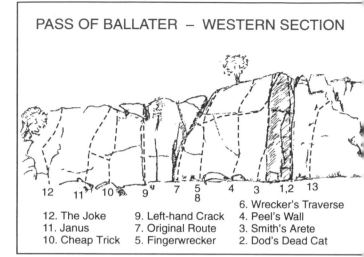

PASS OF BALLATER – WESTERN SECTION

6. Wrecker's Traverse

12. The Joke	9. Left-hand Crack	4. Peel's Wall
11. Janus	7. Original Route	3. Smith's Arete
10. Cheap Trick	5. Fingerwrecker	2. Dod's Dead Cat

19 Jackdaw's Edge 10m E3 5c   (1985)
The right arete of Jackdaw's Groove has some hard moves into the groove near the top. Serious.

20 Crumbling Dice 10m E2 5c   (1977)
This is the corner tucked in underneath Jackdaw's Edge. Climb 6m to a peg, then go up and swing right to finish. Poor rock on the bold lower section detracts from the route.

21 Black Custard 12m E1 5b ***   (1971)
An obvious line 5 metres right of Crumbling Dice, where a quartzy crack slants up left to an black overhanging apex. Climb the crack up to the roof and pull over steeply into an easier groove. A well protected test piece which is the scene of many struggles.
Variation: E3 5c
Start near Crumbling Dice and follow the shallow overlap up right to join Black Custard at its roof.

22 High Steppa 8m E2 6a **   (1980)
The short but fine wall 3 metres right of Black Custard. Make a bold start up a thin crack just right of the arete, which leads quickly to a friendly horizontal break. Move up and step right to attain a standing position. Finish straight up.

23 First Slip 8m HVS 5a   (1982)
Climb the wall rather artificially between High Steppa and Jam Crack.

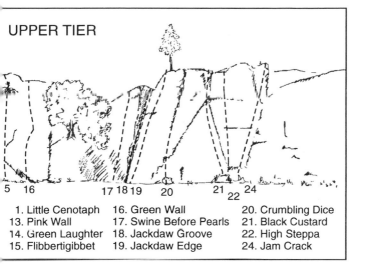

UPPER TIER

5 16   17 18 19   20   21   24
                                    22

1. Little Cenotaph	16. Green Wall	20. Crumbling Dice
13. Pink Wall	17. Swine Before Pearls	21. Black Custard
14. Green Laughter	18. Jackdaw Groove	22. High Steppa
15. Flibbertigibbet	19. Jackdaw Edge	24. Jam Crack

24 Jam Crack 8m Severe   (1960s)
This obvious crack right of First Slip provides a little jamming pitch.

LOWER TIER
Razor's Crack, an obvious feature near the left-hand end of the tier, is described first. The other routes are described proceeding either left or right of this climb.

25 Razor's Crack 8m VS 4c   (1960s)
An interesting little S-shaped crack near the left edge of the tier. The crevasse above the route seems to be getting wider!

26 Skidmarks 8m HVS 5b   (1987)
Start just left of Razor's Crack. Climb the bulge to gain a break, turn the overlap on the left and climb the slab above, avoiding After Shave.

27 After Shave 8m Mild VS 4b   (1960s)
Climb the crack 3 metres left of Razor's Crack, on the left edge of the buttress, to a choice of finishes.

28 Rightguard 8m Difficult   (1960s)
Start at a rowan 4 metres left of After Shave, and go straight up. It is possible to trend right and join After Shave.

29 Swivel Head 8m Difficult   (1960s)
Climb the obvious line with blue paint splashed on it, just left of the rowan.

30 BO 6m Very Difficult
The mossy cracks just left of the edge, 3 metres left of Swivel Head, are steep and rather loose.

The following climbs are right of Razor's Crack.

31 Jumbled Blocks Crack 8m Very Difficult *
The obvious corner and crack 3 metres right of Razor's Crack is also a useful descent.

32 Ping-Pong 8m Severe
The right-hand of the two corners.

33 Close Shave 8m HVS 5a   (1982)
Start 2 metres right of Ping-Pong. Climb a shallow corner and pull over a roof at the top.

About 2 metres right of Close Shave there are two large blocks on top of each other, which provide the starting point for the following three routes.

34 Brut 8m VS 5a   (1982)
Climb the corner left of the large roof at mid-height. Quite dirty.

35 Stinker 10m E1 5b *   (1981)
Climb straight up, taking the obvious crack splitting the roof at mid-height. Well protected but strenuous.

36 Cowardie-Custard 10m VS 4c   (1982)
Take the parallel cracks through the mid-height roof, 2 metres right of Stinker. It is possible to escape right to finish up Fungus Face, hence the name.

37 Fungus Face 8m E1 5b   (1982)
About 4 metres right of the blocks there is a single large stone beneath the slab. Start directly above this and climb up for 2m. Make a few moves up right until it is possible to grasp a jug on the left. Move left and up to finish. Brittle rock and poor protection.

38 Lime Chimney 8m Very Difficult   (1971)
This pleasant route, starting 4 metres right of Fungus Face, is slightly spoilt by a dirty finish.

39 Ton-Ton Macoute 12m E4 6b *   (1988)
The hanging corner 3 metres right of Lime Chimney. Climb the wall to the base of the corner. Make a long reach to a sloping ledge and continue up (crux) to a second ledge and better holds. Finish up the corner continuation (2 peg runners).

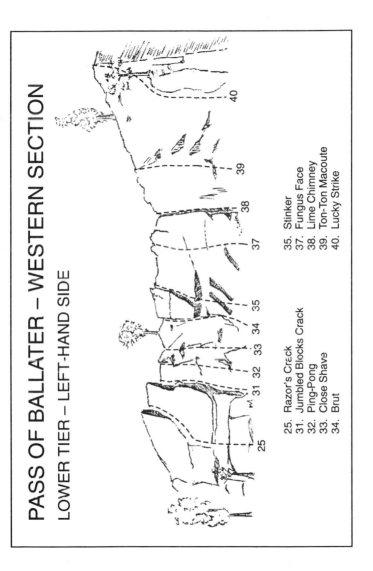

PASS OF BALLATER – WESTERN SECTION

LOWER TIER – LEFT-HAND SIDE

25. Razor's Crack
31. Jumbled Blocks Crack
32. Ping-Pong
33. Close Shave
34. Brut

35. Stinker
37. Fungus Face
38. Lime Chimney
39. Ton-Ton Macoute
40. Lucky Strike

40   Lucky Strike   15m   VS 4c **   (1971)
Another 8 metres right of Lime Chimney there is a very steep black-streaked corner line. Climb this to a spacious ledge and finish up the corner behind the tree. After the polished start on poor rock, the climbing is much better.

About 3 metres right of Lucky Strike an obvious traverse on flakes leads up right across the wall to join the final pitch of Pretzel Logic. This provides an easier but logical start to this route. The traverse can be continued into Rattlesnake to give an exposed HVS.

41   Pretzel Logic   15m   E3 5c **   (1980)
Start at a corner 4 metres right of the flake traverse, just right of the arete. Bridge up the corner until a traverse across the wall gains a crack system. Follow this to the base of the final corner (possible belay), which provides an exhilarating finish.

42   Direct Start   8m   E3 6a *   (1983)
The short steep groove in the true line of the route.

43   Rattlesnake   15m   E3 6a **   (1981)
A little right of Pretzel Logic is one of the most striking lines in the Pass. Climb the initial crux corner either directly or from the right to gain the steep but easier quartzy cracks above.

44   Supercreeps   20m   E1 5b *   (1982)
Start in a small corner a metre right of Rattlesnake. Climb this to pull out right to the left end of the ledge of Medium Cool. Pull directly over the bulge above and go up to a shallow niche. Continue straight up to a small overlap and step up right to join the top of Silent Spring.

There is a crevassed area 12 metres right of Rattlesnake, beneath the large slab. The following two routes start from the crevasse.

45   Medium Cool   20m   VS 4c **   (1971)
From a belay in the crevasse, gain a little tree on the left and then move up to the large overlap. Traverse left to a ledge (runners). Move back right and surmount the overlap. Climb to the tree, then go up behind it on small holds with few runners.

46   Silent Spring   25m   E1 5a **   (1982)
Follow Medium Cool to the runner ledge. From the highest point of the niche gain the upper slab via a scimitar-shaped crack. Move up then right to the tree. Follow the left-trending runnel to the top, serious.

PASS OF BALLATER – WESTERN SECTION, LOWER TIER

THE SLABS

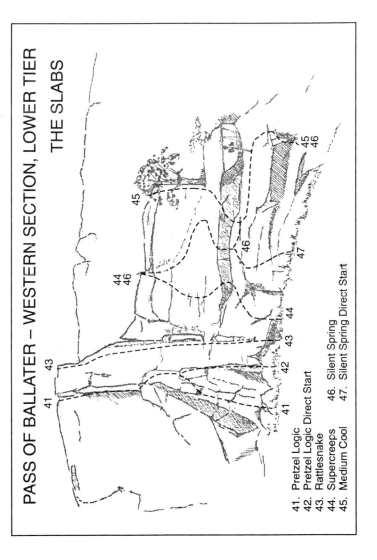

41. Pretzel Logic
42. Pretzel Logic Direct Start
43. Rattlesnake
44. Supercreeps
45. Medium Cool
46. Silent Spring
47. Silent Spring Direct Start

47   Direct Start   5m   E2 5c
Climb the lower overlaps either on the left or centrally (harder) to join the parent route at the niche.
Variation Finish: E1 5a
Climb the slab above the runnel, trending left.

48   Slowly Burning   E2 5c
Follow the direct start and Silent Spring but avoid the traverse to the tree by climbing the slab direct to finish at the top of Silent Spring.

49   Scary Monsters   30m   VS *   (1980)
Good climbing, although the final corner frequently gets choked with pine needles, so some cleaning may be necessary.
1. 10m 4c Follow Medium Cool to the tree and belay.
2. 20m 4c Foot traverse left along the obvious break, then go up and left to the left bounding corner of the slab. Climb this to the top.
Variation Finish: 10m   VS 4c   (1983)
This is the obvious minor corner running up the steep left wall of the main corner.

On the broken tier below and left of Lucky Strike is a slabby buttress.

50   The Wiry Masters   10m   HVS 4c   (1984)
Climb the faint corner in the middle of the slab to a ledge at mid-height. Move left to a curving flange, then follow this to the top. Alternatively climb a crack left of the flange.

51   Tough's Brush   10m   E1 5a   (1984)
Start at the bottom right of the slab. Climb up left to the ledge, go up and right to a pocket to finish as for Wiry Masters.

52   Snowflakes   10m   E2 5b   (1984)
The visionary will struggle up the centre of the slab, avoiding holds on the other routes, for little reward.

On the next piece of compact rock, about 8 metres to the right of the Wiry Masters slab is:

53   Liquid Nerve   12m   E1 5a   (1989)
Start beside three blocks. From the rightmost block climb a quartz vein to a shallow scoop. Go up right to a horizontal break, then climb up and left to a crack and finish on good holds. Poorly protected.

An even poorer route has been climbed using the same start and traversing the lower lip of the slab, then squeezing up the centre of the slab past the horizontal break (E3 5c). Another 8 metres right is:

54   The Dance of the Wu-Li Masters   20m   E1 5b   (1983)
Start directly below the crevasse of the main slab in a small grey corner above
a small slab. Climb the grey corner and continue up the crack above to a small
V-notch. Traverse right to a flake beside a prominent bottomless groove. Go up
this to a small corner on the left. Finish up left.
Direct Finish: 8m   E2 6a *   (1984)
Climb the steep thin crack above the groove. Quite a struggle in a gradually
widening crack.
Right Hand Finish: 12m   HVS 5b   (1987)
From near the top of the groove, traverse right to reach a sloping platform. Finish
up the leaning corner above.

55   Barley's Eliminate   40m   HVS   (1977)
Although this route has been superseded by more direct lines, it provides a good
way up the cliff at a reasonable grade.
1. 20m 5b Follow the Wu-Li Masters to the small V-notch. Continue directly up
the wall above and climb the dirty slab to belay in the crevasse below Medium
Cool.
2. 10m 4c Follow Scarey Monsters as far as the corner. Climb down the corner
a few metres and belay.
3. 10m 5b Continue down the corner and step round left into Rattlesnake. Finish
up this.

CENTRAL SECTION
The central section of crag tapers upwards to the left, merging into the hillside
near the top of the wide-angled gully. The first routes here lie on the upper gully
wall and are described from top left to right.

56   Slope Arms   10m   E4 6a   (1986)
Just right of the broken wall at the top end of the cliff is a thin left-sloping crack.
Climb this, step left and go straight up to finish. Hard to protect.

57   Private Parts   10m   E6 6b *   (1987)
The line right of Slope Arms. Climb up to a poor peg runner. Hard moves past a
small overlap (crux) lead to a good flake. Go up and right to finish by obvious
notch.

58   General Anaesthetic   10m   E5 6c *   (1986)
Down right from Private Parts there is a large overhang. Start just left of this and
climb up a crack to a protruding split block. Carry straight on up the wall beside
a blind crack to reach a welcome jug just below the top. Pulling out left is the
easiest exit.

59   Captain Copout   15m   E4 6a **   (1984)
Climb General Anaesthetic to the split block. Make a right-rising traverse across
the wall to finish up a thin crack. High side runners can be placed before the
traverse.

60   Copulation   15m   E4 6b   (1987)
Essentially Captain Copout direct. Start just left of Isolation underneath a roof.
Move up right on good holds and pull through the roof at a shallow groove. Step
left (peg) then go up to join the parent route.

61   Isolation   12m   VS 5a   (1976)
This route climbs the obvious recessed zone which is located centrally in the
gully wall. Climb the awkward and loose lower wall to the recess and finish up a
corner crack on its left side.

The following routes are right (downhill) of Isolation.

62   The Terrorist   12m   HVS 5a   (1986)
Start just right of Isolation. Climb over the bulge to the right-hand end of the
ledge. Finish directly up the wall. Again, the rock is not irreproachable.

63   Distemper   15m   E5 6b **   (1986)
The small pink corner high on the wall and right of The Terrorist. Climb the small
hollow flakes up to a small roof, then go round into the main corner. Climb the corner
using a high undercling on its left wall (crux). More technical moves gain an
easier finish.

64   Cold Rage   20m   E3 6a **   (1983)
Climb a thin crack just left of Anger and Lust (crux) to a big niche. Move left and
climb straight up to a nose forming the right side of the final slot. Climb the slot
and wall to the top.

65   Direct Start   6m   E3 5c   (1987)
Climb the shallow groove just left of the normal start.

66   Hot Temper   15m   E5 6b ***   (1986)
A direct finish to Cold Rage. Where Cold Rage goes left from the niche, pull
directly through the roof and climb the wall above with difficulty. Strenuous with
reasonable protection, which is hard to place.

67   Anger and Lust   20m   E2 5c ***   (1980)
A classic route taking the obvious roofed corner near the bottom of the gully wall.
A larch tree grows in front of it. Climb the corner to finish sensationally by the
deep crack splitting the left side of the roof. High in the grade.

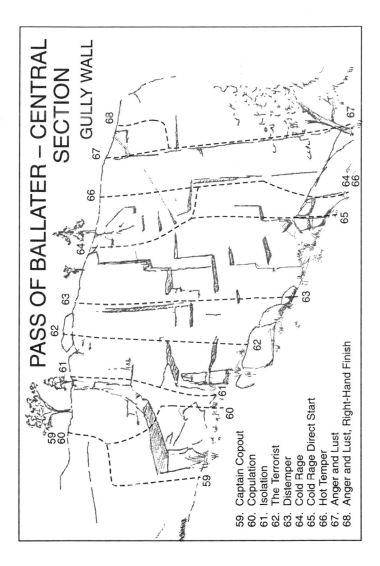

PASS OF BALLATER – CENTRAL SECTION
GULLY WALL

59. Captain Copout
60. Copulation
61. Isolation
62. The Terrorist
63. Distemper
64. Cold Rage
65. Cold Rage Direct Start
66. Hot Temper
67. Anger and Lust
68. Anger and Lust, Right-Hand Finish

68   Right-Hand Finish   6m   E4 6b ***   (1971/85)
The second part of the old peg line. From the bridging rest below the roof,
traverse right along the lip of an overlap to a good jug. Step left and finish up the
corner. Sensational and well protected.

69   Lech Gates   20m   E3 5c   (1983)
Start about 5 metres below Anger and Lust, below and slightly right of a smooth
corner. Climb block-flakes up right to a shallow corner. Use the crack on the
right to move up, then traverse left out of the corner to a poor resting place under
a roof. Take a deep breath, pull round left, and sprint up the crack line to a brutal
finish.

70   Direct Start   6m   E3 5c   (1987)
Climb the thin crack line past a peg runner to join the original line at the resting
place. Using this start makes the route less challenging; not the done thing!

71   Orage   10m   E3 6b   (1987)
Start up Lech Gates. Where this moves left, climb up to the overhang and make
a hard move up the corner to the slab belay of Creak and Squeak. Finish up this.

72   Bottle of Smoke   20m   E4 5c *   (1988)
Climb the arete between Lech Gates and Creak and Squeak. Start at the foot of
the arete and go up to climb a crack on the left, briefly joining Lech Gates, to a
final slot under an overlap (poor thread runner above). Go up right to reach a
good sidepull on the right side of the twin aretes and move up to a tricky exit at
the top. Go up the slab and crack above to finish as for Lech Gates.

73   Creak and Squeak   25m   HVS 5a   (1981)
Start well below Anger and Lust under prominent twin vertical cracks, just left of
the sharp lower nose of the crag. The route climbs up to the foot of these cracks,
moves left, and climbs the long thin groove to belay on the slab above. Climb
straight up a short crack and easier steps above to the top. A well named route
with good situations.

74   Mandrax   25m   Mild VS 4c   (1970)
Start as for the previous route, climb the twin cracks and gain a slabby ramp.
Traverse this away right to finish up rocks just right of a corner crack.

75   The Splits   35m   HVS 5b *   (1983)
Just above the lowest toe of the crag is a small tree. Traverse the hanging slab
above the tree rightwards, then go up to a flared leaning corner. Climb this to
emerge onto the slab above. Continue up to finish via the obvious wide corner,
turning the capping roof on the right.

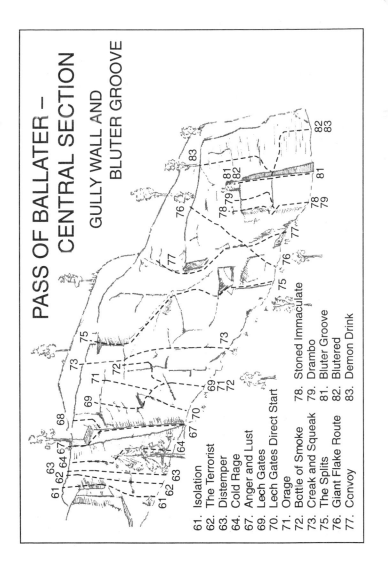

PASS OF BALLATER –
CENTRAL SECTION

GULLY WALL AND
BLUTER GROOVE

61. Isolation
62. The Terrorist
63. Distemper
64. Cold Rage
67. Anger and Lust
69. Lech Gates
70. Lech Gates Direct Start
71. Orage
72. Bottle of Smoke
73. Creak and Squeak
75. The Splits
76. Giant Flake Route
77. Convoy
78. Stoned Immaculate
79. Drambo
81. Bluter Groove
82. Blutered
83. Demon Drink

76   Giant Flake Route   30m   Mild VS 4b **   (1966)
Start about 10 metres right of the tree. Climb a short but hard wall to an easy
ledge system. Go up a crack in a corner to the line of big flakes which crosses
the wall diagonally from left to right. Follow these to the big sloping ledge above
Drambo. Climb onto the big split blocks and continue steeply on big holds up the
groove to the top.

77   Convoy   25m   VS 4c *   (1967)
Climb the groove 4 metres to the right to join Giant Flake Route and follow it to
the big ledge. Go straight up to an alcove and pull over the roof on good holds.

78   Stoned Immaculate   15m   E5 6a *   (1985)
The route climbs the left edge of the wall left of Bluter Groove. Start at some
sloping holds just right of the edge. Climb up leftwards to a horizontal break and
move out left to a rest. Step right and climb the edge, finishing direct. Serious.

79   Drambo   15m   E6 6a *   (1985)
Climb Stoned Immaculate to the rest. Follow the obvious break rightwards into
the centre of the wall (two RP5 runners, the last protection). Climb up to a
handrail and move left along this. Finish up the shallow corner which leads to
good holds. This route is committing and serious.

80   Bluter Crack   15m   E4 6c **   (1965/84)
Climb the desperate thin crack immediately left of Bluter Groove which joins it
higher up.

81   Bluter Groove   15m   E3 6b **   (1982)
The most obvious groove in the centre of the tier. The hard lower section is
climbed initially via the right arete, then step left to bridge up the groove. The
steep upper crack is easier.

82   Blutered   15m   E1 5a **   (1976)
This indirect ascent still provides fine climbing. Start approximately 5m up and
right of Bluter Groove and follow an obvious traverse line across the wall to reach
its upper part.

83   Demon Drink   15m   E5 6b **   (1985)
Climb Blutered to the left edge, then move up right and across to gear. Step left
and go straight up to the next protection. Make a long reach for a knob above
(crux), and go up to the top on superb holds.

84   Doctor Dipso   15m   E4 6a   (1985)
Climb Blutered to the peg runners. Make a hard move up and left to protection.
Climb straight up, then go right on improving holds to finish up the arete as for
Hangover Wall.

PASS OF BALLATER
CENTRAL SECTION

RIGHT-HAND SIDE

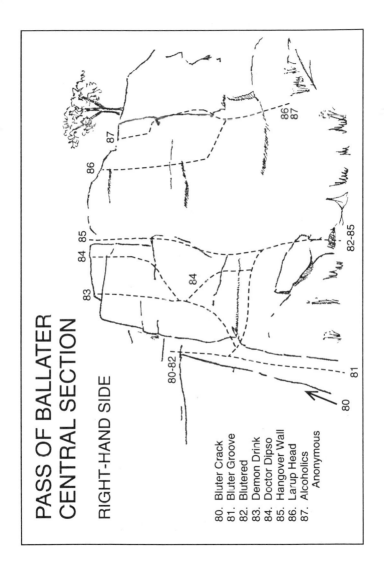

80. Bluter Crack
81. Bluter Groove
82. Blutered
83. Demon Drink
84. Doctor Dipso
85. Hangover Wall
86. Larup Head
87. Alcoholics
    Anonymous

85 Hangover Wall   15m   E2 5c   (1980)
This climb follows the obvious shallow groove line which starts above the traverse of Blutered. There are two pegs protecting the initial crux moves and some of the flakes are quite hollow.

86 Larup Head   18m   E3 5c *   (1985)
Although escapable, this gives a fine pitch up the wall 6 metres right of Hangover Wall. Start at some undercut flakes directly beneath three horizontal breaks. Climb up past these to a good ledge. Move left and climb the wall in a fine position to finish up an obvious crack on the right. Most people use the start of Alcoholics Anonymous, the true start being very devious.

87 Alcoholics Anonymous   15m   E1 5b *   (1985)
Start just right of Larup Head and move up into a shallow niche. Gain the ledge and finish up the corner above (not well protected).

To the right of Alcoholics Anonymous the cliff degenerates somewhat into tiers of broken rock. Up the hill to the right of the broken ground is a clean compact slab which is split centrally by a crack. This is:

88 Strawberry Ripple   8m   VS 5a *   (1980)
This pleasant route climbs the crack up the centre of the slab.

89 Back Slider   8m   HVS 5b   (1984)
Climb the slab left of Strawberry Ripple from bottom left to top right, with a side runner in Strawberry Ripple.

90 Plane Slider   8m   E3 5b   (1984)
The slab right of Strawberry Ripple gives an exciting route, made less serious if a side runner is used.

EASTERN SECTION
This section has two distinct tiers. Although the routes are nowhere more than 12m, it is well worth a visit. The first climbs are on the lower tier. At the bottom right-hand side of the gully dividing the central and eastern sections is a prominent block of rock. Although a number of bouldering routes are to be found here, the landings are atrocious.

Chopped P.O.R.G.   12m   VS 5a   (1987)
About 10m up the gully from Rock 'n' Roll is a steep grey slab behind a small larch tree. Climb the slab to good holds at the top.

Rock 'n' Roll   5m   HVS 5a   (1980)
Climb the prominent thin crack on the green gully wall.

Shivers   5m   HVS 5a   (1981)
Climb the flakes and cracks left of Rock 'n' Roll.

Glue Sniffer   5m   E2 6a   (1985)
The wall between Rock 'n' Roll and the Glaswegian Problem has a hideous
landing with the crux at the top.

The Glaswegian Problem   5m   E1 5c   (1982)
Climb the arete right of Rock 'n' Roll, stepping out right near the top. Try not to
fall off.

Press Up   5m   E1 5c   (1982)
Just round right from the previous route is an obvious cleaned flake. Gain this
and climb the wall above.

Wild Thing   5m   HVS 5c *   (1982)
This is the obvious roof and flakes on the frontal face, just left of an easy
chimney. A good little problem.

All the other climbs are on the upper tier, which is gained by walking up right
from Wild Thing until it is possible to scramble back left under a fine steep wall.
The wall is characterised by a peculiar horizontal band of pink rock with quartz
intrusions. The routes are described from left to right.

Corvid's Chimney   10m   Very Difficult
This is the chimney on the left of the wall. Climb to a platform, step left and finish
up an awkward crack. A useful descent.

Jings   6m   HVS 5b **   (1982)
The obvious crack 2 metres right of Corvid's Chimney provides a fine problem.

Help m'Bob   6m   E5 6c   (1987)
Climb the technical wall between Jings and Hairy Baboon, finishing up a shallow
corner past a peg.

Hairy Baboon   6m   E2 6a *   (1982)
About 2 metres right of Jings a thin crack splits the middle of the upper wall.
Gaining the crack is the crux.

Fat Doris   6m   E5 6b   (1985)
Start just right of Hairy Baboon and climb up to a big hold below a small roof.
Move up right and cross the roof to reach the top. There is no protection, although
it is possible to escape left into Hairy Baboon from the big hold. A very bold sight
lead.

Slender Loris   6m   E1 5c *   (1981)
Climb the fine finger crack behind the prominent tree 4 metres right of Hairy
Baboon.

Crivvens 6m   HVS 5a   (1981)
Climb the wall 2 metres right of Slender Loris to the left end of the overhang, then
continue to the top.

Eek 8m   Severe   (1981)
Just to the right of the overhang is a short deep crack. Climb this, then traverse
round the corner and finish by another crack.

Sooty 8m   Severe   (1967)
This climb takes the deep off-width chimney just right of the finishing crack of
Eek. Either start as for Eek or by a wider crack further to the right.

Aid My Robert 6m   Very Difficult   (1989)
Climb the short steep corner line right of Sooty.

AN CADHA DUBH   *(Map Ref 371 975)*

This is the secluded boulder-strewn hollow about 1km north-east of The Pass.
The climbing arena is a sunny south-west facing crag which is set in a fine pine
forest. The cliff itself supports an impressive variety of trees, some of which are
an integral part of the climbs. Although it is not particularly extensive and the rock
is poor in places, the routes are generally longer and more exposed than those
of The Pass. Reasonable protection can be had with nuts and Friends on most
of the routes. The rock is quite lichenous and takes a long time to dry after rain.

An Cadha Dubh received a facelift in 1987, producing a number of routes.
This has not, however, increased its popularity. For both visitors and locals the
attractions of The Pass prove more magnetic.

Access
The cliff can be reached in about 20 minutes by heading north-east through the
trees from the top of The Pass, or by contouring round the hill from beneath the
eastern tier. The most direct approach is by crossing the burn opposite the
houses at the entrance to Monaltrie House. From here head uphill along a path,
just to the left of a fenced plantation. Where the fence bends right, go straight up
to reach the base of the hollow (10 minutes). If parking is a problem at the
houses, it is possible to park 100 metres along the road to the east. The routes
are described from bottom right to top left.

Toy Crack 12m   Very Difficult
The steep flake crack at the right end of the cliff.

Black Tail 12m   VS 4c   (1987)
Climb the wall between Toy Crack and Dirty Thing. Go up black ledges and the
wall above, trending left then back right. Easy scrambling follows.

Dirty Thing   20m   Severe
This is the easy-looking left-slanting groove some 10 metres left of Toy Crack. It
starts right of the highest part of the broom-strewn bank above some boulders.
Deceptively awkward.

Check the Divot   20m   VS 4c   (1987)
Climb the corner line left of Dirty Thing in its entirety.

Feeling Shattered   25m   HVS 5b   (1987)
Start below and right of the tree-filled corner right of Dark Klepht. Climb up to a
peg, then traverse left to the corner and follow it to the top.

Dark Klepht   30m   E1 5b *   (1987)
A good line taking the obvious chimney and continuation crack 10 metres right
of Run Rabbit Run, with a peg runner below the crux bulge.

Run Rabbit Run   25m   E1 5a *   (1982)
This route climbs the prominent central buttress of the crag. Start up a short flake
corner on the right (under a holly). Traverse left into a curving flake corner and
go up this, then move left to a sapling. Gain the ledge above and continue straight
up the wall, keeping right of a jutting nose, to ledges. Finish up close to the left
edge.
Direct Start: 4m   6a
Climb directly up the short wall to the base of the curving flake corner.

Hare Lip   25m   E2 5c   (1987)
Climb the left side of the Run Rabbit Run buttress to the short hanging corner,
go up this and the leaning wall above to a tree. Climb the slab left of the tree to
finish up a short crack.

The Tink   25m   HVS 5a   (1988)
Start just left of Hare Lip. Gain and climb the obvious flake crack to reach the
ledge. Continue up the curving groove to a point below the final crack of Hare
Lip. Step left here and surmount a roof via a tree to finish up the slab above.

New Gold Dreams   30m   E3 5c   (1987)
Climb the mossy groove left of Hare Lip to gain the top of a block below a
gold-coloured corner. Go up this, step left then go up again to reach the hanging
corner which leads to the top. Sustained.

Crystal Hunter   30m   HVS   (1987)
1. 15m 5a Climb the groove left of New Gold Dreams to a ledge. Climb the wall
above leftwards to another ledge and belays.
2. 15m 5a Follow the ledge system on the right to below the headwall, step left
and go through a pine tree to finish up a groove. Not a good route.

Fall Gold   30m   E2   (1987)
1. 15m 5c Ascend the grey wall 5 metres left of New Gold Dreams to gain a small ledge and go up a short flake crack to belay.
2. 15m 5b Follow Crystal Hunter to below the headwall, move right and finish up a hanging corner crack.

Dwarves' Nightmare   25m   E3 6a   (1987)
Start 8 metres right of Backwoodsman. Climb a tree-filled groove to a grey wall (peg up above). Climb the wall to a hanging corner, then go up this and the wall above to join Backwoodsman.

Backwoodsman   25m   HVS 4c **   (1981)
At the left side of the crag are some impressive roofs. This route turns the main roofs on the right. Start at some trees above a scrappy slab. Go up past a fallen birch into a flake corner. Climb this, exiting right round the roof onto the face in a fine position. Take a direct line to the top, finishing by a big flake. A good route.

The Tramp   10m   E2 5c   (1989)
This climb takes a wall and shallow corner on the small buttress immediately right of where the cliff ends.

PANNANICH CRAG   *(Map Ref 389 962)*

Pannanich Crag faces east high on the slopes south of the Dee, some 2km east of Ballater; it is best seen from the A93 Pass of Ballater turn-off. The cliff is divided into two separate buttresses by an obvious wet gully. High on the left is the short upper buttress and down to its right is the main wall where most of the climbing is concentrated. In general, the routes follow cracks and the rock is sound with good nut and Friend protection. Unusually for granite, an abundance of flat and incut holds is provided and the quality of the climbing is on the whole quite reasonable. The angle varies from slabby on the left to vertical elsewhere and routes average 25m in height with good tree belays at the top. Although it is not the sunniest of cliffs and therefore has drainage problems (especially Freebird), the cliff is sheltered from rogue westerly winds. If a bird of prey is nesting on the cliff in early summer, please be discreet and climb elsewhere. Nature is reclaiming the cliff very rapidly.

Access

On entering Ballater, cross the Dee and turn east to follow the B976 for 2km (1 mile) to a parking area at a grassy lay-by on the right, beside an outcrop of rock. From here, either thrash directly uphill to gain a boulder field which leads up left to the cliff, or walk uphill along the road for 80 metres to reach the second of two storm drains. Go up through the trees, keeping left, to reach a vague path which goes up then right to the crag. Both routes take about 15 minutes. The routes are described from upper left to bottom right.

UPPER BUTTRESS

Gardener's World   8m   VS 4c   (1988)
Climb the wall and thin crack just right of the left edge of the buttress.

Jim 'n' George   10m   VS 5a   (1988)
Climb the short groove and cracks a few metres right of Gardener's World.

Beechgrove Corner   15m   VS 4c *   (1987)
Climb the large open corner a few metres left of the foot of the buttress.

Agent Orange   10m   HVS 5b   (1987)
Climb the corner on the toe of the buttress, then continue left up the obvious line
to the top.

Pannanich Gully   15m   II/III   (1987)
The obvious wet gully dividing the upper buttress and the main wall provides a
rare winter climb.

THE MAIN WALL

1   Wondrous Stories   55m   E1 5b **   (1987)
A worthwhile route which follows the obvious horizontal break, with increasing
exposure, across the cliff. Well protected.
1. 30m 5b Start at the left end of the cliff where the break can be gained.
Traverse to the wide mossy crack and continue, with a step down, to below the
arete of Flush With Pride. Pull round onto the main wall and continue along the
break to a belay to the right of Freebird.
2. 25m 4b Traverse right and up to finish up a wide crack.
Variation Finish: 10m   VS 4c *   (1988)
A better finish than the original. From the belay move back left a few feet to
beneath the large corner. Climb this to the top.

2   The Navigator   15m   VS 4c *   (1987)
Left of a wide mossy crack is a large triangular niche. Climb up to a ledge below
the niche, enter it and exit left below the roof.

3   Top Cat   15m   VS 4c   (1988)
The obvious wide crack right of The Navigator provides a good thrutch for the
masochistic.

4   Cool as a Cat   20m   E3 5c *   (1987)
A bold but escapable eliminate. Climb into an obvious niche, then pull out onto
a ledge. Climb up to a peg and continue up the wall just to its right until forced
left. Finish up a thin crack at the top left of the wall, to pull over beside a large
boulder.

5   German Holidays   20m   E4 6a *   (1987)
From a platform beneath the thin crack left of Flush With Pride, climb a dirty groove to a small sapling and continue up the technically sustained crack to a small roof. Pull over this and go straight up to finish.

6   Flush with Pride   25m   E1 5b **   (1987)
This line links the small right-facing corner near the ground with the upper left-facing corner. Start at the lower corner and climb straight up to the top corner. Climb this by its right edge and finish up the crack line.

7   Pannanich Wall   25m   E3 6a *   (1987)
Start just left of Freebird and move up left to a series of steps. From the third step go up to a ledge and climb the left-hand of two cracks (crux) to the roof. Pull over this on a dodgy block and follow the slanting crack to easier ground.

8   Hot Dog   25m   E2 5c   (1988)
An eliminate without much new climbing but well worth doing. Start at the bottom of Pannanich Wall. Climb the steps, then move up left to the sapling at half-height on German Holidays. Follow the ramp on the left to finish as for Cool as a Cat.

9   The Grateful Dead   25m   E6 6b *   (1987)
Start as for Pannanich Wall. Climb the wall right of the bottom step and go up the wall just left of a black streak to a ledge. Traverse right and go up to a peg runner. Climb the green wall above to join Wondrous Stories. Pull directly over the roof and climb the wall above to finish beside the boulder.

10   Freebird   25m   E4 6a   (1987)
Traverse right to reach and climb the obvious crack on the right side of the face, then move out left just below the top. The crux is the first bulge (poor peg) which unfortunately is very rarely dry. Very mossy.

11   English Tactics   35m   E1 5c   (1988)
Right of Freebird there are two large trees about 10m up the cliff. Below and right of the rightmost tree there is a small arete which leads up to a roof.
1. 25m 5c Climb the right side of the small arete to gain the obvious corner. Climb this, with an excursion out left at half-height, to grass. Belay below the thin crack in the wall above.
2. 10m 5b Climb steeply into the niche and follow the crack above until forced out left just below the top. Finish up the slabby arete. Well protected.

12   Cave Route   30m   Very Difficult   (1928)
The route starts 10 metres right of English Tactics and follows the obvious subterranean chimney. Interesting botanical scenery and an absolute must for budding troglodytes.
Winter: IV   (1987)
Follow the summer route. A head torch is recommended.

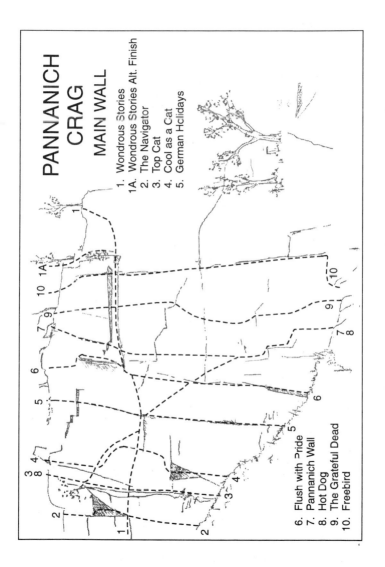

PANNANICH CRAG
MAIN WALL

1. Wondrous Stories
1A. Wondrous Stories Alt. Finish
2. The Navigator
3. Top Cat
4. Cool as a Cat
5. German Holidays

6. Flush with Pride
7. Pannanich Wall
8. Hot Dog
9. The Grateful Dead
10. Freebird

CRAG X   *(Map Ref 394 962)*

This recently developed north-facing cliff lies across the hillside left of Pannanich, on the same level. The cliff is smaller than Pannanich and more lichenous with some dubious flakes. It dries very quickly after rain and there seem to be no drainage problems, so it is a reliable alternative if the main cliff is wet. There is no easy descent down the left side of the crag so it is best to either abseil from the top or descend the heathery right 'shoulder (taking care and avoid the steep grassy gully and subsidiary tower immediately right of No Angel). The cliff is an excellent place to climb on a sunny summer's evening, and is worth a visit.

Access
Contour round the hillside from the foot of Pannanich's upper buttress (5 minutes). The quickest descent is to cut down left to a fire break in the trees. Follow this downhill to its end, then trend left through the trees to reach the road. The routes are in general poorly protected and are described from right to left.

1   Atropine Blackout   12m   E1 5b *   (1988)
Climb the obvious right arete of the crag, keeping as close to the edge as possible.

2   'S Not On   12m   E3 6b   (1988)
Start at some hollow-sounding flakes down left from the arete. Climb the bulge directly above and continue up to a small ledge. Climb the slab above, trending right to finish via a thin crack. Not a good line as the holds lead you to join Atropine Blackout in the middle section. However, the 6b start is fun and well worth doing.

3   Chewing the Bogie   15m   E2 5c *   (1988)
Some 5 metres left of the prominent right arete is a blind crack line. Climb the bulge to reach it, then follow it to the top, finishing beside a small tree. Not well protected.

4   Fungus the Bogeyman   15m   HVS 4c *   (1987)
Climb the wall 2 metres left of Chewing the Bogie, moving left near the top to finish by a hollow-sounding thin flake. Poorly protected.

5   Snotland   15m   E1 5b   (1988)
Left of Fungus the Bogeyman is a right-slanting corner. Climb this to its end, step up left and return right and up to jugs. Finish up the slab above, trending slightly left. Poorly protected, except for the crux.

6   'S Not Again   15m   E1 5b   (1988)
The wall right of 'S Not On has a scarred corner at one-third height. Climb directly up to this and go straight up the wall and groove above to finish up a small arete below a tree. Harder if the slab to the right of the arete is taken. Poor protection.

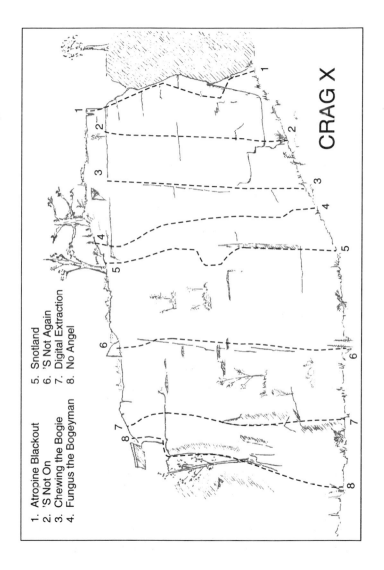

CRAG X

1. Atropine Blackout
2. 'S Not On
3. Chewing the Bogie
4. Fungus the Bogeyman
5. Snotland
6. 'S Not Again
7. Digital Extraction
8. No Angel

7   Digital Extraction   12m   E1 5b *   (1988)
About 6 metres left of 'S Not Again, twin cracks split the wall above one-third height. Climb the wall to reach and climb the cracks, then finish directly up the groove above.

8   No Angel   12m   HVS 5b   (1988)
Just left again is a groove set into the arete. Climb this to its top, move right and finish up a deep crack.

CAMBUS O' MAY QUARRIES   *(Map Ref 397 987)*

These extensive disused granite workings are situated in the old pine and birch forest north of Cambus o' May and are clearly visible from the A93 at Map Ref 400 979. At first sight, the industrial aspect of the crags is somewhat discouraging. This is unfortunate because the routes tend to offer interesting and generally sustained climbing on good rock at a variety of grades. The quarries are currently (1993) being developed as a sports climbing venue, which will render redundant some of the descriptions that follow. Full details of these developments will be made available through topos, the *Aberdeen New Routes* book and the SMC Journal.

The quarries face south and despite some persistent damp patches, tend to offer warm dry climbing, even early in the year, when the cliffs further up the valley are too cold for comfort.

Access
Head towards Ballater from Aboyne, turn off the A93 just before Willows Restaurant (excellent cakes), and take the left-hand track to the new car park (Map Ref 405 981). Go through a locked gate and head north along the track through the forest, passing under electricity power lines. Just after this the track forks. Follow the left-hand track until the western quarry is reached (20 minutes). This is where most of the recent activity has been concentrated. The other quarries have short grotty routes on even grottier bits of rock. The routes are described from left to right.

Scuffer   15m   HVS 4c   (1988)
The steep wall on the left of the quarry is bounded on the left by a slab. Climb the middle of the slab to some cracked blocks, then continue up the edge of the slab above.

The next three routes are on the overhanging west wall.

Boulder Problem   15m   E4 6b   (1988)
Climb directly up the steep wall to the cracked blocks.

No Rest for the Wicked   15m   E5 6b *   (1988)
A sustained line. Start just left of the slanting crack and climb straight up the wall to a small ledge (one peg runner).

Idiot Savant   20m   E6 6b ***   (1988)
Climb the technically sustained crack to underneath the obvious pot-hole at
two-thirds height. Move up left and go across to a thin crack. Climb this to finish
at the highest point on the wall.

Catwalk   20m   E2 5b   (1988)
Climb the prominent slanting corner where the steep wall and the slab meet.
Absorbing climbing (one peg runner).

Mannequin   15m   HVS 5a   (1988)
Start below the large overlap on the slab. Surmount this, via the niche, to gain
the upper slab. Carry on to the common finish with Catwalk.

Hostile Bid   20m   HVS 5a   (1988)
From the centre of the slab climb straight up to the overhang below the tree. Turn
this on the right and continue up corners and slabs to finish.

   All the slab routes are poorly protected. To the right of the slab the angle
increases once more and although the rock is much less steep than the west
wall, the impression of only intermittent difficulties is misleading.

Street Life   15m   VS 4c   (1988)
The wall right of the slab is split by a thin crack. Start directly below this to follow
the crack and a short ramp to the top.

Deathwish 1   15m   HVS 5a   (1988)
Climb the obvious left-facing corner, going up and left awkwardly at the top.

A Walk in the Wasteland   20m   E1 5b   (1988)
Just left of the deep bay is a black prow. Climb this and continue up until a
traverse left to the undercut slab is possible. Move left to the edge of the slab,
then go up to a ledge. Finish as for Deathwish 1. Poorly protected.

Sharp Practice   15m   HVS 5b *   (1988)
A short way along the east wall is a superb flake crack. Climb this to a ledge,
then move right and up (crux) to finish.

Urban Decay   12m   Severe   (1988)
Climb the cracked wall right of the flake to a ledge. Finish up the right-facing
corner.

Quality Street   8m   HVS 5a   (1987)
At the right end of the east wall there is a series of horizontal breaks. Climb these
to finish on small holds; sustained.

CRAIG CORN ARN   *(Map Ref 406 967)*

This small east-facing crag on the long ridge of Pannanich Hill can be seen from the A93 when approaching Cambus o' May from the east. To reach the crag, follow the B976 to park at a track leading to a disused mill near Ballaterach. The crag can be approached from directly below in about 25 minutes. Most of the obvious lines have been climbed, including a cracked arete on the right-hand side (HVS 5a), the crack line and blank wall in the centre (E1 5c), and the bulging twin cracks on the left (Mild VS 4b). The climbs are about 10m long, and although rather mossy, the crag can provide a morning's entertainment. Please avoid climbing here if peregrines are nesting.

Glen Clova

Glen Clova lies in the southern Cairngorms, 40 minutes drive north of Dundee. To reach the glen, drive north on the A929 from Dundee, turning off to Kirriemuir. Pass through the town and continue north, following the signs for Glen Clova. From Aberdeen, the easiest route on first acquaintance is to aim for Kirriemuir. However, the shortest route leaves the A94 at Finavon and goes via Tannadice, Memus and Dykehead. On reaching the Clova Hotel, pass over the narrow bridge marked with a *cul-de-sac* sign and continue up the glen for 6km (4 miles), passing below The Red Craigs which are on the hillside above and right of the road. The glen can also be reached by public transport; regular buses run from Dundee to Kirriemuir, from where a post bus makes trips twice daily up the glen, the morning bus going as far as the Youth Hostel, whereas the afternoon one turns around at the Clova Hotel.

The Red Craigs consist of The Doonie with its upper and lower tiers, sitting above the quarry, while further down the glen are the upper and lower north-west crags and the slabby south-east crag with the steep central crag in between. The climbing and the setting are Lakeland in character, the diorite varying from smooth and angular to rough and rounded, while the crags possess a sense of exposure which belies their roadside nature. They are 10 minutes walk from the road and facing south-west, can be climbed on for most of the year, giving quality pitches of all grades. Other crags in the area are Craig Maud in Glen Doll while Upper Glen Clova contains the granite of Juanjorge and the Altduthrie slabs.

For accommodation, there are two club huts in the glen, owned by the Carn Dearg MC, Dundee and Forfar MC, both of which must be booked beforehand by visiting clubs. The Clova Hotel has a bunkhouse and serves good pub food and an excellent pint. Cheaper alternatives are the campsite beside the car park at the head of the glen or the spacious but draughty boulder-cave below the south-east crag. There is also a youth hostel in Glen Doll.

BRAEDOWNIE QUARRY

The quarry near the road end is loose and dangerous. Despite this, two routes have been recorded:

Agrajaz 20m E4 6a (1986)
Originally a top-rope problem, this line was led after much practise to give a nasty little chop route. Start below the obvious steep smooth slab at the back of the quarry. Move up to a small overlap. Follow this up left to the small corner left of the slab (poor protection). Step onto the slab and move precariously up and right to sidepulls (crux). Pull up to better holds and continue easily to the top.

The Flying Cabbage Heads 15m E5 6a (1989)
A direct on Agrajaz, climbed in the same style as the parent route. Take a direct line up the centre of the slab, passing through Agrajaz at half-height.

THE DOONIE   *(Map Ref 290 758)*

The Doonie is the dome-shaped mass of rock above the quarry, consisting of upper and lower sections separated by a large diagonal terrace.

LOWER DOONIE
The main feature of this crag is the steep main face. To the right of this, the diagonal pink slab of Ant Slab is obvious, while the broken ground to the left contains the tree-filled gully of Jake's Jungle Route. Descent is either by the steep grass to the left of the crag or down the diagonal terrace below the upper crag. The following routes lie on the small crag with the large roof, high on the slope left of the lower crag.

The Cosmic Pump   15m   E3 6a   (1987)
Start at the left-hand side of the roof, below two black hanging grooves. Gain the grooves from flakes on the left. Move right across them to finish up the left edge of the crag.

Solar Wind   15m   E3 6b   (1985)
Climb the central crack in the widest part of the roof, which gives a short but technical struggle, to gain and finish directly up the wall above.

Ion Drive   15m   E3 6a   (1987)
Start right of Solar Wind. Cross the right-hand side of the roof and move left to a prominent tooth. Move up via a niche to finish up the cracked slab on the right.

Sidestep   15m   E1 5b   (1987)
This route takes the hanging pod right of the roof. Begin up the open corner to the right, then swing left into the pod and go up to the top.

The open corner itself is HVS 5a, easiest going left at the top. In the rocks on the right are a VS and a Severe. From the extreme left edge of the lower crag a short blank wall stretches up the hillside towards Solar Wind crag. At the left-hand side of the wall is a tree, from which a narrow ledge cuts back down across the wall.

Jake's Jungle Route   60m   Hard Very Vegetated   (1950s)
An arboreal experience, climbing on vegetation the whole way! Start from the tree at the left-hand side of the blank wall.
1. 20m 4a Follow the narrow ledge right to the arete. Belay on the glacis to the right.
2. 40m 4a Traverse the glacis rightwards into the tree-filled gully-cleft. Battle up this to the top of the crag.

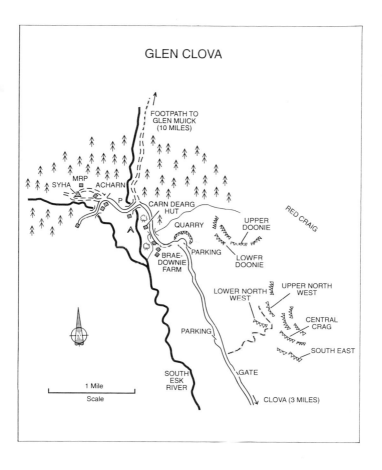

GLEN CLOVA

FOOTPATH TO
GLEN MUICK
(10 MILES)

MRP
SYHA   ACHARN
P
CARN DEARG
HUT
A
QUARRY   UPPER
DOONIE   RED CRAIG
PARKING   LOWER
DOONIE
BRAE-
DOWNIE
FARM
LOWER NORTH   UPPER NORTH
WEST   WEST
CENTRAL
CRAG
PARKING   SOUTH EAST
GATE
SOUTH
ESK
RIVER   CLOVA (3 MILES)

N

1 Mile
Scale

Jug Wall   20m   E1 5b   (1987)
Start midway between Jake's Jungle Route and the right edge of the wall. From
the gully, climb rightwards up the juggy slab and go up cracks in the grey
headwall above to a black niche. Cross the roof above to finish. A right-hand
finish moves right from below the roof via fine cracks to a ledge (E1 5c).

The Thin Wall   20m   VS 4c   (1986)
Start off a block below the shattered orange wall right of Jug Wall. Climb first right
then left to the foot of arete, then go up this or the corner on the right (easier).

The next three routes start off the glacis of Jake's Jungle Route, right of the
left edge of the lower crag, gained via scrambling from the base of the tree-filled
gully-fault 12 metres right of the left edge.

Mandy   15m   E2 5c   (1985)
Climb the obvious sharp arete on the left-hand side of the glacis, starting from
the right.

Lichen Groove   15m   VS 4c   (1988)
Follow the shabby groove right of Mandy to the top.

Ally's Crack   15m   HVS 5a   (1985)
Climb the steep red slightly dirty groove right of Lichen Groove. There is an old
peg runner near the bottom.

Four Corners Route   50m   HVS 5a   (1986)
This route follows the rib right of the tree-filled gully-fault to climb the slab above.
Start 13m up and left from the foot of the obvious grey concave slab (Guinness).
1. 35m 4b Climb the rib via several corners to a ramp leading up to the final
pitch of Guinness. Step left to belay below a hanging slab.
2. 15m 5a Pull onto slab (peg runner) and continue to top.

Summer's Over   50m   E2 5c   (1985)
This takes the flake ladder in the wall between the previous route and Guinness.
1. 35m 5c Scramble up to and climb the flakes to the belay ledge below the last
pitch of Guinness.
2. 15m 5a Guinness, pitch 3.

Guinness   50m   E1 5b ***   (1958/76)
The classic route of the crag gives excellent and varied climbing on good rock.
Start at the left-hand side of the main face, at the foot of a grey concave slab
below a prominent beak overhang.
1. 20m 5a Gain and climb the concave slab directly to a good belay ledge.
2. 15m 5b Attack the black leaning corner above. If successful, continue up and
left to a grassy ledge.
3. 15m 5a Finish up the wide crack on the right (peg runner).

Red Wall, Glen Clova (Climber, Roger Everett)

Variation Finish 1: 5b **   (1960s)
From the top of the black leaning corner of the second pitch, move up and right below the beak overhang to finish up right-sloping cracks.
Variation Finish 2: 5a   (1976)
From the belay at the top of the second pitch, traverse out right on the lip of the overhang to step round the nose. Climb straight up slabs above to finish.
Exit Stage Left: 5a   (1986)
From the belay at the top of the second pitch, climb the groove on the left (peg runner). Surmount a large flake and continue to the top.

Guinless 55m E1 5b   (1985)
A serious and sustained route between Guinness and Special Brew.
1. 20m 5a Guinness, pitch 1.
2. 35m 5b From the right end of the belay ledge, climb the short black corner (two peg runners) to a sloping ledge (peg, possible belay). From the left end of the ledge, gain and climb the vague groove directly above to the top.

Special Brew 70m HVS 5a **   (1950s)
A good route taking an exposed line up the centre of the main face. Start just right of Guinness, below a pink right-sloping ramp.
1. 15m 4a Follow the ramp to a ledge and peg belay.
2. 30m 5a Climb up and left to a small ledge (peg runner) below overhanging cracks. Thug up the cracks to gain a sloping ledge and small corner (peg runner). Traverse horizontally right to a large ledge. Belay.
3. 25m 4c Stand on the large detached block on the right-hand side of the ledge and continue sensationally to the top.
Variation: **The Furstenberg Finish** 5a **   (1988)
From the sloping ledge and small corner of the second pitch, step right then climb directly up till below a "death-niche". Traverse 3 metres left, then continue to top. More sustained than the original.

Special Brew Direct 60m E3 5c **   (1985)
A sustained and well protected direct line through Special Brew.
1. 15m 4a Special Brew, pitch 1.
2. 45m 5c Climb directly up the corner above the belay (first crux) to the large belay ledge at the top of Special Brew pitch 2. Step off the left-hand side of the ledge and continue directly up the wall (second crux) to the top.

Belhaven 60m E2 5b *   (1986)
A good route plugging the gap between Special Brew and Heineken.
1. 15m 4a Special Brew, pitch 1.
2. 45m 5b Step right, then climb directly to a good flake and protection. Step right again and climb the wall directly to the top, passing through a white niche.

Footfall, Ley Quarry (Climber, Iain Lawson)

Variation: **Stella**   5c   (1990)
From the good flake, step left and climb boldly up the slabby wall on good holds
to the large belay ledge of Special Brew. Finish up Special Brew Direct.

Heinekin   65m   E1 5b   (1976)
A slightly contrived route with a hard technical crux.
1. 20m 4c Climb Special Brew pitch 1, then traverse horizontally right to a ledge
beneath a smooth orange diedre.
2. 45m 5b Climb the diedre (crux) to a pedestal (peg runner). Make a long step
left and move up to a ledge (peg runner, possible belay). Climb the black corner
behind and so to the top.
Direct Variation: E1 5b
Gain the ledge below the diedre directly and omit the long step left.

Export   65m   HVS 5b
A rambling route on the right of the main face. Start just left of Ant Slab below a
grey slab.
1. 15m 5b Climb the crack in the centre of the slab (not the vegetated one on
the left) past a thin section to a ledge.
2. 25m 4b Follow the slabby rib on the right to an overhang and move left to a
tree belay.
3. 25m 4c Continue up the obvious chimney-fault through overhangs to the top.

Ant Slab   20m   Moderate *
A superb pitch, hard for the grade, up the obvious narrow diagonal slab on the
right of, and set at an angle to, the main face. Climb by cracks, bearing left at
mid-height to finish directly.

Witches' Mate   20m   Mild VS 4b
An interesting technical snippet up the overhanging nose below and right of Ant
Slab. Climb directly to cracks which lead past a tree to a ledge.

   The roofed corner left of the above route is Hard Severe and the wall behind
the large tree to the right is also Hard Severe (old peg runner).

The Pub Crawl   100m   E1 5b   (1986)
A right to left girdle of the crag gives a superb expedition.
1. 30m 5b Follow Export to its first belay. Move left to the foot of the larger,
roof-capped slab on the left. Climb this and the central crack in the roof to a tree
belay.
2. 10m 4a Move up and left to belay at the top of Heinekin's final black corner.
3. 30m 5b Climb down corner and traverse left to Special Brew's large belay
ledge. Reverse its traverse to a sloping ledge (peg runner). From the left end of
the ledge, move up (as for Guinless) then step left into Guinness Variation 1
below the beak overhang. Belay up and left as for Guinness.
4. 20m 5a Finish up Exit Stage Left.

UPPER DOONIE

This crag contains some fine Extreme climbing. the most obvious feature is the large central alcove with the slanting roof-fault, bounded on the left by the blunt overhanging arete of DRI. Abseil descents can usually be made from convenient trees, or walk off to the left and descend the diagonal terrace.

The following two routes lie on the small stepped wall with a solitary larch tree left of the top of the diagonal terrace and directly above the main face of the lower crag.

Shadow on the Wall   15m   E1 5c   (1987)
Start 3 metres right of the larch tree. Go up an easy crack, then climb the fine slab above via a horizontal break and a shallow diagonal crack.

Larch Tree Wall   15m   Very Difficult *
Start below the central crack, right of the previous route. Follow the vague crack line over three sections to broken ground.

Elliptical Dreams   10m   E2 5c   (1986)
Above the top of the diagonal terrace, at the left end of the crag, are twin stepped overhangs. Grapple with the lower roof at its apex.

Headspread   15m   E4 6a   (1986)
A bold route taking the upper roof at the obvious niche. Climb up to a good protection flake on the slab below the roof. Pull up onto the lip and hand traverse right to cracks that lead to the top.

The Catwalk   15m   E1 5a   (1986)
A cramped pitch up the catwalk between the roofs. Turn the lower roof on the right and climb up and left along the ramp between the roofs to exit left of the upper roof.

Catbird   20m   HVS 5b   (1987)
Climb the curving groove to the left-hand side of the obvious "grass-glacier". Move precariously up and left until below the roof, step right and ascend the short wall to the top.

Henry's Cat   20m   E1 5b   (1987)
Climb the right-hand of two thin cracks right of Catbird to a shallow scoop and peg runner. Move up and right across the hanging slab to join and finish up The Slicer.

The Slicer   20m   HVS 4c *   (1986)
An aptly named route featuring the massive thin flake a little further down the terrace. Stand on the flake, make a scary and committing move onto the wall and scuttle up this to a ledge. Move right to a big block and tree belay.

The Grater   20m   E2 5c   (1986)
Climb the steep crack in the left wall of the huge niche right of The Slicer. Step right above the roof to a thin crack, then climb this until it is possible to move left to a tree belay.

Fastbreeder   20m   E4 5c **   (1986)
The huge niche is climbed by means of trouser-splitting (and filling) bridging. Exit by the obvious flake in the roof, then belay on tree above.

The Making of Bunny   30m   E1 5b   (1986)
Climb the groove in the right wall of the Fastbreeder niche, left of a green flake, until 3m below the roof. Traverse right on jugs to a tree, then move up left above roof to a crack and step back right above the smaller roof to a precarious finish.

Green Bunny   30m   VS 5a   (1987)
An eliminate up the left edge of the green flake right of the Fastbreeder niche. Gain the flake via a groove above the bush. Climb the left edge of the flake to its top, then move left above the top of the flake for 10 metres to the belay tree.

Green Shield   30m   VS 4c   (1987)
Climb the right-hand side of the green flake to join Green Bunny.

Vindaloo   45m   E1 5b ***   (1972/84/86)
This route, described by the direct finish, gives superb contrasting climbing up the clean slabs left of the central alcove. Start 4 metres left of DRI, at the foot of the grey slab below a square black sentry-box. Climb the initial steep crack and the slab above to gain the sentry-box (possible belay). Move out right and over a bulge to a layback crack which leads strenuously to the top. The original finish traversed left from the sentry-box to finish by a sharp arete on the left.

Scoopy Doo   45m   E4 6b *   (1990)
Make some thin moves up the shallow scoop in the slab between Vindaloo and Chitteroo to a horizontal break (protection). Continue with difficulty to better holds beside a peg runner. Hard moves past this lead to easier ground above. Finish up Vindaloo.

Chitteroo   45m   E4 6a *   (1987)
From the large block at the base of DRI, gain the slim niche right of Vindaloo. Move precariously up this to thin cracks in the slab above. Continue up the wall to finish up the layback crack of Vindaloo.

DRI   45m   E6 6a   (1987)
The blunt overhanging arete in the centre of the crag is both serious and sequential. On-sight attempts may well terminate in Dundee Royal Infirmary! Start below steep twin cracks in the right face of the arete. Follow the cracks to

a platform on the front of the arete (protection). Climb the frontal face directly (crux) to arrive with relief on the slab above. Continue up the wall to finish up the layback crack of Vindaloo.

Overhanging Coroner   40m   F4 6a *   (1989)
Climb the dark corner in the left-hand side of the large central alcove to the half-height fault. Follow the continuation above and step right in to The Whoremistress below its overhang. Finish up this.

The Whoremistress   40m   E4 6a **   (1988)
The stunning central line in the alcove gives a very good and sustained outing. Start in the alcove below a recess with a small tree. Climb the recess and V-groove above to a large diagonal shelf. Move onto the ramp above with difficulty (poor peg runner). Either climb directly up to the left-hand side of the overhang (hard) or traverse right across the overhanging wall to a small niche and crack leading to the right-hand side of the overhang (harder). Surmount the overhang directly using a prominent small flake on the wall above (crux). Step into the wide vertical crack on the left and follow it to a ledge and tree belay.

Dancin' in the Ruins   45m   E3 5c ***   (1986)
An excellent route of great character up the wall right of The Whoremistress. Start below the tongue of rock which protrudes leeringly from the roof-fault.
1. 20m 5c Climb the slab, move left and go up to a small wet niche. Swing rightwards through the roof on mega jugs and continue steeply to a tree-belay.
2. 25m 5b Move up and left, as for Cream Cracker, then step right to climb a steep crack with hanging blocks to a metal fence post and belay.

Cream Cracker   40m   E2 5c   (1976/85)
This climbs through the roof at the obvious fault right of Dancin' in the Ruins.
1. 10m 4c Follow the right edge of the tongue to a ledge below the overhang (peg runner).
2. 10m 5c Cross the roof and climb the steep slab on the right to a wall. Move left to a crack and follow this to the tree belay of Dancin' in the Ruins.
3. 20m 5a Move up and left to a short corner which leads to the tree belay of The Whoremistress.

Jungle Warfare   45m   HVS 5a   (1985)
Bungle in the jungle.
1. 10m 4c Cream Cracker, pitch 1.
2. 15m 5a Move up right and climb the wall to a diagonal shelf, continue up right to belay beneath the prominent prow at a sapling.
3. 20m 5a Climb a dirty slab on the right to another tree, then go up the wide crack above to reach broken ground. A bushwhack now ensues to finish at another sapling.

Faulty Towers　75m　E2 5c ***　　　　　　　　　　　　　(1987)
The right to left girdle of the crag gives an exciting journey across the slanting roof-fault.
1. 10m 4c　Cream Cracker, pitch 1.
2. 30m 5c　Climb up and left under the roof to belay in the Vindaloo niche.
3. 15m 5a　Move down and left across the slabs to a peg belay on Henry's Cat.
4. 20m 5b　Step left below the "grass-glacier" into Catbird. Follow this precariously up and left to join and finish up The Catwalk.

HIGH CRAG

This is the small slabby crag high on the hillside above the right end of The Doonie. Although rather trivial, the routes are generally well protected and of good quality. The first route is up and left of the main slab, above a large flake. Pocketeer and the other routes are on the main slab, from left to right.

Wee Slab　10m　Difficult　　　　　　　　　　　　　　(1988)
Gain the slab from below and left.

Pocketeer　10m　HVS 5a　　　　　　　　　　　　　　(1985)
Start at the left end of the crag below large lichenous flakes. Step up right on big holds and cross the diagonal roof on its left-hand side. Good moves on the upper slab lead to an exit right.

Pickpocket　20m　E1 5b　　　　　　　　　　　　　　(1988)
A direct on Pocketeer. Start at the lowest point of the crag. Go up and left and cross a small overlap at 5m to gain a hanging corner (crux). Pull up onto Pocketeer, cross the roof and finish up and left on upper slab.

Centipod　20m　HVS 5a　　　　　　　　　　　　　　(1985)
Climb the obvious central pea-pod groove, then mantel out (crux) and go up the right-hand side of the roof to swing out left above the roof on excellent jugs. Exit right above.

Arachnid　15m　HVS 5b　　　　　　　　　　　　　　(1988)
Start below the pod crack in the right side of the main slab. Gain the pod crack via a dinky face climb up the vague tower below and left of it. Follow it to exit rightwards.

Grunt　12m　VS 5a　　　　　　　　　　　　　　　　(1988)
Right of the main slab are two towers. Climb the left-hand tower using the obvious jam crack.

Geotechnician　12m　HVS 5a　　　　　　　　　　　　(1988)
Climb the central line on the squat right-hand tower over two roofs, then climb the left-hand side of the slab above. Finish over a large perched block.

LOWER NORTH-WEST CRAG

This crag contains some excellent short pitches on good rock. The depression in the centre of the crag contains The Beanstalk and is bounded on the right by the prominent orange rib of Proud Corner. The open corner between this and the steep nose on the right of the crag (Witch's Tooth) is Monster's Crack. To descend, a path leads from the large boulder above Monster's Crack down to the right. The left side of the crag can also be descended.

Twenty Minute Route   45m   Moderate *   (1939)
The broken rib on the left side of the main face gives a series of short interesting pitches with a number of variations.
1. 10m Start at the lowest rocks, below a corner crack. Climb the corner directly to a large terrace and belay.
2. 10m Go up a left-hand sloping crack to a tree belay.
3. 15m Go up rocks behind the tree to a bulging slab, or move left onto the rib and gain the same position by mantelshelfing.
4. 10m Go over the bulging slab then either climb the overhanging crack (Severe) or go left to easy ground.
Variations.
Brenge Wall   Hard Severe
From the top of pitch 1, go up and left to rejoin the parent route below the overhanging crack.
Johnny Milne's Crack   Mild Severe
The jam crack right of pitch 3, gained by:
Middleton's Traverse   Mild Severe   (1950s)
A stomach traverse from Twenty Minute Route into Johnny Milne's Crack.

The broken ramp line left of Twenty Minute Route is **The Catwalk**, Mild Severe, whilst the wall right of Johnny Milne's Crack is **Rowantree Wall**, also Mild Severe.

Gander   35m   VS 4c
A scrappy route with a hard start up the left side of the central depression. Start from a grassy ledge in a shallow overhanging recess in the left side of the face. Break left out of the recess and climb the wall over grassy ledges to the top.

Wander   40m   HVS 5a **   (1957)
A good route following the thin crack and corner line in the centre of the face. Climb the thin vertical crack to a ledge, then move left to the foot of a shallow corner. Follow the corner to a tree (possible belay). Step out right above a lot of space and climb a crack in the steep exposed wall to ledges and the top.

Wandered   40m   HVS 5a ***   (1982)
An excellent route giving good steep climbing and fine positions. Start as for
Wander. Follow the thin vertical crack to the ledge below the corner. The steep
flake crack on the right leads strenuously to the large ledge of The Beanstalk
(possible belay). Climb into a recess on the left, step around the arete and climb
the airy wall on good holds to the top (as for Dander).

The Beanstalk   40m   Mild VS 4b *   (1954)
A tree-mendous outing up the corner in the right side of the central depression,
characterised by a dead tree stump about halfway up. Climb easy rock and a
short chimney to a steep crack. Climb the crack past the dead tree stump to a
large ledge (crux), possible belay. Move up and right to another tree from where
a crack leads to the top. The second tree can also be gained by a rising traverse
from the foot of the steep crack at the same grade.
Direct Finish: HVS 5a
Climb directly from the large ledge up the corner crack above.
Dander Finish: VS 4c
From the large ledge, climb into a recess on the left, step around the arete and
climb the airy wall on good holds to the top.

Proud Corner   45m   VS 4c ***   (1950s)
A tremendous route giving brilliant bold climbing in an exhilarating position up
the crest of the orange rib between The Beanstalk and Monster's Crack. Start
below twin cracks in the right arete of The Beanstalk. Climb either the cracks or
the arete to a large ledge (possible belay, gained easily from the right). Move left
onto the face and climb up the edge to a triangular slab (poor peg runner).
Continue boldly to a small ledge (crux) and finish up the small corner above.

Cinderella   30m   E5 6a ***   (1987/88)
A serious route giving fine strenuous climbing up the impending wall right of
Proud Corner. Start off the large pointed spike on the ledge left of Monster's
Crack. Climb the ragged crack (peg runner) and the ramp on the left to a large
flat hold. Stand on the hold and move up with urgency to clip another peg runner
(good Rock 4 placement beside it). Swing into the corner on the left and step
back right (or pull directly up to the same point) to finish in a more leisurely
fashion. If the top peg is missing this route merits E6.

Rocketman   30m   E2 5b   (1985)
A slightly eliminate route with some good moves. Start off the large pointed spike
of Cinderella. Climb the shallow corner above (peg runner in the crack on the
left) and pull right to a hanging flake. Step back left into a hanging corner and
finish up the arete.

Taken by Force   25m   E2 5c   (1980s)
Thug up the steep jam crack 3 metres left of Monster's Crack to the easier upper wall.

Monster's Crack   25m   Hard Severe   (1954)
Follow the obvious corner crack in the right side of the crag to where it opens out (possible belay). Finish by scrambling out left by an overhanging block, or better, by cracks in the steep right wall.

Monster Munch   25m   E2 6a   (1986)
A poor eliminate up the right wall of Monster's Crack, using side runners in that route and Witch's Tooth, but no holds in either, gives good but contrived climbing. Climb directly up the wall to some hollow flakes. Step left and continue thinly to a rotten ledge. Finish centrally,

Taken With Ease   30m   HVS 5a   (1985)
Another contrived nomadic pitch between Monster's Crack and Witch's Tooth . Gain the hollow flakes as for Monster Munch, then step right into Witch's Tooth. Move up to the right side of the rotten ledge and traverse left to finish up Monster's Crack's right-hand finish.

Witch's Tooth   25m   E2 5b **   (1976)
An excellent technical testpiece up the prominent nose right of Monster's Crack. Unfortunately, the "tooth" fell out in 1988, making the route much harder. Climb the steep crack in the nose to enter a niche (crux). Step left to a corner crack and follow this to the glacis and short wall above. It is also possible to step right from the niche and continue up the steep crack and wall to join the normal route on the glacis.

Cauldron Crack   20m   HVS 5a ***
A superb steep route taking the overhanging recess right of Witch's Tooth, giving athletic climbing on mega-jugs. Follow the steep corner to the capping roof. Turn this on the left and step back right above it (peg runner). Move up right on the lip of the roof to a holly bush and continue to the top.

Halloween   20m   E2 6a   (1985)
A poorly protected trip up the smooth wall between Cauldron Crack and Rander. Climb the wall from bottom right to top left. The crux is near the bottom.

Rander   20m   HVS 5b   (1971)
Follow the steep dirty corner up the gully from Cauldron Crack to a cracked roof. Either climb the roof or turn it on the right and continue to the top.

Wizard's Wall   15m   Hard Severe
A serious route up the short wall right of Rander. Start behind a tree 2 metres right of Rander and climb the wall directly to the top.

Plonker's Passage   80m   HVS 5a   (1987)
A sustained outing, crossing the crag from left to right. Start from Twenty Minute Route, at the top of pitch 2.
1. 20m 4a Cross Middleton's Traverse and continue right across ledges into Gander. Move up this for a few metres before breaking right to the belay ledge common to Wander and Wandered.
2. 15m 5a Follow Wandered up and right into The Beanstalk and follow this to the tree on the right.
3. 15m 4c Hand traverse right to step around the arete and gain the bay of Monster's Crack, tree belay.
4. 15m 4c Traverse along the rotten ledge on the right to belay on the glacis of Witch's Tooth.
5. 15m 5a Move right across Rander to finish up the groove on the right.

UPPER NORTH-WEST CRAG   *(Map Ref 294 757)*

This steep and intimidating crag contains some of the best climbing in the glen. It is characterised by an overhung recess in the middle, out of which cuts the deep diagonal cleft of the High Level Traverse. Right of the recess is the smooth Red Wall, whilst to the left, the large overhang belongs to Roman Candle. To descend from the top of the crag, a path leads up and left to a small cairn marking the top of the descent gully left of the crag.
   The following two routes take lines on the undercut wall on the upper left flank of the crag, above the large roof of Roman Candle.

Sun Goes Down   20m   E1 5b *   (1986)
A good route giving fine bold climbing. Pull onto the wall directly below an obvious niche. Move up through the niche and continue to the top, finishing by an obligatory heel hook.

Jailbreak   20m   E3 5c   (1986)
An athletic route with good but unplaceable protection! Start below twin cracks in the bulge right of Sun Goes Down. Boulder out the initial moves and go straight up to make a long reach for a pod in the right-hand crack. Pull over the bulge before finishing directly up the easy slab.

Just Another Sparkler   15m   E3 5c *   (1985)
The flake line in the steep wall to the left of Roman Candle succumbs to a determined approach. Start below the flake. Strenuously gain and climb it to a difficult exit onto the slab above.

Roman Candle   25m   E3 6a ***   (1964/83)
The crack in the large overhang on the left of the crag is climbed by means of
ape-like manoeuvres. Wander up easy slabs to the corner in the roof. Climb this
(technical crux) and hand traverse to the lip (peg runner). Pull over (physical
crux) onto the slab above.

Zigzag Direct   40m   HVS ***   (1960s/1974)
A good independent start and direct finish to Zigzag, offering an excellent and
exciting outing. Start at cracks in the slab below the large overhang of Roman
Candle.
1. 20m 5a Move up and right across the slab to a large block (peg runner). Pull
over this to follow the crack on the right to an airy pedestal at the top of the deep
cleft.
2. 20m 5b Climb the large open corner above, exiting left at an obvious hand
traverse rail below the capping roof.

Zigzag Double Direct   45m   E2 ***   (1972/85)
A brilliant route giving fine climbing and more impressive positions than the Kama
Sutra! Start directly below the large open corner of Zigzag Direct.
1. 25m 5b Climb the steep crack line through the roof to the large block of Zigzag
Direct. Follow this to its belay.
2. 20m 5c Bridge up the corner above as for Zigzag Direct. Where this chickens
out left, continue up to the capping roof and turn this obstacle on the right (crux)
before stepping up left to the top.

999   25m   E2 5b   (1985)
A bold and strenuous pitch exploiting the weakness between the Double Direct
and Zigzag. Start below the triangular roof right of the Double Direct. Climb easily
up to a spike and pull into the niche below the roof (crucial nut runner). Pull
through the right side of the roof and step left to climb through the gap in the roof
above. Continue up easy slabs to the pedestal belay. This route could be
combined with the next.

The Return of the Living Dead   25m   E1 5b   (1986)
Start from the pedestal belay of Zigzag Direct. Break onto the right wall and lean
into the corner to place a high side runner before gaining the flake in the right
wall. Follow the flake to exit onto the slabs above. Finish up and left.

Zigzag   25m   VS 4c *   (1957)
An awkward little pitch leading up to the cleft of the High Level Traverse. Start at
the foot of a shallow corner containing a small tree (about 15 metres left of the
cleft). Climb the corner past the tree to surmount a small overhang. Continue
straight up (peg runner) to join the High Level Traverse. Follow this to the belay
and a selection of finishing pitches.

High Level Traverse and Direct Finish 60m Hard Severe ***
An epic adventure for the climber-cum-troglodyte, this route follows the obvious deep diagonal cleft slanting left across the face. Start in the overhung recess in the centre of the crag.
1. 30m Follow the cleft and squirm into the upper part. Continue to an airy pedestal belay at the top of the cleft.
2. 30m Make an exposed left traverse on the slab above the large overhangs, stepping round the airy arete, until below a chimney. Climb the chimney, exit left and follow cracks to the top. The normal finish continued traversing below the chimney to easy ground.

A Vanishing Breed 35m E6 6b ***   (1990)
Powerful climbing with reasonable protection up the steep wall between High Level Traverse and The Sorcerer. Start at the base of the cleft of High Level Traverse, gain the wall via a crack. Follow this to where it peters out, then move up and step right to a large sloping shelf and protection (twin RURPs *in situ*. Rock 1 down and right, Tri-cam 1 up and left in crozzly pocket). Climb the wall above, bearing right to join The Sorcerer at the end of its flake.

The crack running directly up to the huge flake of The Sorcerer, left of the proper start, has been climbed at 5c but it is very loose and unpleasant.

The Sorcerer 35m E4 6a   (1985)
This route gains and climbs the huge flake in the steep wall above the start of High Level Traverse. Originally done in 2 pitches (the first serious 6a, the second strenuous 5c), it is probably best done in one run-out. Start at the bottom of High Level Traverse. Climb the wall slightly right, then go left to the large hanging flake (possible belay). Undercling the flake leftwards to its end, then climb directly to the top.

The Supernatural Anaesthetist 35m E4 6a *   (1987)
A sustained technically interesting outing up the steep hanging groove right of The Sorcerer flake. Follow The Sorcerer to the flake (runner). Step right and climb the groove to its top. Finish by a prominent protruding flake.

Sorcerer's Apprentice 35m E2 5c **   (1985)
After a hard start, the soaring crack line in the right side of the overhung recess gives a sustained trip. Start from a perch left of the alder tree, below a steep flake. Climb the flake, then move right to attack the gently overhanging crack. Follow this past a small tree to the top.

Puddin' Fingers 35m E2 5b   (1982/85)
The steep black groove right of Sorcerer's Apprentice is sustained and strenuous. Start by stepping left from the foot of Alder. An awkward move gains the groove which is followed to the top.

Alder   40m   Mild VS ***   (1951)
A brilliant exposed route crossing some improbable ground for the grade. Start behind the alder tree in the right side of the overhung recess.
1. 10m 4b Climb the wide cracks in the corner of the bay to a large ledge and peg belay.
2. 30m 4b Climb first right, then back left and go straight up to the top.

Hanging Chimney   45m   Severe   (1939)
This route starts up the right-hand of two chimneys right of Alder before tackling the obvious hanging chimney left of the red wall.
1. 20m Climb the chimney and slab above before moving right to a flake belay.
2. 25m Climb up to and enter the hanging chimney with difficulty. Move up this to finish rightwards.

At the lowest point of the crag, right of the initial chimney of the above route and below the red wall, is a steep grey wall with a prominent detached flake.

Kremlin Control   45m   E2 5c **   (1985/86)
A good route, described by the direct start, taking the left-hand crack line in the obvious smooth red wall. Start at the left-hand side of the steep grey wall, below some small blocky overhangs.
1. 25m 5c Climb up to a good jug, step right onto the grey slab and reach over the bulge to a spike. Pull up onto the large sloping ledge above and continue easily to a flake belay.
2. 20m 4c Move up left, then go back right under a small roof to the crack. Layback up onto the red wall and follow the crack to the top. The normal start traversed in from pitch 1 of The Red Wall onto the grey slab.

The Red Wall   45m   E1 5b ***   (1976)
An excellent climb accepting the challenge of the central crack in the steep smooth red wall. Start below the steep grey wall.
1. 25m 5b Either climb via the large detached flake (5a) or tackle the steep flake crack on its right (hard 5b and better) to reach the large sloping ledge. Continue up the quartz chimney above to the belay.
2. 20m 5b Step sensationally out right and climb the crack to the top.

The Cold War   45m   E2 5c   (1987)
An eliminate route up the small right-facing hanging diedre right of the top pitch of The Red Wall, with side runners in that route.
1. 15m 5c Follow the Red Wall right-hand start to the large sloping ledge. Move up this to belay at the base of the quartz chimney.
2. 30m 5c Climb the groove right of the quartz chimney. Step right at its top and move up to the hanging diedre. Follow this, stepping right at the top.

Taste Me!   45m   E4 6a   (1988)
A scary excursion up the right arete of the red wall.
1. 30m 5c Follow The Red Wall right-hand start to its belay and continue up pitch 2 for a few metres to a small ledge at the base of the red wall. Belay.
2. 15m 6a Traverse out right on detachable sidepulls and underclings to the arete. Climb this to the top.

Carn Dearg Corner   45m   E2 5c   (1986)
The main feature of this route is a crack in the left wall of the large W+S Chimney.
1. 25m 5c Follow The Red Wall right-hand start to the large sloping ledge. Move up and right across this to belay below a hanging slab.
2. 20m 5c Climb the hanging slab and move up and right past loose blocks left of W+S Chimney. Follow the shallow corner below the jam crack, then jam up the crack to the top.

W+S Chimney   35m   Severe   (1953)
Scramble up into the obvious large V-chimney on the left of the crag, then bridge up it to exit rightwards.

The Magical Mystery Tour   100m   E3 5c *   (1987)
An epic outing of great character, girdling the crag from left to right. Start at the end of the normal finish of High Level Traverse.
1. 20m Reverse the High Level Traverse to the belay above the cleft.
2. 25m 5b Follow The Return of the Living Dead to the exposed hanging slabs up and right. Move down and right across these to belay in the vertical part of The Sorcerer flake.
3. 20m 5b Move up the flake until it is possible to traverse right above it. Make a long reach right for a jug and move across to an overlap. Undercling this rightwards to the corner. Move down and right to the small tree on Sorcerer's Apprentice before swinging round the arete on the right to an exposed belay.
4. 35m 5c Move down and right into The Hanging Chimney. Gain the red wall as for Kremlin Control and step across to The Red Wall. Arrange a high runner before traversing into The Cold War. Finish up this.

CENTRAL CRAG

This fearsome crag is characterised by an impressively steep central wall with a steep nose on its left-hand side. The descent is via a scramble up the steep hillside to a fence. Follow a path rightwards until the scree-filled descent gully is reached.

West Side Story   20m   E2 5b *   (1986)
A good route with contrasting climbing taking the obvious grey wall left of the steep nose on the left side of the crag. Start by scrambling up broken ground to belay below the overhung niche left of the steep nose. Climb strenuously up into

the niche from the right, move up to the apex and pull out right onto the grey wall. Follow the line of holds to a flake crack on the right. Climb up this until it peters out and continue to the top.

Ride my Face to Chicago 20m E2 5b (1990)
Start up and follow West Side Story to the apex of the niche. Step left into a letterbox slot, then move up and left to the flake. Follow this for a few moves, then step right and move up to a vertical crack line. Climb this to the top.

Mearns Wall 25m E4 6a (1983)
Scramble up to start 6 metres right of the steep nose. Step off some loose blocks and gain a recess on the right. Pull over the roof above at a thin crack, follow this for a few moves before stepping right to better holds below a wider crack. Climb the crack until a step left can be made at the top. Belay well back.

Black Adder 25m E4 6a (1985)
A pumpy route bludgeoning its way straight up the middle of the steep wall via some fang-like flakes. Start below some big doubtful blocks (peg runner). Gain the blocks before making some precarious moves up right to a bridging rest in a recess right of the flakes. Swing strenuously out left and climb the hanging flakes to a ledge (belay). Climb the short wall to the top (5a) and belay well back.

Empire of the Sun 30m E4 6a *** (1986)
An excellent route giving well protected aggressive climbing up the shattered orange patch of rock and the steep wall above. Start below the orange patch of rock. Go up slabs and climb directly up the loose orange rock by a crack to a slabby ledge. Grab the flake on the left, then move up and left to a good shake-out at another flake. Move up right along a crack until it is possible to pull up to a small flat ledge (crux). Go straight up to a big ledge and belay. Finish up the short wall of Black Adder.

Gotae Grooves 40m HVS 5a (1971)
This route climbs the right-bounding corner of the steep central section. Start below the patch of orange rock. Climb the slabs to an overhang. Surmount this and follow a heather ramp diagonally right. Either climb a short wall up into the corner or continue right until a groove can be climbed back left. Follow the corner above to the top.

Upper Parapet 40m Very Difficult (1962)
Start from the gully on the right of the crag. Climb a slab and move left to a corner. Climb the recess above to reach a parapet and finish up the wall on the right.

The slabs on the left edge of the crag, above the steep nose, also give an easy climb. There is a second route from the gully of, but beginning higher than, Upper Parapet.

SOUTH-EAST CRAG

The upper section of this crag contains the best low grade climbing in the glen, with three brilliant routes on perfect rock. The best descent is to scramble off to the left. The following routes lie on the white wall down on the left of the crag.

Three J's Chimney   12m   Very Difficult *   (1968)
The obvious chimney close to the left edge of the crag gives an entertaining struggle.

The wall immediately left of Three J's Chimney has been climbed at VS 4c. The chimney-crack just right is HVS 5b if climbed direct, and Severe if reached by traversing in from 5m up Three J's Chimney.

The Spider   20m   E3 5b   (1986)
A necky route taking the ramp and tower 3 metres right of Three J's Chimney. Follow the obvious ramp to a ledge on the right (protection). Step back left and climb the tower, passing a curious hole near the top.

The Wildebeast   20m   E4 6a ***   (1986)
An excellent route on immaculate rock, climbing the technical roofed niche right of The Spider. Step off a boulder and climb directly up the steep wall below the niche to a ledge. Move up through the niche to a juggy finale.

The previous two routes superseded **Clairvoyant Reality** (E3 6a) which took the Spider Ramp and the Wildebeast niche. Right of this wall is a vegetated gully. The steep corner in the right wall of the gully has been climbed, stepping left at the top, at HVS 5b. Immediately right of the gully is a buttress broken by a terrace at 12m. The lower buttress can be climbed almost anywhere at varying degrees of difficulty, but the most obvious line is described below.

Parapet Route Direct Start   12m   Hard Severe
Start above and to the right of the lowest rocks. Climb the corner-crack fault to the terrace.

The following routes start from the terrace, which can also be gained by walking in from the right.

Flake Route   40m   Severe ***   (1939)
Start up a steep chimney at the left side of the terrace. Above the chimney, follow a groove on the left to a perch. Surmount an overhanging block above and continue on top of a large flake (possible belay). From the flake, climb up and diagonally right to a small rounded ledge, then continue to the top on good holds.

Central Crack   45m   Hard Severe ***
Climb the thin corner-crack which runs directly up the face right of Flake Route.

Parapet Route   45m   Severe ***   (1940)
Start below a small corner just right of Central Crack. Climb the corner and
overhanging chimney above. Move obliquely left for 6 metres to a groove. Climb
the groove until it is possible to traverse delicately right to a crack. Continue
straight up to a huge flake (possible belay) and finish up the arete above.
Variation: Mild VS 4b ***
Above the overhanging chimney continue straight up the obvious corner-crack
to reach the end of the right traverse.

The Girdle   45m   Hard Severe   (1987)
A high level girdle of the crag. Start high on the left flank of the crag above a large
recess. Traverse airily above the recess to join Flake Route at the rounded ledge.
Continue right using underclings to the step right of Parapet Route. Move across
the exposed undercut slab on the right to finish up the shallow groove above.

The extreme right edge of the crag gives 100m of broken climbing. The gully
on the right of the crag (the descent from Central Crag) has a steep left bounding
wall. **Comes the Squirmish** (HVS 5b) takes the 15m flake-crack halfway up.

JUANJORGE   *(Map Ref 265 795)*

This curiously named crag lies up the roadless Glen Esk (the right-hand continuation of Glen Clova). It is on the southern flanks of Sandy Hillocks, about 5km
from Braedownie and 2km short of the picturesque gorge, waterfall and larches
of Bachnagairn. The north running glen curves round west after a few ki-
lometres, and the main crag can be seen high up on the hillside across the north
side of the burn. This crag is in general disappointing with only a couple of old
routes recorded. **Diagonal Crack** (Severe) starts from the west gully well up the
left flank of the principal rock mass. **Gimcrack Gully** (Difficult) is the well defined
gully nearer Bachnagairn and starting low down. Low down on the left of the crag
(about 150m above the burn) is a fairly isolated compact 30m wall of immaculate
granite on which the following routes can be found. The best descent is to abseil
off convenient trees.

Granite Heids   25m   E1 5b *   (1987)
Start below the left-hand of two grooves left of the obvious corner line in the
centre of the face (Rhiannon). Climb the groove until it is possible to move out
left onto the edge (crux). Finish out right to a tree belay.

Rhiannon   25m   E3 6a **   (1986)
The obvious corner line in the centre of the crag. Climb straight up the slabby
face below the corner. Pull over a bulge and go up a short groove to flakes right
of the base of the corner. Climb the sustained corner to the top. Tree belay.

Roslin Riviera   35m   E4 6a ***   (1983)
Climb the groove in the toe of the crag to its top, then follow the left-slanting
diagonal crack to a resting place. Continue up the crack until a step left is
possible to another crack, which leads after a couple of moves to a horizontal
break. Finish above a small tree.

Ladies of the Canyon   30m   E4 6b **   (1983)
Climb a short crack and step left into the scoop in the wall 5 metres right of Roslin
Riviera. From the top of the niche make a hard move right to holds which lead
left to a crack. Follow this through the roof to easier ground. Tree belay.

NORTH CORRIE OF ALTDUTHRIE   *(Map Ref 255 785)*

These 100m slabs lie just up the glen from Juanjorge but on the opposite side
(on the same side of the burn as the path). On the lower left-hand slab is:

Solution Socket   35m   E1 5b   (1984)
At the left end of the slab is a prominent crack. Just left is a thinner one. Climb
up to the thin crack and follow it to where it blanks out. Move up left over the
bulge (crux) and climb the final slab centrally. Poorly protected.

Another two routes have been recorded. At the lowest point of the crag, there
is a tree beside the bottom of the slab. The relationship of these to Solution Socket
is unclear.

Unnamed   40m   E1 5b   (1986)
Start beside the tree. Climb the slab to a ledge. Traverse left and climb back right
beneath a bulge. Surmount the bulge then go up a crack in the slabs to the top.

Unnamed   40m   VS 4b   (1986)
Start 15 metres right of tree. Climb the crack and continue up the centre of the
slab to the top.

Angus Area

This section covers the area north of Dundee between the Grampian foothills and the coast. The climbing is located mainly in disused quarries but some exploration has occurred on the sea-cliffs north of Arbroath.

LEGASTON QUARRY *(Map Ref 589 487)*

This extensive quarry provides a useful climbing ground for Dundee and the surrounding region, especially in the summer evenings when time is too limited to travel to more distant crags.

The quarry is popular for training and the extensive use of fixed protection reflects this 'training' aspect. Originally, many routes had peg runners, but after a spate of gear theft in 1987, most of these are being replaced with permanent resin bolts as funds allow. These sport routes have been given French grades only, which reflect more accurately their style and difficulty. The climbing tends to be safe and technical but some exceptions do exist! Unfortunately the quarry has been used as a dumping ground by the local farmer and as such various unsavoury rubbish is sometimes present in the place. However this is kept well clear of the walls, and from May until October it is cloaked in a natural screen of vegetation. During the winter months the quarry can be particularly grim, but several routes are dry almost all year round.

The rock is a very compact sandstone which was used extensively for local building. Due to the compactness of the rock, cracks are uncommon although horizontal breaks and pockets are. This tends to give a very reachy style of climbing. On the less popular climbs the rock can be dusty and lichenous, but in the main it is solid and clean.

Access

The quarry is situated 24km (15 miles) north-east of Dundee, just off the main Arbroath to Brechin road (A933). From Arbroath follow the A933 for 8km (5 miles) until a junction with the B961 is reached (on the left signposted 'Dundee'). Follow the A933 for another 500 metres down a long hill and turn left at the bottom onto a rough track. Park here but please take note of the sign and try to maintain the good relations presently enjoyed with the locals. Walk along the track past a locked gate and round through the trees into the quarry.

The climbing is divided into six separate buttresses; these are described from left to right, starting with Ring Buttress and finishing with Rose Wall. The routes are also described from left to right. A set of steps are cut into the steep earth bank to the left of Ring Buttress to give an easy descent route. Almost all of the sports climbs have lowering-off points at the top, which give the climbing a very continental feel.

RING BUTTRESS

This is the buttress partly obscured by trees on the left side of the quarry. Named after the prominent iron ring at its top, it receives a good share of afternoon and evening sun. The buttress usually remains in good condition all year round.

Left of the obvious wide crack at the left end of the wall are two rather pointless routes (**Grot** and **Choss**), both Difficult.

Ego Trip   10m   Very Difficult   (1970s)
The obvious wide crack leading to a small overhang (crux).

Flightpath   10m   VS 4c   (1982)
An eliminate line up the small slab right of Ego Trip.

Crowbar Crack   10m   Severe   (1982)
The wide crack gives an awkward route on good holds.

The Killing Fields   10m   F6a   (1985)
Another eliminate up the wall right of Crowbar Crack.

Armygeddon   10m   HVS 5a **   (1982)
The obvious bulging groove in the middle of the buttress gives well protected, enjoyable climbing.

Driller Killer   10m   F6b+ **   (1984)
Good climbing up the smooth wall right of the previous route, technically interesting (i.e. desperate!) with a well protected crux move. Climbers of average height or less may find the grade frustrating. First timers are advised to clip the first bolt with the aid of a cheating stick. Lower off.

Flight of the Mad Magician   10m   F6b **   (1984)
The best route on the buttress. Sustained wall climbing leads to a finish up the thin crack above. Two bolts to a lower-off.

Seconds Out   10m   E1 5b   (1984)
The obvious thin crack on the right of the face is quite awkward in the middle and has a long reach at the top. Use of the right arete makes it easier.

Plod   10m   Difficult   (1970s)
The slabby arete on the right edge of the buttress, a useful way down.

Contraflow   15m   VS 4b   (1984)
A high-level traverse of the face. Start at the tree on Plod and traverse to the small ledge on Driller Killer. Move into Armygeddon, then go down and across Crowbar Crack to finish above Ego Trip.

MAIN WALL

The long back wall of the quarry contains a varied selection of routes. In the main there are lower off points at the top of all the routes, which are well bolted. The right-hand section is usually green all winter but the steeper left side can often be dry all year round.

Ratbag   15m   F6a   (1984)
Start from a slightly higher ledge at the left end of the wall. Climb the left-hand end of the wall using the obvious flake, before moving slightly left and up on horizontal breaks. Three bolts to a lower-off.

Hunt the Ratbag   15m   F6b *   (1989)
Start to the right of Ratbag. Climb the wall directly via a series of interesting long reaches to the lower-off of Ratbag.

Death is the Hunter   15m   F6b+ *   (1984)
A hard but well protected wall climb. Start at the paint mark and move up to a break, move up on pockets to the next break, then using small edges reach easier ground to finish on obvious jugs beneath the tree. Four bolts to a lower-off.

Sweet Revenge   15m   E2 5b **   (1984)
An excellent trip back to more traditional times. Climb the obvious left-slanting crack direct, passing a peg runner. At the top break, traverse slightly left to the lower-off.

Junk Man Blues   15m   F6a+   (1992)
Climb the obvious line right of Sweet Revenge past four bolt runners to a lower-off.

Between the Lines   15m   F6a+   (1984)
Enjoyable and strenuous climbing, moving slightly right from the first bolt of the previous route, then continuing direct to a lower-off past two further bolts.

Bomber   15m   F6a+ *   (1984)
This takes the obvious square-cut roof just to the right. Gain a standing position on a glued-on flake below the roof, use finger pockets in the lip and pull over. Swing right and surmount a second small block to finish over a doorstep-sized mantelblock. Three bolts to a lower-off.

Happy Days   15m   Severe   (1982)
A nondescript route up the obvious left-slanting line.

Brian the Snail   15m   F6a   (1985)
Start up Happy Days for 3m before moving out right onto a small flake, step up into a small right-facing corner and climb the headwall directly to a finish on the right. Two bolts to a lower-off.

Brian the Snail Direct   15m   F6c+ *   (1985)
A very difficult direct start to the original route. Start just right of the original and
climb a short wall to a small overlap. Above this the route gets mean. Providing
you don't cheat by using the edge to the right, very hard moves lead up the slab
to the small flake on the original line. Three bolts to a lower-off.

The Rocking Stone   15m   Severe   (1982)
Climb the next diagonal fault on the right. The stone very rarely rocks!

The Head   15m   Severe   (1982)
An awful climb up the obvious fault in the middle of the wall.

Right of this, the wall is less steep and is split into three tiers by wide ledges.

March of Dimes   15m   F6a   (1985)
Just right of The Head is a awkward bulging wall with a small ledge inset at its
top. This route climbs the bulge by an unexpected move. Three bolts to a
lower-off.

Shoot to Kill   15m   F6a **   (1983)
A very good climb up a shallow scoop to the right. Pulling out of the scoop is the
crux. Two bolts to a lower-off.

Overkill   15m   F6b *   (1984)
This route climbs the obvious cleaned line up the wall. The meat of the route is
the middle tier, and tasty it is too! Two bolts to a lower-off.

Desperate Measures   15m   F6b   (1984)
A companion route to Overkill. Start just left of the corner and gain the first ledge.
Move up on small edges, keeping left of the bolt, (or more easily using holds right
of the bolt), then finish direct to the lower-off.

Staircase A   20m   Very Difficult   (1982)
Climb the obvious corner and ledge system leading up and right.

Fire at Will   15m   VS 4b   (1983)
Good climbing up the wall right of Staircase A, but there is no protection on the
middle tier.

Staircase B   5m   Difficult   (1982)
A direct start to Staircase A, joining it below its second corner.

Walking the Straight Line   15m   VS 4c   (1984)
Enjoyable climbing that takes the cleaned line left of the tree stump.

The Rack   15m   VS 4b   (1984)
A right-hand companion to the previous route.

ROTTEN WALL
This wall has seen some advanced cleaning techniques and now sports several
routes on slightly friable rock.

The Golden Shot   15m   F6b+ *   (1986)
Good sustained climbing starting at the left-hand side of Rotten Wall. Start on
the ledge on the left and move right onto the wall, then continue to the top. Three
bolts to the lower-off. The Direct Start is F6c.

First to Fall   15m   F6b *   (1984)
The original route on the buttress, following the obvious line to the lower-off after
a hard start. The first move is far harder than the rest of the route.

Hell's Bells   15m   F6b *   (1989)
A companion route to the previous one, with another very hard start.

Edge of Darkness   15m   F6a **   (1986)
Climb the obvious sharp arete at the right-hand end of the wall, first on the left
face for 8m, then swing right to holds on the arete. Three bolts to a good belay
stake at the top.

FORBIDDEN BUTTRESS
This buttress runs parallel to Main Wall and forms the left side of a small square
extension to the quarry.

Purple Haze   15m   VS 4b   (1981)
Climb the obvious wide crack just right of the arete. Exit left at the top and beware
of nesting birds.

Night-time Sorrows   15m   VS 5a *   (1981)
An enjoyable route up the widening crack right of Purple Haze. Gain the crack
by a reach from the right, or direct over the bulge below (5b).

Virgin Crack   15m   Very Difficult *   (1982)
The shallow corner-crack to the right of above.

Kiss of Death   20m   VS   (1984)
This route takes the obvious layback flake down and right from Virgin Crack.
Climb the flake and up ledges until a traverse left gains Virgin Crack.

   Right of this route the buttress changes character, becoming vertical and
smooth.

No Remorse   20m   F6c ***   (1985)
One of the quarry's best routes, involving technical wall climbing. Start at the
paint mark and climb with difficulty to a small overlap, cross this and gain a good
flat flake. Move up to a second overlap and pull over to the top. Five bolts to a
lower-off.

Mr Access   20m   E3 6a   (1989)
A variation on No Remorse. Climb to the third bolt at the flat flake. Traverse
delicately left for 2 metres to a broken flake, (Friend 2 in pocket on left). Finish
directly up this flake crossing the final overlap just left of a peg runner.

Spandex Ballet   20m   F7a+ ***   (1986)
The harder right-hand companion to No Remorse gives excellent climbing,
desperate for the short. Start right of No Remorse with an awkward move to a
sloping ramp. Ascend this to the thin break, step right to the shot hole, then climb
this to a further break. Continue on pockets until a long reach up and right gains
a tiny edge. Cross the overlap directly and pull onto easier ground. Four bolts
and a peg to the lower-off.

BABYLON BUTTRESS
This buttress forms the back wall of the small square extension. The name stems
from the fact that it once resembled the hanging garden. Unfortunately it takes
longer to dry out than the Dubh Loch and is usually seeping for 9 months out of
12! Once dry, however, it provides several excellent routes and has a good low
level traverse at 6a.

Sign of the Scorpion   20m   E1 5b **   (1984)
Climb the big square corner between Forbidden and Babylon buttresses direct,
with one hard move at the top. Alas it is rarely dry but offers excellent climbing
when it is.

Aerodynamic   20m   F7a *   (1986)
A desperate route which climbs the thin seam splitting the upper half of the wall
5 metres right of the corner. Start up the shallow corners just right of the lower
continuation of the seam and gain the small ledge, (peg runner). Climb the seam
above directly by a very explosive sequence, pausing only to clip a bolt runner
in mid-flight! This route takes a long time to dry. The obvious direct start has been
climbed, but this requires the taps to run dry and the pavements to crack.

Lymphomaniac   20m   F6a   (1985)
This route climbs the fault and ledges just right again. Three bolts to a lower-off.

Roxanne   20m   HVS 4c   (1985)
Start as for the previous route before climbing up and right along ledges crossing
Nymphocyte to reach the Playing with Fire slab. Traverse this in a good position
to finish up Necrosis. A very overgrown climb.

Nymphocyte 15m F6a+   (1984)
Climb the central shallow groove after a tricky wall. Three bolts to a lower-off.

Playing with Fire 15m F6b **   (1984)
An excellent route with varied climbing. Either start from the ground or the boulder and make hard moves to good holds. Move up and left to the obvious flake and pull on to the slab above. Climb the slab to an impending wall and pass this to ledges and an easy finish. Three bolts to a lower-off.

Les Morts Dansant 15m F6b+ *   (1985)
A technical eliminate up the obvious overhung corner and headwall above. Climb the corner directly and pull through the bulge rightwards. Continue on shot holes and pockets to a prominent jug. Make a hard move up and left to a thin break, gain the small ledge above and finish at the lower-off.

Necrosis 15m F6a+   (1984)
Another eliminate line which climbs the nose right of the overhung corner. Awkward moves lead to an overhang. Cross this (thread) and ascend a groove to ledges and the lower-off.

ROSE WALL
This is the far right-hand side of Babylon Buttress which catches the morning sun. There is a stake at the top for belaying.

Rootworks 15m Severe   (1983)
The vegetated left-hand corner is held together by the rootworks.

Exodus 15m E1 5b   (1985)
Climb the smooth wall just right of the corner. Very contrived.

The Weasel 15m F6a+ *   (1985)
An enjoyable little route. Climb the wall directly right of Exodus to a delicate finish. Three bolts to a lower-off.

Remain in Light 15m F6b+ *   (1986)
This eliminate climbs the arete of Caprica, starting on its left side. A hard move past the first bolt leads to better holds on the arete. Continue direct; the ethical and the masochistic will avoid the holds in the corner to the right. Three bolts to a lower-off.

Caprica 15m Mild VS 4b *   (1983)
The obvious corner gives a quite enjoyable climb.

Winky 15m VS 4c   (1983)
Good climbing up the arete right of Caprica leads to a large flake. Finish up this.

Gary's Route   10m   Severe   (1984)
Start round the corner from Winky and climb the slab leftwards to gain the flake
of that route.

BALMASHANNER QUARRY   *(Map Ref 455 486)*

This quarry, which thoroughly deserves its reputation as one of Scotland's best
and most intense sports climbing venues, is situated on Balmashanner Hill just
south of Forfar. The climbing is contained on two separate walls. The left hand
is a bouldering wall whilst the right is bigger and steep. Unfortunately. being a
hole in the ground the outlook from the crag is rather limited although landscap-
ing by the new owner has improved things a lot. Having said that, however, the
routes provide excellent climbing which is well protected and enjoyable. Just
don't bring the family for a picnic!

Most of the climbs are bolt protected, and finish at *in situ* lowering-off chains
just below the top. Continuing above these through overhanging grass to belay
on rotting fencing is not recommended. Please do not remove any of the *in situ*
gear as it is essential, especially at the top.

The rock at Balmashanner is a very compact sandstone, similar to that at
Legaston, although horizontal breaks are less common. The main right-hand wall
has been quarried at a ferocious angle and cracks are few.

Access
The quarry is situated due south of Forfar. From Forfar town centre follow the
Dundee road up out of the town, passing the Guide Dog Centre on the left. About
1km beyond this a track leaves the road on the left marked 'Glencoe Cottage'.
Turn onto this and park alongside the hedge. Please do not obstruct any access
as the locals are friendly at present.

The routes are described from left to right. All of the climbs are well protected
by *in situ* gear, and most of the original bolts have been replaced by resin bolts.
Due to the steepness of the crag, it is a good place to train and 'Hell Bent' is
particularly popular for this. Once the crag is free from seepage it remains dry
during the heaviest rain.

LEFT-HAND WALL
This short wall provides some interesting bouldering, the low traverse giving
good value at British 6a. Towards its right end the wall leads into an area of
tottering overhangs before turning the corner and dropping to a lower level.

RIGHT-HAND WALL
Situated down at a lower level, this is the main feature of the quarry. Continuously
overhanging, it is particularly steep at its right end where it is also at its highest.

Digital Sclerosis   40m   F7b+ *   (1989)
The full low-level traverse of the right wall from left to right, studiously avoiding the resting ledge below Hell Bent.

Rancid Hellspawn   7m   E2 5c   (1989)
Climb the short black roofed groove at the left end of the wall past a peg runner. Finish on the ledge and walk down ledges to the right. A much easier variation leaves the groove for good holds on the right.

Delivery Man   15m   F7a+ *   (1989)
The smooth wall with 3 bolts left of Start the Fire.

Start the Fire   15m   F6b+ *   (1989)
Climb the obvious corner, where the wall begins properly, direct past five bolt runners to a lowering-off chain at the top.

   Right of this route a thin crack indicates potential for climbers of the future. The next crack to the right gives:

Savage Amusement   15m   F7b ***   (1988)
This route gives excellent climbing with some long reaches. Climb the crack with difficulty to a flake, then move up to a big jug (crux). Finish more easily up the shallow groove.

   Right again the next obvious feature is a huge flake which splits the upper half of the wall. This provides the finish for two routes:

Manifestations   15m   F7a+ *   (1989)
Sustained technical difficulty make this the local testpiece of its grade. Climb the smooth wall directly past two bolt runners to reach the base of the flake. Finish easily up this to a lowering point. The crucial pocket is prone to seepage.

Rat Attack   15m   F6c   (1988)
The original route to reach the flake. Climb the thin flake crack just right of the previous route with difficulty to a ledge. Finish more easily up the huge flake (five bolt runners).

Hell Bent for Lycra   15m   F6c+ **   (1988)
A thoroughly enjoyable pump! Climb the shallow groove direct passing five bolt runners. The last move to the big jug just below the lower-off usually proves to be the crux.

Le Bon Vacance   15m   F6c *   (1988)
This one is a little bit more technical but not so sustained as Hell Bent for Lycra. Start in the bouldering pit and climb up and left to good holds. Step left and go straight up to a large jug. Finish by moving right to climb the obvious groove to a lower-off.

Half the Battle   15m   F6c+   (1992)
Another pumper with the crux at the top! Climb the wall just left of the loose cave.
Five bolts to a chain.

The Comfort Machine   15m   F6c   (1992)
Climb to the third bolt of Half the Battle, then hand traverse the lip of the loose
cave. Follow a good ramp past two more bolts to the chain.

Gravity's Rainbow   15m   F7c+ **   (1990)
Superb moves on unnatural holds lead past 5 bolts to the chain.

The Essential Balmashanner   15m   F7c   (1992)
Climb to the fourth bolt of Gravity's Rainbow, then traverse left to finish up the
ramp of Comfort Machine. This gives an easier option with good climbing.

The Niche   15m   F8a+ **   (1991)
The right-hand bolt line passing through the niche gives excellent but vicious
climbing. Six bolts to the chain.

Merchant of Menace   15m   F8b+   (1992)
The even harder line to the right, past seven bolts to a chain.

LEY QUARRY   *(Map Ref 256 377)*

This quarry, the most recently developed of the trio, lies a few hundred metres
off the Dundee road about 3km (2 miles) south of Coupar Angus. Coming from
Dundee, as the road descends the from the S-bends of Tullybaccart there is a
cross-roads; turn right here towards Newtyle. After about 300 metres, just after
the farm of Wester Leys, turn right up a track which leads past a water board
reservoir, bends round to the left, then goes right into the quarry. Relations with
the landowner are good at present, but a specific request has been made that
visitors do not bring dogs to the quarry.
   Most of the routes lie on the back wall of the quarry above the pool. However,
the kind quarrymen left a nice ledge system which provides easy access to the
climbs. Belay bolts have been installed here at convenient intervals, so there is
no danger of falling into the pool. All the routes have been equipped to the highest
standards using resin bolts and *in situ* lower-offs. Overall, the crag has a very
French atmosphere and some very enjoyable climbing. Unlike the other two
bolted quarries, the walls here face almost due south and do not seep. This
means that year-round climbing is possible; in early Spring the place can be
scorching when more exposed crags are damp and cold. It's not just the bolts
that earn it the title of "Le Quarry"!

SMALL WALL
This is the short wall just a few metres from your car door. There are staple
lower-offs, so take a sling to tie into while threading the rope.

Magic Pockets   8m   6b+   (1993)
A short, sharp and very popular lead up the middle of the wall.

Pit Bull   8m   4+   (1993)
The easiest bolt route in Scotland! Climb the right side of the wall.

POOL WALL
Scramble down the steep bank to the ledge system below the wall. The difficulty of access depends on the state of the tide. The routes are described from left to right.

Nectar   13m   6a+   (1992)
An interesting, varied and quite sustained trip up the left side of the wall. "Vertically challenged" climbers may find the move to the chain a bit of a stretch.

Nirvana   13m   7a+   (1992)
Le monodoigt sur la dalle leads to a series of very reachy, sustained and strenuous moves. The upper half is easier.

Five Magics   13m   6c+   (1992)
Excellent sustained wall climbing, with a long reach in the middle.

Footfall   13m   6a   (1992)
The first route to be climbed here, a good introduction to clipping bolts and the stretchy moves so common in the sandstone quarries. Take a sling or a wide gate krab to clip the old quarry bolt.

Not the Risk Business   13m   6c   (1992)
First climbed on a weekend which was meant to be spent in Glen Coe, this very fingery route is not as serious as the more famous route of almost the same name.

Drowning by Numbers   13m   7a   (1993)
The slab to the right is protected by four big bolts.

Darkmoon Rising   14m   6c   (1993)
This starts from a slightly lower ledge, and once again proves a stumpies' nightmare up the prominent groove.

Dropping Like Flies   20m   6b   (1992)
A girdle at two-thirds height. Climb Nectar to the third bolt, then traverse right along the break to finish up Not the Risk Business. There is obvious scope for further extension of this route.

BACKSIDE BUTTRESS

This is the right-hand extremity of Pool Wall, reached by walking round the right-hand side of the pool. It is non-tidal.

Life's a Beach   14m   6b   (1993)
The shallow groove is more sustained than it looks, and requires a rather different style of climbing compared to the other routes here.

THE RED HEAD

This is the most prominent headland on the Angus coast. The head rises 90m vertically from the beach on its north-east aspect and provides an intimidating and serious setting. The rock is an intrusion of red basalt into the surrounding sandstone. This is reasonably sound on the upper half, which is fortunately isolated from the rotten lower section by a small halfway ledge. Due to nesting birds, climbing is banned from March 31st until July 31st and it is in the climbers best interest to observe this.

Access
From the Pub at Inverkeilor, between Arbroath and Montrose on the A92, follow Station Road, for approximately 2km (1 mile). Turn left and continue for another 1km before turning left again. About 1km further on the road degenerates to a farm track. Stay on this and pass through Ethie Barns Farm. About 400 metres past this take a left turn and follow the track to a small clifftop car park. Walk north on an indistinct path to the obvious headland.
   The only route climbs the obvious huge groove. An abseil to the halfway ledge from stake belays is required to start (peg belay, abseil rope backup). Escape from the face once committed is difficult, requiring either prussiking or an abseil to the beach (which is cut off at anything but low tide). One other avenue of escape is to traverse left from the halfway ledge to the prominent narrow arete. This is suicide territory: **Red Head Escape Route**, E3 4c.

The Engine Driver   45m   E3 *   (1987)
1. 25m 5b Climb easily up a short steep crack on dubious rock to a slab, move up a grey ramp just left of the main corner (Friend 2½) before swinging right back into the corner (crux). Follow the corner more easily, passing a large sloping ledge to reach a small cave-like stance (Friend belays).
2. 20m 5b Move up and right until a difficult move leads to the upper finishing crack. An atmospheric pitch.

Minor Crags

A few other crags have been climbed on in this area but it is doubtful whether they are worth detailing. Most are mentioned here to save disappointment rather than to suggest them as alternatives. The quarries of Kemnay and its near neighbour Tom's Forest are worthless and access is not permitted. Tillyfourie, between Monymusk and Alford, has two recorded routes on appalling rock.

Rubislaw Quarry inside Aberdeen is still a stupendous place, although half-filled with water. Several adventurous routes were climbed in the early seventies on the western wall but they have probably never been repeated. The starts of two of them have been cut off by the rising water. This oppressive place is surrounded by barbed wire and access is not permitted. Other quarries are dotted around the North-East but unless described in the earlier chapters they can be ignored.

There are small crags in Upper Deeside other than those described but they are unimpressive, and more importantly they are breeding grounds for sensitive birds of prey, so should be left undisturbed. Already, over-zealous gardening has taken place on Deeside and it should be avoided in the future.

BENNACHIE

Like Clachnaben, this hill has summit tors of granite and the Mither Tap offers two recorded routes and a number of other short unrecorded lines. The following two routes, on which the rock resembles uncut diamonds, lie on a south-facing wall to the south-west of the summit.

Mither Ficker   13m   E3 5c *   (1984)
Climb the obvious right-hand ramp of the wall until it finishes under a roof, then follow a crack through the left edge of the roof to the top.

Finger Ficker   15m   E3 5c
Climb the left-hand of the obvious ramps until it is possible to climb leftwards (mossy) then up to the roof. Traverse right to a niche, then exit here.

The Methlick valley near Gight Castle has some scattered small schist outcrops, but nothing of any real worth.

It is worth mentioning the amazing sea-cliffs of Fowlsheugh, south of Stonehaven, and Dunnottar Castle. Here is a challenge for the future; 45m of grossly overhanging conglomerate plastered with nesting kittiwakes. Like the Pennan crags, these cliffs are worth a visit just to look at.

No list of other crags would be complete without mention of the training possibilities on offer. The Beach Leisure Centre has a good climbing wall, but the others in the North-East but are either very poor or have access problems.

Outdoors, the King George VI Bridge near the Duthie Park in Aberdeen is good but fingery. Also, the viaduct arch beneath His Majesty's Theatre is excellent if less aesthetic. Finally, the Bridge of Don has some fine traversing.

THE MACDUFF CRAGS

The following routes have been developed quite recently, but as they have not been thoroughly checked they have not been included in the main body of the guide.

Access
Take the A98 to Macduff, then follow the coast road leading east to the Tarlair swimming pool.

LANDWARD CRAG   (Map Ref 721 648)
This has sound dark crystalline rock. At low tide approach past the swimming pool and scramble around the shore past a large cave. At high tide go over the clifftop to the golf course green and scramble down the south side of the crag (which faces west).

Tales of Power   10m   E3 5c **   (1991)
This gives very steep climbing up the obvious fault in the centre of the face, protected by small wires and Friends.

THE SEA-STACK
Due north of the landward crag is a small stack, 7 metres offshore, which can be reached at low tide over boulders. Descent from the following routes is by abseil from an *in situ* peg.

Stackattack   12m   E2 5c **   (1991)
Superb, strenuous and sustained climbing on excellent rock. Start at the centre of the west face, right of a rock pool. Climb straight up to a small ledge, then go slightly left then right to an overhang at two-thirds height. Climb through the overhang direct to finish.

Walking the Cod   7m   E2 6a **   (1991)
Climb thin twin vertical cracks right of the hanging corner on the east face. The crux is at the top.

Crighton's Crack   7m   Severe   (1991)
Climb large steps and a crack to the top of the south face.

Oresteg Arete   7m   VS 4c   (1991)
Follow the south-east arete over an overhang to the top.

Rotten Row   7m   Difficult   (1991)
Climb rather loosely up the narrow north face.

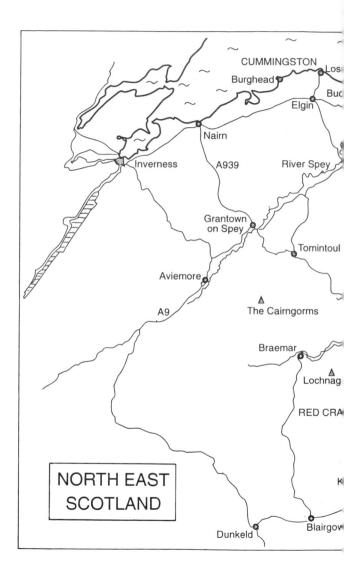

NORTH EAST SCOTLAND

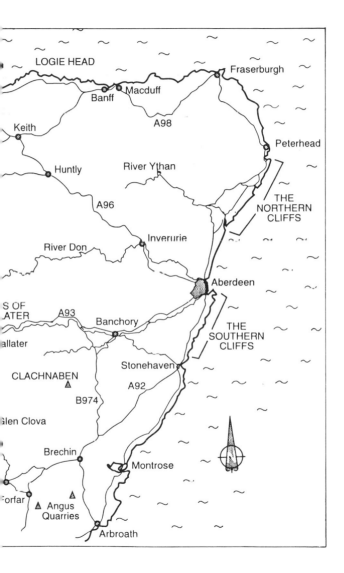